THE FUTURE DESIGNER

During periods of environmental and societal upheaval, design has the potential to be a formidable catalyst towards a sustainable future. However, to unleash its full power, significant shifts in both theory and practice are imperative. This book adopts a unique approach, blending anthropological perspectives with philosophy and cognitive science, and advocates for a thorough transformation of the existing design curriculum.

Supported by a vast body of literature in evolutionary science and design research, the book presents a blueprint for fostering more sustainable patterns of production and consumption. This blueprint is grounded in human virtues rather than vices and proposes a new curriculum tailored towards pro-sociality and sustainability. Leveraging his extensive professional background and expertise in the circular economy, Michael Leube offers practical examples, methods and tools for implementing sustainable approaches in the practical work of experienced designers. Showcasing cutting-edge innovations for pro-social and humanitarian design, the book ultimately argues that if we change the objective of design from creating desire to creating value, we can solve many of the most pressing social problems, from the cooperation of citizens to sustainable cities.

The book will be useful for those studying and teaching design and anthropology, and it will also be an important tool for practicing designers and engineers interested in learning how to design for social and ecological awareness.

Michael Leube, Ph.D., is a design anthropologist who serves as a university professor, author and consultant. Co-authoring two books on the circular economy and contributing to numerous articles in scientific journals, he specialises in design for social innovation and humanitarian design. His unique approach integrates anthropology, ethics and sustainability to shape a forward-looking design education focused on resilience. This approach has garnered invitations to instruct at prestigious design and architecture schools across Europe and to speak at design consultancies like IDEO and Fjord. Notably, he delivered a TED talk titled "Why designers should urgently listen to anthropologists." Leube has held positions as professor of anthropology at IE University, University of California, University of Santa Clara, London School of Economics, Syracuse University and Salzburg University of Applied Sciences.

"Leube pulls on threads from anthropology, design, and ecological justice to braid a compelling story of a future worth fighting for."

Jonathan Chapman, *Professor and Director of Doctoral Studies, School of Design, Carnegie Mellon University, USA*

THE FUTURE DESIGNER

Anthropology Meets Innovation in Search of Sustainable Design

Michael Leube

Routledge
Taylor & Francis Group

LONDON AND NEW YORK

from Routledge

Designed cover image: Samuel ROUX; graphic designer / teacher; Orleans, France

First published 2024
by Routledge
4 Park Square, Milton Park, Abingdon, Oxon OX14 4RN

and by Routledge
605 Third Avenue, New York, NY 10158

Routledge is an imprint of the Taylor & Francis Group, an informa business

© 2024 Michael Leube

British Library Cataloguing-in-Publication Data
A catalogue record for this book is available from the British Library

ISBN: 978-1-032-73555-9 (hbk)
ISBN: 978-1-032-73553-5 (pbk)
ISBN: 978-1-003-46475-4 (ebk)

DOI: 10.4324/9781003464754

Typeset in Times New Roman
by Taylor & Francis Books

This book is dedicated to all my students and teachers, past, present and future in equal parts.

CONTENTS

ACKNOWLEDGMENTS

There is no way, none whatsoever, that I could have done this without my beautiful wife Isa. Thank you for believing in me in times when I was down. "When there was no dream of mine, you dreamed of me." I love you! To our daughters Amelie and Giulia, thank you for being the way you are. Maybe, in tiny part, it is due to the *nurture* Isa and I gave you, but it is your *nature* that I love. I am incredibly grateful to have my parents and brothers. They always supported my strange anthropology adventures. Thank you, Alejandro, for letting me stay at your childhood home. A good chunk of this book was written there, among the waves of grain, in perfect silence under the Castilian sun.

Over three years ago I received an email from an ex-student. Although Markus Petruch was never technically enrolled in my courses, he regularly came to a lecture series titled "Anthropology and Design," at the University of Applied Sciences in Salzburg. Every Thursday afternoon I would hold a talk – or was it a fire and brimstone sermon – on a different topic relating to the two fields. In the email, Markus very matter-of-factly asked if I ever wrote those lectures down. I said no, he said I was an idiot and that was the beginning of this book. Markus, thank you for your sincerity, your drive to change the world for the better and for believing in the power of design infused with anthropology.

I would never have become a *design anthropologist* if not for Günther Grall, chair of the department of Design and Product Management at the University of Applied Sciences in Salzburg. In 2010 in Vienna, you witnessed the ugliest PowerPoint presentations ever, invited me to teach in your department and gave me wings.

Apparently Günther was told by my good friend Rudolf Greger about this weird anthropologist and thus he is the true link between me and the world of design!

Once anyone has read this book, they will have a hard time believing that one of my very best friends is a marketer! Dominik, that dark day over ten years ago brought us together and I am forever grateful to know you! Stay the way you are!

Katarina, I would like to have but a fraction of your energy. Don't give up because one day, you and I will ramble, dance and laugh through those Budapest streets again!

Coming to the world of design was a very steep learning curve for me and there were times when it got very dark. I saw much superficiality, pseudo-philosophy and wasted potential, but Jonathan Chapman's *Emotionally Durable Design* was like a powerful light at the end of the tunnel. I was so moved by it that I wrote Jonathan an email and invited him to my school. We met, held workshops and published together. More importantly, we became friends.

Alex, thank you for always standing by my side no matter how far away.

Samuel Roux: thank you for the beautiful cover, my friend. Ah, la vache!

If it wasn't for those bright nights under the Mojave skies, I might have gone nuts by now: thank you, Phil, for talking sense into my heady ways.

Thank you, Robert, for your friendship and all the late-night sparring sessions over God and the world. Let me be like Markus and ask you to please write down your thoughts. I don't know anyone – young or old – with so much knowledge crammed into a head. Let it out!

Sue Vogel has always been my teacher in all things design. She introduced me to *design for social innovation*, the *sharing economy*, the *circular economy* and so much more in so many music-trenched sessions.

This manuscript was started during the Covid-19 pandemic and although stay-at-home quarantines are good for writing projects, claustrophobia definitely got to me. Thank you, Blair, for our weekly sessions of meeting – often secretly – to talk. In conversations, you always encouraged me to keep writing.

Markus Frauenschuh is proof that you do not need to have a degree in design or anthropology to have a very good understanding of form and behavior. I learned a lot from you.

There is no way I would ever have written this thing if it was not for you David Sloan Wilson. You are a warrior, never faltering in your belief in the power of human cooperation. I have tried in this book to carry your message to the world of design!

There are so many important intellectuals who have inspired me, and this list is surely incomplete: Jared Diamond, Geoffrey Miller, Richard Dawkins, William MacAskill, Ezio Manzini, Michael Shermer, Yuval Harari, Peter Turchin, Robert Wright, Donald Norman, Douglas Murray, John Tooby, Leda Cosmides, Jerome Barkow, Joseph Henrich, Gad Saad, Tim Brown, Michael Easter, Gillian Tett, Nicholas Christakis, Paul Atkins, Steven Hayes … thank you for your clarity, wit and decency in these crazy times. Posthumously, I want to thank Victor Papanek, Elinor Ostrom, E. O. Wilson, Karl Popper and, of course, Charles Darwin for infecting me with "this view of life"!

And then there are the *soul rebels* amongst the intellectuals. Thank you, Sam Harris, Shoshana Zuboff, Michael Shermer, Jaron Lanier, Tristan Harris, John Perry Barlow, David Graeber, Peter Singer, Jordan Peterson, Dave Eggers, Kate Crawford, Annie Leonard, Ellen MacArthur, Jonathan Haidt and Kate Raworth for standing tall and telling it how it is. What takes me semesters to tell, Banksy does in one image. Thank you wherever and whoever you are!

For spiritual nourishment I thank meditators S.N. Goenka, Joana Macy, Sam Harris and Joseph Goldstein, and to all the musicians of the world: When I get confused, I listen to the music play!

Finally, thank you, Christine! A long time ago you said that one day I would write a book. In memory, this is for you!

INTRODUCTION

Just Like Frankenstein

> The sky was overcast at noon-day with clouds of ashes, the sun was enveloped in an atmosphere, whose "palpable" density he was unable to penetrate; showers of ashes covered the houses, the streets, and the fields to the depth of several inches; and amid this darkness explosions were heard at intervals, like the report of artillery or the noise of distant thunder.[1]

Those are the lines of Stamford Raffles, lieutenant-governor of Java, Indonesia writing on the largest volcano eruption ever recorded. Although Raffles witnessed the event from a distance of three hundred miles, it seemed to have been quite a visceral experience for him. On April 5, 1815, on the island of Sumbawa in Indonesia *Mount Tambora* began its eruption. Most animals and plants were killed as lava flows covered the island. Only twenty-six of twelve thousand residents living in the province of Tambora survived. The rest likely died a horrible death of asphyxiation as the volcano threw massive clouds of dust into the air, bringing almost complete darkness to the area for days. According to the geologist Charles Lyell, who collected eyewitness reports of the eruption for his *Principles of Geology*, "the darkness occasioned in the daytime by the ashes in Java was so profound, that nothing equal to it was ever witnessed in the darkest night."[2] When the eruption subsided after a week, Mount Tambora was reduced by a third and the impact of the eruption lasted for years to come and was felt all over the world.

The world's atmosphere was filled with uncountable tons of volcanic material and the sun was blocked almost entirely. Average surface temperatures dropped globally; in North America and Europe temperatures dropped by more than seven degrees Celsius in what was named the "year without summer" or "1800 and froze to death." Freak weather events such as brown

DOI: 10.4324/9781003464754-1

snowfall in Hungary and continuously dark rain clouds swept throughout Europe during what was supposed to be the summer of 1816. Napoleonic troops had plundered whole crops as they retreated and the unforeseen climatic change only exasperated food shortages, leading to Europe's last major subsistence crisis. France, Germany, Austria and Switzerland were hit hardest as prices skyrocketed. Parts of Europe, such as Paris, experienced actual starvation.

But these strange meteorological events also triggered ingenuity. In May of that same year, poet Percy Shelley, his girlfriend and writer Mary Godwin (who a few months later married him to become Mary Shelley), their son William and Mary's stepsister Claire Clairmont, a lover of Lord Byron, traveled to Lake Geneva. Not long after, poet Lord Byron and his personal assistant Dr. Polidori also arrived. Due to the horrible weather the whole group was cooped up in a spooky villa named *Diodati*. This literary circle was a group of romantics, skeptical of the industrial revolution and its effects on human society and melancholic for days gone by. They were also fond of anything supernatural and thus practiced seances to conjure up ghosts. The group did not know the cause of the climate change that summer was a faraway volcanic eruption, and thus the gloomy weather was a mystery to all of them; a claustrophobic, but terribly romantic mystery. The wind and rain bombarded the house. Lord Byron decided to use all this pending gloom, creaking of the roof, and banging of shutters as a catalyst of creativity. Inspired by *Fantasmagoriana*, a collection of German horror stories, he challenged everyone to a competition to write the most bone-chilling tale. Mary was a gifted scribe, but she was only 18 years old; likely all the scary storytelling combined with the raging storm gave her a nightmare. In any case, she woke up early the next morning with the initial idea for the first science fiction novel, *Frankenstein*, in her head. She was clearly shaken up by her nightly vision and wrote the following in the introduction to her book:

> I saw – with shut eyes, but acute mental vision – I saw the pale student of the unhallowed arts kneeling beside the thing he had put together. I saw the hideous phantasm of a man stretched out, and then, on the working of some powerful engine show signs of life and stir with an uneasy, half-vital motion.[3]

In the following days she had crafted the general plot. Its protagonist, the scientist Victor Frankenstein, constructs a creature from dismembered corpses and calls it the *Wretch*. He then animates it, creating an *artificial intelligence*. The novel is the depiction of what in 1816 was an impossible scientific feat but is now essentially recognizable on the horizons of bioengineering or biotechnology. After the Wretch's lights go on, the novel is basically about the so-called *value alignment* or *containment problem* of AI, where we humans desperately try to put a lid back on something that has escaped our control. Victor Frankenstein let his vanity of becoming a world-class scientist overrule his moral compass and created a monster that ends up killing several people including his own brother.

Racked with guilt over his scientific creation, he asks himself: "Had I a right, for my own benefit, to inflict this curse upon everlasting generations?" Guilt, however, is useless because it is retrospective and Shelley forces us to ask not "what have I done?" but rather "what will I do?" before the doing is complete. At the end of the novel the captain says to Victor, "You throw a torch into a pile of buildings, and when they are consumed you sit among the ruins and lament the fall." The novel is based on a counterpoint: a pre-monster, relatively normal world, and Geneva in 1816. In a romantic passage early on, Mr. Frankenstein observes that "It was a most beautiful season; never did the fields bestow a more plentiful harvest, or the vines yield a more luxuriant vintage." But the narrative quickly becomes darker, much darker. It turns into gothic horror complete with murder, psychological terror and a global hunt for creature by creator. All along the weather becomes worse and worse as storms howl, lightning flashes and frost thickens. The novel closes at the end of the world in the Arctic circle. Frankenstein had chased the monster to a frozen hell of jagged ice, wind and snow. He dies there and to him the end of his world looks like a revenge of nature.

It seems that Shelley was so shaken by the climatic anomalies of the "year without a summer" that she produced one of the most chilling novels ever written. But she was not the only one experiencing climate anxiety. Lord Byron's poem, "Darkness" – also produced in the group's involuntary captivity at the villa *Diotati* – epitomizes *dark romanticism*, through its emphasis on human fallibility. Another product from that villa on Lake Geneva was a short story written by Lord Byron's personal physician. It was titled "The Vampyre" and later influenced Bram Stoker to write Dracula. Both *science fiction* and the modern vampire trope were invented under those dark skies inside that villa of that miserable summer.[4]

Dark Futures

I am a big fan of science fiction. I've seen and read hundreds, maybe thousands of fictitious accounts of the future, but I cannot remember one where the things to come are in any way appealing. Instead, the future is filled with smoke hovering over a post-apocalyptic wasteland of death, oppression and destruction. Despite all of that, or maybe because of it, the scenarios are very seductive, especially in the glossy hyper-reality of movies. Aesthetically and thematically, most of current science fiction is of the *cyberpunk* variety, the *film noir* of the genre. First coined by author William Gibson, the genre is usually based on a dichotomy of technological futurism and urban decay or high tech and low life. And in a very Marxian dichotomy, the *cyberpunk* future shows lower classes without any means by which to benefit from technology while the rich not only benefit but control it. Our dark future comes in two basic flavors. In the first, disaster comes from the outside in the form of colonizing aliens, meteors or problems with our powerhouse, the sun. (Incidentally the word *disaster* comes from the French for "bad star.") A second type involves humans not heeding warnings of some eccentric scientist and somehow running civilization into the ground. Usually this is done by destroying biological and human nature through the oppression of most by a ruling few and aided by their machines. Like meteorologists predict a storm by observing the collision of two distinct weather fronts, science fiction visionaries look at the human treatment of earth's biosphere or technology and predict a bleak tomorrow. Both do this by following past and current patterns and extending them like a string into the future. *Anthropogenic* or man-made apocalypse is far more unsettling than the "danger from the outside" variety since here fiasco is caused by our own unique free will. It gives a voice to this anxious feeling that current events are less than ideal and must lead to something worse. If our lifestyles were ecologically, socially and economically sustainable, the catastrophic visions of *Blade Runner* and *Mad Max* would not seem so realistic and so nearby.

Unfortunately, there *are* many reasons to follow strings of bad developments into a bleak future. In other words, the "problems from within" variety of *dystopic* futures is easier to feel. Fear, anger and paralyzing apathy, but also panic attacks, are widespread and stem from knowing that we are all somehow part of all those problems. *Artificial general intelligence* (AGI) will be reached when we are able to code and produce a system, or collection of collaborating systems, that can out-perform humans in most tasks. It will be the day that we have created agents capable of formulating their own goals and designing their solutions, and it is the clear goal of AI research worldwide.[5] But when will we cross this science-fiction-sounding threshold of "singularity"? That exact question was asked in a 2016 survey, where about 350 top machine-learning researchers estimated by what year "unaided machines can accomplish every task better and more cheaply than human workers." The average response suggested that there is a 50 percent chance of that happening by 2061. That is not far into the future![6]

Nuclear Armageddon due to war between great powers is unfortunately also back on the table, which the Russian re-invasion of Ukraine in 2022 has shown. The two bombs dropped on Hiroshima and Nagasaki in 1945 were each 1,500 times more powerful than any weapon known at the time. Today's arsenal of atomic and hydrogen bombs, however, is much larger; it is estimated that the nine nuclear powers have a combined total of 13,000 nuclear warheads, all of which could be launched within 15 minutes.[7] Old-school geopolitics has woken us up form a naive dream of a wall tumbling down in Berlin and a peace that lasts forever.

The COVID-19 pandemic was a horrible scenario right here on earth, one that would have seemed overdrawn science fiction only a few years ago – and not just the airborne pathogen, which killed over 6 million people, but also the radicalized politics and culture wars that happened simultaneously, maybe because of it. It made us think about the very real possibility of engineered pandemics caused by pathogens. *Gain-of-function research* – where biologists studying pathogen behavior can modify a genome to acquire different rates of transmissibility – is practiced by most world powers and research results will likely be published online.[8] And the pandemic was also a healthy distraction for us humans from adding to the mountains of garbage and plastic in the oceans. The current industrial model of literally burning through non-renewable fossil fuels must inevitably lead to an accelerated climate change due to high levels of greenhouse-producing gases and eventual economic stagnation due to the depletion of resources. Fortunately (or unfortunately), there remain relatively large amounts of such resources underground, although they are hard to access, but climate change has undeniably begun. We still have not figured out how to provide clean energy for an increasing global population hungry to consume. We must provide food and basic infrastructural security to a growing number of people in underdeveloped nations while at the same time dealing with an ageing demographic in the developed world.

Abraham Lincoln is credited with saying, "the best way to predict your future is creating it." Any of the above storylines need simply be extended into a future and you get a lot of current science fiction. Much of the genre is also based on some terribly sinister science, involving mind control, genetic modification or technological implantations, as seen in precursory literature by the likes of Philip K. Dick, Bruce Sterling or William Gibson. Science fiction has different aesthetic flavors, but most of it is based on oppressive technological advances coupled with different shades of nostalgia. Thus, steampunk also features dystopian futures, but the machinery is that of the 19th century Industrial Revolution – analogue and steam-powered. Whatever the exact nuances, visions of the future are dark, revolving around societal collapse and omnipotent, monolithic corporations. Lately, an ugly, smoke-filled future, one full of inequality and injustice, is far more salient than one filled with beauty and equity. Unfortunately, such creative representations of life on earth in the future are all we have since no one has ever been there, and, coupled with actual headlines, they set a tone of default pessimism.

The Uncanny

Science fiction is effective as an artistic genre because it is rooted in the human anxiety of being out of sync with its environment. The alien is scary because it kind of looks like us. The post-apocalyptic wasteland is terrifying because we can still detect the fields we remember from childhood. *Science fiction* taps into our human condition of estrangement with nature itself, this mismatch between the way we are and the things we have conceived. Culture has always been a strategy of adaptation through the design and modification of our niche, but the more furiously we build, the bigger the discordance we experience between our nature and our culture. The result is a peculiar human sensation of estrangement best described as *uncanny*, the translation of the German *unheimlich*, or un-homely. We quite literally "live in the wrong home." We feel as strangers in these homes that we designed but were not built for. And the more our built environment changes due to a flurry of designed objects, the greater this estrangement becomes. That is a main theme of this book.

Far weirder than science fiction's fantastic visuals of the future is the fact that we cannot wait to get there. We are leaning into it, head down, hard against the wind. We are completely out of breath as we chase the next moment and its experience. This is an age inflated by novelty and predictions of the unseen. Everybody reading this today "knows" the weather tomorrow, when really such knowledge has few implications for the current moment. Our predictions of the future are intrinsically linked with technology and laced with *technophilia*. Not only do we often use technology to make the predictions, but the predictions themselves are full of new gadgetry and more computing power. For us city dwellers, an analogue life, unaided by smartphones, smart homes and digital assistance, has become a quaint, mildly charming but impossible pursuit. For many of us the present moment is negated through a rich diet of distraction via media channels. We live in so many stories simultaneously as we devour images and fictitious lifestyles by binge-watching series, movies and social media feeds. The latter especially has become a dopamine-fueled feedback loop where we create every next media moment simply by consuming the present. The actual story, the one we live in, we often overlook as we jump into another.

Bad Incentives

Over fifty years ago, industrial design icon Victor Papanek echoed Mary Shelley's warning when he wrote on a dilemma intrinsic to design, stating that few professions have as high a potential for damage. The root of this problem Papanek sees in the very nature of industrial design:

> Whereas architects and engineers routinely solve real problems, industrial designers are often hired to create new ones. Once they have succeeded in building new dissatisfactions into people's lives, they are then prepared to find a temporary solution. Having constructed a Frankenstein, they are eager to design its bride.[9]

This book is *about* all this stuff produced by humans – what we will label the *Anthropocene* – but I am addressing Victor Frankenstein, the scientist, not his created monster. Most of the time (ignoring *Alexa* and *Siri* for a second) we can talk all we want to created objects and they will just sit there, mute, as they clutter up our homes. They affect our lives in profound ways and within my lifetime we will likely address artificially sentient beings as we might address each other. But here I am addressing the masters of those things, who in turn design our lives and behavior, domesticating us.

Frankenstein is a book widely used as a parable of designed things that get out of hand, but apparently Mary Shelley struggled with that title and gave it a second, alternative one: *Modern Prometheus.* Just like the Greek mythological figure Prometheus made humans out of clay and then stole godly fire to give to them, Victor Frankenstein designed a sapiens being using the power of electrical lighting. Although in some versions of the myth Prometheus makes humans, the most important aspect is that he gives them fire, which stands for technology and innovation or civilization. The fire was stolen from the gods and as punishment Prometheus is tied to a rock so that an eagle can eat his liver. The liver, which in ancient Greece was regarded as the place of emotions, grows back, but the eagle returns to eat it again. This cycle of torment continues indefinitely. A common interpretation of the story is that Prometheus, which literally means "forethought," stands for the human quest of scientific discovery. The tale acts as a warning of the risk of overreaching in our emotional obsession to develop and satisfy an unquenchable thirst for experience. But through such obsessions, without regard to sustainability, designers can often make end-users into accomplices in environmental degradation and other weapons of mass destruction. It is for this reason that we need to ask what they are taught in university, how they make money and how they change human behavior. Prometheus has also been romanticized as the lone genius, who becomes enslaved by vanity to be remembered as a great scientist and whose tinkering away results in tragedy for all. Indeed, the most famous Oppenheimer biography is called *American Prometheus.*[10]

I also empathize with consumers running with tongues out, buying things they don't need, with money they don't have, to impress others, to paraphrase Papanek. I want to address an underlying anxiety, a kind of white noise of our modern existence; that feeling we experience when we stuff useless, foreign and aggressive carcasses of packaging into smelly color-coded containers, in ever more frequent garbage runs. I feel the guilt when I realize that more species are dying, that more people are working in abhorrent conditions, that the climate is changing and that all of it must somehow be related. But most of the time we end-consumers stumble through the dark, sure that somehow this must make sense. We are continuously told that we are *Homo economicus,* a self-serving, always rational creature that always wants more, and thus we must throw the old away. Our brief interaction with the garbage can is the only time we are confronted with ugly externalities. If you don't continuously consume nowadays, you are the weird one. It all makes a kind of tautological sense. Humans are fulfilling a fabricated and flawed prophecy of what might be in store for them. Once we believed this about ourselves, *we* also become Frankenstein's monster!

Design became a central driver of consumerist-based capitalism and a popular major for millions of young students, but only because marketing and advertising had long ago taken central stage at the intellectual centers of our world. It is my belief that this ascent brought narcissism, limited empathy, and a thirst for recognition on both sides of the production/consumption divide. Since I lament current consumerist incentives as I see them as the main cause of environmental havoc, I want design to emancipate itself from marketing-driven, faux innovation. My hope is that the anthropological sciences with their methodology and findings are seen as an antidote as they force the focus away from creating user wants and onto solving user needs. Conversely, design as a discipline produces culture and is thus an essential part of anthropology. There exists a *virtuous* cycle between the anthropological sciences – in all their different manifestations – and *design thinking*, a term used here not as a patented process but rather as the purposeful conceptualization and shaping of a given phenomenon.

While tackling many aspects of human behavior, this book is most concerned with the current industrial system, often labeled the *linear economy*. Following broadly the laws of production and consumption, the creation of wealth of most modern nations has been based on aggressive exploitation of earth's biosphere for resources (take), the manufacture of complex, multifaceted commodities (make) and swift disposal of them (waste). Just before the "make" stage of manufacturing, design holds an indispensable role in the conception of our everyday objects. The linear economy as a piece of cultural code can be viewed as malware running its code in perfectly good people. With it, Homo sapiens became the only species on earth to literally *design* garbage. The current economic and industrial order is undeniably linked to biodiversity loss, pollution of water, air and soil and resource depletion, but that link is not a straightforward one. It is the model of human conduct and its exploitation that is so destructive to the biosphere.

But this is not an anti-capitalism book. Approaches of post-growth economic systems are always linked to renunciation and therefore misinterpret the human condition entirely. Rather, emphasis needs to be shifted to selective and qualitative value creation. Production, use and disposal of commodities must be a *circular system* mimicking nature in order to be sustainable while allowing joyous, even conspicuous, consumption. It has to be a system by and for humans, without compromising other biological systems, all of which we depend on for survival. Thus, I will avoid indulging in a political blame game of the left and right, of post-modern grievance babble as well as the maiming pursuit of consumerism for growth in GDP.

This is an anti-marketing book – as far as I know one of the only ones – because the discipline seems to be sacrosanct. Humans are insatiably hungry for novelty and for fitting into a given social order, and when such innate urges are satisfied by consuming and wasting resources, so it will be. The root of current ecological disasters is that we monetize an endless promise of dopamine-and-endorphin-inducing experiences materialized in clunky, non-biodegradable carcasses. It is marketing, advertising and design that feeds our desire to consume. But, if we stop to think for a moment, the tinder of our desires is always a return to natural systems. We are told to have houses, insurance plans and larger cars to feel protected. We are told to change the stuff we wear and hold to be part of a welcoming tribe and to feel the embrace of a desired partner. We are told what to eat, think and say in order to get closer to some kind of ideal of human life. But the closer we get, the further it is removed. The *hedonistic treadmill* has no exit. But if incentives shifted to added value as generated by a circular system, the same media could be used to change towards a cultural paradigm in which conspicuous consumption is despised. As the adage goes, I don't want to "throw the baby out with the bathwater," and we need the powerful machinery of advertisement, marketing and design now more than ever. However, they need to see themselves not as seducers but rather as translators and propagandists of a new system.

Although this book takes a hostile stance against marketing and advertisement, I try to do so with reason and logic. Posing as a scientific endeavor, marketing is not descriptive but entirely prescriptive. It does not study a process of human trade (economics) but rather teaches a program of monetization. By making need and want synonymous, it manipulates human action and skews supply and demand beyond recognition. However, there is another, even more dangerous side to marketing. The world over it has aggressively marginalized important fields deemed as useless (philosophy and developmental work), cannibalized others (behavioral sciences and psychology) and forced the rest into serfdom. The latter is true for design – seen here as a department for the application of art and technology – and now the very mission statement, processes and products of design are largely driven by the logic of marketing. Such assertions sound like naive statements of the obvious, but only because we have taken the incentives of linear economic growth based on obsolescence for granted. Like the fish surrounded by water, we no longer see our culture of waste making.

Only when creative pursuits like design, engineering and architecture turn their incentives to sustainable planetary life and see themselves as sub-disciplines of public policy rather than business can we hope to craft a better future. I want designers to help improve humanity and its civilization. I want them to build a future that brings pro-sociality, sustainability, prosperity and joy to our lives. And I want them to make well-deserved money. I admit to throwing up my arms in despair and opting into buying clothes without approval of their production, or food squeezed into endless and useless layers of plastic. Somehow, all of us were made into culprits of a collective tragedy and I am part of the problem. To paraphrase an old Americana song, just like Mary Shelley and just like Frankenstein, I clank my chains and count my change. I am just trying to walk the line.

Notes

1 Raffles, T. S. (1817). *The History of Java: In two volumes* (Vol. 1). Black, Parbury, and Allen; and John Murray.
2 Lyell, C. (2023). *Principles of Geology: The Modern Changes of the Earth and its Inhabitants Considered as Illustrative of Geology.* Good Press.
3 Just, S. (2021). *Strangeness, Community and Hospitality in "Frankenstein" by Mary Shelley.* GRIN Verlag.
4 Luckhurst, R. (2005). *Science Fiction.* Polity.
5 MacAskill, W. (2022). *What We Owe the Future.* Basic Books.
6 Grace, K., Salvatier, J., Dafoe, A., Zhang, B. & Evans, O. (2018). When will AI exceed human performance? Evidence from AI experts. *Journal of Artificial Intelligence Research, 62,* 729–754.
7 https://www.scientificamerican.com/article/how-many-nuclear-weapons-exist-and-who-has-them/, accessed on December 12, 2022.
8 https://www.samharris.org/podcasts/making-sense-episodes/special-episode-engineering-apocalypse.
9 Papanek, V., & Buckminster Fuller, R. (1972). *Design for the Real World.* Thames & Hudson London, p. 215.
10 Bird, K., & Sherwin, M. J. (2021). *American Prometheus: The triumph and tragedy of J. Robert Oppenheimer.* Atlantic Books.

PART I

Hardware, Software and Malware

1

THE HUMAN CONUNDRUM

Are Humans Good? Well, It Depends …

In bars we are all philosophers. In the pubs of the world, there under dim lights, profound answers to the oldest questions are shared with a conspiratorial wink. Sitting at the bar, you can find out what "they" are hiding from "us" and who is really running the show if only you look at the right sources. Learning that I am an anthropologist, the stranger next to me looks deep into his glass and then asks an incredibly complex question, but rather than waiting for my answer, he repeats the question and answers it himself. "Are we humans good or are we evil? Well *I'll* tell you what human nature is …", self-taught "Plato" begins and then takes a big, meaningful swig of his beer. Apparently, I was too slow or my, "well, it's really complicated and depends on …" did not fit his soft alcoholic haze. As the jukebox plays, his stories follow the old plot line of a corrupt, greedy and selfish human who has always screwed things up and therefore will continue to do so forever. We are doomed and that is why we invented pubs. It is a dark, deterministic and teleological story. It is also quite wrong.

The anthropology of the bar is blaming the state of the world on a human species that is flawed and condemned to repeat failure forever. Current events are seen as the only thing that could have ever happened. The polar icecaps are bound to melt, the robots had to come and in 2007 the iPhone grew out of our bodies. Such reasoning – that history has a goal and direction – is called *teleological*. It also tends to be *theological* and *metaphysical* since it assumes some higher being at the controls. Or is it just pseudo-Zen philosophy? It is what it is! While reality truly is how it is, it did not *have* to be the way it is. To judge the provenance of the universe, we would need to know if other universes are similar; we would need a control group. But, since we are stuck on one planet, in one bar, your argument is invalid Mr. Anonymous!

DOI: 10.4324/9781003464754-3

You, I, all of us are a yapping species; we tell lots of stories and stories are always teleological. In them things happen because of a reason. But, neither the evolutionary process of nature nor culture had to be the way it is right now because, as Karl Popper remarked, "the future is open." The next round is on me.

The guy at the bar is drinking as if to forget that we are all damned. He goes on and on about how we are the world's nemesis. He nods at the news-caster on the big screen telling us how big storms and floods are coming. "We are the killer ape, exploitation and destruction are in our blood, dammit! Right?" Wrong! It is never black or white and to the question on human nature, unfortunately, I must get back to my annoying "it depends." Beha-vior – human or otherwise – always depends on environmental constraints. It does not even make sense speaking of behavior in an imaginary void, because after all what would we behave with? Towards what? Just like all other organisms, humans are equipped with a program to respond to the environment with a specific behavior.

For questions on human nature to even make sense, we must look at *genetic determinism* from the side of *behaviorism*. Even at the very lowest level of complexity, organisms respond to a set of *if* (a certain environment)–*then* (a certain action) rules. For example, *if* you are a fetus severely underweight, *then* for you to survive it makes sense to develop a thrifty metabolism. *If*, as an adult, you find yourself in a very unstable situation with low life expec-tancy, *then* make sure you have lots of kids early. *If*, on the other hand you are in a stable environment with a very long life expectancy, *then* delay having offspring for as long as possible. This, incidentally, is the reason why coun-tries' infrastructural and institutional development correlates with fertility rates and what Thomas Malthus got wrong about his doomsday prognosis of reaching *carrying capacity*. More on that later; for now, it suffices to say: behavioral responses can be virtuous (selflessness, living sustainably, etc.) or they can be vicious (selfishness, thrashing our environment, etc.), depending on the context.

Like Being in the Wrong Movie

Perhaps the most important issue tackled in this book is *evolutionary mis-match theory*. It posits that traits that evolved in an organism in – and for – one environment can be maladjusted or even disadvantageous in – and for – a different environment. To illustrate this, let us first use a non-human example. Female sea turtles prepare for the birth of their offspring. They make nests for their eggs by digging pits into the sand on the higher parts of the beach. Within a few days of hatching, baby sea turtles must make a dangerous journey from the nest into the ocean and to avoid predators and the heat of the sun they usually make the trip at night. But how do they know which way to go? The very first thing they do must be genetically determined since turtle mother cannot communicate any instructions through the membrane of the eggs. The hatchlings depend on their newly opened eyes to turn towards the ocean. But again, *where* is the "ocean" for a creature that has just been born? It seems that it is the *contrast* between celestial bodies (moon and stars) and the open horizon of the ocean that has been written deep into their genes as the correct direction; on an undeveloped beach that contrast tends to be much brighter than its dunes and vegetation, which would be the wrong direction.[1] Such a behavioral algorithm was finely honed by an evolutionary process for hundreds of thousands of years, but at some point in time another species came along. It loves to build villages along the sea, and it wrongly identifies as being nocturnal. It makes light all night long to do stuff. The turtle's behavioral code is misguided by human light pollution, the poor thing waddles in the wrong direction and overheats or gets eaten. Or it is run over by cars.

What about humans? Imagine that you are chosen to play a character in a movie, which takes place in a certain time and space. You were given the part not so much because of your ability to act but because your physical appearance and ways of moving about are a perfect fit for the movie's setting. Excited about landing the gig you take the storyboard home, ready to get to work. You don't even need to dedicate much time to practicing any subtle shades of content, dialect and inflection because the part is made for you. You calculate and plan your move around the movie set. Your worst fear is that on the day of the movie's premiere you are described as a "bad fit," because there is nothing you can do about the way you are. "That won't happen," you are thinking as you arrive well prepared on the first day of shooting. But then a nightmare far worse unfolds. Standing there, waiting for the director's cue, blinded by the light, you look around, searching for familiarity. Panic sets in as your eyes bounce around a space entirely unfamiliar, entirely uncanny. Where is the set you were selected for? Where is the chair you are supposed to sit on, the table with the glass of water, the light switches? You are in the wrong movie! You are in a *mismatch*.

Human birth, just like the sea turtle's birth, is like being cast in the wrong movie or environment. And in both cases the environment was changed by humans. Inside the womb, the baby is floating around like an astronaut; everything needed is provided by a chord attached to their belly, and the outside is only dim shades of light. Suddenly they are forced through an excruciatingly narrow passageway; sounds, images and smells come rushing in as it is pulled into a world that it was not made for. A world made by humans ... and then it is slapped on its back. Like an angel, it opens its eyes – pale blue-colored irises receive light and shadow for the first time. Actually, every iris is unique – not always blue – and comes in most other striking colors. Irises resemble galaxies, but not just in color. When we travel towards an iris' center, we find the pupil, which is a black hole. Literally! Just like many mammals, human babies are born with eyes open, and as light rays enter the pupil they are absorbed by tissues inside the eyeball, sending information to the rest of the brain; "rest of" because technically the eyes are part of the brain protruding from the skull. Light entering from outside goes through the pupil and forms an upside-down image on the retina, which instantly detects the photons of light and responds by sending neural impulses through the optic nerve connected to the brain. The electrical impulses are then processed to create a right-side-up 3D image, giving us visual orientation and depth perception. It is truly miraculous! Biologist Richard Dawkins beautifully demonstrates the evolutionary steps required to craft the human eye by building a model step by step in a must-see YouTube video.[2] The newly born baby's eyes flutter around to find and focus on other eyes, which due to their unique features are easy to track. Our sclera is also the *only* white one; it is extraordinarily elongated and in it floats the iris.

All around the baby are strange objects designed by humans, and they collide with the baby's senses designed by nature, to perceive nature. To the baby all this artificiality – the light, the air, chairs, beds, and all other artifacts – make no sense, literally. The human brain cannot easily compute straight edges, right angles or any man-made features for obvious reasons. Humans were made for an environment that did not have any such features – and instead consisted of a natural habitat, full of fractal features and repetitive patterns – and thus selection pressures did not have to account for the new stuff. Ancestral environments did not change much in generations and so adaptations of earlier generations worked for those coming later. But the *built environment* spread fast and became the modern *movie set* a child is born into. Of course, no environment remains completely constant, but *anthropogenic* (human-caused) environmental change is extreme in both quality and quantity. Hominids living in small tribes of hunter-gatherers evolved patterns of decision-making for archaic – not modern – circumstances, and if those patterns led to their survival, then our heads still hold similar patterns when we try to solve challenges today. They are genetically determined traits, which can be both features or bugs depending on the environment, and – since the alteration of the environment is much faster than genetics – we are increasingly out of sync with our original environment. A constant effort to assimilate rapid changes has left us physiological and psychologically exhausted.

Human cultural and biological evolution is extremely complex because culture is a constant feedback between itself and its makers. It is a process of *coevolution*.[3] We are the masters of *niche construction*, an interactive dynamic in which organisms construct their environments even as their environments constructs them, through natural selection and over multiple generations. Human *niche construction* works along a *feedback circuit*: as we live our lives, we alter the environment, and these alterations in turn bring altered selective pressures on us. Considerations of *niche construction* are a major part of what is called the *extended evolutionary synthesis*, and it challenges theoreticians and practitioners of the built environment alike to take account of the selective consequences it has on humans living in it.

If we just paid attention, we would realize that we are often ill adjusted to the niche we have designed around ourselves for hundreds of thousands of years. The *culture makers* of the recent past have colonized our present at a rate that archaic biology cannot keep up with. Imagine we took some modern campers, shoved them into a time-machine, slammed it closed and shot the outdoor enthusiasts back to the Paleolithic. As our weekend warriors crawl out of the time machine in 40,000 BCE, proud with all their brand-new *Decathlon* gear, their ancestors would likely look at them with skepticism. They would recognize them as being made of the same basic substance and belonging to the same species. Then they would look full of suspicion at their outfits, and all the stuff they are schlepping around with and roll their eyes.

Learning to Become Human

Human birth is a complex and risky process and usually requires assistance. Furthermore, children are entirely helpless at birth; like a plant overwhelmed by its fruit, they cannot even support their own head until four months old. Due to what has been called the *obstetrical dilemma*, our gestation period of nine months is way too short and thus in a very real sense all humans are born prematurely. Natural selection seemed to have opted for early childbirth (at an early stage of fetal development) to allow for large brain size over larger female pelvis size. At birth, human babies have brains less than 30 percent of adult brains so that they can fit through the narrow birth canal. At further maturation, the cranium would simply get stuck. Outside of the womb, brain size nearly doubles in the first year and continues to develop until reaching full maturity at around 25 years old. That explains why humans have the longest period of child dependency of any other species on this planet, why teenagers can act truly strange and why *TikTok* at an early age is not such a splendid idea.

The human mind is not a *blank slate*, empty at birth and ready to be filled with information. Nor is it immutable. We are all born with helpful information for survival (provided by nature), and then we learn a tremendous amount about living in modern groups and settings (provided by nurture). A helpful scientific analogy is that of the immune system, which has both innate and adaptive components, operating synergistically. Very similar to how modern psychology describes the human mind, the innate component of the immune system is modular. Just like macrophages can sense and engulf foreign particles but have no capacity to change their sensory abilities, the human mind can notice and react to thoughts and feelings but cannot turn off sensing. Don't even try it! Innately, we have a sophisticated set of psychological modules that evolved by genetic evolution and are triggered by environmental events. Such *behavioral algorithms* rarely change ontologically, or during one's lifetime. Likewise, the innate component of the immune system can protect against most organisms provoking disease but is paralyzed when something new blocks its automated defenses. The immune system's other, adaptive component has the ability to create an estimated one hundred million different antibodies. Collectively, it is like a toolbox with a hundred million highly specialized tools allowing it to work on just about any conceivable organic surface. When one of these tools (a given antibody) grabs onto an invading pathogen, the innate component of the immune system is told to attack. Thus, the interplay of the innate and adaptive immune system is a complex evolutionary process enabling organisms to ward off diseases and survive.

The similarities of the human cultural and immune system go further still since neither is a centralized control system. As for the immune system, we are seeing a multi-agent cooperative apparatus where dozens of specialized cell types coordinate their activities to achieve the common goal of protecting the organism. No one alive today descended from individuals with immune systems that failed to exhibit teamwork! And on a higher level, no one is descended from individuals living outside of cooperating tribes where cultural adaptation techniques are taught. Our ancestors passed the process of designing and manufacturing things to each and every progressive generation.

Tabula rasa – this idea that just like a little chalk board or slate wiped clean only to be encoded, formed and shaped by our environment – is wrong. This is obvious, because a species would never have survived past the first generation if "put up your hands when you trip over a rock" had to be explained in some ancestral classroom. Behavior such as nursing, blinking or ducking are all directed towards the outside world and provided before birth. In "this view of life," as Charles Darwin referred to the evolutionary framework, the developing human mind along with its physical body is a result of evolution by natural selection.[4]

David Geary pioneered a field called *evolutionary educational psychology*, a Darwinian model of knowledge which differentiates between *primary* and *secondary* knowledge used by humans to make sense of their environment. *Primary knowledge* is that which all humans are predisposed to learn, such as language, categorization of flora and fauna, basic social interaction skills as well as cues on empathy gleaned from reading body language, especially facial expressions. It is not the same as instinct ("put up your hand when you trip over a rock") but information that is learned easily. This goes along Noam Chomsky's belief that the structure of language is biologically pre-set in the human mind and genetically inherited.[5] Simply by being human we can acquire primary knowledge because we have something akin to a template for it. *Secondary knowledge*, on the other hand, consists of the stuff we learn in school and which we would not naturally absorb, such as political science, history, mathematics, etc. According to Geary, the very existence of schools is the gap between *primary* and *secondary* knowledge, where the latter becomes a prerequisite for having a successful life in modern society.[6] Seen in this way, the very concept of "school" is but a symptom of *evolutionary mismatch*. Modern hunter-gatherers don't need schools since their societies don't require their members to know any calculus or Michel Foucault's *Discipline and Punish*. Other societies – ones that have collected an excess of cultural units – do, since navigating through them has become existential.

Geary also speaks of *folk knowledge*, which is knowledge not taught in educational facilities but shared amongst communities of people. It builds on evolutionary templates provided before birth. Thus, *folk physics* refers to an innate understanding of objects moving through space and "taught" to children through practice and play. We don't need to be taught that something thrown into the air comes back down. Basic psychology experiments were done where a very young infant is made to focus on an object such as a teddy bear or a ball and when that object is then dropped the child does not look for it in mid-air but rather, instinctively, looks down at the floor suggesting that it has already at birth been equipped with an understanding of the causality of gravity.[7] Such knowledge has links to inference, user pathway design and simple expectations of how things are supposed to work. *Folk biology* speaks to our ability to classify plants and animals, and other things in nature. Without being taught, most humans and non-human primates can make a distinction between a plant and an animal and by extension classify objects and organisms within their environment into predator and prey, dangerous and non-dangerous. Already at birth, a child masters basic concepts of biology as it can tell the difference between its parents and a stray dog wandering into the hospital room. *Folk psychology* is our ability to read social cues and interact with other humans. It entails the ability to read facial expressions, which can tell us a lot about the people around us. Our ability to feel empathy and sympathy, anticipate violent outbursts and understand what a raised voice or certain body language implies; all are socio-psychological tools that help to build communities and form bonds. As a matter of fact, a child is born with the ability to put the appearances of mouth, eyes, nose and ears into a coherent whole – or *Gestalt* – that is, the face of mother, father or hospital worker. In a nutshell, for most of our evolutionary history, skills were far more important than facts ever will be.[8]

Through a lengthy process called *enculturation* infants learn to live in different cultures, a gigantic conglomeration of designs, a group adaptation. Things that are experienced are stored in the form of images and emotions as memory and reference for similar encounters, as current research on the *predictive brain* supports.[9] Such evolutionary logic is badly needed in the way we train our offspring. This thing that we call "school" – sitting for hours on end in little chairs and getting stuffed with abstract information – is a very recent acquisition in human history and is not natural and does not serve us well. It is newer than agriculture, cities or even written language. In the words of David Lancy, author of *The Anthropology of Childhood: Cherubs, chattel, changelings*:

> Children across cultures and through time have managed to grow to adulthood and learn to become functioning members of their society

without the necessity of schooling. Jump to the 21st-century and we find a world where childhood without schooling is unthinkable.[10]

Schooling has become a necessity, but it badly needs to return its focus from teaching abstract facts about removed phenomena in exclusive silos to teaching tools for young adults to navigate through complexity and to fix a precarious, fragile world. We need to install wonder and awe in the face of an interrelated global system. The *evolutionary mismatch* of modern schooling, as indeed all situations of mismatch, is screaming out for creative solutions.

It is strange that in many languages we speak of birth as "coming into" this world. If anything, babies are born *out* of this world. They are born *into* culture. While it is true that during gestation, they float like space walkers attached to their umbilical cord, they are never aliens. No matter if we look at this semantically, philosophically or scientifically, it is just wrong to assume that we originate outside of the world to somehow arrive in it. We are living creatures and part of the biosphere just as much as a tree, and we don't speak of the tree growing *into* the world. We are equipped along with many other creatures with consciousness, a state of being aware of and responsive to one's inner and outer environment, and most of us have this profound sensation of the outside world starting where the skin stops. Since we envision ourselves as a subject outside of an objective nature, we feel estranged, fragile and defensive. But behavior, being contextual, is dependent on both the inner and outer environment simultaneously, and any attempt to dominate nature is simultaneously an attempt to dominate ourselves.

Human Sciences 2.0

No matter how little sense it makes, the idea of humans molded almost exclusively by nurture has gained a lot of ground in the closing of the 20th century and still represents the status quo today. Referred to as *Standard Social Sciences Model* (SSSM), notions of the *blank slate, relativism, social constructionism* and *cultural determinism* are all doctrines based on nurture. Indeed, most current departments of psychology, sociology or cultural anthropology treat the mind as having little or no role in determining behavior and instead as being determined exclusively by social learning processes plus cultural traditions and environmental contexts. The SSSM also provides a convenient model of human society where oppressive ideologies can simply be overwritten by leftish social justice.[11] As it focuses only on *proximate* explanations of human behavior, ultimate reasons for why we do what we do are often missing. This absolutely holds true for my undergraduate and graduate education in cultural anthropology, where any biological drivers of human behavior were simply ignored. Precisely because of its focus on *ultimate causations, evolutionary psychology* stands as a strong corrective. It explores *why* a particular behavior is displayed, rather than only looking at *how* and *what*.

Evolutionary psychology challenges the methodological framework taught in most social sciences departments. In contrast, it lands squarely on the side of nature. *The Adapted Mind*, edited by John Tooby and Leda Cosmides, the classic text of this young discipline, actually stands as an all-out assault on the notion of the mind shaped almost entirely by forces of nurture.[12] In the words of evolutionary psychologist David Buss, the SSSM is based on the incorrect assumption that:

> the human psychological architecture consists predominantly of learning and reasoning mechanisms that are general-purpose, content-dependent, and equipotential ... That is, the mind is blank-slate like, and lacks specialised circuits that were designed by natural selection to respond differentially to inputs.[13]

Tooby and Cosmides[14] and later Steven Pinker[15] want to replace SSSM with what they call the *integrated model* (IM), which permits both cultural and biological factors to be responsible for the development of the modern mind. Unfortunately, the SSSM includes the entire tradition of *behaviorism* in psychology represented by B. F. Skinner as well as various anthropological traditions that did emphasize the open-ended and evolving nature of human culture, represented by intellectual giants such as Margaret Mead and Clifford Geertz. While Cosmides, Tooby and Pinker threw such helpful traditions out with the proverbial bathwater they did survive as applied psychology, at the level of both individuals (e.g., therapy) and whole societies (e.g., public health).

Evolutionary psychology sees modern minds as modular and shaped by the same forces of natural selection that shaped our hands to have five fingers or our kidneys to work as a filter of toxins. A serious academic endeavor that unifies biology and culture, this discipline has its roots in the 19th century. Long before the systematic evolutionary study of the human psyche began, an evolutionary foundation to human behavior was predicted by Charles Darwin in his *The Expression of the Emotions in Man and Animals*.[16] *Evolutionary psychology* now stands as an explanatory framework with the potential for understanding psychological as well as cultural phenomena and has the following main tenets: (1) our ancestors faced many dire challenges during our species' evolutionary history and natural selection designed our ancestors' neural circuits to solve them; (2) only those ancestors who were able to solve problems passed their genes on and those genes were used to build more successful neural circuits; (3) thus, our modern skulls literally house Stone Age minds; (4) most of the activity in our minds is unconscious and hidden from us; and (5) the mind is modular and different types of neural circuits are all specialized for solving different adaptive problems.[17]

To illustrate the power of *evolutionary psychology*, let us go on an imaginary trip. Picture yourself in a car on a road trip, driving along when suddenly a sign encourages you to pull over. A pictogram of a hopelessly outdated camera and an arrow is telling you that this spot, more than all the others, is the most beautiful. How is that possible? Various researchers have tried to deconstruct our sense of a beautiful environment to arrive at an *ultimate* – not *proximate* – explanation. In other words, it does not suffice to say, "the vista point is beautiful because of all the pretty things!" because that is only a *proximate* and *tautological* argument. A sense of aesthetics can be expected to be innate and deeply connected with a physiological appreciation for habitat. After all, we are primates and we originate from the wild!

Research into why we respond the way we do to our natural environment can be traced back nearly fifty years when in 1975 geographer Jay Appleton published *The Experience of Landscape*, proposing the now famous *prospect–refuge theory* of human aesthetics. It states that an appreciation of beauty is "an acquired preference for particular methods of satisfying inborn desires."[18] The two desires that Appleton refers to are opportunity (*prospect*) and safety (*refuge*). Thus the "vista point" is like the view from a cave, or from under a tree. Open spaces, those with a clear focal point such as groupings of climbable trees, are another preferred landscape feature.[19] Walkable paths, visible water and traces of wildlife also make something attractive and perhaps worthy of a photo.[20]

Humans come from nature and it is very likely that *biophilia*, the love of nature, continues to resonate in us, almost like an archaic homesickness. Perhaps it was Irenäus Eibl-Eibesfeldt, the late German ethologist, who first acknowledged that human aesthetics may have a biological basis instead of just a cultural one, which tends to just speak of "good form."[21] He introduced the term *phytophilia*, the love of plants, as a sub-heading of E. O. Wilson's *biophilia*.[22] Humans have survived because of and with plants since they can be eaten, and provide shelter and shade. Such factors might explain our affinity for plants and explain why we introduce them as much as possible into our built environments. But plants also provide secondary indicators for elements necessary for survival. The mere existence of a plant suggests that there is also water, good soil and relative protection of the elements there. Plus, the plant had apparently not been eaten by what could be a competitor for food or even a predator. Conversely, where there are plants there must also be other animals that could serve as prey. Seen in such a way, *beautiful* is what reminds us of nature or, said more eloquently by philosopher Dennis Dutton, "Beauty is nature's way of acting at a distance."[23]

Let us turn to the so-called *savanna hypothesis*, which argues that a preference to the basic environmental clues of the distant past must still be present in modern minds.[24] Scientific evidence suggests that early hominid evolution took place in the *African savanna*, which provided the most hospitable environment and natural selection would have thus favored a preference among early humans for savannah-like environments, and especially those also containing much drinking water as well as cliffs and caves for shelter.[25] What is startling is that research shows present-day people: (1) to also have preference for savanna-like environments, (2) that savanna preferences are stronger among younger people, who do not have yet acquired preferences for home as much, and (3) that savanna preferences are quite consistent across various cultures and geographic areas.[26] Children always show stronger preferences than adults, a fact that adds a lot of weight to the argument of aesthetics being innate rather than learned tastes, since the latter are more influenced by society and other environmental factors.[27] In other words, there may be innate choices as well as those arising from *proximally reinforcing* ones, like the cultural background we grow up in. In psychological jargon they would be called *operant conditioning*. We long for a time long gone. Almost like a phylogenetic homesickness we are drawn to nature. None of this will go down easy for architects and designers steeped in the ideas of *modernism* and Austrian architect Adolf Loos' anti-ornamental stance. But more on that later.

Likely Loos only opposed it in the human species, but ornamentation of living spaces is not limited to the human species. For example, a bird called the *great crested flycatcher* often adds a shed snakeskin to line their nests. Tree swallows have been observed gathering the largest white plume-like feathers for the same purpose. We are not the only one beautifying our homes. But make no mistake, the bird's nest is considered a *cultural* phenomenon, not a *biological* one. When humans decorate their homes, we say that we do so by simply saying it is beautiful. We stop there. We might argue over it, but "beauty" is simply presumed for its own sake. We beautify our lives with elements of nature as we cater to different types of plants, arrange them in intricate ways to form the ornaments to otherwise boring walls, decks and balconies. Much of such behavior also serves a signaling function, as we are showing off *conscientiousness* by keeping other organisms alive.[28]

Could we explain the human sense of what is beautiful and what is ugly evolutionarily without falling into the pitfall of subjectivity? The short answer is "yes," but first another thought experiment: invited to a dinner party, and as required by etiquette, you want to make a special gift to your host. Should you get a bouquet of freshly cut flowers or a bundle of dead straw? If you are like most humans, the salient answer is, "obviously the former." But is it that obvious? The difference between the two gifts is, we could argue, that the flowers are more beautiful. But why, or rather how do they illicit a positive emotional response? True, technically both are carbon-based, dead plants, but our paleolithic brain sees the former as far more alive and thus romantic than the latter. Was that a jump? Probably not, since there is nothing more romantic than hints of fertility!

Forget the plants. Shiny object are also good gifts, but why? Circular arguments along the lines of "shininess is desirable and that is why our dinner host wants it" begs further questions. Why would young children – unsocialized as they are – prefer shininess? In a classic study nursing-age toddlers were observed to make suckling and licking movements at the horizontal metal mirrors of toys on their hands and knees in a manner not unlike grown-ups drinking from a water source. Maybe, it is suggested, nursing-age children display an innate ability to recognize the glossy and sparkling features of water. Just maybe the human obsession – of both designers and consumers – with the shiny relates to the most important resource for survival: water.[29] In another experiment, blindfolded participants were handed a piece of paper and then asked to rate the paper in terms of quality and attractiveness. In a group of 46 participants, half received a glossy sample and half a matte sample. The ones who held the glossy sheet rated it as higher along both metrics even though they were blindfolded. An interesting follow-up study used *priming* as its methodology. Researchers divided 126 participants into three groups: 1) those who ate dry crackers without any water; 2) those who had the crackers with some water; and 3) those who received neither. Half of the participants then looked at the glossy and half at the matte paper. The majority preferred the glossy pictures, but the group with dry-mouth rated glossy as far more attractive.[30] But the obsession with shiny object is not just a Western idiosyncrasy; remote tribes display a similar affinity. For example, the Yolngu, a Northern Australian Aborigine people, have a key concept in their art that they call *bir'yun*, or "brilliance." It is an effect produced by the finely cross-hatched lines that cover the surface of their paintings, elevating them to something sacred.[31]

But let us not get carried away: extreme caution is required when applying evolutionary theory to explain current phenomena. According to Nikolaas Tinbergen, Nobel Prize winner, together with Konrad Lorenz and Max von Frisch in 1973, a complete evolutionary explanation of any adaptive trait or cognitive system that produces certain behaviors must always be guided by four main questions. First, we must ask, what is the function of the trait or behavior? Second, what is its phylogenetic developmental history? In other words, how did it change over multiple generations? The third question concerns its mechanism: what is the physical basis of a trait or behavior? And finally, we should always inquire what a trait's development is during the lifetime of an organism (ontologically). For example, Tinbergen's first criteria – the functionality of human behavior – allows for both *immediate* and *mediated* pleasure since it can be explained as having *proximal* and *ultimate* functions simultaneously.[32] In this book we will repeatedly use evolutionary explanations for human behavior concerning affinity and aversion leading to and following from design decisions. Tinbergen's four questions require different research methodologies. Readers should remain vigilant of *just-so stories* and his criteria lend themselves to such skepticism. It is important to note that humans also change epigenetically (literally above the genes) by gene suppression and not just variability and flow.

There also exists evidence for a correlation – maybe even causation – between aesthetic sensibility and moral judgment. Ever since Plato's *Republic*, academics have been wondering about such possibilities;[33] even Immanuel

Kant himself acknowledged a link between the awe caused by the inner world (morality) and the other world (the cosmos) in his famous passage: "Der bestirnte Himmel über mir, und das moralische Gesetz in mir" (the starry sky above me, and the moral law within me).[34] It is interesting that expressions such as "heinous crime" or a "beautiful deed," which link expressions of aesthetics and morality, are also very common. Does this have evolutionary roots? Moral psychologists have teamed up with neuroscientists, and using rigorous methodologies they have found that subjects' moral judgments become stricter when exposed to stimuli eliciting disgust, no matter if the moral issue evaluated itself as involving culture-specific triggers of disgust or not.[35] Furthermore, neuro-imaging studies have shown an overlap of active brain regions processing moral and aesthetic judgments.[36]

The Identity Stack

We humans can imagine things that are, things that could be and even things that could never be. We create, categorize and represent experiences – imaginary or real – in symbols. This ability is generally called *culture* and it marks the beginning of what we might call *behavioral modernity* roughly 50,000 years ago.[37] It sounds like a long time ago, but in terms of *phylogenetic* history, culture is a recent biological adaptation to changing environmental factors. That last sentence might seem oxymoronic, as we always juxtapose biology and culture. But really culture can be seen as humanity's greatest trick, and it certainly is much more recent than the things that went into making our bodies. To grasp yourself as both a biological and cultural being, think of yourself as a stack of different identities. In its entirety, the stack makes you look and behave in a myriad of ways, some of them stemming from *nature*, and some of them from *nurture*. The former refers to pre-wiring, influenced by genetic inheritance and other biological factors, and the latter to the culture you grew up in. It includes all kinds of things that shape your behavior, such as the subjects studied in school, the babbling on your smartphone, the interpretation of you standing under the Milky Way, the way you represent yourself and the things you find cool or abhorrent.

From the outside, this *identity stack* is perceived as the *phenotype*. Just like the word "phenomenon," "phenotype" is derived from the Greek "phaino" meaning "shining," or "appearance." It is the stuff that could conceivably be recorded, and includes not only the way an organism looks, but also the way it behaves. The *phenotype* is a result of the *genotype* – the total collection of genes – interacting with the physical and social environment. To illustrate, let us first use an example from the animal kingdom – bowerbirds – because they display a complex suite of *phenotypical* traits. Bowerbirds come in a variety of colors, from green, yellow and orange to white and ash gray. Most of them are *polygamous* and they are renowned for very elaborate courtship behavior, where the males build an otherwise useless structure and decorate it with sticks and brightly colored objects that they find in order to attract females. Besides building the "bowers," the males also perform other elaborate court-ship displays. Biologically speaking, all the above *phenotypical* characteristics are a consequence of the interaction of the bird's genotype and the environ-ment it finds itself in. But, as we can see, that interaction refers to both the bird's *ontogeny* (individual development) and *phylogeny* (species develop-ment). It includes a fancy architectural structure and a dance to impress a female strutting around right here and right now, but the ability to do either one is instinctive. Variation in *phenotype* between individuals is an important indicator of survival and reproductive success and thus a major driver in evolution. This book is not about birds, but it should be easy to see why *phenotype* is an immensely important term for understanding humans and the stuff they design.

Let us return to "culture," a term employed almost like the *joker* in a card game. It is the wild card of conversations because "culture" always works, even when we lack another term. The word has a certain magnetism that attracts all things we cannot really explain but somehow make a difference. To begin grasping how significant culture is in molding who we are, let us use another metaphor. We can see it as an *operational system*, which engulfs us entirely. Made up of all these people behaving, thoughts written into books and millions of objects standing around, this operational system is not static. Instead, it is continuously updated as an adaptation to a prior state. Some of its content is replicated and some of it is dropped, but all of it, during its existence, mutates in form. Such changes happen so fast that it often feels like we cannot catch up, and they are probably the reason why adolescents will always think their parents are so "not updated." Operational systems not only vary across time, but they also vary across space. Ask anyone who has tra-veled. Like the water surrounding the fish (oh no, another metaphor) we are often unaware of our culture. It is all around us, but it comes from within. After all, attitudes, ideas and values become actions. The engineer must first think of a bridge before designing and building one.

Seen as an *operational system*, culture produces objects, norms, even myths that help humans survive and such manifestations survive for millennia. But it also produces maladaptive stuff that dies out quickly and, strangely, it produces maladaptive stuff that survives and thrives. From the *functionalist* school of anthropology, we have the *organic analogy*, where cultural phe-nomena are part of the whole, like bodily organs are part of the body. The heart is necessary when looking at the whole body and only makes sense when seeing its function in it. Similarly, different cultural parts are like organs in a larger system. The most random collection of things, technology, mar-riage, medicine, art, education, family, religion and government: they all influence each other. So far so good, but *functionalism* as a theory breaks down when trying to explain *dysfunction*. There exists a kind of holy mantra in design, *form follows function*, and it can certainly explain the form and design of an atomic bomb, a cultural phenomenon most definitely not adaptive. But does form follow ethics and sustainability? Take fast food: although dramatically raising morbidity rates worldwide, it is a thriving culture that will likely continue to survive and expand. Yes, this book has to do with modern marketing!

Culturally, we are all different, diverse and beautiful, but those differences are rarely categorical or binary, such as those predicted by speciation. We are strong speciesists, as moral treatment towards individuals within different species varies tremendously; juxtapose the horrors of factory farming to the comfort of our household pets.[38] Biologically speaking *race* and *sub-species* are synonymous. Both mean interbreeding populations resulting in *phenotypical* characteristics like skin or eye color, but they also result in cultural idiosyncrasies like the types of music or cuisine enjoyed. Thus, *race* overlaps with the term *ethnicity*, but they are not the same. Because of cultural norms (marriage patterns, religious rules, rules of apartheid, incest taboos), cultural boundaries (frontiers, walls, ghettos), people who look similar tend to also do stuff that is similar. Just think of all the ways we dress, worship and eat. All such means of segregation are designed. Of course, interbreeding populations can also be separated physically by rivers, mountains, deserts or oceans and over time will likely also crystallize culture. I find the term *race* very problematic. Unlike the artificial selection we practice on livestock, humans have fortunately never been "bred." Skepticism, criticism or outright hatred of groups of people who look different is better described using the term *xenophobia*, fear of strangers. Unifying us all, at the bottom of the identity stack is human biology, but assuming designers of the built environment want to provide a good fit for the entire human species, it would be wise to view the whole stack.

Social Life

Paleoanthropologists have combed through all their data sets to piece together the complex story of human evolution, adaptation and variation. And through the study of markers of mutations, geneticists are able to establish when and where groups split off, waxing and waning in size due to environmental conditions. Archeology, the study of human settlements and cultural objects left behind, shows small groups of people living in communities not unlike biological cells with semi-permeable membranes allowing people to move in and out of such groups. The emerging picture suggests that Homo sapiens as a species was geographically united when it first evolved in Africa. Small bands of hominids came up with the major innovations that became the building blocks of civilization and eventually managed the mind-boggling feat of emigrating from Africa constantly iterating those innovations as they adapted to all other parts of the world. There are no descendants of individuals, since they can't have babies alone and thus, we are literally all products of relatively small cooperating, iterating and moving groups. Such is the most natural formation of the human species, and only recently, during the colonial era, did Homo sapiens become reunited again. Whether through coercion, persuasion or consensus, different ideologies gained global reach. Large-scale societies and nation states are thus young stages of human evolution and very recent historical phenomena. Nowadays, we live in a strange hybrid of strong individualism and massive nation states, but by nature we are most definitely tribal.

Named after the evolutionary psychologist, *Dunbar's Number* describes the cognitive limit of people we can have meaningful and stable relations with. This is fascinating because it really puts evolutionary forces on their head; it suggests that human brains evolved as an adaptation to a specific group size, not vice versa. Robin Dunbar has made extensive research with other like-minded scientists and discovered groupings of roughly 150 almost everywhere he looked. The few remaining hunter-gatherer societies tend to adhere to such a number, as do the smallest autonomous military unit in ancient as well as modern armies. The communes of the *Hutterites* and *Mennonites, Amish*-like sects of North America, divide when their numbers exceed 150. But so do the offices of many modern corporations. Dunbar and fellow researchers believe that this was the number of people in the tribes of Homo sapiens emigrating out of Africa. Our modern ability to emphasize with that amount of people is like a "behavioral fossil" of the incredible human ability to overcome hardship in oversee-able groups. This is very significant considering each and every one of us is a descendant of those groups and there exist no descendants of genetic losers.[39] Even online, we conglomerate in numbers close to Dunbar's.[40]

Behavioral traits often pull in opposing directions within groups, causing rivalry, competition and inequality. Indeed, every person has pressing individual *and* social needs to cope with every day, and given a choice, they could meet such needs with either *selfish* or *selfless* behaviors. But let us not forget that we *are* one of the most social species on earth, outperforming even the social insects when it comes to getting along with individuals outside of kin. Biologist E. O. Wilson argues that humans are one of only a handful of *eusocial* species ever to live. According to Wilson, *Eusociality* is the highest, most complex level of societal organization consisting of factors such as many individuals caring for related and unrelated offspring, a multi-generational contract and a strong division of labor.[41] The emerging picture of ancestral humanity is one of *radical egalitarianism* checked by immense peer pressure often shown by displays of *hive-mind*, but this is done through *group self-regulation*, not *individual self-interest*. Teamwork is the signature of this species *because* early humans developed the ability to suppress self-serving behavior and it is there that the secret to successful *management of common resources* lies. In a *Scientific American* article, D. S. Wilson and E. O. Wilson eloquently summarize: "Selfishness beats altruism within groups. Altruistic groups beat selfish groups. Everything else is commentary."[42]

But self-promotion is not always a zero-sum game where one takes as much away from the other as possible. For example, in the *ultimatum game* of experimental economics, two players interact anonymously and are ensured that the encounter will not be repeated. A proposition as to how to divide a sum of money is made by one of the players. If the second player likes the proposal, both walk away with their sum of money, but if the proposal is rejected, neither gets anything. Interestingly, most people prefer something akin to fairness and will not wager below an 80/20 cut. Choosing to get nothing rather than something in the name of fairness shows that individuals cannot be acting *only* under the banner of self-maximization. Why would anyone turn down free money? There are also cultural differences in what is considered fair and ethical, and such differences are likely due to the social conditions of different people and thus concepts of morality likely coevolved with conditions of society.[43] Once again, human behavior is *contextual*, and since context can be designed to be different, that is good news. Really good news! The preferences that we have are not fixed but fluid, depending on environmental and social change. We are not isolated cogs but interconnected units in a vast biosphere. We don't calculate, as *rational choice theory* would like to have it, but approximate.[44]

To be sure, *utility maximization*, the fact that individuals will always choose an action that will enhance the payback of the resources invested is close to axiomatic. Most students of human behavior concede on the question of *utility maximization* of individuals. Although the *Austrian school of economics* is less dogmatic about it than *neo-classical economics*, here they also agree. Even the Buddha said so much in his *second noble truth*: non-satisfaction is caused by a craving to be better off. And there is a clear evolutionary rationale behind it. It is commonsensical and supported by modern research in *evolutionary psychology* and *neuroscience* that nature designed rewards for behavior that fosters self-preservation.

The pleasure an organism receives *cannot* last forever. After all, if the sensation of pleasure after a good meal stayed indefinitely, we'd never seek food again. First meals would be last meals, given that hunger would never return, and this would mean the end of any species. If after a single act of lovemaking, one would just lie around basking in the afterglow of an *oxytocin*-induced high forever, only a limited number of genes would be passed into the next generation. There must be a hangover for any creature that strives to be high. It makes scientific sense that our brains focus more on the pleasure accompanying the attainment of a goal than on the fact that the pleasure will dissipate quickly after reaching such a goal. If individuals focus on the reinforcing pleasure as they try to get to sex, food and social status, they will keep trying, and if they focus on the impermanence of all sensations, they will soon become ambivalent. In the words of evolutionary psychologist Robert Wright, "Natural selection doesn't 'want' us to be happy, after all; it just 'wants' us to be productive, in its narrow sense of productive."[45] On the biochemical level, it is *dopamine*, a neurotransmitter that correlates with pleasure and the anticipation of pleasure. But beyond inner implications of well-being, we must also consider society.

One type of intrinsic motivation, albeit directed outward, is *altruism*, which is regarded as a personal disposition diametrically opposed to selfishness and can be triggered by the right circumstances. Evolutionarily, *altruism* is defined as the behavioral trait of an individual, which brings an advantage to others, and in the case of "strong altruism" actually hurts the carrier of the trait.[46] *Altruism*, as a behavioral trait, logically only starts to make sense when we consider actions on others and consider selection principles at the *group level*. We are not only self-interested but also highly social and reciprocal. When viewed on a higher level of selection, that of the group, than *selflessness* rather than *selfishness* is a winning strategy. Already Charles Darwin speculated about morality on two distinct levels of selection:

> There can be no doubt that a tribe including many members who, from possessing in a high degree the spirit of patriotism, fidelity, obedience, courage, and sympathy, were always ready to give aid to each other and to sacrifice themselves for the common good, would be victorious over most other tribes; and this would be natural selection.[47]

Multilevel selection theory tries to compensate for a discrepancy between local and global processes, while predicting circumstances under which altruism may evolve. The answer as to how that may be possible is to see selection pressures to work on the three different levels of genes, individuals and groups. Thus, the genes for selfless behavior survive even if only a small group of "heroes" hold them. The *proximate* reason we often act selflessly – rather than selfishly – is because it feels good. The deeper, ultimate reason is that it *is* good for us to cooperate.[48] The glue that holds us together as a society is the same glue that holds smaller biological parts together for a greater good.[49] Indeed, the phrase "together we stand, divided we fall," seems to be an axiom of life as we know it. Since small units have a slimmer chance at survival than larger ones, cooperation is likely favored by evolution. As argued by biologist Lynn Margulis, life itself emerged from the very first cooperating prokaryotes making a single eukaryote.[50] At an infinitely higher level of complexity, we find the human species' intense pro-social behavior where the common good is often protected by the ultimate sacrifice of one's own life.

We will wrap this section up with a story encapsulating all that has been said thus far. Very early on the morning of May 11, 1864 the *Invercauld*, a cargo ship with a crew of 25 people, crashed on rocks off Auckland Island, New Zealand. The impact must have been extreme, because the ship broke up instantly and only 19 of the crew members managed to make it to the shore. The survivors had no leader or coordination, they split up several times and left the weakest to die. There was even a report of cannibalism as one member died in a violent struggle and was partly eaten by the aggressor. By the time rescue finally arrived, only three members remained alive. Fascinatingly, this *natural experiment* of survival strategies had a control group. Another ship, the *Grafton* crashed on the other side of the same island in the same year. In a strange twist of the *prisoner's dilemma*, the two crews did not know of one another and thus could not communicate or share crucial information. The survival strategies of the *Grafton* were different as they helped each other until the end. They even designed a kind of makeshift school learning and teaching each other while waiting for rescue. They had at their disposal what Nicholas Christakis called a *suite of behaviors*, apparently superior – evolutionarily speaking – because everyone surviving the original crash also survived on land.

Besides these horrible incidences of 1864, much other research shows humans coming together not in times of leisure and prosperity but actually during dire straits. All humans – no matter their gender, race or other groupings – share cooperative social tendencies, including the ability to learn, relationships of friendship and love, as well as mutual trust. Such traits are crucial for adaptation and survival, as is the human ability to develop, improve and preserve culture. They are a *behavioral suite* that serves as a blueprint for cooperation.[51]

Artifacts

Everyone alive today is a descendant of cultured and tool-making ancestors. We hold both their genes and their tools. Of course, we are not born with anything in hand but most definitely with the potential to conceive, craft and use things. We are specialists in constructing our own niches like a beaver constructs a dam, termites construct mounds and birds construct nests. The blueprint for the things we design – hand axes, houses and smartphones – is never genetically anchored, but the potential to shape existing matter into new forms and in new ways likely is. Within every population of organisms there exists a huge pallet of *phenotypic variation* with respect to morphology, physiology and behavior. But not everyone has the same chances, and different traits confer different rates of survival and reproduction, a concept known as *differential fitness* in biological anthropology. Truly, the entire *theory of evolution* is based on diversity on every level from groups of individuals to individual molecules. Different traits, too, are passed from generation to generation.

But what about humanity's most complex survival skills – ideation and innovation; how are they a result of evolutionary processes? For *Homo habilis*, which literally means "handy man," the trump card was the design and manufacture of tools, but this was surely not done on an individual level. Of course, there exists an abundance and continuous change of Paleolithic tools over the past two and a half million years. *Paleolithic archaeology*, which has existed as an academic discipline for over 150 years, has collected, categorized and given names to different cultures and industries, but the question as to how things were made is often neglected. Strange, because it undeniably is biological and behavioral capacities and cultural innovations that evolve, not the artifacts themselves.

Human-made things are usually immediately distinguishable from things found in nature. They send a code for their recognition and use and thus the *techno-sphere* (inhabited by man-made things), just as much as the *biosphere* and *geosphere*, also falls under the jurisdiction of *biosemiotics*. In a brilliant argument, historian George Basalla posits that all *artifacts* come from other already existing artifacts. Following evolutionary logic, the first one would then come from a *naturfact*, and an altered *artifact* is different insofar as it doesn't reproduce but *is* reproduced by humans. The reproduction of artifacts works on the *phenotype* and in true evolutionary fashion follows the same principles as seen in nature: *variation, selection* and *retention*. According to Basalla, selective pressures operate on technical entities just like on biological ones; some are selected positively to be used and reproduced, and others are selected negatively and discarded. The direction of selection always depends on better or poorer fit to environmental conditions. Concerning artifacts, economic, military, social and cultural factors are involved in determining their fate.[52]

Michael Schiffer, an *experimental archaeologist*, made the key observation that any new technology requires much more than simple invention. It foremost requires a series of steps, most of which are experimentations in refining the processes or forms for local circumstances. Most importantly, a novel behavior must be copied beyond a small sphere of specialists or early adopters; many people must be aware of its utility and copy it.[53] It seems that the archaic process of ideation, manufacture, distribution and communication of the first gadgets could only have happened through teamwork and continuous feedback between "designers" and users.[54] It is tempting to see all the material stuff left behind as results of individual, ancestral designers, but when rigorously studying the archaeological record design surely was participatory and sources open! The processes and conditions allowing people to learn new ways of doing things had to be just right before any of them decided to emulate them. "Social learning parasitises innovation," noted Richard McElreath, an *evolutionary ecologist*.[55] Epistemologically speaking, for any of this to happen a large proportion of a population had to process the necessary cognitive processes underlying the creative act.

In the classic *The Design of Everyday Things*, cognitive psychologist, engineer and designer Don Norman muses about such things as he stayed up late drinking beer with his friend. Psychologist J. J. Gibson was a pioneer of *ecological psychology*, which claims that the mind directly perceives environmental stimuli and then computes an appropriate interaction with them. Although the two "disagreed about almost everything," one very important concept about human interaction with things arrived in the world of design:

affordances, or the meaning conveyed by objects about how to use them.[56] In the words of Norman, "Knobs afford turning, pushing, and pulling. Slots are for inserting things into."[57] We drink from a bottle's neck, because that is how we get to the liquid. We sit on a couch because that is what it was made for. It is the action offered. A "button" on a webpage *affords* me to interact with it like I might with a physical one. *Constraints*, on the other hand, are restrictions imposed by internal and external factors. Unfortunately, the couch might be too small for a nap. The design elements on artifacts that convey that message Norman called *signifiers*.[58]

Things as Mediators

I wander the city. I am alive today but am part of a species whose vast majority of evolutionary history was tribal, nomadic and radically different to all these colors, sights and smells around me. To me, all this was always here. I am not responsible for it. I am reminded of a poem by Alfred Housman, "I, a stranger and afraid in a world I never made."[59] Like most people alive today, I spend the vast majority of my lifetime inside this built environment, surrounded by artificial ground, light and air. But all these structures and artifacts are more than just brick and mortar. They play a kind of dramaturgical role in their relationship with me, their user. I wrap myself in these material edifices just like in semantic ones. Albeit not in words, the buildings and squares, hammers and cars also tell me stories. They actively co-shape my perceptions, experience, actions and existence on this planet. I use them to defy reality. They tell me what to do.

Armed with the latest technology, I refuse to admit that I am lost. How can I hope to find meaning in life; because of expectation of the perfectly planed, my mind has been coddled. I have a harder time dealing with annoyance. Technology is advancing at an incredible speed around me. Inertia creeps. By abandoning agency through app-aided walking, I stop absorbing many key elements of the built environment. Built-in *affordances* and *constraints* become obsolete. Who needs an information board? Road sign? Why talk to the indigenous? I am told to stay safe, within my comfort zone and away from anything strange. Am I becoming fearful of strangers, are my applications turning me into a *xenophobe*? In this city, everything is decided by techno-scientific determinism, and I am ushered like a zombie via algorithms and the hive's recommendations. I resist and keep on walking! Or, as read by poet Ras Jabulani, "walkin', walkin' away from the material, simple soul that I am."[60] *Psychogeographers* – those studying the effect of place on human emotions – have long advocated purposefully becoming lost in the city. They call it *dérive*, or "drift." It is the *flâneur*, or city stroller, who walks about urban streets, with no obvious purpose other than to simply wander. Iain Sinclair[61] and Will Self[62] drift through the cities; they report their thoughts in their elegant books. An equally beautiful but more scientific treatment of *psychogeography* can be found in Colin Ellard's *Places of the*

Heart.[63] But it is all psychological schools, east and west, that agree that human joy comes from overcoming hardship and solving problems.

The *artifice* is not just *artifacts*, idle lying around. *Artifacts* are in fact mediators in a relationship between humans and the world. Already in 1927, Martin Heidegger understood inanimate objects as embodied relations in their "readiness-to-hand"; they are incorporated, becoming an extension of their users.[64] In biological terms, Richard Dawkins sees them as part of the *extended phenotype* where genes do not only control protein synthesis inside an organism's body but also affect the organism's environment through that organism's behavior.[65] The philosophy of technology offered by Don Ihde speaks of another relation to artifacts, a *hermeneutic relation.* Here technologies do not provide a direct and incorporated access to reality, but rather they act as representations of reality. A wristwatch, for example, establishes a relationship between humans and reality by keeping track of the passing of time. Since technologies radically change our relationship with reality, it can be said to have agency, even intentionality.[66]

French philosopher, sociologist and post-constructivist Bruno Latour went further still, arguing for an "object-oriented democracy," where the role of technology, even science, must be reframed and linked with politics.[67] Latour famously asked for the creation of a "parliament of things," which should not be understood literally but metaphorically as a place where non-humans and humans stand at eye level, represented adequately.[68] We enter a very complex philosophical terrain here because, after all, *how* can we know what things really *are* or *want*, when humans increasingly have a hard time distinguishing between centuries of social constructions and different political ideologies? We can't even begin to know anything without recourse to language.[69] To make any sense of Latour's *parliament of things*, it is wise to focus on the *parliament* rather than the things, the relationship rather than the property. Latour does not make a plea for less technology or a return to untouched nature void of things, but rather for a more thoughtful use of technology.

Latour did not invent this kind of "anthropology of things," and it does have a considerable history. At the end of the 1800s Émile Durkheim, for example, already used his term *social fact* to mean equally a thing and a structure.[70] Marcel Mauss's *Gift* of 1950 gave a solid foundation to this analytic of things and is enjoying a kind of rebirth in current discussions of *post-capitalistic economies.*[71] And thus also can be understood Daniel Miller's analysis of material culture in his book *A Theory of Shopping.*[72] What sets Latour's approach apart, however, is the symmetry he draws between human and non-human entities. Here, society is seen as humans assembled around things instead of vice versa! The heavy barriers between the realms of nature and of culture that we have learned to accept are more like semi-permeable membranes. Even the age-old dualism of subject and object becomes fuzzier. Madeleine Akrich has pointed out that all artifacts contain "scripts," which dictate their use and configure their users, albeit in an ongoing process. These scripts are written in the imperative and it takes years of meditation to stare at a pen and see only a raw amassment of molecules and not an object to write with. Similarly, a single-use coffee cup has inscribed a script that says, "throw me away right after use," whereas the ceramic cup "wants" to be cleaned, handled with care and used again.[73]

Framed slightly differently to Akrich, Latour suggests "programs of action" encoded in artifacts and accessed when a given artifact is being used. The user also has such a program of action encoded by nature, culture and experience and when he/she enters a relationship with the artifact, the original *programs of action* of both are turned into a single new one. When that conversion is seamless, then design goes far beyond making shiny objects and matches necessity with utility, need with demand and feasibility with possibility. There is a wrinkle however, since the perfect melting of human and machine programs of actions does not necessarily lead to good outcomes. Take fast food. When a person's action program is to "upload massive amounts of sugar, salt and fat quickly," and this program meets that of a touchscreen menu at McDonald's ("fulfil desire for sugar and fat conveniently"), the new action program of the machine/human actor might be "eating junk food, alone and often."[74]

Modern Prometheus

This book talks about people, things and people transmuted to *users* and *consumers*. Primarily, however, it is about conceivers of things. I see designers as the bringers of culture or the "Prometheus of the everyday" as Italian designer Ezio Manzini has called them.[75] At the dawn of speciation, culture was synonymous with design and the designers have changed human trajectory by thinking in the auxiliaries of *could, would* and *should* in order to get away from what *is*. Countless millennia ago, hominids started on a trajectory from holding a rock to thinking about how that rock "should," "would" or "could" become a tool. And then they made what me might call a "hand axe" or "spear" for us to find and puzzle over.[76] Those hominids we labeled *Homo habilis* – literally handyman – were Promethean because, like in the Greek myth, they gave us culture. They were the original designers! They kindled a fire that kept burning until today, made camps and began to reconstruct their environment, their niche. We are so good at reasoning based on design from birth onward that it is very likely a genetically evolved adaptation.[77] Each one of us is a designer, *literally*. Humans have failed to evolve many offensive and defensive characteristics, such as a tough exoskeleton, claws or fangs, but we have gone far beyond mere biology and produced the most sophisticated culture on earth.[78] We made decisions with an eye on likely outcome, and if certain societal phenomena are unattractive, then the environments surrounding those phenomena were re-designed. Here, designers are seen as a Platonic ideal, as they are the ones who shape the world.

Of course, *design thinking*, as opposed to *designing*, refers to a specific methodology with a clear aim to foster creativity for problem solving but on a purely theoretical level, the crucial steps of design thinking are surprisingly similar to evolutionary theory.[79] The first step of *design thinking* is *generation*: here variation, and consequently innovation with a given set of ingredients, must be generated. The ingredients themselves must either mutate or recombine. Then comes *selection*: analogous to nature, the undisputed grand master of prototyping, patterns of information (or ingredients) that have been generated must now be tested under changing environmental contexts. While the genotype represents the genetic information of an organism, *natural, sexual* and *artificial* selection happens on the level of *phenotype*, which is what is represented. Finally, we have *retention*: in both biological evolution and *design thinking*, a pattern of information must be stored and reproduced. For living things this is accomplished through inheritance and breeding, and for ideas, they must be retained in the mind, written down or otherwise recorded. Culture travels *intra* (across) and *inter* (between) generations, which is to say (in fancy language) the transmission of the *phenotype* works both genetically and culturally. *Brainsstorming* – I believe the term should be in the plural since singular *brainstorming* is just an individual going mad – is an important part of design's *ideation* stage. But neither the brain nor many brains will have any creative output if ideas are not saved. In this vein, founder of IDEO David Kelley praises the *Post-it* as a retention tool.[80] For digital, remote work tools like *Figma* or *Miro* are immensely useful for teams. In *design thinking*, testing of assumptions is done repeatedly through prototyping. To make yet another analogy to biology, a concept or idea is the *genotype*, while its prototypical representation is the *phenotype*.[81]

The process of design and product management is like the biological process of inheritance. The designer must try and understand what is done and desired on the level of phenotype, and some of the best available theories to make sense of the human mind and body are broadly the principles of *natural* and *sexual selection*. The third principle, *artificial selection*, helps when trying to understand cultural evolution. An artifact is ultimately chosen by a customer based on appearance, signaling and use agency. Products that impress aesthetically and functionally will likely be selected over others and sometimes first-to-market commodities mark a *path dependency*. The current industrial system is analogous to but relies strongly on a perversion of the Darwinian principles outlined above by making commodities seem inadequate, unrepairable and "so last year" in the combination of two terrifying realities: *conspicuous consumption* and *planned obsolescence*. The destiny of a product's use or waste is influenced heavily by the machinery of marketing-driven design, which decides it's *desirability, fashionability* and *user-friendliness*. The more those three metrics increase, the more desire is created and the more *user-data* we have. It is for this reason that I treat marketing-driven design along ethical lines. The "success" of much of modern design depends on sales. For end-users, buying decisions are often based on a delusion that bought product reduces the gap between what they are and what they are expected to be. The bigger the gap between what is "in" and what is "out" – a kind of Gini coefficient of status – the bigger the incentive. If the means of marketing-driven design is to create such incentives, does its end not become repugnant on *utilitarian* grounds?

Buckminster Fuller wrote, "a designer is an emerging synthesis of artist, inventor, mechanic, objective economist and evolutionary strategist."[82] But they can't be any of that if they are told an erroneous story of human nature. It seems so obvious that to change anything, creatives must be shown the sustainable, equitable and cooperative side of Homo sapiens in order to design that which reenforces such behavior in a virtuous cycle. Designers have the incredible power of *telling* another story by *making* it. I am hopeful, as I am seeing more and more designers who show courage through all the trials and tribulations they face when shaping a better story! In a truly Jungian sense, they can be heroes, who set out on a journey, are tempted and antagonized, but in the end triumph through reason and truth. Infinitely easier said than done, the current challenge is to design for a corrected story that prioritizes cooperation and sustainability. It is my ambition to help tell such a story for those designing for its protagonists.

Design Curricula

I now work in many different design universities across Europe. On a semestral basis I teach at the *IE University* in Madrid, *University of Applied Sciences* in Salzburg, *Moholy-Nagy University of Art and Design* in Budapest and *Strate School of Design* in Paris. I have held various courses and workshops at *ELISAVA School of Design and Engineering* in Barcelona, the *Hochschule für Gestaltung in Schwäbisch Gmünd*, the *Joanneum University of Applied Sciences* in Graz, *IED University* in Madrid, *Nottingham Trent University* and others. The departments I teach at are always in schools of design with different qualifiers, such as *product, interaction, transportation, strategic, Internet of Things, fashion, communication*, or *interior*. They are mostly master's degree programs, although at some of them (*IE University, Hochschule für Gestaltung, ELISAVA*), I also teach bachelor students. The courses I teach to design students include "Anthropology and Design," "User-centered Design," "Qualitative Research Techniques," "Ethnography," "Strategic Design," "Circular Economy" and "Social Design."

As you can see, I get around. At most of these schools, I am alone in teaching social science and humanities courses. That is great, you might think. You found a niche! To the contrary; I am shocked by how little support there is for such subjects, so important for the *future designer*. I need back-up! Concerning other design schools around the world, I decided to research what kind of courses await young design students, or at least what is on offer on their webpages. I looked at the ranking of design universities in the US, Asia, Australia and Europe, picked the best schools and made an *Excel sheet* of courses advertised in the human sciences (anthropology, psychology, demography), regenerative design (circular economy, biomimicry, material sciences) and ethics. The results were devastating. Ethics is wholly missing with notable exceptions of semester courses such as "Ethical Decisions and Leadership" or "Equity and Politics," and for the human sciences I found rather vague titles such as "Cultural Studies," "Design and Diversity" and the like. Fortunately, sustainability is becoming much more widespread, but it seems to focus mostly on material sciences.

The Archipelago

Different disciplines work in their respective *disciplines* on their specific interests to describe their findings using their specialized jargon. There seem to be some historical reasons for the divisiveness of university disciplines. Postmodernist Michel Foucault wrote of a kind of "archeology of knowledge," where different phenomena can be found in different *strata*, along with other seemingly unrelated phenomena. He discovered that the word *discipline* does indeed have two notions arising at roughly the same time: the word in the sense of domination and control on one hand, and universities becoming more and more fragmented and isolated on the other. Somehow, the different academic tribes controlled their subject matter, but then morphed into their fractal shapes, forgetting to communicate with each other. Political scientists write in their journals and preach to their converted circles while the psychologists over in the other department do pretty much the same.

The lack of communication between different disciplines is very real, but the famous metaphor of the pure yet lofty and removed *Ivory tower* does not adequately describe it. Evolutionary biologist David Sloan Wilson aptly changed the metaphor to the *ivory archipelago*, describing different academic disciplines in their isolated academic ecosystems. Used geologically, *archipelago* refers to an extensive group of islands, extremely interesting for the study of diversity since it offers proof of evolution both biological and cultural. Within it, every island hosts a unique interplay of environmental variables, becoming natural laboratories of what can arise, why, when and how. Not coincidentally, Darwin found the inspiration for his grand theory of variation through selection on the Galápagos Islands. Cultural variations, innovations and idiosyncrasies can also be observed and understood more readily on islands. Thus, some of the first ethnographic fieldwork by Bronislaw Malinowski conducted on the Trobriand archipelago taught us about distinct systems of trade, kinship and magic.

It has become painfully clear that some of the truly wicked problems – climate change, biodiversity loss, energy prices – can only be solved through a multidisciplinary and systemic approaches, yet we continue to live and work on our separate islands in the *ivory archipelago*. This is tragic since, in the words of the late evolutionist E. O. Wilson:

> Most of the issues that vex humanity daily ... cannot be solved without integrating knowledge from the natural sciences with that of the social sciences and humanities. Only fluency across boundaries will provide a clear view of the world as it really is.[83]

Notes

1 Wilson, D. S. (2007). *Evolution for Everyone: How Darwin's theory can change the way we think about our lives.* Delta.
2 https://www.youtube.com/watch?v=2X1iwLqM2t0, accessed on February 15, 2024.
3 Chudek, M., & Henrich, J. (2011). Culture–gene coevolution, norm-psychology and the emergence of human prosociality. *Trends in Cognitive Sciences*, 15(5), 218–226.
4 Tooby, J., Cosmides, L. & Barkow, J. (1992). *The Adapted Mind: Evolutionary psychology and the generation of culture.* Oxford University Press.
5 Chomsky, N. (2002). *On Nature and Language.* Cambridge University Press.
6 Geary, D. C. (2012). Evolutionary educational psychology. In *APA Educational Psychology Handbook, Vol. 1. Theories, constructs, and critical issues* (pp. 597–621). American Psychological Association.
7 Bjorklund, D. F., & Pellegrini, A. D. (2000). Child development and evolutionary psychology. *Child Development*, 71(6), 1687–1708.
8 Geary, D. C. (2002). Principles of evolutionary educational psychology. *Learning and Individual Differences*, 12(4), 317–345.
9 Barrett, L. F. (2020). Forward into the past. *APS Observer*, 33.
10 Lancy, D. F. (2014). *The Anthropology of Childhood: Cherubs, chattel, changelings.* Cambridge University Press, pp. 327–328.
11 Somit, A., & Peterson, S. (2003). *Human Nature and Public Policy: An evolutionary approach.* Springer.
12 Tooby, J., Cosmides, L. & Barkow, J. (1992). *The Adapted Mind: Evolutionary psychology and the generation of culture.* Oxford University Press.
13 Buss, D. M. (Ed.) (2015). *The Handbook of Evolutionary Psychology – Volume 1: Foundation.* John Wiley & Sons, p. 6.
14 Cosmides, L., & Tooby, J. (1994). Beyond intuition and instinct blindness: Toward an evolutionarily rigorous cognitive science. *Cognition*, 50(1–3), 41–77.
15 Pinker, S. (2000). The blank slate, the noble savage, and the ghost in the machine. *Tanner Lectures on Human Values*, 21, 179–210.
16 Barrett, P. H. (2016). *The Works of Charles Darwin: Vol. 23: The expression of the emotions in man and animals.* Routledge.
17 Dunbar, R. I. M., & Barrett, L. (Eds.) (2007). *Oxford Handbook of Evolutionary Psychology.* Oxford University Press.
18 Appleton, J. (1996). *The Experience of Landscape.* Wiley.
19 Kaplan, S. (1992). Environmental preference in a knowledge-seeking, knowledge-using organism. In *The Adapted Mind: Evolutionary psychology and the generation of culture* (pp. 581–598). Oxford University Press.
20 Orians, G. H., & Heerwagen, J. H. (1992). Evolved responses to landscapes. In *The Adapted Mind: Evolutionary psychology and the generation of culture* (pp. 555–579). Oxford University Press.
21 Eibl-Eibesfeldt, I. (1997). Human ethology: Origins and prospects of a new discipline. In *New Aspects of Human Ethology* (pp. 1–23). Springer.

22 Wilson, E. O. (1986). *Biophilia*. Harvard University Press.

23 Dutton, D. (2009). *The Art Instinct: Beauty, pleasure, and human evolution*. Oxford University Press.

24 Orians, G. H., & Heerwagen, J. H. (1992). Evolved responses to landscapes. In *The Adapted Mind: Evolutionary psychology and the generation of culture* (pp. 555–579). Oxford University Press.

25 Pigliucci, M., & Kaplan, J. (2010). *Making Sense of Evolution: The conceptual foundations of evolutionary biology*. University of Chicago Press.

26 Ulrich, R. S. (1986). Human responses to vegetation and landscapes. *Landscape and Urban Planning*, 13, 29–44.

27 Balling, J. D., & Falk, J. H. (1982). Development of visual preference for natural environments. *Environment and Behavior*, 14(1), 5–28.

28 Miller, G. (2009). *Spent: Sex, evolution, and consumer behavior*. Penguin.

29 Coss, R. G. (1990). All that glistens: Water connotations in surface finishes. *Ecological Psychology*, 2(4), 367–380.

30 Meert, K., Pandelaere, M. & Patrick, V. M. (2014). Taking a shine to it: How the preference for glossy stems from an innate need for water. *Journal of Consumer Psychology*, 24(2), 195–206.

31 Morphy, H. (1989). From dull to brilliant: The aesthetics of spiritual power among the Yolngu. *Man*, 21–40.

32 Burkhardt, R. W. (2005). *Patterns of Behavior: Konrad Lorenz, Niko Tinbergen, and the founding of ethology*. University of Chicago Press.

33 Gould, S. J. (2011). *Life's Grandeur: The spread of excellence from Plato to Darwin*. Random House.

34 Immanuel Kant: Kritik der praktischen Vernunft, Riga 1788, hier Kapitel 34, "Beschluß."

35 Schnall, S., Haidt, J., Clore, G. L. & Jordan, A. H. (2008). Disgust as embodied moral judgment. *Personality and Social Psychology Bulletin*, 34(8), 1096–1109.

36 Zaidel, D. W., Nadal, M., Flexas, A. & Munar, E. (2013). An evolutionary approach to art and aesthetic experience. *Psychology of Aesthetics, Creativity, and the Arts*, 7(1), 100.

37 Klein, R. G. (1999). *The Human Career: Human biological and cultural origins*. University of Chicago Press.

38 Singer, P. (2004). Animal liberation. In *Ethics: Contemporary Readings* (pp. 284–292). Routledge.

39 Dunbar, R. (2010). *How Many Friends Does One Person Need? Dunbar's number and other evolutionary quirks*. Harvard University Press.

40 Saad, G. (2013). Evolutionary consumption. *Journal of Consumer Psychology*, 23 (3), 351–371.

41 Wilson, E. O. (2012). *The Social Conquest of Earth*. W. W. Norton & Company.

42 Wilson, D. S., & Wilson, E. O. (2007). Evolution: Survival of the selfless. *New Scientist*, 196(2628), 42–46.

43 Henrich, J. (2020). *The WEIRDest People in the World: How the West became psychologically peculiar and particularly prosperous*. Penguin.

44 Shermer, M. (2008). The mind of the market. *Scientific American*, 298(2), 35–36.

45 Wright, R. (2017). *Why Buddhism Is True: The science and philosophy of meditation and enlightenment*. Simon and Schuster, p. 8.

46 Wilson, D. S. (2015). *Does Altruism Exist? Culture, genes, and the welfare of others*. Yale University Press.

47 Darwin, C. (1888). *The Descent of Man, and Selection in Relation to Sex*. John Murray, p. 166.

48 Shermer, M. (2008). Don't be evil. *Scientific American Mind*, 19(1), 58–65.

49 Wilson, D. S. (2015). *Does Altruism Exist? Culture, genes, and the welfare of others*. Yale University Press.

50 Gray, M. W. (2017). Lynn Margulis and the endosymbiont hypothesis: 50 years later. *Molecular Biology of the Cell*, 28(10), 1285–1287.
51 Christakis, N. A. (2019). *Blueprint: The evolutionary origins of a good society.* Hachette.
52 Basalla, G. (1988). *The Evolution of Technology.* Cambridge University Press.
53 Schiffer, M. B. (1992). *Technological Perspectives on Behavioral Change.* University of Arizona Press.
54 Mithen, S. (Ed.) (2005). *Creativity in Human Evolution and Prehistory.* Routledge.
55 Sih, A., Stamps, J., Yang, L. H., McElreath, R. & Ramenofsky, M. (2010). Behavior as a key component of integrative biology in a human-altered world. *Integrative and Comparative Biology*, 50(6), 934–944.
56 Norman, D. A. (1988). *The Psychology of Everyday Things.* Basic Books.
57 Norman, D. A. (1995). The psychopathology of everyday things. In *Readings in Human–Computer Interaction* (pp. 5–21). Morgan Kaufmann.
58 Norman, D. A. (2008). The way I see it: Signifiers, not affordances. *Interactions*, 15 (6), 18–19.
59 Housman, A. E. (1924). *Last poems.* CUP Archive.
60 Up, Bustle and Out. (2002). *Urban Evacuation.* Unique Records. Liner notes.
61 Sinclair, Iain. (2018). *Living with Buildings: And walking with ghosts – on health and architecture.* Profile Books.
62 Self, W. (2007). *Psychogeography: Disentangling the modern conundrum of psyche and place.* Bloomsbury.
63 Ellard, C. (2015). *Places of the Heart: The psychogeography of everyday life.* Bellevue Literary Press.
64 Van Den Eede, Y. (2011). In between us: On the transparency and opacity of technological mediation. *Foundations of Science*, 16, 139–159.
65 Dawkins, R. (2016). *The Extended Phenotype: The long reach of the gene.* Oxford University Press.
66 Ihde, D. (1990). *Technology and the Lifeworld: From garden to earth.* Indiana University Press.
67 Latour, B. (2005). From realpolitik to dingpolitik. In *Making Things Public: Atmospheres of democracy* (p. 1444). MIT Press.
68 Latour, B., & Roßler, G. (2001). *Das Parlament der Dinge.* Suhrkamp.
69 Kelly, K. (2011). *What Technology Wants.* Penguin.
70 Durkheim, E., & Durkheim, E. (1982). What is a social fact? In *The Rules of Sociological Method and Selected Texts on Sociology and Its Method* (pp. 50–59). The Free Press.
71 Pyyhtinen, O. (2016). *The Gift and Its Paradoxes: Beyond Mauss.* Routledge.
72 Miller, D. (2013). A theory of shopping. In *Emotions* (pp. 307–310). Routledge.
73 Fallan, K. (2008). De-scribing design: Appropriating script analysis to design history. *Design Issues*, 24(4), 61–75.
74 Latour, B. (1992). Where are the missing masses? The sociology of a few mundane artifacts. In *Shaping Technology/Building Society.* MIT Press.
75 Manzini, E., & Cullars, J. (1992). Prometheus of the everyday: The ecology of the artificial and the designer's responsibility. *Design Issues*, 9(1), 5–20.
76 Simon, H. A. (1988). The science of design: Creating the artificial. *Design Issues*, 4 (1/2), 67–82.
77 Wilson, D. S. (2011). *The Neighborhood Project: Using evolution to improve my city, one block at a time.* Hachette.
78 Lorenz, K. (1964). Ritualized fighting. In *The Natural History of Aggression* (pp. 39–50). Academic Press.
79 Thoring, K., & Müller, R. M. (2011, October). Understanding the creative mechanisms of design thinking: An evolutionary approach. In *Procedings of the Second Conference on Creativity and Innovation in Design* (pp. 137–147).

80 Kelley, T., & Kelley, D. (2013). *Creative Confidence: Unleashing the creative potential within us all*. Currency.
81 Thoring, K., & Müller, R. M. (2011, October). Understanding the creative mechanisms of design thinking: An evolutionary approach. In *Proceedings of the Second Conference on Creativity and Innovation in Design* (pp. 137–147).
82 Buckminster Fuller, R. (2001). *Your Private Sky: Discourse*. Springer Science & Business Media, p. 301.
83 Wilson, E. O. (1998). The biological basis of morality. *The Atlantic Monthly*, 281(4), 53–70.

2

SIGNALS

Interactions with Our Surroundings

The Spirit of Things

It is striking that designers often speak of the *spirit* of good design. That *spirit* is their decisive goal, yet it escapes definition, description and often evades discussion. From the Latin *anima* ("breath, spirit, life"), animism refers to the belief in the possession of a spiritual essence or soul of non-human entities such as animals, plants or inanimate objects. Interestingly, the vast majority of cultures do not have a term for such a belief and even the described practitioners of *animism* do not use the term, suggesting that the phenomenon is little more than a construct of 19th century Europe. Communicating with inanimate objects is nothing new and humans have likely done it since the beginning of our species, but what was a one-directional monologue has in recent years transmuted into a full-blown dialogue. Would a person alive during the first Industrial Revolution think it possible to send information through thin air to be received by a magical box that then squirts out rows of material and makes an object? What we now call 3D printing involves a complex interaction between users and machines. It is also an example of the archaic tug of war between the two.

Already in 1877 Thomas Edison, thirty years after Max Weber's introduction of *Entzauberung*,[1] made his "talking machine" to reproduce "Mary Had a Little Lamb," which he had just sung into a cylinder. For the first time one was able to listen to the magic of the reproduction of one's own voice. An ensuing discussion ran counter to the Weberian concept and caused widespread anxieties about a spirit world hidden in electrically animated objects. One can only speculate on the reaction of the same people to what we have now. As our tools' communication improves, users move in a little closer to listen and respond. We already pinch, tap, touch, hold and talk to our

DOI: 10.4324/9781003464754-4

devices, and it seems that, ironically, modernity has returned to a kind of *animism*. With hindsight it seems that Weber's concept did not age well and industrial technology has re-enchanted the world. Every day the impossible happens. *Wiederverzauberung?*[2] Anthropologist Alfred Gell calls the spell that speaking, beeping and flashing objects have on us the "enchantment of technology." He writes that this is "the power that technical processes have of casting a spell over us so that we see the real world in an enchanted form."[3] When the animated objects around us become interconnected – like the *Internet of Things* (IoT) – our living rooms turn into living entities and we turn into modern shamans staring in disbelief. Indeed, it has become more normalized to be animistic, as the things around us are gaining "souls." Our phones communicating with our cars, thermostats, washing machines and us has become a present scenario; the relationship we have with everyday objects is changing with what might be described as a kind of renaissance of animism. Of course, things have still not literally been animated, but the distinction between life and death has become a little trickier and more complex to manage. As the things around us become "alive," is it not feasible to expect more emotionality and experience?

Edward Tylor first articulated the term *animism*, calling it the "idea of pervading life and will in nature."[4] According to him, animism was part of a non-dualist stage of belief systems, which strongly suggested spiritual or supernatural perspectives and came before the development of organized religion. Tylor's *animist stage* of belief was followed by a *polytheistic* and final *monotheistic stage*. Tylor's animism had no institution (e.g., a synagogue, mosque or church), no infallible doctrine (e.g., a belief in a son of God) and no sacred literature (e.g., the Hebrew Bible, the Quran, the New Testament). In fairness, Tylor did not propose a clear-cut division between animists and non-animists. He did concede that the strange animistic rituals that we continue practicing are *survivals* of times past. Examples include the knocking on inanimate wood in order to expel any bad spirits that might interfere with future plans, or the widespread use of talismans and lucky charms. His definition of such *survivals* – processes, customs, opinions and so forth – which have been carried on by force of habit into a new state of society different from that in which they had their origins, thus remain as proof of an older condition of culture out of which a newer one has been evolved.[5]

Animism now stands for traditionalism; for an outdated, even absurd practice no longer done. The term also became part of a larger construct of the notion of a time before and after bestowing souls onto material things, a time before and after modernity. It was a rejection of an eternal dualism as proposed by René Descartes and today it is anchored in the esoteric, non-scientific traditions. In his *Primitive Culture*, Tylor clearly laid out the task of cultural anthropology to discover "stages of development or evolution" and thus became one of the most important *unilinear evolutionists*.

In a quick excursion, it is important to stress the danger and far-reaching consequences of the ideas behind *unilinear* evolution. They are intrinsically related to *modernization theory*[6] via the writings of the so-called *neo-evolutionists*, which suggest that civilizations imperatively have to move through the same stages of development. They are linked to the very idea of humanitarian efforts of world development conducted by European culture. Together with a blind faith of ever-growing GDP and deregulated markets they have dire consequences. But, if we really have moved beyond a spirited world save for a few vestibules, if we really have modernized, when did it happen?

Ever since Descartes's *Discourse on Method* modern Europeans have decided to think dualistically in terms of subject and object.[7] But such a mode of classification was just that: a classification. To a large degree *modernism* is based on objectifying nature, of doing away with any notion of a subject–subject based relationship. Another intellectual tradition born of the 19th century, positivism, raised technology to Godly heights and with it created a semi-religious faith in techno-scientific progress and empirical methods. It is interesting to note Auguste Comte, a staunch atheist who aimed to raise a secular and scientific worldview to the height of a competing Catholicism.[8] For Comte, Tylor and the 19th century scholars, there simply was no room for a worldview that regarded all natural phenomena on par. Therefore, it seems there are two problems with the original perception of *animism*. First, the belief system was wrongly defined, and second, the so-called developed world, the West, isn't really Cartesian.

The Eyes of the World

Until recently, the core of anthropological literature saw indigenous knowledge as mistaken epistemologies, as un-scientific and irrational worldviews. However, currently the tables are turning, and indigenous thought is used as a critique of Western epistemology of modernization. And so, anthropologists and comparative religion scholars have re-defined *animism* to mean something different.[9],[10] Our very relationships with the world, and the frontiers between human and non-human – even between living and non-living – are being reconsidered. Nurit Bird-David (1999) and Philippe Descola (1994) have shown that not only ancient but also contemporary people with diverse systems of subsistence continue to approach their non-human environments through what is now being called a *relational stance*.[11],[12] Radically, such *posthumanism* has spawned discussions on building a new modernity after the present world order.[13]

Stewart Guthrie, in an extensive and comprehensive discussion of animism and anthropomorphism, defines animism as humans "attributing life to the non-living" and anthropomorphism as "attributing human characteristics to the nonhuman."[14] Animism is now treated as an alternative, relational ontology allowing a rethinking of the problem of matter and agency and as a worldview that goes beyond human exceptionalism and superiority; one that embraces all non-humans. For Descola animism is considered an understanding that all classes of beings (human and non-human) exchange signs, similar to the tenet of the field of *biosemiotics*, where everything that occurs in the universe is a semiotic event.[15] What emerges is a scientifically sophisticated animism, which understands all things as related in their nature as signaling entities, but different in their physical appearances or phenotype. Entities such as plants or even rocks may be approached as communicative subjects rather than the inert objects perceived by rationalists. And indeed, smartphones and microwave ovens that beep and blink are signaling entities, and if we respond to them in a purposeful manner, then communication is complete. This new perception of animism is important because it overcomes the 19th century conundrum of animism as nemesis to modernity. Bruno Latour writes: "There is no way to devise a successor to nature, if we do not tackle the tricky question of animism anew."[16]

Let us return to this curious notion of the *parliament of things*. It is probably the most radical notion emerging in a discussion on a new animism.[17] Latour argues that modernity was never more than a mode or ideology of sorting and that *pensée sauvage* (primitive thinking) was not displaced by a dualistic *pensée modern* (modern thinking). Of course Latour writes in accordance with structural anthropologist Claude Lévi-Strauss, who thought the savage mind did not belong to primitive people but was a kind of mind untamed by rational domestication.[18] Thus, we have actually "never been modern" and the notion of modern people cleanly separating the world of subjects and objects might have been an illusion from the start.[19] If all matter has spirit, then the Cartesian duality of mind and matter and that of society and nature become senseless. Modern society seems to have rested on a collective self-delusion from the start. There is no before and after in history. A modern, rational mind never replaced a superstitious, primitive one, just like the conquistadores of various eras and nations never found savages on lower evolutionist strata. In short, mistaken epistemologies aren't replaced. In the words of Latour:

> If there is one thing to wonder about in the history of Modernism, it is not that there are still people "mad enough to believe in animism", but that so many hard-headed thinkers have invented what should be called in-animism and have tied to this sheer impossibility their definition of what it is to be "rational" and "scientific". It is in-animism that is the queer invention: an agency without agency constantly denied by practice.[20]

It is not that we have no relationship with our things. Modern, industrialized Westerners animate objects around them more than the so-called animists, and in reality humans everywhere attach animacy and personhood to things. We talk to our cars and give them anthropomorphic forms. We have favorite trees, houses, cars and teddy bears. We curse at our computers, give our boats names and – at least children – sleep with inanimate forms resembling animals. According to Latour, such hypocrisy must be addressed by first accepting that the Cartesian dualism we are socialized to accept is phony in order to then recognize a new *parliament of things*. He writes:

> However, we do not have to create this Parliament out of whole cloth, by calling for yet another revolution. We simply have to ratify what we have always done, provided that we reconsider our past, provided that we understand retrospectively to what extent we have been modern, and provided that we rejoin the two halves of the symbol broken by Hobbes and Boyle as a sign of recognition. Half of our politics is constructed in science and technology. The other half of Nature is constructed in societies. Let us patch the two back together, and the political task can begin again.[21]

Closet Animism

Interesting for the discussion on whether humans have animist tendencies is the psychological phenomenon called *pareidolia*, which lets humans wrongly perceive a random visual or auditory stimulus as significant. Seeing animals or faces in clouds or the man in the moon, and hearing messages on Black Sabbath records when played in reverse, are examples of this sub-category of *apophenia*, the perception of patterns within random data. *Faces in the Clouds: A new theory of religion* actually sees *pareidolia* as part of *animism*, positing that this might be a fitting evolutionary explanation for the birth of religions.[22] It seems that we might be wired to see life rather than no-life in things. In the (critical) words of anthropologist Tim Ingold: "Thus we have all evolved to be closet animists without of course realising it. Intuitive non-animists have been selected out, due to unfortunate encounters with things that turned out to be more alive than anticipated."[23]

Another fascinating line of research suggests that we attach more significance to "original" artifacts than to copies, as if the former somehow bestows a soul or spirit. Psychologist Brandy Frazier and colleagues have found that college students consistently preferred "authentic" objects (paintings, signatures ...) to imitations even when the two cannot visually be differentiated.[24] Similarly, in a 2008 study, Bruce Hood of Bristol University demonstrated that school-age children were fooled into believing that an object can be "copied" but always preferred the original one to the "copied" one.[25] Hood and his team of scientists demonstrated in three separate studies that the destruction of a photograph of an object dear to the subjects produced significantly more electrodermal activity than the destruction of photographs of other control objects.[26] Another interesting study found that subjects do not like to wear a pullover – even after being thoroughly washed – when told that the garment belonged to Hitler.[27] Similarly, I was hesitant to buy an old ambulance van to convert into a camping bus, imagining all the suffering that took place in that vehicle. Too many ghosts!

Signaling Theory and Impression Management

With the publication of Charles Darwin's *The Expression of Emotions in Man and Animals*, the discussion moved well beyond merely explaining biodiversity to accounting for all the wonderfully superfluous detail in nature's designs.[28] Take an apple tree. To spread itself, nature has come up with an incredible system of *coevolution* where the information for the next tree is hidden inside a delicious shiny fruit, which can only be enjoyed if taken away from the tree. If an animal eats the entire apple – seeds and all – it even carries them off somewhere else to be dropped with an added heap of fertilizer. Yes, self-promotion and self-marketing are everywhere in nature for the simple fact that individual organisms need to be noticed by others of the same or another species. Very often organisms also need to stay hidden, and by blending in or being covered they stay alive. Such incognito techniques are just as much part of signaling as silence is part of a song. In *biosemiotic* fashion we can see the entire universe as a symphony of appearing and disappearing signals, *sounds, sights, tastes, smells* of living and non-living entities foremost as senders of signals to be perceived.

As for the "designing" process of nature, we must introduce sexual selection, introduced by Charles Darwin first in *On the Origin of Species* (1859)[29] and later in *The Descent of Man, and Selection in Relation to Sex* (1871),[30] as an addition to the mechanisms of *natural selection*, which are unable to account for many adaptations that don't help or even hinder in survival. *Mate choice* is intersexual competition and refers to human and non-human animals of one sex responding selectively to the other according to phenotypical (observable) stimuli. In plain language, before we engage with a potential sexual partner, we check them out – obviously because we want to see if particular traits are beneficial for us. The other main component of sexual selection is *intrasexual* competition of members of the same sex for access to members of the opposite sex. It is manifested by opulent display of resources – biological and cultural – as well as violence. In the words of evolutionary psychologist Geoffrey Miller: "Sex became the foundation of almost all complex life because it was so good at both short-term damage limitation … and long-term innovation."[31]

Signaling theory from biology now boasts a 30-year history and is likely the best tool for understanding animal communication, mating strategies and sexual dimorphism amongst animals (why males and females tend to look very different). Take the male deer, or buck, for example. We often get things entirely wrong when trying to explain why the male and not the female deer has this ridiculous gadget, aka antler, attached to its head. It is not to fend off other species preying on their families. Rather, the true function of the antler is signaling a very counterintuitive and silly sparring behavior. The buck will gather speed and then charge head-first against another male deer in order to hit the head containing the most important organ (the brain) against that of the opponent. This is done repeatedly, and as proof of victory, the antler grows branches like a tree, becoming tokens for establishing dominance in their herd and for competing for female mates, which in many ways amounts to the same thing. Stunted, broken antlers are proof of defeat. Such strange displays of strength make sense when compared to the alternative, which is actually fighting to get rid of competitors. Advertisement will always be cheaper than destroying the competitor. Amotz Zahavi, an Israeli biologist, developed the *handicap principle* to explain that only animals with very high-quality genes can afford to ostentatiously signal. Here, the signal's cost – not its meaning – becomes a good indicator for physical health.[32] Let us look at the classic example of the peacock, which sports a massive tail that can be fanned into and incredible display of color and ornamentation. That tail, however, is disadvantageous in a life-treating situation since it impedes both fight and flight. Neither does it have any added value in reproduction. The very fact that it is in the way, that it is a handicap, counterintuitively makes the peacock attractive to the peahen. The tail of the former is basically communicating, "in spite of this enormous thing tangling behind me, I'm still around to talk about it" to the latter. The signal works because the signaler is still around in spite of it. If it leads to reproduction, then the resulting offspring will have the genes for just such a tail. And probably also for telling the tale (pun very much intended).

There is a reason we started with examples from the non-human animal world. It is simply a more efficient approach since no one gets upset and starts picketing for animal sexual liberation or deer feminism. No doubt, there would be plenty of reason to, since sexual discrimination, iniquitous labor division and domestic violence are all rampant in the animal kingdom, but it is nearly impossible for us to escape our species-centric worldview. Humans are also animals, and they also fall into a basic biological framework: it is generally males who compete and females who select. Women and men have different strategies when it comes to mate choice, since an entirely different set of resources are at stake for either one. They follow basic rules of signaling and thus painting or piercing our faces is done by self, on self and for self – take a deep breath – only in terms of promotion. The antlers of the buck are kind of like the heavy bling worn by '90s-style rappers, and they are exactly like the heavyweight boxing belts worn by the one who remains standing. You are probably thinking of "the mirror argument" right now. I put on makeup to feel pretty, and I got that tattoo for myself, and I can see it in the mirror. Correct, but there is still a sender (you, facing the mirror) and the mirror is only a gadget that sends the image back to be perceived by you. Perhaps the semi-opaque windows of shops have the double function of displaying fabulous mannequins wearing a desired outfit and bouncing back an inadequate image of self, wearing something drabber. *Signaling theory* is a helpful framework for understanding patterns of digital communication. There, an important concept is that the cost of deceiving the receiver keeps signals within a limited range of honesty.[33] It is the *simulacrum* of you and your life that gets you the job and the date.

Of course, body ornamentation is only indirectly for self. Take tattoos. No matter how emotional inked people get about their skin art, its artist and the circumstances of the image, the tattoo is foremost a symbol for others to make sense of. If that beautiful image of the Buddha on your biceps is meant for you – the bearer of the canvas – then how come you did not have it drawn for me, the receiver to be upside down and you right-side up? Seems to me that your *samadhi* is only skin deep. Whether conscious or not, the ultimate function of body ornamentation is to signal to the outside world. We could call this one-upmanship *conspicuous rebellion,* where individuals try to signal their critique by displaying cultural capital. It is a difficult game because extremely subtle shades of gray could mean the difference between really bad-ass and mainstream. In his 1979 book *Distinction*, French post-structuralist Pierre Bourdieu wrote on the social logic of taste that "social identity lies in difference, and difference is asserted against what is closest, which represents the greatest threat."[34] As for tattoos, Polynesian-themed flora is not quite as "gangsta" as *familia* written in Chicano font, which in turn is suburban compared to a prison-style pen inking. How far do you let the images creep? Even the bearer of a full-sleeve tattoo ending at the cuffs likely thought of a future in an office. Do you write on the face? How far dare you stretch your earlobes? Small, medium or large? Or are we talking post-gauge, tangling lobe? Albeit concerning architecture, Adolf Loos understood this with his radical repudiation of ornaments. He realized that ornamentation is little more than an attempt to join inner and outer worlds in a coherent whole. The phenotype communicates the genotype. By getting rid of ornaments, Loos argued, the illusion of a harmonious unity is abandoned.[35]

We humans are very concerned about the state of our hair. Since it is an honest indicator of health and age, and since it is usually the only hair that we show, a lot of effort has always gone into hairstyles. It can be used to show (or hide) gender, age and race. Besides biological cues of immunity, nutrition and reproduction, it is also a way to illustrate a level of civilization or coun-ter-civilization, uniformity or rebellion. One important style of grooming amongst the creative class of the early 21st century was the *undercut*, and thank God that is now outdated. Granted, the *undercut* has recurred so many times it is now ideology-free, the Hitler hairdo is still making me ill. And then there is the *man bun*! Grown out only to be tied up, carefully piled to look carefree, it is truly oxymoronic. I see so many designers learning to make industrial products, services and applications for a future consumer society looking like Indian sages of renunciation. Really! But unlike the *sadhus* on the banks of the Ganges River, they crave lots of stuff and have no intention of overcoming their ego any time soon.

In his classic sociological text, "The Presentation of Self in Everyday Life," Erving Goffman employs helpful metaphors from the world of theater, describing individuals as "actors" on a "stage" called life.[36] The great efforts we all make in presenting ourselves as favorably as possible becomes obvious when we understand humans walking in modern cityscapes with Paleolithic algorithms in their heads. We are all just characters playing "roles" and united only by a "script" to appear like we are modern and living in the present tense. Of course, we want to look smart, attractive and well-off because at the end of the day there are only two purposes to life: to survive this life and any future life by passing our genes on. The tricky part is that all these signals range from honest to deceptive and hardly ever are they balanced. To leave a good impression, we truly "fake it all the way until we make it." We are far more likely to signal virtue than vice.

Already in 1890 – two decades before the ascent of modern marketing – American godfather of psychology William James wrote about the relationship between the acquisition of material possessions and a definition of the self. In his words:

> In its widest possible sense, however, a man's Self is the sum of all that he can call his, not only his body and his psychic powers, but his clothes and his house, his wife and children, his ancestors and friends, his reputation and works, his lands, and yacht and bank account. All these things give him the same emotions. If they wax and prosper, he feels triumphant; if they dwindle and die away, he feels cast down, not necessarily in the same degree for each thing, but in much the same way for all … An instinctive impulse drives us to collect property; and the collections thus made become, with different degrees of intimacy, parts of our empirical selves.[37]

In James' writing, the term *extension of self* was pioneered, but it was made popular by consumer researcher Russell W. Belk a century later. In his influential essay "Possessions and the Extended Self," Belk states that "knowingly or unknowingly, intentionally or unintentionally, we regard our possessions as part of ourselves."[38] Belk's work is not only methodologically dictated by consumer research, but has accelerated the consumption of certain objects by showing how their acquisition and utilization can help people express themselves through material goods. Thus, pursuits of self-enhancement and self-esteem seem to influence the buyer decisions of material goods. Recent research has shown that shopping goes well beyond the acquisition of necessities and towards signaling features.[39]

Signaling with Artifacts

Not just the production but also the acquisition of aesthetic objects brought our ancestors a survival advantage. Philosopher Dennis Dutton believes that all types of designing are innate and calls it the *art instinct.*[40] As we have seen, body aesthetics are easily explained through sexual selection theory and mate choice theories. But aesthetics is not only displayed via the *phenotype* (the body and/or behavior), but also the *extended phenotype* (products and other artifacts) an individual organism makes and is then associated with. This is not limited to animals alone. In a pioneering study of products as fitness indicators, anthropologist Marek Kohn and archeologist Steven Mithen have independently come up with an extraordinary twist on *sexual selection* theory to account for the exact symmetry and razor-like edges of Paleolithic hand axes. Such hand axes, varying little over vast temporal and geographical distances, were found in abundance and often lacked signs of abrasion. Strange as it may seem, their functionality may have moved beyond cutlery and to signaling attractiveness of the user.[41] Maybe the hand axe follows Zahavi's handicap principle on a meta-level. It is a materialized indicator for physical attributes since it is a costly process to produce and/or acquire it. Just like the owner of a flashy new smartphone, some Paleolithic guys (flashing resources correlates significantly more with males) wanted to be seen with one of these gadgets. Let us revisit the Australasian male bowerbird, which stays at and in the vicinity of the bower created by him for years. The bower is attended, maintained and improved on a daily base to display a beautiful collection of parrot feathers, blue berries and various shiny objects.[42] Humans take such conspicuous display much further and use housing, clothing, jewelry, even their own skin as canvas. In artistic expression the skill required to make something often *is* the show. A gymnast or skater may be physically fit, but the essence of their projection is skill. It is what impresses us, what separates something from routine and what has led to judgmental categories such as *higher* and *lower* art.

As we saw in the previous section, ironically, the latter can be seen as attractive because it is a *conspicuous waste* of resources. The challenge of our consumer society is to see how one agent can tell whether the signal sent by another is a truthful representation of a situation. Conversely, how might the signaler persuade the receiver that the truth is being communicated, no matter whether the situation is true or not? Such questions can potentially arise whenever there exists an asymmetry in information.

In the seminal *The Theory of the Leisure Class*, Thorsten Veblen combines economics and Darwinian theory to explain why we conspicuously consume.[43] The idea itself is very simple but its novelty is the mixing of evolutionary with economics theory. As individuals of a population 1.0 go through the trials and tribulations of life, striving to satisfy the basic needs of drink, food, shelter and finding reproductive partners, they will always be competing for finite resources. When a large number of these individuals have gone from *hand-to-mouth* lifestyles to ones where they can afford some luxury, Veblen calls them the *leisure class*. This population 2.0 might have been the hardest working or just the most lucky. In any case, the principles of selection don't stop and now individuals will go out of their way to demonstrate their status by conspicuously consuming more than their share of resources. This model not only explains why we overeat but also why we wear a Rolex watch, drive shiny cars or wear fancy clothes. Or boast about our house having five bathrooms when at end of the day you can only use one of them and trying to use all five would have disastrous consequences. Ironically, those who waste the most resources seem to find the most reproductive partners and climb up social ranks better than everyone else, and it is for this reason that we will signal our place in society. Greed is sexy! By encouraging *conspicuous consumption*, we are encouraging individuals to take utility maximization to go well beyond need. We are asking for *tragedies of the commons*. But, more on that later.

The most glamorous display of richness frequently comes from people who have a hard time paying their overhead costs. The display of wealth obviously is a prime example of *conspicuous consumption*, but what is especially interesting is its juxtaposition with the down-and-out poverty of the 'hood. It is a much larger sacrifice of resources for a person living in abject poverty to display an expensive car or jewelry than it would be for Bill Gates. As a matter of fact, the super-rich often go out of the way to show simplicity and modesty. There definitely is a correlation between conspicuous consumption and income, which correlates with race. In 2007, a US economic study revealed that African Americans and Latinos spent 25 percent more of their disposable income on jewelry, cars and apparel than those in white neighborhoods. However, this was only true when comparing poor neighborhoods with wealthy ones, and as soon as we look at blacks and Hispanics living in more affluent neighborhoods, we find that they spend much less on *conspicuous consumption*. It always depends on who we compare ourselves with. In terms of sustainability, we obviously also overcompensate for poor behavior in what is known as greenwashing. It is done on webpages but also on other, material facades of cars and houses. Put simply, the lighter something looks, the heavier it often is in its CO_2 footprint.[44] When trying to understand anything at all about the culture of consumerism, we always must look at the unit of selection.[45]

Something has gone terribly wrong when Jack Dorsey – Twitter CEO until the end of 2021 – with his trademark tattoo, nose-piercing and hipster-beard, could easily pass for the local lumber-sexual barista making foam art. Over-and-under-representation of self can be confusing, and I can think of no better example than the San Francisco Bay Area. By no coincidence does it also have an *absolute Gini coefficient of income inequality* score of over 70 percent, where zero percent is total equality and 100 percent means that one person gets everything and everyone else nothing. But there in Silicon Valley, even – or especially – the leaders of the most powerful tech companies are sporting eccentric leisurewear as, for example, Mark Zuckerberg with his iconic hoody over tight Lycra. It is easy to forget that he is CEO of *Meta*, and one of the richest and most powerful men on earth. He is part of a mighty elite running our world and refusing to wear anything remotely business-like. Walk into the *Googleplex, Apple Park* or a design consultancy and you notice flat hierarchies and laid-back dress codes as well as free espresso, ping-pong tables and nap cocoons, but the signal sent is most definitely not lavish wealth. Forget ties, shirts and old age! Here come the colorful, disruptive and eternally young. This is an example of *countersignaling*, whereby the more wealthy prefer to look cheap. In the words of psychologist Bruce Hood, "It has become almost a point of honor in Silicon Valley not to wear expensive clothes or suits, but rather jeans and trainers, which signals that you are more interested in tech than status."[46] As we know, behavior is contextual and false modesty works well in the right context. In a fascinating study conducted in high-end designer boutiques of Milan, shop assistants were asked to rate two shoppers, one of which was wearing pricy clothing and the other gym sweats. The assistants correctly rated the latter as more likely to buy expensive items.[47] Of course, those ferociously ugly *Yeezy* sneakers can cost thousands of dollars depending on their (fake) scarcity. Just ask a teenage *hype beast*, waiting for days for some sneaker to drop. All of this would be trivial if creativity was not so damn important. The stuff conceived in design and tech companies is changing the world at break-neck speed. Fake it until you make it and then move fast and break it.

By combining biological *signaling theory* and *conspicuous consumption* we can explain the Porsche Cayenne. The modern human has spent a lot of time driving around and they have found this to be an excellent opportunity to signal their worth. But now they must use the metal shell they are stuck in as their canvas. If you see a clean SUV (those actually used in dirty off-road situations are exempted here) maneuvering around cities with tiny streets it is a safe assumption that its driver is flaunting *conspicuous waste.* The argument is basically the same as above with the peacock, the difference being that the colossal metallic *extended phenotype* weighs three tons, and the carbon-based phenotype of feathers weighs about 300 grams. While it is estimated that about 3 percent of a peacock's daily energy budget goes into growing and maintaining its tail, humans likely spend much more energy making money in order to buy cars and gas. In times of peak oil, an inefficient, clunky SUV is definitely a handicap. Humans display richness, in the form of houses, cars and jewelry, not wealth, which, although it may be enormous, is invisible. I have seen several master's theses dedicated to and money invested by the automotive sector in researching the mere perception of car parts. To be perfectly clear, the question is usually not how production and use of a car can become efficient, durable or sustainable, but rather what form and appearance to give a car in order for it to *appear* all of those things. Frankly, to a naive non-designer, such research is mind-boggling in its Darwinian simplicity. There are armies of young and passionate minds dedicated to creating designs acting as signals to be received by people mostly outside of the vehicle. The driver cannot see all the gorgeous shapes of his or her car while driving; it would be dangerous and hopefully illegal to lean out of the window while roaring down the freeway to marvel at them. Take car rims: the shape and order of the spokes are invisible even from the outside while a car is moving. They are but a blur and can only be seen when the car is standing still. Likewise, a sticker on my car is not for myself either since I am already very much aware of the meaning of the sticker. Rather, I am following a strong desire to let other people, stuck in traffic behind me, reckon with that symbol. It is a car tattoo!

Consuming the World by Displaying the Self

Thou shalt covet! Thou shalt want very much your neighbor's house! Thou shalt want very much your neighbor's wife, or his male or female servant, his ox or donkey, or anything that belongs to your neighbor! Such sentences should sound very uncanny. I changed the last of the Ten Commandments into an imperative and the word "covet," due to its antiquity to "want very much." In its original, this commandment arguably is the cornerstone of Judeo-Christian civilization because it acts like a seal, which, when broken, might lead to breaking the others. The Torah (the five books of Moses) were apparently revealed to Moses sometime at the end of the 13th century BCE But the Talmud and Quran also explicitly warn about yearning for the property – wives of the ancient world were considered as such – of others. The intention here is not to moralize but it is blatantly obvious that the tenth commandment has been radically inverted in modern society.

Whether or not archeologically authentic, seeing the Ten Commandments in the context of a group of nomadic pastoralists on an excruciating journey through the Sinai desert can be helpful. Viewed evolutionarily, it makes perfect sense to demand of this group to agree on one God as a metaphorical father, to refrain from spreading falsehoods behind the person's back, to not sneak into the neighbor's tent at night to sleep with someone else's partner or to steal someone else's stuff. And none of those things would be a problem if we did not covet (want very much) each other's belongings. Christopher Boehm posits *radical egalitarianism* as a cultural adaptation for groups to suppress rivalry and conflict and lay the foundation for altruism to prosper genetically. His studies among current foraging hunters and gatherers as well as primate groups conclude that those individuals who desired and took more than their share were subject to social sanctions including gossip, ostracism and even homicide, although in a hostile environment, the latter two amount to the same thing. Small human groups are amongst the most cooperative and egalitarian thanks largely to cultural (or moral) dictates that suppress bullying and self-serving behaviors. If a situation makes it hard for individual members to dominate at the expense of each other, then another main avenue is to succeed as a group. Such success might be decided brutally on the battlefield, or in times of peace through the production of more offspring. In any case, a cultural norm of egalitarianism (such as the tenth commandment) suppresses within-group selection and magnifies variation among different groups, shifting the force of evolution to between-group selection.[48]

In pre-industrial times, not everyone could have everything, yet everyone knew each other and so coveting was a far more intimate problem, as it led to more violent conflict. Now it is a *tragedy of the commons* as it leads to global environmental consequences. The underlying psychological phenomenon, however, is the same: we *covet* artifacts because we *envy* the people with those artifacts. Most philosophical, spiritual and religious traditions would agree that envy is one of the very worst human emotions. The word itself is often preceded with qualifiers such as "vile," "repugnant," "green" or "deadly" and is the stuff of the world's myths. Out of envy for God's approval Cain kills Abel. Lucifer envies God's supremacy and is cast out of heaven to become Satan. Salieri envies Mozart's talent and apparently tried to poison him. The Wicked Queen envies Snow White's beauty and tries to take her out. And on and on it goes. Envying others usually leads to unhappiness and psychological crisis as well as toxic *Schadenfreude* – when we actually get pleasure from someone else's losses. Perhaps it is the most complex human emotion: Aristotle pointed out a distinction between *malicious envy* (where we resent the success of others) and *benevolent envy* (where we look up to and copy the success of others). Although not rational and not fit for standard economic theory, the latter version undeniably leads to competitiveness and has been employed as a main driver of consumerism.

Furthermore, it is no secret that the art of advertising commodities can be found in the *bandwagon effect*, according to which we behave in a certain way simply because others behave that way.[49] This effect can be a remarkable marketing strategy, when celebrities – the modern version of royalty – flaunt something material.[50] Nescafé did so well in part because George Clooney is shown sipping coffee, and to the archaic brain Clooney is an alpha male stakeholder. Such things are written deep into our DNA, and in this sense asking people to avoid or do things for the planet that lower their status, prestige and chances for sex is anti-natural. Indeed, marketers have long exploited the tribal nature of people. Is it not time to work with that same nature but skew benefits towards end-users?

More than other primates, we are an intensely hierarchical and status-seeking species. That is the bottom line. While it likely has always been the case that access to food, shelter and shiny objects got us ahead in society, easy access to all three got us into a kind of arms race of status. As we have seen, costly signaling that increases status and thus chances for romantic encounters is a peacock tail in the language of sexual selection theory. Person A often buys something because an envied consumer B already has it. A lot of purchasing decisions are made to "keep up with the Joneses"; to conspicuously display what others display. Thus, there seems to exist a strong link between human archaic desires and what has been called the *Anthropocene*. For example, a deep-seated need for status – from a gasoline-devouring yacht to constantly changing fashion accessories – can be directly linked to greenhouse emissions and pollution in waterways, which in turn propel climate change.

By seeing what, where and how things are consumed, we can maybe get to the big *why*. Geoffrey Miller's *Spent* stands as one of the most important books on this subject.[51] Products, services and experiences – all objects that humans interact with – exist basically for two reasons: they give us pleasure whether or not anyone knows we have them, and they display our desirable traits and bring status when we own them. We have forgotten the actual point of life – of first being and then having more beings. In a strange neo-Malthusian twist of fate, this species has maneuvered itself into a situation where neither is sustainable. Instead, we live lonely lives, with few children and to fill the void we consume. What the consumer wants to advertise could likely be psychological traits which are perceived as positive. Emotional content, feelings, thoughts, ideologies are all worn – quite literally – on the sleeves of the people walking around us. It is all there, pushed to the surface by the pumps and levers of marketing. Right there in front of us.[52]

Gad Saad of the Concordia Business School in Montreal is another pioneer in this type of thinking as he partially founded the field of *evolutionary consumer psychologist* with his book *The Evolutionary Bases of Consumption* in 2007.[53] Marketing schools around the world teach how to best sell the "sizzle rather than the steak," but no one seems to be interested in *why* something is desirable. Mental associations (the sizzle) have become far more important than the physical object (the steak). As a matter of fact, the entire point of marketing and advertisement is Pavlovian, by making things appear better than they actually are. Already in 1972, media critic John Berger wrote:

> Publicity is not merely an assembly of competing messages, it is a language in itself, which is always being used to make the same general proposal. It proposes to each of us that we transform ourselves and our lives by buying something more.[54]

Commodities themselves don't fetch nearly as much money as our mental constructs of them, and thus our attention is always held fast on the carrot at the end of the stick. Annie Leonard, the founder of the excellent *The Story of Stuff* cartoons and movies, demonstrates this vividly. If, for example, tap water costs us taxpayers a fraction of a cent, a marketed product called *Evian* is sold for several euros. Companies obviously try to shift from selling *commodities* to *products* when the margin to be made is exponentially higher.[55]

The *extended self* when scaled to the aggregate of society is one major cause of the global environmental crisis. But not only to the outer world, also for our inner world, consumerism is detrimental in its futility. Material abundance does not guarantee emotional and social abundance, and we have fallen prey to what Geoffrey Miller has called the *fundamental delusion of consumerism*. As marketing and advertising promises a delusional, narcissistic bliss produced by the subjective pleasure of consuming goods and services, we believe: (1) that below-average behavioral traits can be compensated by above-average commodities, (2) that consumption leads to lasting happiness and (3) that the display of clothing or products is a better way of signaling our natural fitness than simply introducing oneself to a stranger and explaining one's traits. The first two beliefs follow an erroneous logic since immaterial phenomena (behavioral traits) can never be compensated by anything material. If it were possible, we would have stopped consumption after reaching perfection. There must be something that keeps us feeling inadequate. Finally, all this signaling that we do with our cars and clothing and housing is in vain. Emphasizing and sympathizing with a fellow human being is a much more efficient form of communication.[56]

Truly tragic, the delusion persists even when understanding its empty promise. As the so-called *Easterlin paradox* suggests, after a certain point additional income does not guarantee happiness. It is named after the first economist who dared to include research into happiness in economics, Richard Easterlin. Turning citizens into consumers is dangerous on another level; unlike the former, the latter can only find self-expression by engaging in markets.[57] Consumerism thus benefits the economy, while undermining democracy, as the financial crash of 2008 showed. A fix to an innate need to display wealth and possession was advertised as subprime mortgages, which allowed low-income Americans to become homeowners. They had no chance to pay back loans and consequently caused the biggest housing bubble in history. Indeed, the very idea of credit is based on an idea of instant gratification of our desire to own and display but often does not address or alleviate basic living requirements. Only very few of us have enough liquid assets to buy a large house, fancy car or dress.

Consumerism is uniquely human, and although the term tends to have a negative connotation, it has become the most important aspiration in our societies. It acts as mirror to a complex being that *needs* to survive and reproduce and *wants* to purchase products to express success in both. Marketing 101! We will revisit this topic later, but for now it suffices to say that we live in a culture where more and more individuals express themselves through energy-hungry products and experiences. From the first tools used as artificial extensions of the human body all the way to mega-cities, humanity's *extended self* is changing the planet. The externalities of ever-faster fashion cycles of commodities conceived as single-use are not accounted for but seen in environmental degradation. Dawkins' *extended phenotype* has been commodified. Thus, the incentives to purchase commodities and experiences to flaunt phenotypically are diametrically opposed to environmentalism. These incentives are based on a strong desire to show how great we are by holding nifty gadgets, and they are pushed by marketing, advertisement and design. All of this is likely offensive for designers due to an aversion to Darwin and outward attraction to Marx. But truth be told, the motivation for hard work is not always building a better society but rather making money to buy stuff to show off with. Victor Papanek, firmly established in the pantheon of industrial designers, said it much better: "Advertising design, in persuading people to buy things they don't need, with money they don't have, in order to impress others who don't care, is probably the phoniest field in existence today."[58]

The statement is reckless in its honesty, but cuts to the reality of phenotypical signaling known throughout life on earth. So, you might wonder, what is it that humans desire? Sorry, but don't look at me for answers. Forget about anthropology, behavioral sciences or psychology. By nature, humans are insatiably hungry for novelty and for fitting into a given social order, and when such innate urges are not satisfied, we are left with the consumption and wasting of resources.

Notes

1 From German, it refers to the disenchantment that comes with modernity. Max Weber borrowed the term from Friedrich Schiller.
2 From the German for "re-enchantment."
3 Gell, A. (1992). The technology of enchantment and the enchantment of technology. In *Anthropology, Art and Aesthetics* (p. 44). Clarendon Press.
4 Tylor, E. B. (1871). *Primitive Culture: Researches into the development of mythology, philosophy, religion, art and custom* (Vol. 2). J. Murray.
5 Ibid. p. 63.
6 Rostow, W. W. (1990). *The Stages of Economic Growth: A non-communist manifesto.* Cambridge University Press.
7 Descartes, R. (1975). *Discourse on Method.* Barnes & Noble Books.
8 Comte, A. (1858). *The Positive Philosophy of Auguste Comte.* Blanchard.
9 Bird-David, N. (1999). "Animism" revisited: Personhood, environment, and relational epistemology. *Current Anthropology*, 40(S1), S67–S91.
10 Ingold, T. (2000). Evolving skills. In *Alas, poor Darwin: Arguments against evolutionary psychology* (pp. 273–297). Crown.
11 Bird-David, N. (1999). "Animism" revisited: Personhood, environment, and relational epistemology. *Current Anthropology*, 40(S1), S67–S91.
12 Descola, P. (1994). *In the Society of Nature: A native ecology in Amazonia* (Vol. 93). Cambridge University Press.
13 Hardt, M., & Negri, A. (2009). *Commonwealth.* Harvard University Press.
14 Guthrie, S. E. (2020). Religion as anthropomorphism. *The Oxford Handbook of Evolutionary Psychology and Religion* (p. 48). Oxford University Press.
15 Barbieri, M. (2009). A short history of biosemiotics. *Biosemiotics*, 2(2), 221–245.
16 Latour, B. (2010). An attempt at a "compositionist manifesto." *New Literary History*, 41(3), 471–490.
17 Simons, M. (2017). The parliament of things and the Anthropocene: How to Listen to "Quasi-Objects." *Techne: Research in Philosophy & Technology*, 21.
18 Wiseman, B. (2007). *Lévi-Strauss, Anthropology, and Aesthetics.* Cambridge University Press.
19 Latour, B. (2012). *We Have Never Been Modern.* Harvard University Press.
20 Borck, C. (2012). Animism in the sciences then and now. *E-flux Journal*, 36, 10.
21 Latour, B. (2012). *We Have Never Been Modern.* Harvard University Press, p. 144.
22 Guthrie, S. E. (1995). *Faces in the Clouds: A new theory of religion.* Oxford University Press.
23 Ingold, T. (2006). Rethinking the animate, re-animating thought. *Ethnos*, 71(1), 11.

24 Frazier, B., Gelman, S., Wilson, A. & Hood, B. (2009). Picasso paintings, moon rocks, and hand-written Beatles lyrics: Adults' evaluations of authentic objects. *Journal of Cognition and Culture*, 9(1–2), 1–14.

25 Hood, B. M., & Bloom, P. (2008). Children prefer certain individuals over perfect duplicates. *Cognition*, 106(1), 455–462.

26 Hood, B. M., Donnelly, K., Leonards, U. & Bloom, P. (2010). Implicit voodoo: Electrodermal activity reveals a susceptibility to sympathetic magic. *Journal of Cognition and Culture*, 10(3–4), 391–399.

27 Rozin, P., Haidt, J. & McCauley, C. R. (2008). Disgust: The body and soul emotion in the 21st century. In *Disgust and Its Disorders: Theory, assessment, and treatment implications* (pp. 9–29). American Psychological Association.

28 Darwin, C., & Prodger, P. (1998). *The Expression of the Emotions in Man and Animals*. Oxford University Press.

29 Darwin, C. & Kebler, L. (1859). *On the Origin of Species by Means Of Natural Selection, or, the preservation of favoured races in the struggle for life*. J. Murray.

30 Darwin, C. (1872). *The Descent of Man, and Selection in Relation to Sex* (Vol. 2). D. Appleton.

31 Miller, G. (2012). Sex, mutations and marketing: How the Cambrian explosion set the stage for runaway consumerism. *EMBO reports*, 13(10), 880–884.

32 Zahavi, A., & Zahavi, A. (1999). *The Handicap Principle: A missing piece of Darwin's puzzle*. Oxford University Press.

33 Hancock, J. T., & Toma, C. L. (2009). Putting your best face forward: The accuracy of online dating photographs. *Journal of Communication*, 59(2), 367–386.

34 Blok, A. (1998). The narcissism of minor differences. *European Journal of Social Theory*, 1(1), 34.

35 Loos, A. (2019). *Ornament and Crime*. Penguin.

36 Goffman, E. (2016). The presentation of self in everyday life. In *Social Theory Re-Wired* (pp. 482–493). Routledge.

37 James, W. (1890). *The Principles of Psychology* (Vol. 1). Henry Holt and Co., pp. 291–292.

38 Belk, R. W. (1988). Possessions and the extended self. *The Journal of Consumer Research*, 15(2), 139–168.

39 Nandy, S., & Sondhi, N. (2022). Brand pride in consumer–brand relationships: Towards a conceptual framework. *Global Business Review*, 23(5), 1098–1117.

40 Dutton, D. (2009). *The Art Instinct: Beauty, pleasure, and human evolution*. Oxford University Press.

41 Kohn, M., & Mithen, S. (1999). Handaxes: Products of sexual selection? *Antiquity*, 73(281), 518–526.

42 Frith, C. B., Frith, D. W. & Barnes, E. (2004). *Bowerbirds*. Oxford University Press.

43 Veblen, T., & Galbraith, J. K. (1973). *The Theory of the Leisure Class* (Vol. 1899). Houghton Mifflin.

44 Ellard, C. (2015). *Places of the Heart: The psychogeography of everyday life*. Bellevue Literary Press.

45 Charles, K. K., Hurst, E. & Roussanov, N. (2009). Conspicuous consumption and race. *The Quarterly Journal of Economics*, 124(2), 425–467.

46 Hood, B. (2019). *Possessed: Why we want more than we need*. Oxford University Press, p. 98.

47 Bellezza, S., Gino, F. & Keinan, A. (2014). The red sneakers effect: Inferring status and competence from signals of nonconformity. *Journal of Consumer Research*, 41(1), 35–54.

48 Boehm, C., & Boehm, C. (2009). *Hierarchy in the Forest: The evolution of egalitarian behavior*. Harvard University Press.

49 Campbell, C., & Campbell, C. (2018). *The Puzzle of Modern Consumerism. The Romantic Ethic and the Spirit of Modern Consumerism* (New Extended Edition), pp. 77–105.

50 Lindstrom, M. (2012). *Buyology: How everything we believe about why we buy is wrong.* Random House.
51 Miller, G. (2009). *Spent: Sex, evolution, and consumer behavior.* Penguin.
52 Miller, G. (2009). *Spent: Sex, evolution, and consumer behavior.* Penguin.
53 Saad, G. (2007). *The Evolutionary Bases of Consumption.* Psychology Press.
54 Berger, J. (2008). *Ways of Seeing.* Penguin, p. 131.
55 Leonard, A. (2007). Story of stuff, referenced and annotated script. *Journal of Occupational and Environmental Health*, 13(1).
56 Miller, G. (2009). *Spent: Sex, evolution, and consumer behavior.* Penguin.
57 Easterlin, R. A., & O'Connor, K. J. (2022). The easterlin paradox. In *Handbook of Labor, Human Resources and Population Economics* (pp. 1–25). Springer.
58 Smith, D. (2020). Lessons from the Archive: Still relevant 50 years later. In *Advances in Interdisciplinary Practice in Industrial Design: Proceedings of the AHFE 2019 International Conference on Interdisciplinary Practice in Industrial Design, July 24–28, 2019, Washington DC, USA 10* (pp. 214–219). Springer.

3

STORIES

How We Turn from Narrators to Protagonists

The Power of Stories

We are the *symbolic species*.[1] Humans have a fantastic capacity for symbolic thought, which can provide an inheritance system with a similar combinatorial diversity as genetic recombination and antibody formation. Just like the immune system adapts to new environmental threats, by learning, so does cultural evolution. Cultural innovations are group efforts, and they are the cultural analogues of genetic mutations. Economic competition is analogous to ecological competition in the biological world and the survival of the most adapted institution is assumed to benefit society as a whole. Let us start with semantic edifices. Ask yourself, how much of your life do you spend consuming stories? Are you lost in thoughts? Are they not stories too? In the words of the great anthropologist Clifford Geertz, "the drive to make sense out of our experience, to give it form and order, is evidently as real and as pressing as the most familiar biological needs."[2] We are so good at telling stories that we move from storyteller to story-maker, from narrator to protagonist. When stories are especially moving and when masses of people become protagonists in a single storyline, they can change history, to become history. Books like the Bible, the Quran or even the Harry Potter series have actually changed history. They have also changed our understanding of our place, our role and identity in this universe. As literary critique Jonathan Gottschall points out, a narrative always has a darker side as self-fulfilling prophecy. It is also dangerous to juxtapose elements of stories as this and that, or good and evil.[3]

With a 24-hour news cycle, the restless social media frenzy, millions of books, and movies and series on demand, there are indeed many stories told by this human species on this planet. But really, all of them boil down to only

DOI: 10.4324/9781003464754-5

two plots. One is about unrequited love. As we have seen, people go to great lengths to make themselves attractive to others. But right now, let us turn to the other story. It is called "good versus evil" and is played out in hundreds of thousands, perhaps millions, of iterations on theater stages, movie sets, in writing, in lectures and on podcasts. This battle of moral virtuosity against malignancy is probably the most powerful narrative ever; we see it acted out everywhere both inside and outside of us. Human warfare is the brutal reality of that story, and each group has obviously always seen themselves on the side of righteousness. But we also have both sides at war inside our own psyche. They are conflicting strategies; we know how to get to something we desire, but we also have a voice in our heads that says, "no you can't have that!" Who wins? If there is a dialogue in the head, does that mean there is a free will and a free won't?

It is not so much every plot twist of the story that we are concerned with, but its power as social cohesion. Akin to a swarm of fish mimicking one larger fish, humans rally around one narrative when they must accomplish larger feats. Together we stand, divided we fall. It is what religious traditions have said for millennia, and with the sole exception of Ayn Rand's *objectivism* – I do consider it to belong to this grouping – no religious organization holds ruthless selfishness as its foundation. The word *religion* is likely a translation of the Latin *religare*, which means "to bind fast," or bind together a group of individuals. Already in 14th century Andalusia, Ibn Khaldun wrote about sociological ideas very similar to those of classical sociologists such as Auguste Comte, Émile Durkheim, Ferdinand Tönnies and Karl Marx. Especially the notion of *asabiyya*, popularized by Ibn Khaldun, is now a standard concept of social solidarity with an emphasis on unity, group consciousness and a sense of shared purpose and social cohesion. Many current scholars have picked up on the theme of interconnectedness as key for the strength of modern nations, such as Jared Diamond, Robert Putnam, Peter Turchin and others.[4,5,6]

For better or for worse, how are these narratives made? Humans use signs, marks and words that represent ideas, objects and even relationships. They can be words, paintings, flags, brands and things, and they give us humans a kind of superpower since they allow us to transcend reality by linking radically different concepts and experiences. They are magical, universal and probably unique to us. Symbols detach themselves from the surfaces they are written on, and thus a traffic sign has the power to make people slow down purely because of what it signifies to the driver, not because of its material presence. Symbols are omnipresent since all communication is based on them.

The symbol is always more than the sum of its parts. The father of modern sociology Émile Durkheim said, "The soldier who dies for his flag dies for his country, but as a matter of fact, in his own consciousness, it is the flag that has the first place."[7] An amusing pedagogical quirk of mine illustrates the Durkheimian axiom of the symbol being more than the sum of its parts. One day in class, I was trying to make the simple point that the flag becomes charged with the emotional collective of an entire nation. It can cause individuals to feel a whole plethora of emotions ranging from warm and fuzzy to ashamed, intimated or angry. The flag can also result in action, making people fight and kill. My students followed what I was saying, in their mind deconstructing their flags into poles, canvas, paint, a design and little more. They seemed bored with this commonsensical assertion, and so it was time to test the assertion. The classroom I was teaching in was part of a Jesuit university, where each classroom comes equipped with a wooden cross on the wall, which I spontaneously decided to use as an illustration of a symbol. I took the crucifix and held it out in front of me, thrusting it towards my students. There was a shudder felt through the room of mostly religious young Americans. Then my class turned a little silly. I stood there, one hand holding the cross and the other dramatically held in the air as I have seen singers of black metal bands and preachers alike do. And then, ever so slowly, I proceeded to invert the cross slowly, painfully in front of my students, all the while adding some screeching sounds that I had heard in various horror movies, such as *The Exorcist*. The pregnant silence burst when one student vehemently defended his sacred symbol. He said that I cannot do that, that what I was doing was sacrilegious. I asked him what the problem was since I was just holding two sticks that are glued together in the middle making a cross. He said: "But it stands for the Son of God, redeemer of the world!" I said: "Bingo! You understood today's lesson!" Alas, symbols are extremely powerful as any religious or political leader – and brand consultant – will attest.

A helpful term increasingly used in the anthropological literature is *symbotype*, referring to a whole set of symbolic relations that result in the phenotype of a culture. So, like the genotype dictates appearance and behavior of an organism, the *symbotype* is the whole suite of rules, norms and worldviews characteristic of entire cultures. And just like genotypes, *symbotypes* are extremely diverse. When looking at a community as a whole, the *symbotype* replaces the *genotype* as the carrier of information into the future. They are based on the recombination of different elements, and also evolve based on the environmental changes of societies.[8] *Symbotype* – although similar – also differs in many profound ways to Richard Dawkins' *meme*. We have to be quick to mention that here the term is used in its original, referring to massively successful and often irrational cultural complexes like "Christianity," and not its current demotion of a *Tik Tok* video on a smartphone's screen. (Dawkins himself complained about this misunderstanding.)[9] In his *Selfish Gene*, Dawkins suggested that cultural traits resemble physical genes especially in their role as "replicators" going from human brain to human brain.[10] Although the term referred to immaterial ideas, *meme* was very much part of Dawkins' gene-centric views. *Symbotype* differs in as far as it addresses culture at the phenotypic, surface level. It is definitively possible for cultural traits to reproduce systemically without the need for gene-like replicators.[11]

Part of the problem is that often the story is much stronger than what it represents. Experience usually precedes the story; it is prior to *logos*. It is as if we humans forget that there is an actual reality outside of stories, a fact that is true epistemologically (there exist millions of other sentient species) and evolutionarily (for hundreds of thousands of years hominids were around but likely told no stories). Stories are often entirely fictitious, corresponding entities are not found in the real world, but as *symbotype*, they still survive as long as they motivate the right behavior at the right time. According to this *pragmatist* view of religiosity, crazy, unnatural fantasies such as a person defying the laws of physics and walking on water or an angel dictating an enormous book to a merchant sitting in a cave in Medina have not only survived for millennia but continue as behavioral architecture for billions of people.

Malware

It seems counterintuitive: good people with bad ideas is far worse than bad people with good ideas. Let me explain. When we look at culture as a kind of operating system, which manages software – the content of the minds of people – we see how powerful *symbotypes* really are. Some bad people are like bad hardware and no matter what software you feed them, and provided you let them roam freely, they will probably cause havoc. But what happens when healthy hardware is fed some bad *malware*? Then we have a far bigger problem, because the good majority is now motivated by a bad story. We are dealing with a simple statistical truth: since belief motivates behavior and since there are far more good people alive than bad ones, bad stories are far more dangerous than bad people. In both scenarios, I am speaking of ideas, which are subjective fiction. If you think this is all philosophical bullshit, please reconsider and think about the horrors of history due to bad ideas in the heads of perfectly good people. Think about Medieval witch-trials, the ideas of racial superiority and eugenics. Think about modern jihadism!

The terms *good* and *evil* are kind of silly, because there exists no metric to measure either one of those qualities. There are some people – estimates lie between 1 percent and 3 percent of the world population – who are considered *psychopaths* and have a very limited ability to empathize with others and may even receive pleasure from hurting others. To avoid any lengthy discussions of moral philosophy or metaphysics (there will be plenty of that later), let us settle on labeling them as "bad." But since they are rare, they are not really the definition of bad. "Bad people" are the ones who think we are bad. As infantile as it sounds, such is the stuff of our myths old and new. Indeed, it is not actually bad people we need to worry about. Far more dangerous are bad stories! As Hannah Arendt remarked at the Adolf Eichmann trial in Jerusalem, the *banality of evil* is committed by good people acting under the spell of bad stories. It is done by people simply doing their job but at the aggregate it culminates in many historical atrocities, in the name of cultural constructs such as nations, flags, gods and economic ideologies.[12]

Like *genotypes, symbotypes* vary infinitely, because they are a recombination of specific elements, and they evolve based on what they make societies do. The *symbotypes* are full of rules on how to behave and how not to behave. We might label them etiquette, and they can certainly differ from culture to culture (it might be okay to spit on the street in one and not okay in the other), but driven by globalization they can also become the status quo. However, not only thoughts, words and soundbites are the carriers of stories. It is also objects and services and automobiles and clothing that can carry ideas, good and bad. If all those things are carried in the name of, under the flag of, a bad story, each one of them is an embodiment of an idea, good or bad. Their designers are either on the side of those stories or apathetic bystanders. Designers embody ideas. There is the word, the artifact and the artifice, and we need to know what those things have as an end objective. Their means are clear: it is the objects themselves.

Welcome to the Anthropocene

Imagine for a second sitting somewhere high above and looking down at earth. Imagine also that you somehow have the ability to see everything unfold as a time lapse. Seasons would come and go and daylight would just shutter by as the geology of earth would sit there motionless except for an occasional volcanic eruption or tectonic shift. It would be impossible to focus on humans as they are rushing about way too fast, but you see big machines rapidly "pistoning" into the earth to take out stuff, which is taken elsewhere to be combined with other stuff and formed into things. For an ever so brief instance you see people holding their stuff and then tossing them onto huge mountains or burning them up. You see these great apes obsessed – no, possessed – with changing nature and making things that they manage to permanently mark their territory. They are living in the Holocene, an interglacial interval, marked by unusually stable and mild climate conditions, said to have started 11,700 years ago, but now they have a new term for the most recent geological epoch. As expected by the aggrandizing nature of the human spirit, it is all about them. But does it stand for something beautiful, like planetary harmony or ecological equilibrium. No, instead it describes one great ape gobbling up the planet's resources, killing its species, and leaving behind pharaonic buildings built to last and trash made to break. Welcome to the *Anthropocene*!

Terms are examples of symbols; they act as placeholders for reality. While it certainly isn't my aim to question anthropogenic change to earth's systems, "Anthropocene" is a *term* for an epoch. It is a term for the ages. And in its inevitability and grandeur, this most recent chapter in the story of the planet is truly biblical. As the term was introduced to mark a break with nature, complete with a date, it comes awfully close to the story of *Paradise Lost*. Cast out of Eden, we are the villain combatants, "afraid and strangers to this world."[13] It is the consequences of the human insistence of seeing themselves as outside the world and looking in that are manifested in the *Anthropocene* and that have dire consequences for the global biotope. From the Greek *human* (*Anthropo-*) and *new* (*-cene*), the term first surfaced in a 2000 paper by Crutzen and Stoermer simply entitled "The Anthropocene."[14] In 2002, Crutzen wrote another essay in *Nature* called "Geology of Mankind" with much wider circulation and attention.[15] Basically, the term suggests that most earth systems – atmospheric, geologic, hydrologic and biospheric – are now altered by humans. Impossible as it may sound, all the things we have made and left behind – the *technosphere* – is literally heavier than the biosphere. Human-made, dead stuff outweighs all the stuff alive! Very shocking as all this might sound, it is the stories of the anthropocene's origin that are most consequential no matter how factual they are. They help legitimize current power structures as they narrow the scope of possible futures.

The common street version of the *Anthropocene* goes something like this: once upon a time, small hordes of hominids were tossed around by nature. When they could, they sat around in great discomfort. They utterly lacked any critical thought or even visions of how things could improve and thus nothing much happened for most of prehistory. Finally, a great trajectory started with the birth of agriculture and the construction of the first cities in the Fertile Crescent and culminated in the Enlightenment and the Industrial Revolution. And now we sit around conveniently. But everything is polluted. Because we are bad. There are two main versions of this story, both of which were fabricated in the 17th century. Both revolve around a *social contract*, a kind of deal made by groups to band together to affront nature. The first one comes from Thomas Hobbes, who saw the lives of hunters and gatherers as "solitary, poor, nasty, brutish, and short" until the invention of the modern state and rule by law allowed progress.[16] It follows the pessimistic mantra on human nature as "red in tooth and claw," domesticated only by human institutions.[17] Another version – from Enlightenment philosopher Jean Jacques Rousseau – sees indigenous life as harmonious, peaceful and full of love until the arrival of Europeans changed everything, as it forced the *noble savages* into servitude.[18] Both versions assume that the only current option we have is to make small political adjustments but that truly wicked problems such as climate change and resource management are here to stay forever. Either way, the species took a wrong turn.

Hard to believe after so many thousands of years of telling it, but the human story has a few extra twists. Fatalist views of human nature subside when we see that history never was teleologically moving from simple and beautiful to complex and nasty. Instead, it seems that we did not permanently live in small, egalitarian hordes in an endless present but rather changed continuously as the environmental context demanded. For instance, the architects of Göbekli Tepe, the world's oldest known megaliths, have been dated to between 9500 and 8000 BCE, way before what is generally considered the agricultural revolution. It seems our hunter and gatherer ancestors weren't dumb brutes but engineers and architects as they conceived and shaped enormous structures. Its pillars are decorated with incredible details, providing archeologists with insights into prehistoric life or at least a vision of life. And all of this was done three thousand years before Stonehenge! As David Graeber and David Wengrow demonstrate in their monumental *The Dawn of Everything*, throughout history, humans have adopted several different subsistence patterns and have even changed between them on numerous occasions.[19] In their 526-page opus (not including 62 pages of bibliography) the authors don't deny ecological determinism but rather try to balance it with human agency. Perhaps the most important part of this new appraisal of the past is its ability to widen our scope of possible futures.

It goes without saying that much of the *Anthropocene* is marvelous; humans have made airplanes, satellites, dishwashers, personal computers and electric guitars. But let us go back up to that higher ground in the beginning of this section. As you sit up there and observe human industry you glimpse something else and before you resort to your usual, myopic vision you realize that all the artifacts are simply a particular bundling of molecules in a moment of time. They have a lifespan as a product but their parts live on infinitely elsewhere. Everything, every last thing that we produce, is here forever and we cannot throw anything away. All this stuff – from egomaniac structures designed to last to the waste of the things designed to break – is still here, albeit in different shape or form. Some of it lies around idly, some of it has been recycled into something new and most of it has been dissolved into the earth and air. Of course, a lot of the built environment remains in use until eventually we try to get rid of it, but cleaning efforts are merely an outsourcing of responsibility and denial of reality. When we look closer, the destruction of our commodities is paid for by massive crowdfunding efforts we simply call taxation. It is also done invisibly: in the still of the night, when the last bar has closed and we go to sleep, governmental cleaning efforts come alive, and we wake up to pristine streets and empty garbage bins.

Living in the *Anthropocene* we are confronted with another story: James Lovelock's *Gaia*. Proposed in 1972, this hypothesis suggests that all living entities interact to form one self-regulating system that maintains the climatic and biochemical conditions of this planet.[20] Here nature is non-dual. Everything is part of the same thing and interacts in infinitely complex ways with everything else. Not new, it is a permanent condition. In the words of Isabelle Stengers: "no future can be foreseen in which [Gaia] will give back to us the liberty of ignoring her."[21] The *Anthropocene* is real. It is straightforward to understand. A society based on consumption relies on dead goods while a society based on reproduction relies on things to be alive. As pointed out by anthropological great Marvin Harris, that is the precise reason why the cow has a holy status in India and is chopped up into hamburgers in the United

States. Indeed, the Anthropocene is a non-fiction story, and it is hard to tell how it will end. There are many attempts to draft a global moral code, but while everyone is speaking about universal human ethics no one is addressing its application. A Jain monk (concerned with the welfare of every sentient being) follows a different story about the world than an Ayn Randian zealot (seeing egoism as a rational code of ethics and altruism as destructive) and will thus act distinctly. The very fact that we can construct an artificial niche so omnipresent that it has altered the entire system known as earth holds many dangers. As the late E. O. Wilson remarked: "The real problem of humanity is the following: We have Paleolithic emotions, medieval institutions, and godlike technology. And it is terrifically dangerous, and it is now approaching a point of crisis overall."[22] Over and above a new geological time, the *Anthropocene* can be seen as a new attitude towards the world. The *Anthropocene* is the greatest story ever told as it describes the sum of all man-made entities, all of which themselves tell stories. It is also the most ironic: after hundreds of thousands of years objectifying nature, we are forced to become its subjects again.

Notes

1 Schilhab, T., Stjernfelt, F. & Deacon, T. (Eds.). (2012). *The Symbolic Species Evolved* (Vol. 6). Springer Science & Business Media.
2 Segal, R. A. (1988). *Interpreting and Explaining Religion: Geertz and Durkheim.* Soundings, p. 35.
3 Gottschall, J. (2021). *The Story Paradox: How our love of storytelling builds societies and tears them down.* Hachette.
4 Diamond, J., & Renfrew, C. (1997). Guns, germs, and steel: The fates of human societies. *Nature*, 386(6623), 339–339.
5 Putnam, R. D. (2000). Bowling alone: America's declining social capital. In *Culture and Politics: A reader* (pp. 223–234). Palgrave Macmillan.
6 Turchin, P. (2005). *War and Peace and War: The life cycles of imperial nations.* Pi.
7 Schatz, R. T., & Lavine, H. (2007). Waving the flag: National symbolism, social identity, and political engagement. *Political Psychology*, 28(3), 329–355.
8 Witoszek, N., & Sørensen, Ø. (2018). Cultural evolution and symbotypes. *Sustainable Modernity: The Nordic model and beyond* (p. 36). Routledge.
9 Solon, O. (2013). Richard Dawkins on the internet's hijacking of the word "meme." *Wired UK*, 20.
10 Dawkins, R. (2016). *The Selfish Gene.* Oxford University Press.
11 Henrich, J., Heine, S. J. & Norenzayan, A. (2010). The weirdest people in the world? *Behavioral and Brain Sciences*, 33(2–3), 61–83.
12 Arendt, H., & Kroh, J. (1964). *Eichmann in Jerusalem* (p. 240). Viking Press.
13 This is a slightly altered version of a line in the poem "The Laws of God, The Laws of Man" by A. E. Housman: "I, a stranger and afraid in a world I never made."
14 Crutzen, P. J. (2006). The "Anthropocene." In *Earth System Science in the Anthropocene* (pp. 13–18). Springer.
15 Crutzen, P. J. (2016). Geology of mankind. In *Paul J. Crutzen: A pioneer on atmospheric chemistry and climate change in the Anthropocene* (pp. 211–215). Springer.
16 Hobbes, T. (2008). *Leviathan.* Oxford University Press.

17 This is a widely used phrase credited to Alfred Lord Tennyson, describing merciless competition in nature.

18 Cranston, M. (1991). *The Noble Savage: Jean-Jacques Rousseau, 1754–1762.* University of Chicago Press.

19 Graeber, D., & Wengrow, D. (2021). *The Dawn of Everything: A new history of humanity.* Penguin.

20 Lovelock, J. E., & Margulis, L. (1974). Atmospheric homeostasis by and for the biosphere: The Gaia hypothesis. *Tellus,* 26(1–2), 2–10.

21 Stengers, I. (2015). *In Catastrophic Times: Resisting the coming barbarism.* Open Humanities Press, p. 47.

22 Ratcliffe, S. (Ed.) (2014). *Oxford Essential Quotations.* Oxford University Press.

4

MODELS

On Flawed Representations of Humans

Evolutionary Models

As we sat around the table, inside and warm, the colored board lay in the middle under our gaze. Pictured on it was a mustached character with a cylinder hat and cane, arms thrown wide open in celebration. He was obviously rich since money was flying all around. Unusual, considering that we are four boys, my brothers and I rarely competed and never fought, but when we started playing *Monopoly* all that changed. Then, only self-serving, aggressive behavior came out in all of us simply because the objective of the game is driving every other player into bankruptcy by owning all the real estate. An interesting historical footnote is that the boardgame was originally designed to teach economic and social justice. Elizabeth Magie, creator of the game's original version *The Landowner's Game*, gave it two separate sets of rules. The first set was anti-monopolistic where players were rewarded when wealth was created for all. Based on the ideas of economist Henry George, whom Magie admired, the rules put a burden of a single federal tax on wealthy landowners to discourage speculation and encourage equal opportunity. Magie wanted to demonstrate the validity of such policies in her game. As we all know it was the other set of rules – create monopolies and crush opponents without regard to consequences – that became such a fixture of modern households. Incidentally the idea was stolen and rebranded as *Monopoly*. But no one went to jail! And a footnote to the footnote: although he later rejected Georgian economics in his *Constitution of Liberty*, Nobel Prize laureate Friedrich von Hayek did write in 1926 that "It was a lay enthusiasm for Henry George which led me to economics."[1]

As we have seen, human behavior can be understood as *behavioral algorithms* that interact with a contextual matrix and result in a program of action. In the

DOI: 10.4324/9781003464754-6

example of *Monopoly*, ruthless and self-serving behavior – call it algorithm 1 – is brought to the surface simply because the objectives and rules of the game encourage it. But if we played it using rules and objectives of the greater good, then selflessness – call it algorithm 2 – triumphs. To be sure, such algorithms were written countless millennia ago by nature and not by modern society. The role of modern society is to engage with and amplify one archaic piece of code, the desire to consume and to improve one's rank through consumption, on both sides of the point of sale. Often, it does so through empty promises of satisfaction. Out in the street, in the real world, but just like in *Monopoly, individual maximization of relative fitness* within the group is also advertised as the winning strategy. And analogous to the board game, where a player's actions do not have repercussions beyond the table, limits, or boundaries of earth as a life-supporting system, are also ignored entirely both in public and political spheres. In an economic order based on outsourced responsibility and over-consumption, ethical and sustainable citizenship has become a weak evolutionary strategy; the upright person became a defector. If the context of modern society is such that unsustainable and unethical consumption is encouraged cognitively and made easy culturally, it will become the most widespread behavior. Living carbon-neutral, free of plastics and without hurting other sentient beings far removed, on the other hand, is strongly disincentivized and made harder through limited consumer choices. All this is relevant here, because it is design that gives such incentives agency through the lure of splendidly novel, beautiful and convenient objects. Design is a culprit.

Thus, this book is concerned with a grand narrative, a *symbotype* that spreads to all corners of the world and has turned much of world citizenry into its protagonists. It is full of sanctions, incentives and norms for citizens to squander resources, and it is purposeful insofar as it serves capitalist accumulation. However, this is not a conspiracy theory. I am not suggesting that a powerful and coordinated economic cabal conditions humans through a complex system of socialization to consume. But it is a fact that economics, the study of how humans deal with resources for production, distribution and consumption, has been dominated by a particular model of humanity, and just like any model it assumes certain parameters. In this case the assumptions are the reduction of human needs to individual materialism and a total ignorance of the social fabric. Such assumptions are utterly wrong, but this model has nonetheless dominated our economic discourse. So, grudgingly, we must now turn to *Homo economicus*, a fictional protagonist, which always acts perfectly rational, cares only about maximizing its personal utility and is never influenced by anyone else's preferences. "If you look at economics textbooks," behavioral economists Richard H. Thaler and Cass R. Sunstein muse, "you will learn that *Homo economicus* can think like Albert Einstein, store as much memory as IBM's Big Blue, and exercise the willpower of Mahatma Gandhi."[2]

Homo Economicus: The Story of a Truly Bad Story

Like a stubborn weed with long roots, this story of pathologically selfish and always rational humans is hard to yank. Its idea goes back to 1705, to the *Fable of the Bees*, where Bernard Mandeville makes an analogy of human society as a buzzing, productive beehive, with every bee as selfish as can be.[3] In his parable, Mandeville's emphasis was on both the *self-organization* of the beehive and the *self-interest* of the individual bee. Adam Smith, founder of the field we now call *economics*, picked up on such thoughts and postulated in his *Wealth of Nations* that in society the conglomerate of individual self-interest – not benevolence – makes all of society better.[4] *Utility maximization* was seen as the base of all human behavior, an erroneous thought that centuries later led to *rational choice theory*. The ideas of Smith became immortalized as the *invisible hand* magically guiding the market economy and together with the ideas of Thomas Malthus it influenced Charles Darwin and Alfred Russel Wallace in their development of the theory of *natural selection*. However, *Homo economicus* becomes problematic – as indeed any model – when taken to explain human reality. Just as Newtonian physics describes the motion of the celestial bodies, the argument went, so could mathematical techniques describe the motion of human minds in the economy. The logical conclusion was that regulatory efforts from governments are simply superfluous, but the story of *Homo economicus* and the *invisible hand* still needed to be placed on a loftier foundation than other human sciences such as anthropology or psychology. It needed to become a "hard science" like physics. That became the obsession of economist Leon Walras and others who constructed a model of the economic order by including lots of assumptions of human behavior, many of which are still taught today.[5]

In December 1946, Friedrich von Hayek sent personal invitations to fifty-eight economists, historians and philosophers, all of whom where staunch defenders of classical liberalism, to attend a historic meeting. It would take place in April 1947, at the Hôtel du Parc in the Swiss mountains. Besides Hayek, thirty-nine intellectual heavyweights including Karl Popper, Ludwig von Mises, George Stigler and Milton Friedman made the pilgrimage to a village ironically called *Mont-Pèlerin*, or "Mount Pilgrim." The task at hand was urgent and perhaps noble for Hayek. He had just published his *Road to Serfdom*, an articulation on how popular democracy could give rise to fascism and totalitarian states as witnessed in Germany, Italy and Spain.[6] The members of the *Mont-Pelerin Society*, as the meeting was called, were rightfully worried about a centralized government and consequently ideas such as deregulation and minimal state control were systematically seeded in universities, think tanks and other institutions of Europe and the United States. Most notably, Milton Friedman advanced Hayek's ideas in powerful ways at the University of Chicago in the 1970s. Just think of the *Chicago Boys*, Chilean economists studying free market economics in Chicago and then implementing their curricula with the help of authoritarian dictator Pinochet.

By the mid-20th century economics was scrambling to become a scientific field but had as its foundation some very flawed assumptions about human nature. Any attempts to self-correct became compromised by the growth of an ideological agenda with a lot of powerful financial interests supporting it. For example, *Mont-Pelerin* fellow Milton Friedman is considered the godfather of the *shareholder primacy model* of business, which has been enjoying a steady, hardly challenged run since the '70s. Here the primary objective of business to make money and raise the income of *C-level employees* is directly linked to shareholders' behavior on the stock market. Obviously, your only focus as a business is to maximize profit, which in turn only works when every *day-trading* individual wants to maximize theirs. Back then evolutionist and economist theories of humanity moved in lockstep in what can be labeled an *individualist* worldview. Thus, Richard Dawkins' *gene-centric* approach for the theory of natural selection seemed to support and legitimize the liberal economics of Milton Friedman or even the *objectivism* of Ayn Rand. The idea of billions of *homines oeconomici* running around trying to self-maximize and guided only by an *invisible hand* is good because it is natural, right? Wrong! It is not even a *naturalistic fallacy* – where biology is destiny – because it isn't based on a correct assessment of human nature. I don't want to say it, I really don't, because it might take away credibility, but instead all this looks awfully close to a *Ponzi scheme*.

True global, political success for *liberal economics* came in 1980 with the election of Ronald Reagan in the United States and Margaret Thatcher in the UK. In 1987 the "Iron Lady" Thatcher famously said that "there's no such thing as society."[7] With that quote, she represented the Z*eitgeist* of the political and economic arena in the late '80s. That same year, selfish utility maximization at the expense of the group became perfectly embodied by the fictional character Gordon Gekko. In the movie *Wall Street*, Gekko holds a speech making the ethos of "greed is good" a powerful meme, shaping ruthless, real-life practices in the financial sector. So many years later, much of mainstream economics remains spellbound by this story and continues defending deregulating markets. According to the most recent edition of the *New Palgrave Dictionary of Economics*, for example, "laissez faire leading to the common good [is] the first fundamental theorem of welfare economics."[8] The consequence of encouraging bankers, CEOs and financiers to act in such ways without regulation directly led to the financial crash of 2008, one of history's five worst financial crises, with an estimated global economic loss of more than US $2 trillion. As we have seen, the true potential of stories unfolds when large groups become their protagonists, and so it is with this global narrative of the human individual as selfish, ruthless and the only unit of measurement.

But there is hope. The story of *Homo economicus* started to come apart in the 1950s, when Nobel Prize–winning economist and cognitive psychologist Herbert Simon introduced the concept of *heuristics*. This was a major break from the fashionable *rational choice theory* because it suggests that human judgment is subject to cognitive limitations. Purely rational decisions, it was argued, cannot be the driving force of momentary decision-making since weighing every single variable of potential costs and possible benefits would overload human cognition. Instead, people are always constrained by time, energy, resources and information to make choices. Where finding an optimal solution is impossible or impractical, *heuristics* simply speed up the cognitive process of finding a satisfactory solution or making the right decision. Humans might be reasonable, but they are definitely not rational.[9] The true death blow to *Homo economicus* came with Vernon Smith and Daniel Kahneman in 2002, when they received the Nobel Prize for their work in *behavioral economics*.[10] That year can also be seen as the birth year of a new field called *evonomics*. Here, the focus lies on human behavior beyond graphs, fiscal policies and numbers, and instead has its foundation in simple experiments based on *evolutionary theory*. *Behavioral economics* has adjusted for many of the wrong assumptions by addressing *heuristics* and *cognitive biases*, both of which dictate much of our behavior. Few designers are into radical selfishness, but they *do* design for the experience of a single user at a time. Then designs are scaled, as explained by Adam Smith and practiced by Henry Ford. The collective experience, and the collective impact of design, it is assumed, will take care of itself.

WEIRD

We have been using a faulty model of humans, but even when we study real ones our methodologies seem to be skewed. Joseph Henrich, chair of the Department of Human Evolutionary Biology at Harvard, has spent over a decade researching the oddity and anomaly of the people behavioral and social scientists saliently call "normal." He uses the acronym WEIRD to describe *Western, educated, industrialized, rich* and *democratic* people. Clever, because it is both descriptive and provocative, the acronym most definitely antagonizes. *The WEIRDest People in the World: How the West became psychologically peculiar and particularly prosperous*[11] is a *big history*, with a macroscopic sweep comparable to Jared Diamond's *Guns, Germs, and Steel*[12] or Yuval Harari's *Sapiens*.[13]

In Henrich's book, WEIRD people are described as highly individualistic, self-obsessed, control-oriented, analytical and non-conformist. Most of the world's cultures today have a notion of nature being alive and to be part of it, but to the Western mind such notions are considered infantile superstition. Many Westerners have children very late (if ever) and live in a kind of suspended state of adolescence stretching well into their thirties. In other societies, people not only have families much earlier but are given guidelines as to when adolescence is finished according to specific rituals. The Western mind is plagued by self-absorption and ethnocentrism, focused primarily on itself confronted by the world. Rather than relationships and social roles, in the

West attributes, accomplishments and aspirations are measured as individualistic. The Western mind is far more hedonistic, pursuing pleasure and avoiding pain as much as possible. Western people have tended to be more isolated spatially but also in terms of age, spending most of their time in their specific age-group cohort. Much of Western identity is formed through patterns of consumption. Even the Westerners' incredibly sedentary lifestyle – spending most of their time indoors and surrounded by screens – is not normal in the statistical sense but actually WEIRD.[14]

The people we consider "normal," with their "normal" biases, actions and reactions, are quite unusual. Consequently, perceptions of human society are often derived from studies of "a-normal" subjects, which flips the terms around, rendering all the others as exotic. Henrich argues that edicts of the Catholic church systematically undermined "natural" kin-based human society through regulations of marriage beginning as early as the 4th century and thus created the more individualistic and analytical thinking so prevalent in Western societies today. Especially after the Protestant Reformation of 1517, in what Henrich calls a "booster shot," European society increasingly lived in closed, nuclear families and trusted institutionalism, education and industrialization for advancement. Thus, Western civilization is a very idiosyncratic cultural concoction with a massively skewed self-perception. The following quote from Henrich warns of the perils of learning from such a sliver of a population:

> The fact that WEIRD people are the outliers in so many key domains of the behavioral sciences may render them one of the worst subpopulations one could study for generalizing about Homo sapiens. … WEIRD people, from this perspective, grow up in, and adapt to, a rather atypical environment vis-à-vis that of most of human history. It should not be surprising that their psychological world is unusual as well.[15]

Indeed, many psychological traits have been treated like axioms when really they are peculiarities. Experimental psychological research, with its roots going back to the Germany of the mid-19th century, was originally designed to uncover universal truths, but instead, it may have only uncovered truths about a thin slice of our species – people who live in WEIRD (Western, educated, industrialized, rich and democratic) nations.[16] As part of a wider crisis of replication, sometimes decades-old test results have not been verified by looking at other groups and contexts. Of the top journals in six sub-disciplines of psychology, 68 percent of subjects were from the US and an amazing 96 percent from "Western" industrialized nations (European, North American, Australia and Israel).[17] Putting the numbers a different way, that means a 96 percent concentration on 12 percent of the world's population.[18]

Also in the field of social psychology many classic studies were conducted exclusively by European professors on their European undergraduates. For example, the famous *fundamental attribution error* – an individual's tendency to attribute another's actions to their character or personality, while attributing their own behavior on external contextual factors – is definitely a phenomenon. But it is basically non-existent in other cultures. Thus, non-WEIRD societies, dominated by kinship-intensive social relationships, offer fewer social niches; variety of personality combinations are constrained culturally. Researchers also found some very "physical" traits, like the perception of visual illusions to be far more common among US college students than people from many other cultures, such as the San foragers of the Kalahari. It is not that everyone falls for such illusions; actually, the ones who fall for them are the exception to the norm. This is surprising. But the reason for the surprise might be a Western treatment of biology as the only realm subject to evolutionary forces. Besides *nature, nurture* also changes us. It is now commonly accepted that a complex interplay of the two is at work and thus *epigenetics* is the field studying how an individual's behavior as well as their environment can have changes that affect human gene pools. Joseph Henrich suggests that if such basic processes as visual perception can be altered by cultural evolution, then it makes sense that others can, too. The relevance of such views in this book are obvious.

Notes

1 Andelson, R. V. (2004). 29 Hayek: "Almost Persuaded." *American Journal of Economics and Sociology*, 63(2), 433–440.
2 Beinhocker, E. D. (2006). *The Origin of Wealth: Evolution, complexity, and the radical remaking of economics*. Harvard Business Press, p. 6.
3 De Mandeville, B. (1992). *The Fable of the Bees*. Jazzybee Verlag.
4 Beinhocker, E. D. (2006). *The Origin of Wealth: Evolution, complexity, and the radical remaking of economics*. Harvard Business Press.
5 Walras, L. (2014). *Léon Walras: Elements of theoretical economics: Or, the theory of social wealth*. Cambridge University Press.
6 Hayek, F. A. (1994). *The Road to Serfdom* (50th Anniversary ed.). University of Chicago Press.
7 Interview September 23, 1987, as quoted in by Douglas Keay, *Woman's Own*, October 31, 1987, pp. 8–10.
8 Newman, P. (Ed.) (1998). *The New Palgrave Dictionary of Economics and the Law*. Springer.
9 Simon, H. A., & Newell, A. (1958). Heuristic problem solving: The next advance in operations research. *Operations Research*, 6(1), 1–10.
10 Kahneman, D., & Smith, V. (2002). Foundations of behavioral and experimental economics. *Nobel Prize in Economics Documents*, 1(7), 1–25.
11 Henrich, J. (2020). *The WEIRDest People in the World: How the West became psychologically peculiar and particularly prosperous*. Penguin.
12 Diamond, J. M., & Ordunio, D. (1998). *Guns, Germs, and Steel*. Vintage.
13 Harari, Y. N. (2014). *Sapiens: A brief history of humankind*. Random House.
14 Henrich, J. (2020). *The WEIRDest People in the World: How the West became psychologically peculiar and particularly prosperous*. Penguin.
15 Henrich, J., Heine, S. J. & Norenzayan, A. (2010). The weirdest people in the world? *Behavioral and Brain Sciences*, 33(2–3), pp. 79–80.

16 Henrich, J., Heine, S. J. & Norenzayan, A. (2010). Most people are not WEIRD. *Nature*, 466(7302), 29–29.
17 Arnett, J. (2008). The neglected 95%: Why American psychology needs to become less American. *American Psychologist*, 63(7), 602–614.
18 Henrich, J., Heine, S. J. & Norenzayan, A. (2010). The weirdest people in the world? *Behavioral and Brain Sciences*, 33(2–3), 61.

5

CONSEQUENCES

Human Conduct with Finite Resources

Why Don't We See the Whole Earth?

Somewhere in San Francisco, on a back porch sat Stewart Brand who waited for a vision. It was February of 1966 and a few weeks earlier he had co-organized the *Trips Festival*, which would unite a nascent Bay Area hippy movement by giving the stage to the Grateful Dead, Jefferson Airplane and other psychedelic rock bands. As a graduate of biology from Stanford University and a self-described Darwinist, he saw the forces of selection work on every imaginable scale, means and end. He was also influenced by designer and architect Richard Buckminster Fuller, who argued that a global environmentalism can only ever succeed if our planet were seen as a hermetically sealed entity with finite resources. Moved by such thoughts and aided by 100 milligrams of L.S.D, his vision came, and Brand *floated* out of his chair to see and experience the whole world's curvature and finitude below him. His experience resonated with Buckminster Fuller's assertion that the reason humanity misbehaves so much is that people perceive earth as flat and infinite. What was needed was an inverted vision, as if floating in a tin can far above the world. But how to broadcast such a vison? Perfectly capturing the urgency and paranoia of the 1960s hippy movement he proceeded to print buttons with the simple question "Why haven't we seen a photograph of the whole earth yet?", circulated them and formally urged NASA, the Russians or anyone, really, to take such a photo. Brand also sent the buttons to Marshall McLuhan, Buckminster Fuller and members of Congress. It was the Cold War and the US and the Russians raced for nuclear dominion on earth and a first landing on the moon. What was needed, Brand thought, was an inversion of the lens to look back at ourselves. Whether it was due to his campaigning we will never know, but a picture was supplied: On November 10,

DOI: 10.4324/9781003464754-7

1967, a NASA satellite captured history's first photograph of the whole earth. Brand was very excited and used it for the cover of the premier of the *Whole Earth Catalog*, a kind of bible of '60s counterculture and analogue forerunner to the *World Wide Web*. The book, which really wasn't a book, acted as a web of like-minded people.[1] It heavily influenced the evolution of Silicon Valley.

The true global turning point came at the very end of 1968, a horrible year that saw the assassinations of both Martin Luther King and Robert Kennedy, an escalation in the Vietnam War and violent student protests across the globe. On Christmas eve, astronauts Frank Borman, James Lovell and Bill Anders traveled further away from home than anyone before them. As they left earth's orbit, they looked back and filmed. What they saw was televised and arguably caused a global leap in consciousness as millions of people sitting in their homes watched their own planet from the outside. But the biggest television show ever was grainy and somehow uncanny. It was *Earthrise*, the photograph the astronauts brought back three days after, that captured all our imaginations. The first picture taken of the whole planet became the symbol for the first *World Earth Day* in April 1970 and still stands for an awakening to the reality of an intricate interconnectedness of all life on this planet. Psychologist Frank White has called the cognitive effect experienced by astronauts during spaceflight the *overview effect*.[2]

The Tragedy of the Commons

Equally important for the year 1968, and published just a few days before *Earthrise* was taken, is Garrett Hardin's "Tragedy of the Commons," a pessimistic allegory of human resource use outside of private fences. His model consisted of a parable of villagers each selfishly adding extra cows to the common pastures outside their own property. The sum of all their selfish actions was overgrazed, barren and useless resources. Suggested by its title, the essay denies that a group ever stands a chance of successfully managing common resources. In a situation of individual users with open access to resources and unregulated by social structures or formal rules, Hardin argues, the depletion of the resources through their uncoordinated action must be the inevitable result. We are dealing with a kind of *tug-of-war* between individual *utility maximization* and group welfare. No side wins, but the outcome is always tragic.[3]

Commons can be defined as "a general term for shared resources in which each stakeholder has an equal interest.[4] It is a derivation of an old English legal term for *common land*, also known as *commons*. In this most basic sense, the *commons* are those lands that are neither owned by the government nor by private citizens, although before its more recent usage, the term described shared – but privately owned – agricultural fields, grazing lands and forests. The Roman legal system distinguished between the categories *res communis* –

resources to be used and enjoyed by everyone – and *res publica*, applied to public property managed by the government.[5] Thus, any discussion of the commons inevitably also deals with *resource allocation*, which has been studied by anthropologists, psychologists and historians for centuries.

A painful, direct experience of this phenomenon is the daily traffic jam. The road – whether public or private – is a common resource with a utility of getting vehicles from A to B. When it is open, its utility is high, and the mind is free. But when the road is clogged, its utility drops towards zero and the mind contracts into a toxic stew of claustrophobia, impotence, impatience and guilt. Basically, traffic jams begin with many individuals choosing to use public roads in order to serve their own needs of transportation and end with pollution of the air we all breathe, and the shared roadways of daily transportation rendered useless. One might yell, "God damn traffic!" – essentially telling some supreme God to please punish everyone, except of course oneself. Such a reaction – although perfectly human – is as senseless as a drop of water in a swimming pool complaining about all the surrounding water.

Who can we blame for the traffic jam? Is it poor transportation design? Partly, and hopefully soon we will see the obscene myopia of taking fossil fuels out of the ground and burning them up to propel tons of vehicular matter, plus passengers and their stuff. Maybe the city planners should make bigger roads! Wrong – that would likely invite more cars to circulate. Should we instead point our finger at the business model of car companies benefiting from selling cars as units for private property, all of which are going in the same direction at the same moment? Sort of. As we point at all these possible culprits, three fingers are pointing right back at us, the driver. Roads are a good place to start a discussion on *common resource use* since in many countries they are still state-owned. But public roads are exclusive, not *inclusive*, since they require a state-sanctioned driver's license and – in many cases – a *TÜV-approved* vehicle.

Another example are the open waters of our oceans, considered *global commons*. In them live fish. When pulled out of the water they don't have price tags, but when sold on the marketplace they certainly do. When millions of fishermen and fisherwomen become stakeholders in the common oceans we are left with oceans depleted of fish. The longevity of the COVID-19 pandemic is another illustration of the *tragedy of the commons*. Individuals insisting on the non-adherence of social-distancing and masking and/or refusing vaccination caused increasing *incidence* and *prevalence rates* of the SARS-CoV-2 virus. All diseases are demographic phenomena and not privately owned, and pathogens are designed by nature to ignore the boundaries between what we call individuals. During the COVID-19 pandemic, a person acting selfishly was thus vandalizing a true *public common* called *health*.

Management of the commons often ends tragically, and most tragic of all is the management of the planetary ecosystem. To mitigate the worst scenario outcome, immediate action by people, companies and nation sates is required.

The economic cost of doing something about it or ignoring will be paid by everyone inhabiting the future. The required actions are extremely disruptive to the current economic order and so no nation wants to take a first step, because unless every nation changes simultaneously, the early adopters are quickly out-competed by those waiting on the side. As a result, the global climate crisis remains unaddressed. Alas, it is becoming hard to deny that an unregulated pursuit of self-interest in terms of consumption is toxic for the common good. Vandana Shiva, an outspoken critic of globalization, explains how:

> The destruction of commons was essential for the industrial revolution, to provide a supply of natural resources for raw material to industry. A life-support system can be shared, it cannot be owned as private property or exploited for private profit. The commons, therefore, had to be privatized, and people's sustenance base in these commons had to be appropriated, to feed the engine of industrial progress and capital accumulation.[6]

Shiva is referring to processes of enclosure in nature. However, a similar process is now occurring with *machine learning*, a subfield of *artificial intelligence*. As we will see in later sections of this book, there is a new *gold rush* under way to extract not nature but *human nature* by enclosing fields of human knowledge, feelings and actions. This is done through the capture of users' data, which is then sold to private entities. While a data set – such as a bunch of people's faces gleaned by facial recognition technology – may still be publicly owned, the meta-value of the data is sold between private companies. In the words of media critics Kate Crawford and Vladan Joler, what we are dealing with is a: "future where expert local human labor in the public system is augmented and sometimes replaced with centralized, privately-owned corporate AI systems, that are using public data to generate enormous wealth for the very few."[7]

Efforts made to preserve common goods benefit all users in equal measure, whether or not they have made necessary sacrifices. Conversely, change, depletion or destruction thereof negatively impacts each and every user equally, regardless of their contribution. In economic terms, beneficiaries of the *commons* receive the full *marginal benefit* from their use but bear only part of the *marginal cost*. The problem is the incentives. For each individual user to make sacrifices for the benefit of common resources, they are far less than they would be if the resources were privately owned. If we pursue an open society where humans enjoy the right for "life, liberty and security," and we agree that many current *externalities* negatively affect all three aspects, then producers and consumers of so-called *externalities* must be held accountable. Rogue individuals, corporations and nations do what is best for their self-interest, care little for a greater good and are excluded from accountability.

In essence Garrett Hardin's *tragedy of the commons* tries to disprove the classical economists' claim that rational decisions made to promote one's self-interest will always lead to the best outcome for the common good. In a similar vein, in 1966, biologist George C. Williams argued that adaptations for the good of the group are seldom advantageous within groups and would therefore require group-level selection to evolve, a process he found unlikely. E. O. Wilson, the father of *sociobiology*, also stresses that maximizing relative fitness within a group seldom maximizes the fitness of the group.[8]

Game theory models also show that cooperative strategies were usually weaker and more vulnerable than self-serving strategies. After all, the dilemma – in the *prisoner's dilemma* – is caused by the inability to communicate and clearly makes self-interest the best strategy. The *prisoner's dilemma* illustrates why two individuals, who might be perfectly reasonable and rational, fail to cooperate even when doing so would favor both. Although originating from the Cold War think tank RAND, it was Albert W. Tucker who is responsible for cloaking the dilemma into the following story and naming it the "prisoner's dilemma": two criminals are arrested and thrown into solitary confinement. The police do not have proof to convict the two of the crime they were caught for, but they have evidence of prior, less serious offenses. Thus, they offer each prisoner a deal whereby either they can betray their confederate by pointing their finger at them, or cooperate by remaining silent. Let us not forget that the actual reason for solitary confinement is for prisoners not to communicate. The possible outcomes are:

- A and B betray each other: both have to serve two years in prison.
- A betrays B but B remains silent: A will be set free and B remains in prison for a maximum sentence; and vice versa – the situation is the same.
- Both A and B remain silent: both will only serve one year in prison.[9]

It was not until 1981 that the *prisoner's dilemma* was made famous through the publication of *The Evolution of Cooperation* by political scientist Robert Axelrod and evolutionary biologist William Hamilton. For the book, Axelrod ran tournaments where algorithmic computer programs competed against each other in the prisoner's dilemma hundreds of times. The program that did best was "tit for tat," where every move was countered with the same but only when the opening move was cooperation. It assumes players to be rational information processors.[10] A big assumption! But, fortunately, life is not a model.

In sum, cooperators are losers. They finish last; everyone knows that. That is why it is so much easier to explain *vice* than *virtue* in the world. Why should humans not act in ruthless, self-serving ways? Or the better question might be, why do they? Whereas religions struggle to explain the creation of evil by a benign creator god, evolutionary scientists often have a hard time explaining the "problem of goodness." How could behavior that does not bring an evolutionary advantage to the bearer be passed on genetically? Elliot Sober and David Sloan Wilson review such frameworks as "inclusive fitness," "multilevel selection theory" and game theory.[11] *Inclusive fitness theory* as formulated by Hamilton in 1964 usually applies where sender and recipient of selfless behavior are related or at least know each other. Basically, it is argued that the further removed individuals are genetically or platonically, the less they care for each other.[12] The pessimism of all above conclusions stems from an unwillingness to consider functional organization at a level above the individual.

Spaceship Gaia

Life itself can be seen as a series of events whereby members of groups become so cooperative that they appear, indeed, become higher-level organisms. As we saw above, the idea of *major evolutionary transitions* was championed by cell biologist Lynn Margulis in the 1970s to explain how nucleated cells evolved from *eukaryotic* cells, which themselves evolved from a symbiotic relationship of *prokaryotes*, or bacteria. *Endosymbiosis* – as this hypothesis is called – is well supported by studies of mitochondria and chloroplasts, both of which likely evolved from bacteria living in large cells.[13] The idea is very powerful: individual entities working in such harmony towards a common goal that they form a larger, more effective unit. Individual, multicellular organisms can thus be seen as groups and eusocial insect colonies as individuals. Human evolution, too, can be seen as a victory of group collaboration.[14] *Endosymbiotic* associations seem to have had an evolutionary advantage over other strategies and thus cells "collaborated" to form organs, body systems and populations.[15] Regarding human evolution, a fascinating question gets louder and louder: could it be that human evolution might undergo another major evolutionary transition towards one, functioning whole, beyond the nation state? For those now jumping out of their chairs exclaiming that such is not human nature, let me remind you of your hubris in assuming that evolution is complete when we are not even past the half-life of the sun.

A year after Hardin's essay, in 1969, Buckminster Fuller published his book *Operating Manual for Spaceship Earth*, which describes our planet as a spaceship flying through the cosmos. Buckminster Fuller was many things and "architect," "designer," "systems thinker" and "futurist" are really just unnecessary partitioning of his persona. In this book, Buckminster Fuller offered an actual operational manual for the linked relationships of everything on planet earth. The following quotation, which refers to fossil fuels, clearly reflects his holistic approach:

> we can make all of humanity successful through science's world-engulfing industrial evolution provided that we are not so foolish as to continue to exhaust in a split second of astronomical history the orderly energy savings of billions of years' energy conservation aboard our Spaceship Earth. These energy savings have been put into our Spaceship's life-regeneration-guaranteeing bank account for use only in self-starter functions.[16]

Buckminster Fuller describes the whole earth as a mechanical vehicle in need of maintenance. In the '70s, influenced by both Buckminster Fuller and space photography, biologists Lynn Margulis and James Lovelock went further and postulated the above-mentioned *Gaia hypothesis*, which violates conventional scientific wisdom of life merely adapting to pre-existing planetary conditions. The hypothesis is named after the Greek earth goddess and suggests that all biological beings have a regulatory effect on the earth's environment, while earth itself is homeostatic in its support of life-sustaining conditions. Thus *Gaia*, unlike *Spaceship Earth*, is not just a vehicle for life but the very force of life.[17] Now we have all witnessed the whole earth, we know all the facts and we know what needs to be done. We use *Earthrise* as logos, pins and brands but still somehow fail to see it. *Anthropogenic climate change* suggests that humanity increasingly affects and threatens to undo *Gaia*'s homeostasis. Lynn Margulis, Richard Buckminster Fuller, Stewart Brand and James Lovelock would probably all agree that the current conundrum requires stewardship.

It goes without saying that the human species long ago took a strong turn towards *materialism*. Understood as an epistemological stance aimed at the outside, objective world that is true, but taken to mean an affinity for material possession, the term is misleading. True, the average Western household owns about 10,000 different items, most of which are made worldwide and shipped, but that is only an observation and not an explanation. *Materialism* is only wishful thinking as it implies that we cherish, repair and take care of the physical objects surrounding us. Were we really *materialists*, most of us privileged Westerners could no longer move in our apartments due to all the stuff we'd have collected. Instead, we easily neglect and fall out of love with stuff, discarding objects as precious as, for example, smartphones. The root of the current ecological disaster is that we still sell endless promises of *dopamine*- and *endorphin*-inducing experiences in the form of clunky, non-biodegradable carcasses. Humans can decide neither their genetic makeup nor their cultural upbringing, the so-called *ultimate links of causation*, but they can make *proximal* choices. The breadth of choices – what is commonly referred to as free will – is narrowing due to rampant use of marketing, as we are conditioned to purchase materials as we chase the dragon of satisfaction. *Proximately* we are *materialists*, but ultimately we are consumerists!

What is happening is truly tragic: the state of the world is caused by decent people responding to perverse incentives. Human nature is inherently pro-life, and no one wakes up in the morning, rubs their hands and exclaims, "today I am going to trash the planet." But together we all do! We do it in an economic system that is bent on novelty, beauty, convenience and obsolescence with a lot of human inadequacy in its wake, and thus the tone of the rest of this book can turn sad and angry. To be perfectly clear it is not over-consumption itself but its consequences that I lament and the constant encouragement of such behavior that I take a moral and economic stance against. What we are seeing is not simply human nature and neither is it all learned behavior. Far more complicated, it is the human predisposition of desire made all too easy to quench. But since desires due to their nature cannot ever be quenched permanently, we are dealing with grave consequences.

The challenge of averting the worst repercussions is to generate new *symbotypes*, which prioritize sustainability and influence processes of cultural selection. Granted a gigantesque challenge, it is a *design* challenge. But for such a daunting task, a robust image of a possible and preferred future must be the target of selection. Following the basic ingredients of evolution – variation, selection and replication – we can hope to achieve cultural change. Regenerative models such as the *circular economy* with its heart of *cradle to cradle*, the *sharing economy* involving *open-source* software and hardware and *design for pro-sociality* are all ideas that students should be expected to master. Through countless replications, such ideas can be scaled to different circumstances. The creatives – designers, architects and artists – could do much in taking on the role of stewardship for a transformation. But first, they need to desire change towards cleaner, more meaningful products, fairer working conditions and a brighter future. And for that to happen, their incentives must change. If we want to avoid collapse, collectively we ought to construct a more sustainable niche for humans. The very first sentence of the first issue of Stewart Brand's *Whole Earth Catalog* is: "We are as gods and might as well get good at it."[18] Or, on a humbler note, I want to share the ethos of my late friend John Perry Barlow, internet pioneer and creative soul: "I want to be a good ancestor."

Notes

1   Obst, L. R. (Ed.) (1977). *The Sixties: The decade remembered now, by the people who lived it then*. Random House.
2   White, F. (2021). *The Cosma Hypothesis: Implications of the overview effect*. Hybrid Global Publishing.
3   Hardin, G. (2009). The tragedy of the commons. *Journal of Natural Resources Policy Research*, 1(3), 243–253.
4   "Digital Library of the Commons." dlc.dlib.indiana.edu, accessed on September 7, 2021.
5   Basu, S., Jongerden, J. & Ruivenkamp, G. (2017, March 17). Development of the drought tolerant variety Sahbhagi Dhan: Exploring the concepts commons and community building. *International Journal of the Commons*, 11, 144.
6   Shiva, V. (2001). *Protect or Plunder? Understanding intellectual property rights*. Zed Books.
7   Crawford, K., & Joler, V. (2018). Anatomy of an AI System. Retrieved September 18, 2018.
8   https://davidsloanwilson.world/online-content/the-tragedy-of-the-commons-how-eli nor-ostrom-solved-one-of-lifes-greatest-dilemmas/, accessed on May 6, 2020.
9   Lacey, N. (2008). *The Prisoners' Dilemma*. Cambridge University Press.
10 Axelrod, R., & Hamilton, W. D. (1981). The evolution of cooperation. *Science*, 211(4489), 1390–1396.
11 Sober, E., & Wilson, D. S. (1999). *Unto Others: The evolution and psychology of unselfish behavior*. Harvard University Press.

12 Dugatkin, L. A. (2007). Inclusive fitness theory from Darwin to Hamilton. *Genetics*, 176(3), 1375–1380.
13 Margulis, L. (1970). *Origin of Eukaryotic Cells*. Yale University Press.
14 Smith, J. M., & Szathmary, E. (1997). *The Major Transitions in Evolution*. Oxford University Press.
15 Cooper, G. M., Hausman, R. E. & Hausman, R. E. (2007). *The Cell: A molecular approach* (Vol. 4, pp. 649–656). ASM Press.
16 Buckminster Fuller, R. (2008). *Operating Manual for Spaceship Earth*. Estate of R. Buckminster Fuller, p. 40
17 Lovelock, J. E., & Margulis, L. (1974). Atmospheric homeostasis by and for the biosphere: The Gaia hypothesis. *Tellus*, 26(1–2), 2–10.
18 Brand, S. (1968). *Whole Earth Catalog*. Point Foundation.

PART II

Amongst the Prometheans

6

AN ANTHROPOLOGIST ENTERS THE WORLD OF DESIGN

Entering the World of Design

The seeds for this book were planted in 2010 when I traveled to Vienna to give a lecture called simply "anthropology and design." It was my first time speaking at a design conference, and I was way outside of my comfort zone of the human sciences. Instead of pretending to know anything about either design or business, I went out on a limb and compared the creative process to evolutionary theory. I talked about *artificial, natural* and *sexual selection, signaling theory* and *conspicuous consumption*. Always up for a little provocation and knowing full well what kind of cars were parked outside the conference building, I compared the lavish plumage of the peacock to a Porsche Cayenne. Retrospectively, I believe that my very cluelessness in what is commonly understood as design gave me an objective point of view and status as a maverick. In 2013, Günther Grall offered me a job as a full-time social scientist at the University of Applied Sciences in Salzburg, Austria and I was finally given the chance to make a practical change in the world. That year was the beginning of a new life in what can be considered applied anthropology. I am forever grateful for the chance.

On my first day at the new job, I remember looking around for something appropriate to wear. Before arriving at the school, I was forming mental images of my expectations. I was in a foreign field here, and the natives all around me seemed so content and adjusted. I sat down and tried to mimic office sounds like hammering some random rhetoric into the keyboard or clicking the mouse. Everyone was staring at me, and I could almost hear their questions out loud: what is an anthropologist doing here? Or, more paranoid: what is he *doing* right now? Truth be told, I was not doing anything much at all. The occasional office banter made no sense, with words like "rendering,"

DOI: 10.4324/9781003464754-9

"mock-up," "prototype," "target group," "persona" and "iteration" floating around. They were like husks, meaningless and severed in space. This was a design school. Oh, what a misfit I was!

The first lecture was the perfect excuse for me to leave my desk. With a horrible combination of insecurity and compensatory arrogance I walked into a shiny, high-tech classroom, the like of which I had never seen before. It was brightly lit with every single spotlight fully engaged. I walked to the front of the room, the heels of my penny loafers clicking on the wooden floor, my students watching every step with faint amusement. What is this thing anthropology? What does it have to do with design? I reached a podium resembling a DJ deck. There were knobs, levers, switches, cables and microphones, but none of them were marked with any kind of instructions or visual cues. Under the buzzing spotlights I was starting to sweat and so I walked back to the entrance to dim them. I found some sort of panel – again no instructions, icons or anything except several buttons much smaller than even my pinkie. The students' eyes and the bright ceiling lights remained, silently staring me down.

Incidentally, this inability to work the technology has been the same in the auditoriums of the many design schools I have taught at since. I should have no problem working this stuff, but since I receive no feedback from randomly pressing the switches, only the sour feeling of inadequacy and stupidity remains. Non-responsiveness to intuition is exemplary of "the psychopathology of everyday things," in the words of Donald Norman. The shape and placement of switches should never make the user feel inadequate or stupid but rather in control and capable. Especially in a lecture room, designed for multiple and diverse users a switch plate needs only provide two types of information: which of the many electrical objects in the room do they correspond to, and which object is controlled by what switch. The switch panel is the interface between me and the switches, but its design caused not luminous and only bad emotional energy. Ever since that first day, I call those designer light switches "Norman switches." I did not yet grasp that struggles with certain designs are great opportunities for *user research* and product improvement.

I had to call a technician. Then I started my worst class ever, a lecture on "scientific work," a class intended to teach students how to go about researching a specific problem, forming a hypothesis and testing it. Standing beneath the first PowerPoint slide projected onto the massive screen, I heard chairs moving and lots of whispering. Some students laughed. Was it my technical inadequacies? Was it that I looked different? Was it the subject matter? In reality, it was none of that, but only the *way* the subject matter was written, the font that I used. My class was on the scientific method of deductive reasoning, starting with a theory, and then empirically investigating a social phenomenon to falsify or verify a given hypothesis. Easy enough, and something we all do intuitively. Or so I thought. But I literally did not get past the superficiality of my letters. Admittedly, "Scientific Work" written in the not-so-cool slab serif font Copperplate Gothic really looks horrible. But then I also broke every other graphic design rule. I used a punch of different fonts, including Comic Sans (with shadows). I had never thought much about format, and I have to admit that my presentations were crowded collections of pixelated and grainy stock images in fridge magnet effect. My visual skills fell dismally below the expectations of my students.

Even beneath the surface, my lecture would have never worked. I know now that the classic scientific method is almost entirely useless in the context of design and that a hypothesis can only be formed much later after vigorous observations in the field. The exception might be a project where a designer proposes, and then tests, a new material for its superiority in each task. But such insight lay on top of a very steep learning curve and that day I headed back to my desk, highly discouraged. Feeling so far out of my comfort zone, I was looking for an anchor, something familiar, and so I began a general overhaul of my classes, starting with the *phenotype*: the appearance of my PowerPoints. So scared of being judged for typeface, fonts, color theory and composition, I just dropped it all. From that day on, my slides feature only one striking image and one word. No one missed any of my PowerPoint art and neither did anyone miss any writing. Everything that I now say comes straight from my head, and yes, sometimes I repeat myself. But PowerPoint is just an overrated public cheat sheet anyways.

I headed over to Google images. My very first slide needed to be an info-graphic of *evolutionary mismatch theory*. As our bodies and minds struggle in tiny increments to adapt to our surroundings, the surrounding itself is changing at warp speed. Rapid cultural evolution – fueled by design – in contrast to a painfully slow biological evolution has produced a strange conundrum for us humans. There must be a picture for that, I thought. I tried many different prompts, ordered in novel sequences, in German and in English, with no satisfying results. What I really wanted to find visually was this mismatch between "ancient bodies and brand-new commodities," and this being before ChatGPT, I typed those words into Google and hit *search*. And there, among the first hits, one Banksy image stared back at me with lucid clarity. An abstract representation of archaic hominids standing in the barren savanna with spears in their hands attacking a few empty shopping carts was my first triumph in wedding design with anthropology. In that moment of looking at that image, everything surrounding me – the computer screen, the hard drive, the chair, table and ceiling – changed. I realized fully that I am living in the designs of the past and that everything artificial that the future will hold is conceived by my students now. You cannot design for the present.

I ordered the print and a week later received and framed two enormous panels. I hung them side by side in the staircase of the university building and regularly pulled colleagues and students in front of them to explain my fascination … and to mark my territory. The left panel has the empty shopping carts, as if waiting to be filled by designed commodities. The other one shows the three hominids in a threatening stance. Their amygdala hijacked, they stand frozen but ready to charge the shopping carts. Together, the two pictures address the mismatch between culture and biology: the interface of things and the users of things. And they scream of the immense responsibility of designers to conceive and produce commodities for total strangers inhabiting an unknown future. They also speak of the total impotence modern humans have in providing for themselves. In an act of self-domestication, we have created a world that we are struggling to comprehend and on that cold winter day I understood that I had landed in the workshop of culture. Thank you, Banksy, whoever you are!

With my mission statement firmly hanging on the wall, I rolled up my sleeves and went to work. But who is this new tribe that I found myself in the middle of? Aware of culture shock, I have always been a kind of connoisseur of it. I love its unsettling nature, the anxiety resulting from leaving my comfort zone and being truly lost in the streets of New Delhi, Nairobi, Kathmandu or Buenos Aires. This will not surprise anyone, since stripping away as much of my ethnocentric sense of self and trying to make sense of the new and strange is a crucial part of any anthropologist's training. Confronted with the Other, questions tend to first have an inward and not outward direction; when all sense of familiarity is peeled off, we ask about ourselves. What is it that I do as a user and consumer of things? And then, slowly starting with the superficial, I looked at how designers communicate their designs and themselves.

Amongst the Promethean

Anthropologist Clifford Geertz noted that ethnographic accounts are fictional, not in the sense of being false but in the sense of being fabricated by the storyteller. So here too I am spinning a yarn of how I first entered the world of design, and these being first observations, they are caricatures. *Design* is a fuzzy term made of different disciplines, traditions and philosophies, and its actors are not in fact a uniform grouping ready to be pushed into a neat story. However, in this world one can find such an abundance of information bootstrapped to what Erving Goffman called "sign-vehicles," that a rough sketch is possible. Of course, the information received is always computed against previous experiences with similar individuals resulting in stereotypes, which in essence are untested mental shortcuts.

The senders of signs, knowing that they make a public impression, are expected to devote much effort to conveying themselves in the best possible way. Impressions that people project range from fairly accurate to totally fabricated, depending on what is at stake in each situation. Especially in the world of design, social media, dating applications and portfolios weigh heavily, and so it should not be surprising that the levers have been moved towards deceitful glorification of self. When everyone tries so hard to be awesome and says "nice" all the time, maybe ethnographers can be excused for using clichés and perhaps they can also be forgiven for mockery. I continue to have the outmost respect for design and as the architecture of the human niche, it deserves all of it. As a newcomer, naively, I expected designers to display a kind of stoic apprehension or gravitas as stewards of things to come. Unfortunately, over ten years later I still only rarely see any such thing. Oh, and much of this is an account of things I saw and interpreted when I first contacted this world. So, yes, all this has a real Tumblr vibe. It's so 2013!

Let us revisit that day when I was humiliated due to the way I wrote words. In the world of design, the written word is used sparsely, but when there is text it tends to follow certain patterns. Fonts of the serif category – the ones with a small line or stroke at the edges of the letters – are viewed as conservative and generally disliked. Also, many of my colleagues refuse to use capital letters in emails and memos, a behavior that probably is anti-establishment and a sympathetic nod to the *Bauhaus* movement that made lower case writing its program. Austrian and American graphic designer Herbert Bayer designed a letterhead for Walter Gropius, director of the Bauhaus, which explains Bayer's insistence of avoiding all capital letters. Literally a manifesto, the letterhead included the line: "why capitalize when you can't speak big?"[1] Incidentally, the massive admiration of the *Bauhaus* as *Gesamtkunstwerk* (comprehensive piece of art) helps settle some of design's paradoxes I was struggling to understand. After all, the German movement of the 1920s and 1930s did make it their explicit goal to wed individual artistry and mass production as well as aesthetics and functionality. Perhaps writing all lowercase is a form of *virtue signaling* of the anti-imperialism of Otl Aicher, the great German graphic designer.[2]

Typefaces have been associated with empires, with national character and also with emotionality, and apparently, due to the writing I used in my presentations I was typecast (excuse the pun) as dictatorial, serious and not really very fun. That is not me and so I adopted a very common one in the world of graphic design, Helvetica, designed in 1957 by Max Miedinger for the Haas'sche Schriftgiesserei in Switzerland. To appear especially elegant (and "designy") I use the "Neue" variety. From a design standpoint, matching my typeface with the content of what I am writing is not trivial and rather important if I want to get my message across. I now know the difference between fonts and typefaces, where the former is one is the mechanism of delivery, and the second is a creative item. Studies show that the way you write is as important as the message. The use of supercool fonts is great, but it should not eclipse content.[3]

Let us turn to the way designers dress and act, or their *impression management*. Design schools look like dress-up parties with a theme of contradiction; the stuff worn is mostly void of any temporal, geographical or cultural connection. In an age where *Instagrammability* is more important than rebellion and novelty, I guess we are left with nostalgia and cynical irony. It is as if the fashion industry is auto-cannibalizing: in a kind of protest of itself it is capitalizing on its own mishaps. In any case, the student body in schools of applied arts is celebrating the ugly, cheesy and ridiculous. Thus, '80s-style windbreakers, a Led Zeppelin shirt, *Sound of Music* rucksack, Mr. Potato Head socks and Vans is a perfect outfit for someone who is too young for everything mentioned and most certainly does not skateboard. (The absence of ollie-induced wear on the Vans is an instant giveaway). Parents and the status quo won't understand but their fashion-forward friends will. It is *cultural appropriation* to the highest degree, but while *old-school* gets a lot of credit, my old age certainly does not. Pronouncing cultural references correctly by placing them into a historical context is usually met by deaf ears and rolling eyes.

And what is it with the faux simplicity? #craftmanship? Considering that design is all about moving forward on and on into some bright techno future, full of innovation and novelty, the old-fashioned-ness is ostentatious. Like traveling back to the early 20th century, I looked around campus and saw vests, tweed flat-caps, Budapester shoes and Harry Potter spectacles. Modern craftsmen with handlebar mustaches were whizzing by on old-fashioned (looking) bicycles with their pants rolled up as if to protect them from chain grease. Funny thing is, after parking their fixies, their pants stayed up. Vintage workwear, meant as an understatement, comes across as such a strong statement just because it is absolutely not the bourgeoisie of capitalist society that is mimicked here. Instead, it is the proletariat, the underdogs of the machine and the good side of creativity. It is a celebration of a golden age before everything went south. Perhaps this too can be traced to the Bauhaus movement, where the likes of Hungarian design legend László Moholy-Nagy preferred wearing overalls to flowing Bohemian outfits. Whatever the reason, don't ever mention capitalism!

Like the anachronistic aesthetics of *steampunk*, the markings of designers must be described as *retro-future*. Visually this produces a striking effect, not unlike *Black Mirror* episodes: technological novelty is exaggerated while the clothing, hairstyle and accessories of the cast are decidedly old-fashioned. Similarly, while to the outside they appear old-fashioned and *slow life*, my students indulge in total connectivity, via the latest smartphones, tablets and wearables. Lifestyle design – and its army of influencers – is pushing hard to catch the attention of a generation accustomed to spending hours scrolling quickly and mindlessly and so all this signaling is fed into an endless feedback cycle. Infinite glimpses, experiences and moments are interrupted to pose, recompose and record.

Much like a director typecasting the "creative" in a movie on capitalism, I desperately needed a term to trigger something similar in the minds of my students, a kind of instantly recognizable caricature. And much like a marketer describing a *target group* by jamming lots of data points into one fictitious character, I basically searched for a *persona*. Maybe it is an example of the law of large numbers, or maybe it is just an overused stereotype. At this point it is outdated. Whatever the reason, *hipster* became my term of choice. There is no better word for playfully mocking designers' superficiality and egocentrism without ever attacking anyone personally, which, incidentally, was never really a problem since no one ever identifies as a hipster – at least not until many years from now when musing over selfies of the past. *Hipsters* like to pretend that they are inventors or at least first-adopters of new styles. Students themselves use the term pejoratively for someone overly concerned with appearing un-trendy. "He's a fake, he's just a hipster," the hipster might hiss. Of course, it isn't a new cultural phenomenon and dates to at least the amphetamine-fueled jazz scene of the 1940s and the reactive literary sub-culture known as the *beatniks.* Celebrating the rootless anti-hero, I guess Neal Cassidy in Jack Kerouac's *On the Road* [4] or William S. Burroughs' pseudo-nym William Lee in *Junkie*[5] were hipsters. But if the term still applies to counterculture and progressive thought, I am witnessing an obvious paradox because *hipsterdom* went mainstream. I don't think it is punk to wear vegan Doc Martens, the Che Guevara shirt from Amazon is only red in color and the Grateful Dead hoody at H&M is not drop-out but throw-away. What happens when behind every coffee bar in town hangs the faux-handwritten, mixed-font chalkboard? How can my *macchiato* be advertised with a clash of *Oldiez family and Cypress Hill gangsta* writing? Insane in the membrane.

Call Andy Warhol a *hipster* but don't dare call designers pop artists! Ironic, because design schools are very reminiscent of the pop art factory of the '60s, as they crank out beautiful objects with the explicit goal of scaling for mass consumption. Let us settle on designers as "artists without angst." Of course they are because they – unlike artists – peddle functional easy-to-monetize stuff. The *hipsters'* appearance can be read as a claim of authenticity and uniqueness. Their consumption patterns – at least those that are signaled – are pure commodification of counterculture. While suggesting a simultaneous creation of the new and consumption of the old, they are strangely sincere. It is a kind of rage against the machine that they feed! But the rage is on aes-thetic and technological rather than ideological grounds. This is perfectly understandable since the very nature of design is the destruction of now. Every generation rebels against the establishment and the mainstream and creative movements probably all come from a kind of oedipal revolt, but with designers it is stranger, more abstract. Admittedly all this is likely a failed attempt at pigeonholing a population. It is simply a list of observed patterns, which I coded and analyzed to classify. By the time this book is published my observed patterns won't be trending anymore, which is my point exactly.

Left, or Right? The Strange Politics of Designers

Next, as I looked beneath the surface, I puzzled over ideologies. Spoiler alert: I witnessed design students and practitioners all over the world oblivious to economic theory and philosophy. "How many of you know Adam Smith?" I regularly asked in class, only to see one or two hands raised timidly in response. "But he is your God!" I would exclaim. "Without Adam Smith, there is no Henry Ford and certainly no logic of scalability and outsourced supply chains!" Let us try someone from the left. What about Karl Marx and his ideas of *super-structure* or *surplus value*? Okay, how about someone a little later. Who knows Maynard Keynes and the post–World War II world order as established at Bretton Woods? Bretton what? What about current authors like Kate Raworth, Thomas Piketty or David Graeber, whose respective work on the *doughnut economy*, the wealth divide and an analysis of debt are all so important for designers? Okay, let's go back to the right, to Keynes' nemesis Friedrich von Hayek, the father of modern liberal economics. Anyone know him? Nope! It did not matter: I received blank faces bordering on boredom and apathy! Why are we not teaching political science and economic theory to the students making the future?

Retrospectively, all this seems terribly naive, but back then it was very confusing to be the lecturer of design students. As the anthropologist hired to bring humanitarianism, ethics and ideas of social justice to the table, I found myself defending a kind of libertarian position of a lean state with minimal regulation. When dismantling dangerous ideas like *Homo economicus, rational choice theory* or the concept of the *tabula rasa*, the general reaction tended to be faint surprise caused by the realization that perhaps this is something important. Again, it is ironic considering that design as a very capitalist creed, working in lockstep with industrial partners, conceives and makes things and services to be distributed at scale. Dear designer, why do you never admit to being in it for the money? It is okay! Really! Throughout history, technology and design were always strongly linked to capital accumulation. Technology has made our lives so much easier and longer, but it has also always been used to capture money. The entire point of patents is to freeze an innovation to capitalize on its sale and use. It is okay to be in it for the money – we all are to a certain extent – and I don't think a greener, more equitable world and capitalism are mutually exclusive concepts. In this discipline so firmly in the throes of capitalism, hell-bent on creating novelty and the desire of end-users to own more and more, I suddenly found myself shifting to the right, antagonizing the *snowflakes* on the left.

But do terms such as left and right still hold any merit? In a 2005 essay titled "The end of left and right," Andrew Kelly asks just that question. He asks, "is Osama bin-Laden left wing"? Or:

> Who has a more left-wing approach to women's sexuality: Pope John Paul or Hustler magazine? Consider Fidel Castro. He persecutes homosexuals, crushes trade unions, forbids democratic elections, executes opponents and criminals, is a billionaire in a country of very poor people and has decreed that a member of his family shall succeed him in power. Is Castro left-wing or right-wing? Explain your answer.[6]

As a provocation, this essay published in *Spectator* magazine is important in a long overdue discussion on political polarization. Clearly, many right-wing ideologies got us into the current mess of climate change, species extinction and ocean garbage patches, making top-down regulation mandatory. But can personal liberty and freedom be guaranteed when behavior is designed, monitored and curtailed? And so, it goes back and forth between the political left and right. Conservatives want to retain traditional culture and civilization, they value stability, safety and continuity. They want to limit change and allow only the kind that is clearly "better" in the engineering sense of the word. Building a better mousetrap is fine; reforming public policy not so much. Many conservatives reject modernism and would like to turn the clock back to times when things seemed simpler, when everything and everybody was in its proper place. They presume an innate human nature that is relatively unchangeable. Conservatives dream safe. Progressives, on the other hand, value equality, human rights and progressive reform, and are willing to change and even cast aside traditions and institutions in the service of making things better for those who are not currently served well by them. Liberals are willing to experiment, even if the outcome isn't certain. Liberals believe humans can and must change to create a better, more egalitarian world for all. Liberals dream big. Jonathan Haidt's *The Righteous Mind* explores the psychological phenomena of *confirmation bias* and the *general error of attribution*. It explains very eloquently why people will spend their entire life on the so-called left or right but rarely out of intellectual conviction.[7] Like a boxer needs an opponent to hit, we actually need the other side, in order to legitimize our own ideology. Fritz Breithaupt, a literary scholar, has called this phenomenon *emphatic sadism*.[8] David Sloan Wilson has also researched and written on possible genetic dispositions for leftish and rightish thinking.[9]

Their political stance did not really seem based on anything, but I saw the designer leaning forward with a distinct arch to the left. Might this be virtue signaling to compensate for white, capitalist guilt? Are we talking about solving all the problems of the world, without considering that we WEIRD people caused most of them? Like Silicon Valley, the creative ideology is not easily explained in binary but as a strange brew. Especially in the creative sector a new form of political correctness called *wokeism* is on the loose. I am very familiar with its origins – both its animosity towards injustice and its alliance with high tech – as I grew up in the San Francisco area and there is no better place to study the origins of this ideology.

In the Southern Bay stands Hoover Tower on the Stanford campus and technically above the Hoover Institution, a think tank known for promoting economic liberty, free enterprise and limited government. In the Eastern Bay stands the Campanile tower on the campus of the University of California at Berkeley, or the "People's Republic of Berkeley" as it is called due to its strong leftist leaning and history as the epicenter of '60s hippy rebellion. Always safely cloaked by political correctness, Berkeley's departments of social science are perhaps more aptly called departments of social justice, the university's gatekeepers – departments of admission and human resources – practiced affirmative action until 1996. Of course nowadays such departments are called "Diversity, Equity and Inclusion", or DEIs. Along with public policymakers and progressive media, Berkeley spread a powerful narrative of repairing the wounds of the past. At its core is a deep skepticism of an economic system bent on unbridled individualism and relentless growth in GDP.

While my parents mingled in circles of classical liberalism around the Hoover Institution, I enrolled in cultural anthropology at Berkeley. The Berlin Wall had just fallen, the last colonial regimes had retreated and the Cold War seemed to be over. While Francis Fukuyama short-sightedly called it *The End of History* by declaring the victory of Western liberalism and capitalism, social science turned to undoing wrongs committed in the name of both.[10] But the idea of reparation of the past is an incredibly difficult ethical and impossible logistical problem since the present citizenry descends from both slavers and slaves, victims and victors. Of course, I had to read classic anthropologists like Marcel Mauss, Bronislaw Malinowski, Franz Boas and Claude Lévi-Strauss, all of which focus on culture and reject racial models of human differences. But the curriculum was also loaded with white man's remorse, historical materialism, postmodernism and ecofeminism, all in search of social equity. At Berkeley and other schools, classical social sciences departments spawned "cultural studies," "identity studies," "gender studies" or "critical theory," which are firmly rooted in the '60s postmodern take on "theory." The common denominator of such "grievance studies" is problematizing all aspects of culture in more and more detail, to oust power differentials and systemic oppression rooted in identity.

Awakening to see history as an inhumane mess of oppression and plunder, which continues to manifest, including in our smallest actions, hearts and minds, in principle is a good thing. "Be woke," an old phrase from African American Vernacular English (AAVE), meaning to be alert to racial prejudices, started to dominate discourses and was used as a rallying cry against all forms of discrimination. Unfortunately, having awoken also implies a righteous juxtaposition to those deeply asleep and ignorant to societal evil. The enlightened *woke* crowd often tries to cancel the rest with vengeance, fueled by fear and hatred. As John McWhorter has pointed out, *wokeism* can be called a new religion[11] complete with orthodoxy, dogma (books like *White Fragility*[12] and *How to Be an Antiracist*),[13] thought police (college campus speech codes as mandated by the DEIs) and the cancellation of heretics. Going out of one's way to publicly show piety and moral convictions has always guaranteed a favorable ranking for individuals; during times of the Spanish Inquisition, for example, it literally was a matter of life and death. In *wokeism*, inequalities are cloaked in intellectual-sounding but hollow concepts such as *intersectionality* or *critical race theory* and thrown around by the masses prancing around like political peacocks. In short, it is *virtue signaling*.[14]

Everything is seen through a lens of power differentials, and thus the woke movement polarizes by providing fuel for today's palpable culture wars between right and left, straight and queer, black and white, man and woman. It also includes a decidedly anti-science stance and legitimized Donald Trump as a good candidate for 53 percent of the US population. *The Madness of Crowds,* an excellent book by Douglas Murray, makes sense of recent, truly puzzling social phenomena like the massive spike in teen gender dysphoria or Black Lives Matter marches during an airborne viral pandemic.[15] It seems that what started as critical knowledge provided by the study of social science had become inflationary, superficial and mainstream. It is especially big in the creative sectors and suddenly tech nerds who have never taken a humanities course in their lives care deeply about systemic oppression. To use a very *woke* term, we are dealing with a serious case of *cultural appropriation*! But, perhaps the most fascinating aspect of *wokeism* is that its fanatic, no fascist tendencies come from the left and not the right! We are not dealing with a tiki-torch-touting right minority but a left mainstream and, as we shall see, moral outrage spreads exponentially on social media.

Wokeism is especially rampant in the creative class. Since many of the WEIRD traits are also shortlisted to stand for male toxicity and patriarchal hegemony, *wokeness* amongst the creative class is a like the Freudian *projection,* where inner complexes are cast outward and vilified. Any hint of coming from a Western, educated, industrialized, rich and democratic culture is suspicious. If you show some gratitude for being dealt favorable cards at birth you risk cancelation. This is what happened to me at a design school of Switzerland. After speaking without notes almost continuously for six hours on the most design-relevant aspects of history, I turned to the humanities. I remember that unlike other design classes, that day, I dug deep into cultural anthropology proper and talked about such topics as the horrors of colonialism and slavery as well as the omissions of income disparity and unpaid work of women in measurements of GDP per capita. As we wrapped up class in the final question-and-answer session, a woman asked me why I used the masculine version of "designer." The lecture was in German, which unlike English uses pronouns for everything and I should have used the gender-inclusive Designer*in, where the final "in" denotes the female gender. I don't lecture in German much anymore and never for six hours straight. I apologized and said that mentioning masculine, feminine and transitional gender forms for every profession would have robbed me of my flow. Never mind that the entire day I was defending women, people of color and anyone else disfranchised and oppressed. The pardon was not granted, and she added that I should have addressed the non-binary and genderqueer designers as well. I responded that the little asterisk between the word "designer" and the ending "in" was unpronounceable – by definition – since it stands for silence. I regret that comment because it was only received as cynicism and to cut the story short and I was not invited again to teach at that school.

I guess I had my little *Jordan Peterson moment* as I stood guilty as charged with original sin and for things I did not choose. There is no trial in cancel culture. The woman in the audience was shooting down a white, cis, heterosexual male for not using correct pronouns and she was doing it right in front of her classmates. She must have marched to the dean, who in a later telephone conversation said I was convicted of being neo-liberal. Clearly one of the strongest cognitive biases planted into our minds in deep evolutionary time is that of thinking in the binary of inside and outside groups. Us and them. Unfortunately, we often forget that our hatred is actually directed at a person's words, not the person. The latter just embodies the former. Thus, I am not embittered by my student, and I welcome discussion, but I also noticed how adrenaline-laden she was, how righteous her voice was. Designers want to overthrow the patriarchy. Great! They also want to go *post-human, post-growth, post-everything*. Also great, I guess. Nothing should remain how it is, and everything must be burned to the ground, but aren't such efforts usually just a desperate search for yet unexploited market segments? Design has incredible power for finding solutions; I am just not sure it is used for the right problems.

Creative Destruction

Sustainability means "the ability to sustain," and closely related to conservation, "the act of conserving," which sounds kind of like the right side of the political aisle. Conservation tends to protect nature and artifacts from humans, whereas sustainability counts on human intervention. Of course, sustainability and conservation are not synonymous, and it makes sense that designers, with their built-in drive to change things, talk about the former and never the latter. In any case, the preservation of natural systems requires both. I thought the left was all about disruption and revolution – just think of Che Guevara or Lenin – but there exists an obvious paradox between disruption and sustainability. Yet, I hear all this babble coming from students, teachers and keynote speakers, like a whole lexicon of newspeak, with all these fancy-sounding, empty words like "disruptive innovation," "start-ups," "incubators," "hubs," "unicorns," "agile" and "scrub." Great, but how do such concepts pair with sustainability that everyone was going on about at the same time. As my opening statement for an online podium discussion on *sustainable fashion,* I once said that the two terms are oxymoronic. Of course, that did not make me very popular, but I wanted to address that the very concept of fashion was based on obsolescence. Something – no matter if we are talking about clothing or anything else – becomes fashionable *because* it is not the thing preceding it. Fashionability is not material; if it were, then trends would not change all the time. Fashion is based on the fact that new things make prior things *look* dumb. Marketing-driven fashion cycles *is* planned obsolescence.

All this seemed like the economist Joseph Schumpeter's nightmare. Let me explain: by far the most impressive and unique aspect of the designer's personality is the willingness and ability to change things. Unlike us dusty and passive academics, they go beyond words to action. As we have seen above, designers are artistic and free, and they come off decidedly liberal and left wing in dress. But also ideologically, I experienced strong resistance to anything remotely hinting at libertarianism or anything else small-statist.

Once, at some design event with a glass of champagne in hand, I thought I could score some points in a circle of designers by telling the anecdote of meeting Friedrich von Hayek as a boy. He was my father's teacher and together with his wife they often socialized with my parents. The memory is sweet: it was at a holiday resort in Tyrol. Hayek was quite old at this point, frail, one hand resting on a cane. I remember his kind eyes and warm touch as he gave me some coins and pointed me towards a place for ice cream. Friedrich von Hayek, Nobel Prize laureate and one of history's most famous economists, invited me for ice-cream! The anecdote did not make much of an impact and the conversation moved towards publicly funded research projects. I moved towards the bar.

I witnessed an oxymoronic blend of positions. You cannot create *fashions* and be *sustainable. Value added by design* was rightfully taken for granted, but nobody talked about any theories of *marginal utility.* Entrepreneurship and design start-ups where highly praised but then so were heavy taxation. I learned that patents and intellectual copyright laws are crucial for designers, yet the open-source movement – be it in the digital or material realm – is also championed. Mysterious to me, as it seems threatening for the creative sector; even OpenAI, as a business model, is celebrated. Unsustainable design practices concerning materiality, manufacture, marketing and distribution can only happen in a system of utter deregulation, yet the designers I mingled with are all in on governmental interventions and subventions. I have not done a survey, but from the countless conversations I had, I would guess that most designers vote left of the center and green in color. While American business jargon like *awesome, nice, game changer, next level, burn-out, bigger picture* and *out of the box* are liberally sprinkled into non-English conversations, there also exists a strong anti-Americanism.

In short, I had naively assumed that design – more than any other discipline – fits the continuous innovation and *creative destruction* popularized by Joseph Schumpeter. The evolutionary economist used the famous term to describe business cycles, but he used it cautiously, such as in Part 2 of *Capitalism, Socialism and Democracy*, where he argues that capitalism would meet its demise as a system if the creative-destructive forces go unchecked. Schumpeter saw the interplay of innovation and imitation as the main engine of capitalist competition.[16] His model is intrinsically evolutionary because it features the elements of variation, selection and replication. In the words of Christopher Freeman, a scholar of Schumpeter's work: "the central point of his whole life work [is]: that capitalism can only be understood as an evolutionary process of continuous innovation and 'creative destruction'."[17] For Schumpeter, economic change revolves around innovation and entrepreneurial activities, and he aimed to prove that innovation-originated market power can provide better results than the invisible hand and price competition. He did not, however, think that many innovations are significant enough to be deemed *mutations*. For that to happen an innovation needed to stay around, be sustainable and not just be random and opportunistic novelty for someone to get rich off of and waste materials with. In any case, designers absolutely love to speak about innovation and novelty, but by and large they are not ready, willing or able to speak about Schumpeter and the Austrian School of Economics proper. I thought design is based on cycles of *obsolescence* and *novelty*. It is, to use a typical Silicon Valley euphemism, *permission-less innovation*, or, to put it as Facebook's old slogan, "move fast and break things." Like I was saying, designers are simply leaning forward into the future, and towards the left.

Designers Are Kinda WEIRD

For my focus on a place inside the current industrial order closely associated with human innovation and material throughput, I looked at appearance and behavior of those who design. My first observations were superficial, and I needed to find some pattern, common denominators. I was not yet aware of Joseph Henrich's work, but my observations mapped perfectly onto the people now referred to as WEIRD. Designers, practitioners and students alike are generally raised in a society that is Western, educated, industrialized, rich and democratic. An important tool for measuring personality traits, the dominant one in social and personality psychology has been the Big 5 model. Usually referred to by its acronym OCEAN's 5, the independent dimensions of one's personality traits – openness, conscientiousness, extraversion, agreeableness and neuroticism – are often visualized using a spider diagram. Each category is a continuum of possibilities on a spectrum of two extremes. Whether someone tends to be overly outgoing and sociable or socially reclusive and introverted, for example, can be seen on the scale of extraversion. The five positions of an individual make up someone's personality, and most people stay true to their dimensions across their lifetimes. Of course, the Big 5 model itself is based on observations of overwhelmingly literate, college-age students in urban settings and thus it is skewed; so much so that Joseph Henrich has renamed it the WEIRD 5. In any case let us put on our psychology hats and look at designers a bit closer.

Although much empirical research exists on creatives in general, I found none on designers specifically. I will guess that good designers would be high in most Big 5 categories, but let us start with openness. The higher someone scores in openness, the higher the chance he/she appreciates aesthetics since that requires being open to the world. Indeed, aesthetics and openness define the life of creative minds like painters, actors or designers. Because only a small percentage of all people are high in openness and even fewer have any aesthetic affinity, designers are kind of outliers and through their lifestyle choices they tend to refine and distil their taste further. It is also interesting to consider that at least in openness artists and scientists are similar. A large meta-analysis of over 83 research studies on creative and scientific personality types found the strongest positive correlations to creativity being with openness. Strongest negative correlations were found with scales of 1) neuroticism, meaning they are in general more neurotic – in the OCEAN model neuroticism is scaled opposite to the rest – or what we might label control freaks, and 2) conscientiousness, which in turn correlates highly with conservatism, meaning they are less likely to finish mundane tasks since too many curious projects are open. Creativity also reliably correlates with extroversion, which might be a surprise if we think of the lonely, brooding artist.[18]

But, if behavior is part of the phenotype and if conceiving products and services of the extended phenotype, then designers, at least empirically speaking, are extroverts. They are taking ideas found inside themselves and they manifest them to the outside world. In such a light, they are the interface between subject and object. Extroversion is characterized by high energy, positive affect, sociability, enthusiasm, novelty seeking, dominance, self-confidence and assertiveness, all of which I see amongst designers. In general, creatives are far more open to novelty, less conservative and less conscientious, quite self-confident, driven and ambitious. They are also quite dominant and impulsive. To me designers are sometimes kind of like hippies in their openers but the opposite when they get anxious, which is when they try to control the future.

The Pregnant Silence

If designers were a tribe, it would die out in just a few generations. In that sense they are also a mirror image of greater, WEIRDer society: they are worshiping the new but forget about having the young. I am not basing this on statistical evidence and only my informal observations and conversations with designers; but from all designers I know, I have never met *any* with more than two kids. (Remember that the replacement rate of any population to remain stable is 2.1.) My ex-students who do have kids are extremely rare and the current students all shudder at the thought of having to share their lives with a child. Recently in a workshop for Parisian master's students, we were speculating about future urban scenarios. "Imagine yourself with your kids in 10, 15 years …", I said, but could not even finish my prompt when a student burst out with "That's a horrible thought!" The class laughed in agreement. Design students, especially of the Generation Z sort, are very clear about family planning: nothing is planned except not to have kids! Yet – and this is the strange, pregnant silence – everyone wants to build new objects for shiny, happy people. If designers had more kids they might empathize better with us, my wife and I, parents of two teenage girls in our futile battle to shield them from very unwholesome technology packaged into those shiny objects.

There also exists much confusion around demography in design. I have seen countless design presentations where there is talk about women, men, generations, morbidity and migration, but such terms are all too often used only for selling strategies. Consider for a second one nasty piece of marketing jargon: *target group*. What an undignified, shameless and – worst of all – anti-scientific word to describe a group of Homo sapiens peacefully minding their own business. It never means the study of groups as they are. It stands for a group to be made into customers, for the simple fact that they stand as idle resources to be used. Groups display behavior that sets them apart and makes them recognizable, employing what are called *social markers*, and to the designer/marketer they are fodder. But is defining a target group and then reducing it to a *persona* not by definition creating a sampling bias in research? And once strategies and designs go into action are we not deliberately changing – or more aptly, priming – that target group to consume further.

To sharpen the focus, a fictitious conglomerate of the stereotypical *target group* called *persona* is created. And yes, the *personas* – fictional characters crafted from user research – have an age range, job description and marital status. But caricatures such as "Caucasian," "brown-haired" and "living in Berlin" are individual attributes and not demographics. Demography describes not individual agents but the aggregate. While *personas* – vestibules of old marketing techniques – are often based on short-sighted, over-simplified images coming uncomfortably close to stereotypes, demography is the statistical study of human populations. Personas are little more than attempts to create identity politics based on consumption. They are creations of images using demographic data to fine-tune marketing techniques to turn people into customers and users. After all, the target is a group of customers with shared demographics, identified as the most likely customers of a company's product or service. It is the foundation for the implementation of a successful marketing plan of anything new. On it hinges *brand positioning* and *demand creation. Lead nurturing* – another nauseating marketing term – is providing potential customers with a unique experience to make them feel special, keeps them coming back for seconds and eventually converts them into influencing consumers to the rest. And then comes the so-called *conversion funnel*, which is like a pipeline of content provided to guide people through stages in becoming buyers. But I must change topic now because I am feeling a bit queasy.

Turning Away from Papanek

Between 2018 and 2021, the *Vitra Design Museum* and the Victor Papanek Foundation of the University of Applied Arts Vienna hosted an honorary exhibition entitled "Victor Papanek: The Politics of Design." Its purpose was to raise awareness of the great designer's vision of his creed as a powerful agent. Over fifty years ago, his *Design for the Real World* was supposed to be a call-to-arms for industrial designers as he wanted them to tackle real rather than constructed problems.[19] Design has only gained in agency since Papanek's writing, and thus there is reason for optimism.

Under the banner of *design thinking*, designers have entered distant arenas, heretofore inhabited exclusively by lawyers, management consultants and policymakers. Broadly labeled *strategic design*, this movement boldly goes beyond making shiny objects or pushing pixels for social media, but projects tackling environmental or social problems are still fringe. Even the promising concept of listening to many different voices in a business ecosystem, *industrialized empathy*, has become mainstream. After analyzing more than 100,000 executive-level design decisions across 300 publicly held companies, consulting giant *McKinsey* found that those that had rigorous design thinking strategies at their core had 32 percent higher revenue and 56 percent higher shareholder returns compared to those that did not.[20] Today massive corporations (i.e. IBM, Apple and Nike) and even governments (ie. Finland, Estonia and France) are using *design thinking* to improve their output or institutions, respectively. Eventually, quite literally all the big tech companies (*Alphabet, Hewlett-Packard, Oracle, Intel, Cisco, Meta, X* (formerly *Twitter*), *Adobe, Broadcom, LinkedIn, eBay*, etc.) moved in. As is the case in any system, so it is in our society of consumerism: if the goal is an ethical and sustainable future, then everyone needs incentives to get there. Instead of looking away, designers must develop sensitivity to real problems, realize the absurdity of "modern" production cycles, go out into the world, gain rapport and through participant observation become part of different tribes. That is the only way to empathize.

Real problems of supplying food and shelter vanished as we developed. But as we turned from *people* to *consumers*, we truly turned into Veblem's *leisure class*, conspicuously consuming and signaling. Struggles and ideologies of justice and equity disappeared, or rather transmuted into identity politics. Like Saint George, the dragon slayer was forced into retirement when the last of his nemeses disappeared, we started to shout, tweet and hashtag about struggles that only marginally affect us. Why is no one shouting and *hashtagging* about marketing's capture of creativity? We all know something is going terribly wrong and that our hedonist pleasure wheel is run on externalities, but apparently we want to do nothing about it. In the words of David Graeber, "It was a guilty awareness that lay beneath the postmodern sensibility and its celebration of the endless play of images and surfaces."[21]

In September 2014 I was on the way to Johannesburg, South Africa. I was excited to be able to contribute a research paper to a conference titled "Design with the other 90%," but had no idea what a turning-point the event would prove to be. Just the title deserves attention because it holds the key to *modern humanitarian aid*. The word *design* shows that societal change is purposeful and demands a target, monitoring and replication of best practices. It goes well beyond simply addressing and analyzing issues and straight to solving them. The word *with* – as opposed to *for* – shows a marked difference to old fashioned *post-colonial* humanitarian aid. By focusing on such notions of inclusivity and altruism the conference explored the role that design plays in addressing problems of the under-served communities, which are rarely benefactors of the work of artists and designers. The conference gave me hope, and it is also where I met Ezio Manzini, the godfather of *design for social innovation*.

We discussed efforts of participatory design and he agreed with me that anthropology, with its mountains of research on when groups of people best collaborate, might be a crucial addition to solve the "wicked" problems of this world. Manzini's distinction of *diffuse* and *expert design*, where the former comes from a public of non-designers and the latter from trained designers, also maps nicely onto the anthropological concepts of *emic* and *etic* information, respectively. Interdisciplinary research shows, for example, that true humanitarian design is possible only when driven by local knowledge and that the role of local institutions (for example, ineffective delivery of services) are key drivers of inequalities of material well-being.[22] Integrating *users* into the design process (e.g., within *co-creation)* has proved to be stimulating in helping victims of accidents and humanitarian crises alike. Thus design, production and marketing with its lines of ethnicity, kin and class strongly affect a country's potential for economic development.[23] However, design students, while learning the required skills of rendering and modeling products, launching them onto and keeping them in the marketplace, rarely apply such skills in the sectors and/or communities that need them most. Let's teach all the important skill sets but let's apply them in the real world. Let's have a revival of Papanek.

Design Disconnect

I have been part of a certain "design disconnect" between the built environment that designers and architects prefer and the built environment that most non-designers prefer. Sitting on sunny terraces in Zagreb, Sarajevo or Budapest, sipping my beer, my designer friends, my teachers in things concerned with style, will point at some buildings or objects that stand out brilliantly. I turn to look, scrambling to say something sophisticated, because actually I think they are counterintuitive and ugly as hell. The same applies exponentially to fashion shows. In discussions I mention *A Pattern Language* by Christopher Alexander as well as my usual drone of evolutionary theory. My friends then turn to me with faint pity and say that I just don't have the eye yet. Absolutely true, I have not been trained, but such comments scare me. To get "the eye" you have to disconnect from the real? That is like complaining in a restaurant about the quality of the food and the chef reassuring you that I just have not developed the correct palate yet. In the case of the cook, I am the client paying, and no matter how primitive, I am right about my tastes. Is there some strong bias at work here? Is design education a priming exercise, to the point of forming an in-group (those who see things in certain ways) and an out-group (those who don't)?

Perhaps the most famous study on this phenomenon comes from psychologist David Halpern. In 1987, he showed a group of UK students – they were a mixed bunch of architecture and non-architecture students – photographs of people and buildings they were not familiar with. When asked to rate them in terms of attractiveness, a fascinating pattern emerged amongst the informants. Everyone had similar views on which people were attractive, but the views of architecture and non-architecture students diverged diametrically when rating the attractiveness of the buildings. Basically, architecture students loved some buildings, which were exactly the ones the non-architects hated. And vice versa.[24] A 2015 online survey of 283 respondents, of whom 37 percent worked as architects, planners or in other creative fields, by the webpage *Create Streets* seems to replicate Halpern's findings.[25]

Adolf Loos, author of "Ornament and Crime," is turning in his grave. His famous essay – originally published in French and then in 1929 as "Ornament und Verbrechen" – was an attack against *Art Nouveau* in general and the *Austrian Secession* in particular. The essay was moralizing and proved important to the *Bauhaus* design studio; it helped define the ideology of *modernism* in architecture as anti-natural. In his days it was in vogue to apply evolutionary logic to cultural contexts, and Loos sensed a linear and upward progress in architecture. Like so many *unilinear evolutionists* in the century before him, his stance was a teleological turning away from nature. Loos firmly distinguished between *architecture* and *dwelling* and thus separated interior from exterior world. He practically assigned exterior and interior architects separate chores and advocated for the visible, exterior-facing appearance of a building to be as plain as possible. He wrote: "The evolution of culture marches with the elimination of ornament from useful objects." Loos argues that "the evolution of culture is synonymous with the removal of ornament from objects of daily use." He found ornaments unacceptable and believed that truly contemporary people should feel the same. To him, the production of decorative designs, as in the *Secession*, was degenerative and pretentious. His writing antagonized and his architecture got him in trouble with the law. When he designed a building completely void of ornamentation opposite a palace, he eventually conceded to requirements by adding flower boxes to the windows. It was literally a legal fight over *phytophilia*, the love of plants.

Emancipate Yourself!

Designer, emancipate yourself! You are too important to subjugate yourself to the mental slavery that the logic of *runaway consumerism* implies. The lure of beauty, convenience and novelty dictates the curricula of design education, which are geared to train young creatives to conceive products and services. They distract. Since our current economic order is based on buying new units for display of private ownership, we are not training our creatives to conceive things to be repaired or recycled. For designers, the incentives are obviously stacked in favor of producing novelty at the expense of ethics and sustainability. Making stuff that allows people to be wholesome, ethical and sustainable sans cumbersome detours would surely lead to more fulfilling and purpose-driven lives, which in turn would protect us from falling for cheap thrills of further consumption, but living such a life is harder to monetize. And that is why a lot of design is geared precisely towards preying on *vices* rather than *virtues* of humans – obviously, because a lot of money can be made with the promise of permanent satisfaction of a desire that will never, ever go away! Every year thousands of bright young minds enroll in design schools ready to learn how to conceive, model and sell more stuff. Design is so much more than just embodied marketing.

In trying to create new needs, marketing has become closely entangled with design. I cannot agree more with David Graeber, who wrote, "As marketing overwhelms university life, it generates documents about fostering imagination and creativity that might just as well have been designed to strangle imagination and creativity in the cradle."[26] Classically, the marketer asks what will please the greatest number of people, whereas the designer asks how a specific end-user might be thrilled enough to tell others about a creation. This marketing ethos discourages everything adventurous or humorous and – aided by the internet – kills innovation immediately. As media critic and science fiction author Neal Stephenson put it:

> Most people who work in corporations or academia have witnessed something like the following: A number of engineers are sitting together in a room, bouncing ideas off each other. Out of the discussion emerges a new concept that seems promising. Then some laptop-wielding person in the corner, having performed a quick Google search, announces that this "new" idea is, in fact, an old one; it – or at least something vaguely similar – has already been tried. Either it failed, or it succeeded. If it failed, then no manager who wants to keep his or her job will approve spending money trying to revive it. If it succeeded, then it's patented and entry to the market is presumed to be unattainable, since the first people who thought of it will have "first-mover advantage" and will have created "barriers to entry." The number of seemingly promising ideas that have been crushed in this way must number in the millions.[27]

Biologist E. O. Wilson argues that looking towards the future with hope itself is a uniquely human asset.[28] In that sense, designers are especially human and they are downright contagious in their light, fun and carefree approach to the world. Playful and breezy, their mannerisms radiate optimism. To me as an awkward outsider on high-tech campuses, in design consultancies and even at conferences I always feel conservative, stiff and overdressed. Designers are powerful. The best ones are potent mixtures of engineers, artists and social scientists. They think in terms of solutions instead of mulling over problems all day, like my kind.

In the next chapters we will explore how design entails some of the most powerful means known to move people. I am trying to move it towards more fulfilling ends.

When they turn to real problems, designers' ability to find solutions is mind-bending. Take the following example from consultancy IDEO, where designers bravely tackled the ultimate Western taboo: death. While we can't predict, not to mention prepare for, the inevitability of dying, we can help make life a richer, more dignified experience especially towards the end. Hospice worker B. J. Miller, is a faculty member of UCSF, where he is leading an important conversation on *patient-centered* care. He also works at San Francisco's *Zen Hospice*, which hired the design consultancy to work on the end of life of terminally ill patients. Together with IDEO's Shoshana Berger, they researched directly in the hospice and developed an application that allows patients and their friends and family to address this most real subject.

In general, hospital patients have long been exemplary *lead users* and increasingly they are part of a design movement towards inclusion, called *patient innovations*.[29] The core of such research is the development of new treatments, therapies or medical devices not by doctors but by patients or their acquaintances. In contrast to professional corporations (medical or pharmaceutical), which introduce novelty for the sake of commercialization, affected individuals invent remedies to benefit themselves, to raise their life quality or simply to survive, all of which are highly effective drivers for innovation. Only when design turns to helping underprivileged people help themselves can there be a reciprocal benefit. In the moment that the underprivileged are given the capability to change their own fate can design flourish again as an agent of problem solving.[30]

Notes

1 Lupton, E., & Cohen, E. L. (1996). *Letters from the Avant-Garde: Modern graphic design*. Princeton Architectural Press, p. 68.
2 Poon, S. T. (2019). Typography inspirations in 21st-century: Social and cultural roles of modernist Bauhaus in graphic design. *International Journal*, 2(7), 23–37.
3 Asif, A., & Burton, O. (2021). Comic Sans or common sense? Graphic design for clinical teachers. *The Clinical Teacher*, 18(6), 583–589.
4 Kerouac, J. (2011). *On the Road*. Penguin Books.
5 Burroughs, W. S. (2023). *Junkie*. Modernista.
6 http://archive.spectator.co.uk/article/5th-february-2005/14/the-end-of-left-and-right, accessed on May 12, 2021.
7 Haidt, J. (2012). *The Righteous Mind: Why good people are divided by politics and religion*. Vintage.

8 Breithaupt, F. (2019). *The Dark Sides of Empathy.* Cornell University Press.
9 Wilson, D. S. (2007). *Evolution for Everyone: How Darwin's theory can change the way we think about our lives.* Delta.
10 Fukuyama, F. (2006). *The End of History and the Last Man.* Simon and Schuster.
11 McWhorter, J. (2021). *Woke Racism: How a new religion has betrayed Black America.* Swift Press.
12 DiAngelo, R. (2018). *White Fragility: Why it's so hard for white people to talk about racism.* Beacon Press.
13 Kendi, I. X. (2019). *How to Be an Antiracist.* One World.
14 Miller, G. F. (1996). Political peacocks. *Demos Quarterly,* 9–11.
15 Murray, D. (2019). *The Madness of Crowds: Gender, race, and identity.* Bloomsbury.
16 Schumpeter, J. A. (2013). *Capitalism, Socialism and Democracy.* Routledge.
17 Freeman, C. (2009). Schumpeter's business cycles and techno-economic paradigms. *Techno-economic paradigms: Essays in honour of Carlota Perez,* p. 126.
18 Feist, G. J. (1998). A meta-analysis of personality in scientific and artistic creativity. *Personality and Social Psychology Review,* 2(4), 290–309.
19 Papanek, V., & Buckminster Fuller, R. (1972). *Design for the Real World.* Thames & Hudson.
20 Design, M. (2018). *The Business Value of Design.* McKinsey Design.
21 https://thebaffler.com/salvos/of-flying-cars-and-the-declining-rate-of-profit, accessed on May 24, 2023.
22 De Beukelaer, C. (2014). The UNESCO/UNDP 2013 Creative Economy Report: Perks and perils of an evolving agenda. *The Journal of Arts Management, Law, and Society,* 44(2), 90–100.
23 Gereffi, G. (2001). Beyond the producer-driven/buyer-driven dichotomy the evolution of global value chains in the internet era. *IDS Bulletin,* 32(3), 30–40.
24 Halpern, D. (1995). *Mental Health and the Built Environment.* Routledge, pp. 161–162.
25 https://createstreetscom.wordpress.com/our-work/research/surveys/, accessed on November 11, 2023.
26 https://thebaffler.com/salvos/of-flying-cars-and-the-declining-rate-of-profit, accessed on May 24, 2023.
27 https://www.wired.com/2011/10/stephenson-innovation-starvation/, accessed on May 24 2023.
28 Wilson, E. O. (2004). *On Human Nature.* Harvard University Press.
29 Canhão, H., Oliveira, P. & Zejnilovic, L. (2017). Patient innovation – empowering patients, sharing solutions, improving lives. *NEJM Catalyst,* 3(5).
30 Leube, M., & Gugg, M. (2014). Design education for a world out of balance: A case study. In Design with the other 90%: Cumulus Johannesburg Conference Proceedings (p. 286).

7

THE IMPACT OF DESIGN ON HUMAN BEHAVIOR

Shaping the Future

Sometime in the late 1960s, Martin Cooper was working in the lab of Motorola. One day he felt especially tired and decided to take a break. He walked over to another room and slumped down in a sofa to watch some TV. A Star Trek episode was on where Captain Kirk uses a wonderfully blinking flip-device called *Communicator* to frantically call the *Enterprise*. Spock was injured and needed help. Inspiration hit him brightly that moment, and Cooper jumped out of his sofa. He just had to bring such a device to reality; eventually he became the inventor of the mobile phone. In 1973 Cooper, then general manager of Motorola, did get on such a phone to call Joel Engel, general manager of AT&T, and said "Joel, this is Marty Cooper, I'd like you to know that I'm calling you from a cellular phone." The race for the first cell phone was over. It is a beautiful story, although not entirely true.

Cooper's inspiration did not come from Star Trek. The truth is actually an even better story and goes something like this: once upon a time there was a comic book illustrator by the name of Chester Gould, whose most famous creation was a terribly cool, tough and intelligent detective-agent called Dick Tracy. This guy was decked out in trench coat over suit and tie and always had his hat drawn deep onto his face. He wielded baseball bats, pistols and machine guns to fight crime on the gritty streets of a city resembling Chicago. Besides his weapons, he had a very cool gadget: a two-way wrist radio that got him out of many near-impossible situations. It was that device that inspired Cooper to invent the cell phone and ironically preceded the first Apple Watch by nearly 70 years! Star Trek *did* inspire other products we now take for granted. For example, *The Next Generation* featured a computer reproducing a digital music file, which inspired the MP3 player. And of

DOI: 10.4324/9781003464754-10

course, the iPad's (future) ancestor was the PADD, acronym for *Personal Access Display Device.*[1]

In the book *Speculative Everything: Design, Dreaming, and Social Dreaming*, the authors speak of a whole spectrum, a "taxonomy of futures." They include possible, plausible, probable and preferable futures, which is interesting since usually we divide what has not yet happened simply into a dystopia (bad) and utopia (good).[2] Anthony Dunne, professor of interaction design at the Royal College of Art, and Fiona Raby, professor of industrial design at the University of Applied Arts in Vienna, coined the term *speculative design* and popularized the concept in their book. It is an important book showing that designers shouldn't just address issues of today, indeed they cannot, but must speculate about the future. Importantly, we are neither talking about predicting the future nor the oxymoron that is future research (you cannot research something that has not yet happened) but speculating about possible, plausible, probable and preferable futures.

While authors of fiction create scenarios that can become realities by the mere fact that people have been exposed to them, inventors and designers take such scenarios and make them tangible. A story is *verbalization* whereas design is *objectification* of thought. But a designed object goes far beyond that. Linguistically, a declaration is a way of speaking or writing that creates a fact out of thin air, creating a new reality where there was none before. Design is a declaration of behavior. The can of Coke I just bought is a result of some past design decisions that the people of their future should drink up to 355ml of soda. When we sit down in a chair, they declared how our body would be suspended. The design process goes from what is to what could be and finally to what will be, and thus designers producing artifacts and services change the possibility of futures. More precisely, they manipulate future behavior whether it is through a smartphone (industrial design), a check-in process (service design), a shopping mall (shop design), a museum (exhibition design), a webpage (interaction design) or a healthier lunch box (design for social innovation). While stories are powerful tools for transporting ideas from head to head, currently many designs are powerful tools for transporting commodities from sketch to hand. Unfortunately, the hand all too often then throws the designs onto a landfill.

As we will see in some detail, we have moved far beyond the simple logic of supply and demand, and future markets will be filled with products that citizens were never asked about. They cannot be asked for the simple fact that they have not been born yet. Thus, in a very real sense the noble ambitions of *user-centered design* can only be as myopic as the length of a human lifespan. Future people cannot be asked, but they will have to reckon with all the stuff conceived now. Even if we stopped making anything at all now and future generations were to remain totally abstinent of consumerism, they most certainly will have to deal with the *externalities* of current production, use and disposal of things. Just the word "externality" is by definition a cynical affront to anyone removed from a current economic transaction by space and time because the resources that we use now are a loan from the children of our children's children. Again, you cannot design for the present and you cannot design without affecting the future. In a very real sense, makers of things – designers, architects and engineers – and users of things are fighting over the right for the future; or, as Shoshana Zuboff has called it, "the right for the *future tense*" (emphasis added).[3]

Imagine asking a civil engineer to design a bridge that will not collapse. It is an absurd request because spanning a river is the bridge's function, even definition. And if a bridge does not fulfil basic safety standards, then it is a design failure, and its engineer would face liability. Through their role in cultural production, designers also have tremendous responsibility, but rarely are they held accountable. Perhaps exercising accountability is trickier in design than in engineering proper since consequences of design objects are not seen until much later. Does a product designer's responsibility end with a customer standing at the point of sale? Or is it when a user interacts with a new device? Is it morally sound to transfer all responsibility of a product – its production, distribution, use and disposal – to the customer at the point of sale? What about marketers, advertisers, designers and policymakers? Should they not also share responsibility? Apart from moral considerations, it also seems economically unwise since customers rarely have enough information on products' long road to and from the shelves to carry such a heavy responsibility. They know next to nothing about production and distribution, and other than the four-colored recycling bins don't even know where to put their stuff when they're done with it, let alone how it is treated. If we extend a designer's responsibility beyond a product's lifespan and all the way to residual management, then ironically the predominance of *marketing* and *planned obsolescence* in design has massively increased its own moral and economic debt to the future. It is ironic, but not at all funny.

Consider our mobile phones. When Steve Jobs unveiled the first iPhone in early 2007, a before and after was marked in human history. Daydreaming and boredom died that January 9th in San Francisco. Now, fifteen years into this world-wide social experiment of humans hooked on smartphones with personalized media streams, we are seeing how a small artifact with all its application and physiological and societal consequences will likely reach far into the future. In the journal *Psychology Today* it is stated that, "There is ... little doubt that all of the new technologies, led by the Internet and digital technology, are shaping the way we think in ways obvious and subtle, deliberate and unintentional, and advantageous and detrimental."[4] Our attention span will likely be affected and, as some studies suggest, shortened.[5]

The data is coming in, but governments refuse to acknowledge *marketing* and *planned obsolescence* as false indicators of supply and demand by not regulating it. For those two strategies to be beneficial for us in the developed world we obviously need to outsource any nasty external factors. In a dizzy display of math, for example, it has been estimated that a child working in the Democratic Republic of the Congo would need around 700,000 years of work to earn as much as Jeff Bezos makes in a day.[6] It goes without saying that the combination of such design-drivers also causes literal mountains of waste. The world's largest multinational center concerned with waste from electrical and electronic equipment (WEEE for short) estimated roughly 5.3 billion mobile phones/smartphones to drop out of use in 2022. To illustrate this horrendous number, stacking all the flat and abandoned phones would make a tower 50,000 km high.[7]

It seems obvious for a designer to question whether their creations directly serve the interests of the military or the abuse of animals and humans. But do they question whether the production of their devices calls for undignified labor conditions? Do they question the role of extraction and exploitation of resources used in the production of our material culture? Does an urban planner consider whether their spaces are safe for marginalized and disenfranchised people? Some people were favored by the designers of the past because they might now have the spending power to buy their creations, and some were left behind, simply because their bodies cannot properly use their creations. Women – accounting for nearly half of the human population – were simply not accounted for by past designers. Our love-affair with touchscreen phones simply does not consider the fact that women's hands are smaller. Or take waiting lines for women's bathrooms. Is it not strange that anatomical differences account for different user cases in such a way that waiting times are far longer? How is that acceptable? Caroline Criado Perez's excellent book *Invisible Women: Exposing Data Bias in a World Designed for Men* reads like a catalogue of facts and instances of persistent gender inequalities in society. In countless ways half of the planet's population is just not thought about or represented in the built environment.[8] But not just along binary gender lines, biased design manifests itself in countless ways, making large parts of our demographics invisible. What about my wheel-chaired friends: how could we have excluded them from the joys of seeing a concert or film? Is that not a design failure? Why, given all the data on inequality, inequity and disparity, is so little done to fix things? Human diversity must be taken seriously *before* anything is conceived for them, not after!

The future always comes in different flavors. According to science fiction writer and internet theorist Bruce Sterling, those flavors are: "'Gothic Hi-Tech', where Steve Jobs-like characters create something brilliant, which may bring health hazards, and 'Favela Chic', where all things material as well as job prospects have been lost, but one is wired like crazy and really big on Facebook."[9] Such scenarios should be taken very seriously because an uncharted future is currently staked out along lines of exclusivity, power and accumulation. The way we will walk around a room ten years from now is decided now. The way we communicate, work, eat and live will be as well. Inventing robots to order food and do our housework will only be worthwhile in a system no longer divided into the super-rich or the desperately poor willing to do their figurative and literal dirty laundry. Only then can design begin to be directed towards human needs. Just as the gadgets, spaces and buildings around us right now were all designed by thinkers and makers of the past to colonize the present moment, shape, form and price of the human niche of tomorrow is parceled out now.

Akin to colonialism, many Native Americans did not have a concept of private property, and so when it was declared who the new owners were, they were quickly conned out of their land. Before I go any further with this analogy of colonialism, I am systematically opposed to the conquistadors of the 15th and 16th centuries, not design. It is just that I am concerned about the flag under which we sail into the future. Should it be in the name of equity and development, or should it be in the name of marketing and obsolescence? Should we really be giving this awesome responsibility and power to brightly dressed dandies who say "amazing" far too often? Sure, but then why on earth are we not training them in ethics?

The Power of Design

Design is incredibly powerful. It is everywhere. The interface between business and its customers used to just be more people, but design has promised to actively specify that interface, which makes it easy to scale. Scale is treated uncritically and measured only along lines of positive and necessary value for success, and not incorporated into the design process itself. Everyone – designers, businesspeople and users – know we need to produce things that are *user friendly*. As of late, design has indeed taken a sharp turn to UX (user experience) and UI (user interface) by focusing on how emotional connections can be built between objects and their users. As the world has shifted to focus on production towards marketing, it is the end-users who push revenue. Such an approach – championed by most industrial sectors and firmly at the core of most design schools – has been labeled *human-centered design*, and it dominates today. However, what at first sounds like a very welcoming move towards human emancipation is seldom born out of corporate care and empathy. The bottom line is: designing products and services around researched people's needs is just more competitive and profitable. It is based on the fact that we need to cater to humans to make money. Authors Cliff Kuang and Robert Fabricant in their book *User Friendly* describe how qualitative methods for user research rely on empathy to get to innovations. *User experience, human-centered design* and *design thinking* – all are based on the simple truth that there is no one genius that always knows exactly what everyone wants. Users do.[10] It is interesting to note that around the same time – in the 1970s, '80s and '90s – more and more self-reflective anthropological literature concluded that ethnographers similarly stand in their own way, and that nothing is harder to overcome than *ethnocentrism*.

The disruptive ideology of "move fast and break things" is epitomized metaphorically and literally by e-scooters. It happened suddenly. One day in 2017, thousands of slick but somewhat cute scooters appeared everywhere, as if dropped by helicopters into the cities of the world. We all woke up and there they were, all around, piloted by very average citizens whizzing by. Very modern Insta-hipsters were saving time now, because before they might have used public transportation, the bicycle or – heaven forbid – their feet. Yes, the times they are changing, there is something utopian in the air, we are all sharing in this economy and showing a clear signal that we have had enough already! Our ties are now flapping in the wind, and they point to our brand-new but up-cycled tote bags. Putting cynicism aside, obviously net-carbon emissions went up all over the world because these scooters and their lithium batteries need to be produced and their success hinges on the obsolescence of prior modes of transportation.[11] This "innovation" is not limited to scooters. There are also looters and vandalizers and traffic offenders, but Silicon Valley start-ups like *Lime* don't seem to care much about all of them. They just threw all the cards way up in the air, saw how they landed and watched from the sideline as users and regulators tried to catch up.

Much of modern design seems intent on burning the old and introducing the new. Is this *creative destruction*? As an anthropologist trying to understand all this rapid culture change led by technology, I thought Schumpeter would be a good conversation starter. An icebreaker for a coffee-break discussion. Here I was in this new world of design, a discipline that stands for innovation, and I tried to start a discussion I thought would be well received. It was not and it was then that it dawned on me: all my confusion was over the *libertarian, tech-utopian* and *woke Kool-Aid* they are serving over in Silicon Valley. Is this the same cocktail that produced the commodified design process called *design thinking*? To find out, I had to revisit Palo Alto, the place I spent my youth.

Californication

"Mellow" is the term I would use to describe the California I grew up in. As a teenager of the early '80s, my home was simply the San Francisco Bay Area, an easy and sheltered place with good weather and clean streets, perfect for skateboarding. *Silicon Valley* is a term from the '70s to reference silicon transistors, but I never really heard it used much until the mid-1980s. Our house lay quietly somewhere between the garage where the first Apple computer was born and the house were Steve Jobs died. None of this entrepreneurial lore mattered to me since the PC was but a specter in our dads' offices and I was far more interested in riding the ramp that we built in front of *our* garage.

A little later, at the cusp of the new millennium, Mohandas Gandhi, the Dalai Lama, Nelson Mandela and other revolutionaries looked down at Bay Area drivers from massive Apple billboards telling us to "think different," when I thought I was already. It seems that Californian ideologues Steve Jobs and Steve Wozniak were using such social justice warriors to help them preach a bizarre gospel of hippy anarchism, economic liberalism and lots of technological utopianism. The signs were a powerful juxtaposition of radical social disruption and Silicon Valley's "innovation without permission" sold simply as a life more comfortable. But back then social media was little more than notes passed in class. Like countless generations before, we experienced the archaic dynamics of teenage rank, the anguish of not belonging to certain groups and the violence of bullying and mobbing. But those things were natural, and they made us stronger. We were sheltered, sure, but we were not coddled and had no helicopter parents following us at every step. Mostly, it was carefree and clean fun under the Californian sun.

As one part of the San Francisco Bay Area became spectacularly rich, another dwindled into poverty and homelessness. What followed was a kind of digital caste system divided into those working for extremely high wages, those just barely getting by on fixed contracts of an older age and those living in American favelas of tent and tarp under bridges and off-ramps. During what is known as the *dot-com bubble*, people making hundreds of thousands of dollars a month, rushed past the homeless in SUVs, looking like immense armored carriages of tinted glass and chrome. The freeways became riddled with potholes, but *Caltrain* – the rail system running along the north–south axis of the peninsula – is but a poor alternative as it makes the trains in underdeveloped countries look state-of-the-art. Investors ignored all that and through a combination of fad-based investment and abundant venture capital funding, poured their money into internet start-ups. It was truly another gold rush! And what about all the hippies, people in motion with flowers in their hair? They had morphed into yuppies and turned from real societal problems to an oxymoronic mixture of collective harmony and dogmatic egoism.

Until quite recently, I was oblivious to the important chapter of design history written in Palo Alto. There is, for example, PARC (Palo Alto Research Center), formerly Xerox PARC, established in 1970. There is the first personal computer; the graphical user interface; the computer mouse; the laser printer: all these things I now take entirely for granted and use as I write this text were developed right there on Coyote Hill Road. Was I involved? No, but I pedaled past them all the time on my way to the best mountain bike trails.[12] One anecdote illustrates well the irony of growing up in the thick of Silicon Valley, gleefully ignorant of its significance. In our early twenties, my friend Chris and I would visit the house of Bill Moggridge, but our mission was anything but design-related. We were there only to pick up his son Erik for his thrash-metal band *Epidemic*, which as a matter of fact opened for death-metal gods *Death* and *Cannibal Corpse* in the city that night. It wasn't until decades later that I found out Erik's dad was a real big shot in the world of design. Late, great Bill Moggridge designed the first mass-produced laptop, for the love of God! Moggridge himself has said that tinkering around on the prototype of a clam-shelled laptop made him realize that no one cares about edges, levers and handles when working on the machine. No one cares about hardware because it is software that demands our attention, and keeps our eyes glued to the screen and hands hammering away on the keyboard in that dialogue with the machine. Frustrated, he conceived a whole new subfield of design called *interaction design*. Good design is good interaction because it is that dance with the object that dictates use and non-use.[13] All these important insights I so full-heartedly embrace now, but all I can remember is that Bill Moggridge's two little yapping dogs were called "Ozzy" and "Osbourne." I still grapple with the fact that my beloved Palo Alto, which I remember only as idyllic and care-free, is the birthplace of so many design decisions that have forever altered life on this planet.

But the true heroes of Silicon Valley were not philosophers and not designers. They were the original, anti-authoritarian hackers. Franklin Foer of *The Guardian* writes that they,

> were technically virtuosic, infinitely resourceful nerd cowboys, unbound by conventional thinking. In the labs of MIT (Massachusetts Institute of Technology) during the 60s and 70s, they broke any rule that interfered with building the stuff of early computing, such marvels as the first video games and word processors.[14]

Besides hi-tech entrepreneurs, "the techno-intelligentsia of cognitive scientists, engineers, computer scientists, video-game developers, and all the other communications specialists" formed a new "virtual class" of digital craftsmen.[15] Of course, product design was also important as it helped transform clunky and scary machines into slick and seductive objects; Apple, better than all the rest, successfully differentiated its products from functional but ugly competitors. The galleon figure there was champion of LSD and Zen, design god Steve Jobs. Media theorists Richard Barbrook and Andy Cameron gave Silicon Valley's strange ideological brew a name with their 1995 essay "The Californian Ideology." In their words, "this new faith has emerged from a bizarre fusion of the cultural bohemianism of San Francisco with the hi-tech industries of Silicon Valley … the Californian Ideology promiscuously combines the free-wheeling spirit of the hippies and the entrepreneurial zeal of the yuppies."[16]

The abhorrent plundering of natural resources and labor of the underdeveloped countries under unregulated global industrialism is the same, but somehow the reputation of high-tech Silicon Valley remained untarnished. This sector is somehow perceived as different, more ethical. *The New York Times*' Ross Douthat believes that Silicon Valley corporations have been playing the "greed is good" capitalism since the 1980s, but now include a new leftism to keep governments and consumers happy. He writes that, at an accelerating pace our corporate class is trying to negotiate a different kind of peace, a different deal from the one they struck with New Deal liberalism and Big Labor. Instead of the Treaty of Detroit we have, if you will, the Peace of Palo Alto, in which a certain kind of virtue-signaling on progressive social causes, a certain degree of performative wokeness, is offered to liberalism and the activist left pre-emptively, in the hopes that having corporate America take their side in the culture wars will blunt efforts to tax or regulate our new monopolies too heavily.[17]

The *wokeness* of high tech was illustrated in 2017 when Google engineer James Damore circulated an internal company memo called "Google's Ideological Echo Chamber" about Google's culture and diversity policies and was promptly fired.[18] Like Damore, Antonio García Martínez was let go by Apple in 2021 when his fellow employees circulated a petition highlighting the supposedly misogynistic tone of his 2016 tell-all book *Chaos Monkeys*.[19] Not mixing politics and work is no longer considered commonsense and companies now actually make headlines by declaring themselves politics-free. Basecamp – a small co-working application provider – and Coinbase – a cryptocurrency exchange site – are recent examples. While Damore was concerned with Google's HR policies, we should be concerned with its product, as a short experiment in the *Google Images* search engine will demonstrate. Type in "white couple" and you will get pictures of black couples or mixed couples. Now type in "straight couple" and amongst the first hits you will be greeted with gay-pride flags. The algorithm itself is programmed to be *woke*!

Like the ideological promiscuity mentioned by Richard Barbrook and Andy Cameron, internet pioneer Jaron Lanier has called the techies of Silicon Valley "ideology sluts." They freely switch their philosophy, whenever convenient. Silicon Valley has become very politically correct, but it has strayed from its roots of minimal statism as a growing creative class of gentrified and urbanized liberals, is supporting policies that embrace hard-core capitalism *and* a benevolent government! Let us not forget that the state of California only thrives through massive community-based funding for irrigation systems, highways, schools and other important infrastructure. Capitalist entrepreneurs rarely give recognition to the contributions made by the state, their labor force or the wider community within which they are celebrated. Just look at Elon Musk, often hailed as the most innovative, entrepreneurial venture capitalist. His companies *Tesla, SpaceX, SolarCity* and recently *X* (formerly known as Twitter) have gobbled up billions of dollars from the US government in the form of loans, contracts, tax credits and subsidies. According to a *Los Angeles Times* investigation, the money was estimated to be as much as $4.9 billion in government support by 2015, and funding has not stopped since.[20]

For Big Tech, the state has long ago become a partner by either investing directly in lucrative industries or allowing them leeway when they become useful in the control of a population. Thus, aided by historical events such as 9/11 and the ensuing "war on terrorism," modern citizens' vulnerability was exploited by the likes of the US *Patriot Act*. A steady encroachment of surveillance followed, and through governmental ties, lobbying Congress and very close relationships with US presidents such as George W. Bush, Barack Obama and Donald Trump helped shield companies from federal regulation. In the crucial early years of Google and Facebook, their founders were basically given a free pass – by stockholders and regulators alike – as they consolidated control of their companies and grew to dominate markets they themselves had created. Section 230 of the US Communications Decency Act of 1996 has liberated Big Tech companies by protecting online platforms from legal liability for content provided by others. The sacred First Amendment of the US Constitution was truly weaponized![21]

Palo Alto is also where the concept of *design thinking* was conceived and commodified. To find out what all the hype surrounding this process was about, I enrolled in a *design thinking bootcamp* at Stanford University's Hasso Plattner Institute of Design, or simply *d.school*. More than a school, it is a program that integrates law, business, medicine, the humanities and social sciences with traditional engineering and design. The *d.school* is based on radical collaboration as it unites students, faculty and practitioners from whatever discipline and background imaginable to learn the methods of *design thinking*, which roughly follows the *double diamond* popularized by the *British Design Council*. Proposed in 1996 by Hungarian American linguist Béla H. Bánáthy, the two diamonds, through their shape, stands for divergent and convergent thinking, where a problem is explored widely and deeply and then focused action is taken to solve the problem. Typically, such a design process is divided into four phases of *discovery* (understanding an issue through qualitative and quantitative research), *definition* (insights gathered from the discovery phase help frame a challenge clearly), *development* (coming up with several solutions for the clearly defined problem) and *delivery* (testing out solutions, rejecting the unfeasible and improving the feasible).[22]

Dividing the design process into a problem space of discovery and definition, and a solution space of development and delivery, makes sense and it gave me hope as it supplied a long-missing link between the problems of the world and their solutions. However, I must admit that I was filled with cynicism (great, now Big Business has appropriated anthropology) and arrogance (I have a PhD in the subject; what are they going to teach me?). Indeed, the *empathy* model developed by the d.school can be uncharitable and somewhat offensive to cultural anthropologists who spend their entire lives observing and reporting on other people. Adding insult to injury is the imperative tense that design thinkers use for the noun *empathy*, the holiest of grails in anthropology. Empathize! Hold on guys, it's not that easy and takes a long time, much love, curiosity and patience. How can some hipster meandering around Stanford and stalking strangers constitute ethnography? Tech writer Lee

Tinsel is even tougher in his language: "The Empathize Mode of Design Thinking is roughly as ethnographic as a marketing focus group or a crew of sleazoid consultants trying to feel out and up their clients' desires."[23] Ouch! Plus, these bootcamps are so expensive that the underprivileged people we are supposed to help are kept out. Nonetheless, thinking of design as a participatory, emphatic discipline calls for optimism but it is not new. While the research is largely *social science thinking, design thinking* goes further by solving issues. Interdisciplinary, inherently optimistic and constructive, design thinking is a strong candidate for tackling some of societies' wicked problems.[24] *Design thinking* always claims to cater to the needs of the people and to put humanity at the center of its ambitions, but is it really all that "human-centered"? If there is one thing we have learned from anthropology, it is that the human experience is extremely varied. How can a single design ever approach all its many shades and hues? "Human" and "user" have of course become synonymous; both are at the center of a non-negotiable new world of designed objects sold for hard cash. Is *design thinking* just thinly veiled marketing? Those were the questions racing through my head as I was walking around sunny Stanford University before starting my course. I have to admit, however, that the bootcamp – highly overpriced and commodified social science technique it may be – taught me a lot of anthropology.

The following is a good example for illustrating the power of this process. Students of the *d.school* were told to find a social innovation for a truly wicked problem: they were asked to help lower infant mortality rates, an extremely important world development indicator, in rural Nepal. It is important since it reveals social and infrastructural conditions that allow a child to survive its first year. The team traveled to Nepal to start its fieldwork, because rather than just assuming something the young designers needed to understand it. Around the streets of Kathmandu they met as many involved people as possible. The plan was to build an incubator for premature children, but during the research they learned they were not going to the root of the issue or, in the words of engineer Paul MacCready, their "problem was the problem."[25] Kathmandu had lots of incubators, provided by the state and donated by NGOs and philanthropes, many of them standing around idly. After days of observing the neonatal units of city hospitals, the team turned to the treatment of premature infants in rural areas. They needed more data and learned that, most of all, premature infants were born not in the city but in remote, rural areas. The root problem was that infants never made it to a hospital. Because of weather conditions, work, gender roles or whatever other reason, few mothers visited the remote hospitals. With the reframing of the problem the *design brief* changed: to build an incubator that allows mothers to stay in their villages and continue their work. If mothers did not go to the incubators in Kathmandu, then incubators had to be brought to the mothers. The product would have to be light and work without electricity, be intuitive, easy to keep clean and culturally appropriate. And – if that brief was not hard enough – it had to be inexpensive.

The *d.school* students turned to local knowledge of keeping babies and designed a first prototype they called the *Embrace Incubator*. Looking something like a tiny sleeping bag, it wraps around premature infants. The babies' bodies are kept at the right temperature for about four hours, after which the pouch could be "recharged" by dunking it in hot water for a few minutes. The prototype was improved in several iterative cycles and the final product was light and easy to clean and use. Most impressively, it cost 800 times less than a standard incubator of US $20,000.

But even the best of all ideas and products are considered a failure if they don't survive the *delivery* phase; if they don't reach users. The *Embrace* team pushed on and presented itself as a non-profit start-up, worked out a business plan and applied for funding. Because of its ingenuity, *Embrace* won awards, received media attention and gained seed funding from business plan competitions.[26] For me, this is a story of great design but also of applied anthropology.

The *d.school* was founded by David Kelley, who cofounded IDEO in 1991 through a merger of *David Kelley Design, Matrix Product Design* (founded by Mike Nuttall) and London-based *Moggridge Associates* and San Francisco's *ID Two* (both founded by Bill Moggridge).[27] IDEO probably was the first consultancy that wedded empathy with industry. Its credos – design research before any ideation – is an indispensable part of the design process.[28] They have developed their own Human-Centered Design Toolkit, with a strong emphasis on a cooperative design process between visiting designers and locals, as well as their Circular Design Guide.[29] For me, IDEO CEO Tim Brown's book *Change by Design* resides up there with *Designing for the Real World* by Papanek and *Pattern Language* by Christopher Alexander.[30] IDEO. org specializes exclusively on design for social innovation and sustainability and openIDEO is a platform for anyone with a good idea to compete in finding solutions to some of the world's most wicked problems. Indeed, I have much respect for this consultancy, but when I gave a talk on anthropology at IDEO's headquarters in San Francisco there was something missing. As the creatives around the table were taking notes, I felt I contributed something, but my audience was not much interested in the evolutionary roots of empathy. Furthermore, there was something dogmatic, sectarian about this group, a sense that I also got when I visited the IDEO Munich headquarters. As I walked around, all the doors were quickly shut as if I would glean something important from all the colorful Post-its.

Before we leave the San Francisco Bay Area let us take a journey into Palo Alto's Apple store. Positioned in the center of one of the most important cities on an unimaginably expensive piece of real estate, we are first struck by the physical beauty and elegance of the interior. It is an excellent example of choice architecture both metaphorically and literally speaking. The display of all these toys lying around to be touched, swiped and fondled preys on what social psychologists call the *endowment effect*. Once you touch and make a machine intuitively perform a function of your brain, you're very much closer to buying the piece of machinery because giving up something that has been yours is much harder.[31] The iPad thus quickly turns into the *myPad*. Although refurbished Apple products are now available on their webpages you will not find anything secondhand in their stores. No, here we have exclusively new shiny objects on display to be fetishized.

Their logo – a combination of the forbidden fruit with a bite missing and a name stolen from *The Beatles* franchise – is on prominent display in the vanishing point of a person entering a store, like the crucifix in the church. Does my analogy with religion bother you? What are hordes of Apple devotees camping for days in front of a flagship store if not on a modern pilgrimage? The people in Apple stores can easily be divided into three groups: sectarian zealots dressed in blue, those who have been there many times before and curious newcomers. The latter are repeat offenders of *commodity adultery*, willingly seduced to caress and purchase a hotter, newer model of a phone they have and that likely works perfectly well. Again, let me put (scare)-quotes around a biting Lee Vinsel: "It's the annual model change of some consumer electronic, slightly reconfigured in the name of planned obsolescence and unveiled at CES as a 'New Revolution' in whatever. It's iShit."[32] In the Western world of abundance, when we open our drawers, attics and cellars, we find staring back at us multiple electronic items in what I call the *limbo of things*. When we get around to spring-cleaning – the *purgatory of things* – we ship them to their last station, the incinerator, or *hell*. Apple boasts a very robust story, which involves a design god Steve Jobs, a philosophy of life and aspirations for the future. The story of glamorous modernity given to the end-user, however, is very different to that involving real production, ethics and sustainability. Apple is a very good example of the before-mentioned power of the symbol as it specializes in transporting meaning. It is a technical *transmigration of the soul*.

Their business model was always based on exclusivity – no matter if they adorned themselves with the faces of the Dalai Lama or John Lennon – and it is undeniable that Apple has become rich by installing the interfaces of our lives. If you use their products only, your life will be smooth as silk. Dare to mix operating systems and it will be turned into hell as the software and hardware are designed to cannibalize each other. Contrary to an open innovation process, in their closed system the boundaries – or "membranes" to borrow from biology – are not permeable, making the exchange of information with other systems cumbersome or impossible. That is why people live in worlds of Android *or* Apple and rarely both. A Bay Area friend and I have a running joke where we rename the most "Babylonian" aberrations using Rastafarian *Iyaric* and thus it is the "*I and iPad*." The minuscule "i" is one of Steve Jobs' many legacies and a fixture of globalized tech talk. Although it apparently stands for many things simultaneously – internet, individual, instruct, inform, inspire – it epitomizes our self-obsessed, narcissist society. I and I, we both have very conflicting opinions about Apple products. Most of the time, I intuitively understand their logic. I celebrate the pure aesthetics –the shininess, clear symmetry and simplicity – and intuitive functionality of Apple products. The perfectly slick and elegant design with their patented off-whites and pastels captures perfectly the Californian attitude copied by countless other tech companies around the world. But my other side hates Apple's notorious closed-system approach, regarding it as the antithesis of a regenerative industry.

The Cult of Cargo

All over the world creative consultancies attempt to emulate the raging success of Silicon Valley start-ups. They stock their offices with brainstorming rooms, bean bags, toys and sticky notes, and their walls are filled with lofty bullshit statements like "be your awesome self!" Though a business run on a flat hierarchy with lots of creative chatter on sofas and around espresso bars is contagious, even desirable, simply building the same vestibules of office environments in the hope of success is often unrealistic. Similarly, the unreflected adoption of random activities from the *agile management* portfolio, like stand-ups or weekly planning sessions, with the hope of reaping benefits without understanding any of their reasons, will probably result in a waste of time. At many consultancies, there also exist certain rituals to usher in success. Apparently, team members euphorically yell when their prototypes fail early, and periodically each one of them gets to show their magical, funky selves in elaborate show-and-tell events. Some of them even leave the team for some days to go on semi-esoteric *change management* seminars in the hope that upon their return they "infect" everyone with creativity. As of late, mind-altering drugs like LSD, psilocybin and MDMA are enjoying a renaissance, but in Silicon Valley it is to boost creativity in the name of late-stage capitalism.[33] Everyone must wear hoodies, and the interior has to be festooned in pastels and hues of gray! After everything is in place there is a countdown for creative breakthroughs. (Is this going to age well?) One, two, three … innovate!

By merely mimicking the appearance of something that works elsewhere, it unfortunately amounts to little more than what in anthropology circles is called *cargo-cult thinking*. Let me use the wonderful first scene of the 1980s movie *The Gods Must Be Crazy* to explain. A !Kung man out on a long walk finds a Coke bottle lying on the ground. To him, the strange artifact is mysterious, alien and senseless in its surrounding. He looks up, shakes his head and then for a lack of a better explanation figures it must have come from the gods. And they must be crazy to throw this weird thing down. What is it good for? What is the writing on it? What a succulent shape it has! Is it magic? The protagonist takes the bottle back to the village and the narrator tells us that it was, "the strangest and most beautiful thing they have ever seen." It turned out to be a very useful kitchen utensil and hammer. The pilot of the plane, on the other hand, did not think much at all as he carelessly chucked the thing out of his cockpit window. To him, the Coke bottle – a classic first designed by Raymond Loewy in 1915 – had become commonplace and something to discard.

With its plot based around a piece of material culture falling from the sky and subsequently changing social life on the ground, the movie is a reference to the *cargo-cults,* one of the most colorful displays of anthropological literature. Indigenous *millenarian* beliefs, such as the *cargo-cults,* were based around performance rituals supposed to bring about a realm of abundance and beauty through delivered goods. To the people of the central highlands of New Guinea the arrival of Europeans – who used the islands as bases during the world wars – was a sign of the fulfillment of a long-awaited prophecy. It literally meant the end of the world as they knew it. They were so certain of the coming apocalypse that they not only butchered all their pigs – the principal source of subsistence – but also abandoned their crops. Typical for *millenarian movements,* the islanders applied an apocalyptic timetable to the changing of the world where an imminent, cataclysmic event ushers in a millennium (read by believers as simply a very, very long time) of utopia.

They set up mock antennae consisting of bamboo and rope and listened patiently for any "news" of the coming "cargo," or commodities brought from supernatural sources. The natives had observed the arrival of supplies in ships and airplanes but did not understand the logic of colonial bases. Above all other modes of delivery, it was the stuff that came from the sky that had the biggest impact on the natives' psychology. Like a divinity, aircraft descended from the sky and air-dropped crates full of clothing, tools and canned foods. The islanders had literally never seen anything like it before and thus put "cargo" in the realm of the sacred. *Landing strips* and *watchtowers* were made out of tree-trunks, branches and straw were built in preparation because it was believed that simply mimicking the mode of delivery would suffice. It would invite tribal divinities and ancestors to return with more cargo.

Obviously, the planes, landing strips and watchtowers made by the South Pacific islanders did *not* result in more food and supplies, but the actions of the *cargo-cultists* start to make sense if we sympathize with people wanting to replicate desirable outcomes without knowing the full story. Every one of us, at some point, behaves in irrational, empty and irrelevant ways. Building all these structures out of wood and straw didn't result in future gifts any more than blindly mimicking celebrities results in personal success. Yet we are all running after the "cargo" that our celebrated elites so effortlessly display in glossy magazines and social media posts. Just like the islanders waited for their airdrop, fanatic *hypebeasts* are camping out for days for the latest Nike Air to "drop." Don't we wear the stuff and paint our faces the way the *influencers* are telling us to in hope of magically morphing into them? Fringe groups aside, most of us have become entirely estranged with the complexities of material culture, thinking of it as *a priori*, or something that just kind of appears out of nowhere to be used and disposed of. But, unlike esoteric beliefs such as the *cargo-cults* have it, culture does not fall from the sky.

Design Fetishism

I distinctly remember a pair of scissors that always floated around my child-hood household. The grip was comfortable and slid ergonomically around my index finger and thumb. As if the scissors knew that I was going to use the right hand, their *affordances* and *constraints* made them painful to use in the left. They were made of glossy, beautifully orange plastic that led down to the metal blades, a pair of stainless-steel knives that when sliding against each other made a clean hiss that was somehow intimidating through its precision, and forty years later, on a university trip to Helsinki, I saw them again. I found myself staring at *Fiskars* best-known product, which was introduced in 1967 and has become iconic in the world of design. It was in that moment that I learned an important lesson: industrial design is far from arbitrary and the objects cluttering our lives go far beyond function.

At the *Fiskars Pavilion, Pentagon Design* created a space to display some of *Fiskars'* most famous objects in what is called a *brand land.* By completely downplaying the building's architecture, the focus falls on design objects displayed in artistic installations, woven into the interior, and becoming the décor. Here, these objects are completely divorced of their function, and one sees only their shapes, forms and colors. There are garden tools used as staircase railings, some of the wall art is made of cutlery and, of course, dozens of my childhood's orange-handled scissors hanging as a kind of chandelier from the ceiling.

The *Fiskars Pavilion*'s scissors, axes and cutlery fit the definition of *fetish objects*, as those believed to have magical powers above and beyond other objects. In the pavilion I saw for the first time that design culture is a complex system driven by objects that stand for much more than the sum of their parts. Thus, design goes well beyond aesthetic and function and becomes super-human, prodding and nudging us to behave in a certain way and not another. Design, seen this way, also comes close to the other kinkier definition of *fetishism* as outfits and objects that coerce users. Sam Jacob, professor of architecture at the University of Illinois in Chicago, writes that, "it is as much about constraint and control as it is about freedom and liberation. You can keep your dungeons, there's really nowhere kinkier than a *Vitra* showroom."[34] I am forced to agree, having been to several *brand lands* since my trip to Finland, including the *Vitra* showrooms in Milano and Madrid.

As an anthropologist, wandering through the *Fiskars Pavilion* and seeing modern mundane objects raised to cultish statues was fascinating. Any display of human-made objects must be part of anthropology, even if the objects were designed by predominantly Western designers under democratic conditions of artistic expression. But in my pre-design life I have only seen arcane objects from far-away cultures labeled *fetish* or *totem* behind dusty vitrines of stuffy ethnography museums. Displays of farming tools, domestic products and farmhouses are displayed for their ingenuity and beauty but always in an archival effort. But there is one massive difference: all those artifacts, no matter if they are valuable or not, are never for sale nor do they advertise copies for sale. The *brand land*, on the other hand, is a very complex display of corporate identity, brand recognition and flaunting of design skills. "Is this a strange stage of marketing where capitalism itself is fetishized?" I asked myself as I exited through the gift store.

In the first chapter of Karl Marx's *Das Kapital, Volume I* we can find a short section devoted to the question of *fetishism*, "The fetishism of commodities and the secret thereof." In the afterword to the second German edition, Marx writes about that section.

> A commodity appears, at first sight, a very trivial thing, and easily understood. Its analysis shows that it is, in reality, a very queer thing, abounding in metaphysical subtleties and theological niceties ... The mystical character of commodities does not originate, therefore, in their use value. Just as little does it proceed from the nature of the determining factors of value.[35]

It seems that Marx, writing in the waning 19th century, was already alluding to the added value that design brings to the boardroom. But are those "metaphysical subtleties and theological niceties" added by design and then capitalized, or is it the other way around? Does the *fetishism* of objects only happen in capitalism? It turns out I had a kind of control group in the industrial design exhibition in Belgrade, Serbia. Another fetish object – this time in a deeper yellow – again stirred up deep childhood memories. This time, I was looking at the old *Iskra ETA 80* telephone, a Slovenian design classic of 1979. It was commissioned by the Tito administration of Yugoslavia in the *Secretariat for Industrial Design of the Federation of Associations of Applied Arts Artists and Designers of Yugoslavia* (SID SPID YU). Around the same time the Russians of the former Soviet Union also had a centrally planned, top-down research institution called *All-Union Scientific Research Institute for Technical Aesthetics* (VNIITE), founded in 1962.

At first, the two words *Soviet* and *Design* seem mutually exclusive: a massive manufacture of goods was crucial to improve the well-being of the Soviet population, while *commodity fetishism* and division of social groups along the ownership of commodities was very dangerous to the fabric of society. True to Marxist philosophy, which always urges workers to overcome dehumanizing *alienation* associated with industrial production, the word "design" was frowned upon and used only to describe unworthy capitalist "styling," where form and color are used primarily to fetch more money in the marketplace. Instead, the Soviets used the term "technical aesthetics" as "a science of the laws of artistic creativity in the field of technology." Such a "science of design" was to be integrated with central economic planning in order to censor and steer aesthetic aspects of technology, which under capitalism were said to arise irrationally and spontaneously. An explicit goal of the VNIITE, however, was to lessen the gap between the Soviet Union and the West. Ironic as it may be, the *Soviets* were far more *user-centered* in their approach to heavy research on consumer demand, psychology, ergonomics and anthropometrics than the West.[36]

Can top-down design work? To avoid *commodity fetishism* and *conspicuous consumption*, a world was conceived where consumer goods were primarily designed to make the Soviet bloc stronger. It seems that the communists wanted desperately to design a collective utopia for a real world of individual differences and collective desires. The *Design Center* in Belgrade helped me re-evaluate design products forever associated with the drab iron curtain. But is that another gross example of wasted creative potential and capabilities, or is it "Plato's Academy of Design"?[37] As we know with hindsight, when the Berlin Wall came down most of the Eastern bloc could not wait to adopt Western-style consumerism, and in an evolutionary sense the Western approach to design *won* the arms race. The real question becomes: what is first, the desire for an object or a system creating desire? Is it the golden egg or the golden hen? That same evening, I visited *Nova Iskra* – or "new spark" – a design and innovation hub in Belgrade. I saw Serbian design alive and well but becoming kind of WEIRD!

Design and Alchemy

Alchemy is value proposition. It claims to produce perfection through the purification of "base metals" and their transmutation into "noble metals," such as gold. The means of this *proto-scientific* practice of wide parts of Asia, the Middle East and Europe, however, were always hidden. Processes and rites were rarely disclosed and kept safely behind cryptic symbolism. Analogously, contemporary use of minerals in devices are protected behind NDAs, trade secrets and sealed carcasses. Indeed, the ever-increasing complexity and miniaturization of our electronic products and processes is strangely like the ambitions of early medieval alchemy.

Devices such as laptops, smartphones and wearables contain so-called *rare earth elements*, which allow for products smaller and lighter. Color displays, camera lenses, loudspeakers, rechargeable batteries and hard drives all depend on them. They are also indispensable elements in our communication systems, from signal amplification in mobile communication towers to satellites and GPS technology and fiber optic cables. But, as end users we have been excluded entirely from all phases of material culture, as we are banned from their midwifery as well as morgue and remain only momentary handlers of material composites, entirely ignorant of the logistics behind their delivery. At the end of their excellent "Anatomy of an AI system," Crawford and Joler write:

> The scale required to build artificial intelligence systems is too complex, too obscured by intellectual property law, and too mired in logistical

complexity to fully comprehend in the moment. Yet you draw on it every time you issue a simple voice command to a small cylinder in your living room: "Alexa, what time is it?"[38]

From the dismally slow geological process of elemental development to their excavation, smelting, mixing, molding and logistical transport, our products have crossed thousands of kilometers and billions of years.

But instead of spelling that out, they are sold to us as simply magical. Through the shop window, we look at them in awe. Then we get them, handle them for a brief period before we carelessly toss them into the bin.

Design and Magic

Right around the time of crossing the magical threshold into a new millennium – from 1997 to 2007 – a young wizard took the world by storm. Generation Zs were born or came of age as this series of seven fantasy tales unfolded. Written by J. K. Rowling, the series tells of the life of outcast Harry Potter, and plays out as an archetypal *hero's journey* full of complexity and epic battles of good versus evil. The protagonist and his friends Hermione Granger and Ron Weasley are all students at the Hogwarts School of Witchcraft and Wizardry where they learn magical rites and formulae, and most importantly how to become magicians.

I first became aware of a striking similarity between Hogwarts and design schools when in presentations of final projects "good" students were praised for giving their designs a *magical quality*. The overt goal of design is the creation of something that triggers awe, mystery, amazement and rituals, and it employs symbolic logic, but the actual *magic* occurs with the end-users who wish and receive a promise. Good designers craft the interface between object and its users, not just the objects themselves; great designers make that interface disappear ... *magically*. Design clearly adds value to most business ventures, but it often evades metrics; while most can recognize good design, no one can tell why. That is magical! The magic of design is powerful but, as Donald Norman laments, "the design of everyday things is in great danger of becoming the design of superfluous, overloaded, unnecessary things."[39]

The field of magic might be the least understood human phenomenon, probably due to its very essence of working invisibly. There are lots of ways to even think of the word. Biologist Richard Dawkins, for example, addresses a kind of *poetic magic* that stands for the mysteries we are confronted with every second of every waking hour.[40] In the same vain, design causes emotions and exaltations. According to the *Encyclopedia Brittanica, magical thinking* "presumes a causal link between one's inner, personal experience and the external physical world."[41] Designed objects – whether physical or digital – touch us at the core and through us they change the course of events in the physical world. They are ethereal objects with the power to move people in every imaginable direction and that is ... *magical.*

Over a hundred years ago anthropologist E. B. Tyler tried to banish magic into the past by calling it "one of the most pernicious delusions that ever vexed mankind."[42] What an ethnocentric, anachronistic and arrogant claim! Ever since *structuralist* Claude Lévi-Strauss, we instead see societies as living simultaneously in a world of primitive and rational thought. Let us not forget that, had we not been taught through an education based on the Enlightenment, humanism and technology, we would not hesitate to call an airplane in the sky – or the internet – magical. They seem to defy everything else that makes sense. Around the same time as Tyler, James Frazer divided magic into *sympathetic* and *contagious*.[43] The former – just like homeopathy – operates through a promise that "like affects like," or that one can impart characteristics of one object to a similar object or person. The most famous example would be the use of voodoo dolls. As pointed out by Russell W. Belk, possessions are part of our *extended self* – our cherished objects – and we infuse them with magical qualities and would suffer greatly when lost.[44] Mihaly Csikszentmihalyi and Eugene Rochberg-Halton suggest that when directing our efforts and attention to objects we "charge" them with "psychic energy," since they have grown or emerged from the self.[45] Such energetic objects can also link individual persons (wedding rings, *Swifty* bracelets) or cement in-group solidarity (soccer jerseys, flags, music T-shirts). *Contagious magic*, the belief that two things that were once connected retain a link and can affect their related objects, should also ring a bell. Most people today think the entire world functions according to such mimetic or homeopathic principles, and in that sense we have not evolved much. Just marvel at the way you tell your *iPhone* to download a distant friend's playlist to play on your wireless *Sonos* speakers! Has the internet of things (IoT) not cast a magical spell on humanity? And is the super annoying moment of not being able to pair objects via Bluetooth not a violent disruption of technological magic?

For Marcel Mauss, history's most renowned anthropologist on magic, all magical systems require three elements: magicians, magical representations and magical rites.[46] The best modern designers prove their brilliance by being able to create out of thin air objects, services and experiences, but to pull off that magic trick he or she needs the participants to go along. They need to believe the result to be true, especially in situations of otherwise risky and uncertain conditions. We are talking about an act of faith since here the audience isn't employing rational thought, but rather emotional association. Rather than rationally explaining and demystifying curiosities, novel commodities also offer enchantment and require blind faith. Since design – almost by definition – relies most frequently on non-verbal communication, such recourses to emotional realms become understandable. Of course, a narrative is needed to convey the marvels of new designs and *storytelling* has become a viral buzzword, but good design does not rely on many words. The presentations of new wondrous trinkets are like *magical rites* designed to not only affect *disruption* of the ordinary but also to mark the exact time and place for this to take place, and thus the yearly unveiling of new Apple gadgets has become a cultural institution. In a good presentation, the audience is taken to an abyss, beyond which lies a miraculous innovation, but just like the mentalist, the designer never shares the inner workings of anything. Steve Jobs understood this all too well, and it is no wonder that he has reached mystical status in and around the world of design.

Magical thinking cannot and should not be equated with religious thinking. Neither should the magician be confused with a deity, and thus besides being an undisputed genius of design, Jobs was also a master magician. In its essence, magic is an emancipation from a supernatural entity since the magician doesn't rely on the heavens for something awesome to happen; they promise the impossible right here on earth. Marcel Mauss notes, "it is their profession which sets them apart from the common run of mortals, and it is this separateness which endows them with magical power."[47] Ethnographer Bronislaw Malinowski wrote that magic is used in "the domain of the unaccountable and adverse influences, as well as the great unearned increment of fortunate coincidence," going against the 19th century view of magic exemplifying non-rationality.[48] In his classic study of the *Kula Ring* in the Trobriand Islands he observed that his subjects knew perfectly well how to plant their gardens for a rich crop just as they knew about static and hydrodynamics for the use of their catamaran-type boats. It was only in uncertain, precarious situations that they resorted to all kinds of acts of magical thinking simply because success of their sea voyages and their work on the fields depended on a series of uncontrollable factors such as weather, predatorial animals or the whimsical attitudes of their neighbors. Malinowski's theory is reminiscent of Tylor's *survivals*, remnants of an older world, ruled by a magical *Weltbild*.

In most of humanity's past, just the right amount of weather ingredients meant the difference between life and death, and so it is not surprising that this is still a matter of concern for us today. Do we, today, not find comfort in looking at our weather predicting apps, in a world that seems totally out of control? Of course, few people today believe that the app on their iPhone *produces* the weather, but most of us accept that we can somehow report about the future. It is dumbed-down pseudoscience that is displayed on our screens, and it does cause us to change our future through our behavior. In situations of uncertainly, the emotions of anticipation, imagination and fantasy play a key role in the use and acceptance of magic today. Don't we still knock on wood in times of uncertainty, knowing full well that there are no sinister specters to be chased out of the table surface? We say *mantras*, cross our fingers in weird *mudras* when we try to find that one magical parking spot in a clogged city. In an uncertain, fragile world modern science can only help, but never fully satisfy the human need for order and rationality.

As Arthur C. Clarke famously stated in his *second law*, it gets harder to distinguish between technology and magic the more advanced a civilization is.

Because magic "speaks to realms other than material reality," it engenders a sense of enchantment in our modern world.[49] A "magical consciousness" accesses hidden, unseen forces, or acts at a distance, as a prime vehicle for firing the imagination. Diametrically opposed to such enchantment stands Max Weber's *disenchantment* to describe a world devoid of magic, a world predictable and calculable. Weber's *Entzauberung der Welt*, first used in 1919, was a concept borrowed from Friedrich Schiller's poem "Die Götter Grie-chenlandes" of 1788. Both Weber and Schiller addressed the consequences an overly rational worldview dawning during the Enlightenment might have, and the resulting romantic longing for the magical and unexplored times of the past. They insinuated that while the European mindset had accepted that the things surrounding them where devoid of magic rationally, on a more archaic and basal cognitive level the human mind had not been able to keep up with the rapid technological advances brought by industrialization. Unknowingly they hinted at the mismatch between our sense apparatus and the complexity of the things surrounding us.

Good magic is all about jumping a gap of uncertainty or bridging that little moment when the most important trick is being used, yet the whole event comes across as a seamless string of causality. That is the very essence of the magicians' sleight of hand. When we stand on the street corner tapping on our Uber app and moments later we see a little digital car approaching our location represented by a pinpoint on our screens, and then we look up and a real car is pulling up and waits for us to get in – that is good magic! And that is why the century-old institution of taxis doesn't stand a chance. What the end-user does not see is that there is a very real person sitting in some remote place of the world checking drivers against their IDs to make sure they match. In the gaps of modern transactions is an invisible segment of the labor market, hundreds of thousands "on demand workers." In a recent book researchers Mary L. Gray and Siddharth Suri focus on the people who per-form "ghost work" in the technology industry that algorithms and AI alone can't do. Ghost workers fill the gaps between what AI and other forms of technology can accomplish and what end consumers expect in an on-demand economy. They are hired by companies that mix application programming interfaces (APIs) – the technology that allows two different applications to communicate – and artificial intelligence (AI) and realize that there is some-thing missing. The proverbial "ghosts in the machine" for tasks as disparate as delivering Uber Eats, reviewing online photos and texts or captioning videos are bike riders and home office workers the world over. Legions of hired hands also apply ingenuity to problems that software cannot yet solve by cleaning *training data* – the data fed to machines to learn – by fixing typos, adding descriptive tags to images and other tasks to make information digestible to our machines. In this magical, modern world, the work must be done fast and on demand.

Ghost work may consist of "micro-tasks," such as the Human Intelligence Tasks (HITs) on *Amazon's Mechanical Turk* platform, which comprise actions as small as tagging an image. Workers on Upwork and Fiverr facilitate "macro-tasks," like copyediting or website design. Full-time staff members at hiring companies often manage on-demand workers. They draw a historical line from marginalized workers doing piecework in sweatshops to today's gig workers, an important analogy since on-demand work is likely the future of employment. Gray and Suri advocate legal and societal changes to make gig work viable for workers and businesses.

At Amazon distribution centers, vast amounts of *cargo* are shelved along millions of shelves in algorithmic and opaque order. The position of the items is not organized in the way you might find books in a library, along lines of subjects and the alphabet. Instead, they are stowed randomly along a complex mathematical matrix of time (of orders) and space (of delivery). With the help of electronic bracelets workers are directed through airplane hangar–sized warehouses to pick out the specific items with robotic drive units. One Amazon invention – US patent number 9,280,157 – has made the news recently as a stark illustration of worker alienation in an age of machines. It stands for a metal cage, a kind of exoskeleton to the workers standing inside it, which can be moved through the warehouses along vertical and horizontal axes to reach items. "Here, the worker becomes a part of a machine ballet, held upright in a cage which dictates and constrains their movement," as stated by Crawford and Joler in their important article "Anatomy of an AI system."[50] The global spread of information technologies allowed for new ways for logistics, such as the containerization of shipping and industrial jobs, to be outsourced to less developed countries with the availability of cheap labor and less stringent laws of environmental degradation.

As problems are solved, more humans are displaced. At the same time, the process of drawing on human skills will repeat, and we will likely see a rapidly oscillating creation of labor markets as new automation services are offered and new tasks required. Especially in the IoT sector, sensors and gadgets, more still unimaginable on-demand services and products, will hit the market and they all need new lines of *ghost work* – people working away, hidden from view. Since human needs and wants are fuzzy, and are designed by evolution's deep history, machines can only approximately satisfy them. Self-filling refrigerators or Google Translator are made possible by ghost workers, but they are grossly undervalued and rendered invisible, by the magical design of the machines we build to do what humans can do. In our on-demand economy, part-time, super flexible and docile contract workers are thus indispensable, and they are found on crowdsourcing platforms like *Crowdflower* and the above-mentioned *Amazon Mechanical Turk*, the latter cheekily named after the 18th-century chess-playing automaton that toured Europe and beat both Napoleon Bonaparte and Benjamin Franklin.

The slick applications, services and gadgets sold to us have dirtier secrets yet. Snuff movies, pornography and hate speech are uploaded on YouTube every day, but somehow we never see any of it. That is because real, carbon-based humans get paid to see them and pick them out elsewhere, where we're not looking. Those magical transactions that deliver your pizza or even the news, the push notification telling you when and what is *trending* – they involve AI, APIs and people. Automation is marching ahead at frightening speed, and by the time anyone is reading these lines it might well have gone much further, but it will not be "fully automated" any more than the *Mechanical Turk* chess machine was just a contraption with a person underneath the tablecloth moving the chess pieces. It is disappointing to realize that our gadgets are not as artificial or intelligent as we are told; Dorothy and her friends were also really shocked when they realized that the great Wizard of Oz was only a run-of-the-mill, normal man pulling levers from behind a curtain. Is it reassuring to know that full automation still takes human intelligence? In the wake of the creation of technological advancement there will always be people working in the shadows. The question is, how much should we recognize and value them? However, this is no place to ponder the fairness of working conditions, but rather to point out that the seductive power of magic in design has done an incredible job in hiding what is going on in the shadows. And meanwhile, over at Amazon, hundreds of scientists, aerospace engineers and futurists have been working hard to develop *Prime Air*, a drone-based delivery service. Isn't it ironic: cargo will soon be falling from the sky.

Emotional Design

In 2016 I was invited to speak at a conference on design and emotions in Amsterdam. Emotions are probably the most elusive and vague of our human sentiments. They might also be the most important drivers of human action; they are part of our cognition, triggered by internal events like thoughts or memories but also external stimuli. Emotions often precede thinking, speaking, writing and behaving, and so while they inhabit our most private spheres of consciousness, they can erupt into the public sphere. They color our everyday experience, but when harnessed as social aggregates they can cause the biggest social movements imaginable. Finally, emotions, without a doubt, are the sweet spot of good design.

To say that I was intrigued to see how responsible designers harness human emotions is a big understatement. However, emotionally (pun intended), I changed quickly from excitement and curiosity to shock when an eccentric electrical engineer and professor at the University in Tokyo took the stage as keynote speaker and introduced the *Kissinger*, a device that provides a virtual reality experience of kissing someone not present. The following description of the gadget is taken directly from the professor's webpage:

A multimodal interactive system for remote kissing interaction is developed. The kissing device is designed as an attachment device for mobile phones, allowing users to kiss each other remotely while having a video chat using their mobile phones. It measures and transmits real-time lip pressure over the Internet. The device consists of force sensors that measure the contact force between the lip surface of the device and the user's lips, as well as a linear actuator array to produce accurate force feedback and lip movements during user interaction.[51]

After his presentation, which also hinted at some very dubious "user research" with his female lab assistants, the room roared with applause. The room was charged with emotion! What novelty! Thankfully, I was given the microphone and asked how this technophile device could possibly close the gap between estranged lovers in a cold and distant society. Did we not become emotionally bankrupt *because* of electronic gadgetry? His smile was smug when he responded with the obvious: "we have to educate society on how to handle this technology!" No kidding! I could not agree more.

Thank God for people like cognitive scientist and designer Donald Norman, whose research into *emotional design* also has a serious side. Credited with putting *human-centered design* and *user experience* testing on the map, he not only understands the responsibility designers have, but holds them accountable. Emotions are actually the Holy Grail of design, since success and failure depend on how the end-user feels when engaging with an object, service or experience. According to Norman, users have different cognitive processes going on all the time and designers address at least three levels of behavioral responses: 1) visceral reactions are what we usually call gut reactions because they are felt in the body usually below the head and above the knees, so how a design makes us feel; 2) behavioral reactions are really evaluations of how a designed object helps or hinders us from reaching our goals; and 3) reflective reactions are intellectual, analytical appraisals of how a design object performs for us, so does it make us look good? Was it worth the money?[52]

Notes

1 Fung, B. (2012). Make it so: What *Star Trek* tells us about how to make tablets. *The Atlantic*, July 26.
2 Dunne, A., & Raby, F. (2013). *Speculative Everything: Design, fiction, and social dreaming*. MIT Press.
3 Zuboff, S. (2023). *The Age of Surveillance Capitalism: The fight for a human future at the new frontier of power*. Profile Books, p. 20.
4 J. Taylor (2012). How technology is changing the way children think and focus. *Psychology Today*. www.psychologytoday.com/blog/the-power-prime/201212/how-technology-is-changing-the-way-children-think-and-focus.
5 K. McSpadden (2015). You now have a shorter attention span than a goldfish. *Time Health*. http://time.com/3858309/attention-spans-goldfish.

6 Glum, J. (2018). The median Amazon employee's salary is $28,000. Jeff Bezos makes more than that in 10 seconds.

7 https://www.bbc.com/news/science-environment-63245150, accessed on November 14, 2023.

8 Perez, C. C. (2019). *Invisible Women: Data bias in a world designed for men*. Abrams.

9 http://www.sweetspeeches.com/s/13939, accessed on October 20, 2015.

10 Kuang, C., & Fabricant, R. (2019). *User Friendly: How the hidden rules of design are changing the way we live, work, and play*. Random House.

11 Hollingsworth, J., Copeland, B. & Johnson, J. X. (2019, August 2). Are e-scooters polluters? The environmental impacts of shared dockless electric scooters. *Environmental Research Letters*, 14(8), 084031.

12 Smith, D. K., & Alexander, R. C. (1988). *Fumbling the Future: How Xerox Invented, then ignored, the first personal computer*. William Morrow & Co.

13 Kjeldskov, J. (2012). Interaction design. In *Mobile Interactions in Context: A designerly way toward digital ecology* (pp. 19–31). Springer.

14 https://www.theguardian.com/technology/2017/sep/19/facebooks-war-on-free-will, accessed on April 20, 2022.

15 Kroker, A., & Weinstein, M. A. (1994). *Data Trash: The theory of the virtual class*. New World Perspectives, p. 15.

16 Barbrook, R., & Cameron, A. (1996). The Californian ideology. *Science as Culture*, 6(1), 44–72.

17 https://www.nytimes.com/2018/02/28/opinion/corporate-america-activism.html, accessed on May 19, 2022.

18 https://web.archive.org/web/20170809021151/https://diversitymemo.com/, accessed on May 20, 2022.

19 Martínez, A. G. (2016). *Chaos Monkeys: Inside the Silicon Valley money machine*. Random House.

20 https://www.latimes.com/business/la-fi-hy-musk-subsidies-20150531-story, accessed on April 20, 2022.

21 Zuboff, S. (2023). The age of surveillance capitalism. In *Social Theory Re-Wired* (pp. 203–213). Routledge.

22 Gustafsson, D. (2019). Analyzing the double diamond design process through research & implementation. https://core.ac.uk/download/pdf/224802861.pdf, accessed on January 26, 2024.

23 https://sts-news.medium.com/the-design-thinking-movement-is-absurd-83df815b92ea, accessed on October 13, 2023.

24 Buchanan, R. (1992). Wicked problems in design thinking. *Design Issues*, 8(2), 5–21.

25 http://www.azarask.in/blog/post/the-wrong-problem/, accessed on September 12, 2016.

26 http://dschool.stanford.edu/extreme/impact/embrace_02.html, accessed on September 12, 2016.

27 Kelley, T. (2001). *The Art of Innovation: Lessons in creativity from IDEO, America's leading design firm* (Vol. 10). Currency.

28 Brown, T. (2008). Design thinking. *Harvard Business Review*, 86(6), 84.

29 Mucha, H., & Nebe, K. (2017). Human-centered toolkit design. In *HCITools: Strategies and best practices for designing, evaluating and sharing technical HCI Toolkits, Workshop at CHI* (Vol. 17).

30 Brown, T. (2010). *Change by Design*. Lian Jing/Tsai Fong Books.

31 Shermer, M. (2009). *The Mind of the Market: How biology and psychology shape our economic lives*. Macmillan.

32 https://onezero.medium.com/giving-up-apple-in-the-name-of-repair-and-the-environment-dbd53bc2fa26, accessed on November 11, 2023.

33 https://www.ft.com/content/0a5a4404-7c8e-11e7-ab01-a13271d1ee9c, accessed on November 10, 2023.

34 https://www.dezeen.com/2015/04/14/kink-and-fetish-much-to-teach-mainstream-design-culture-opinion-sam-jacob/, accessed on September 25, 2021.
35 Marx, K. (1996). *Das Kapital* (F. Engels, Ed.). Regnery Publishing, p. 81.
36 Cubbin, T. (2018). *Soviet Critical Design: Senezh Studio and the communist surround.* Bloomsbury.
37 Azrikan, D. (1999). VNIITE, dinosaur of totalitarianism or Plato's Academy of Design? *Design Issues*, 15(3), 45–77.
38 Crawford, K., & Joler, V. (2018). Anatomy of an AI system. Retrieved September 18, 2018.
39 Norman, D. A. (1988). *The Psychology of Everyday Things.* Basic Books.
40 Dawkins, R. (2012). *The Illustrated Magic of Reality: How we know what's really true.* Simon and Schuster.
41 https://www.britannica.com/science/magical-thinking, accessed on March 5, 2022.
42 Bidmead, J. (2016). Making magic: A comparative perspective. In *Invest Your Humanity: Celebrating Marvin Meyer.* Pickwick Publications, p. 53.
43 Frazer, J. G. (1900). The Golden Bough: A study in magic and religion. *Revue des Traditions Populaires*, 15, 471.
44 Belk, R. W. (1988). Possessions and the extended self. *Journal of Consumer Research*, 15(2), 139–168.
45 Csikszentmihalyi, M., & Halton, E. (1981). *The Meaning of Things: Domestic symbols and the self.* Cambridge University Press.
46 Mauss, M. (2005). *A General Theory of Magic.* Routledge.
47 Moeran, B. (2014, October). Business, anthropology, and magical systems: The case of advertising. *Ethnographic Praxis in Industry Conference Proceedings*, 119–132.
48 Malinowski, B. (2013). *Argonauts of the Western Pacific: An account of native enterprise and adventure in the archipelagoes of Melanesian New Guinea [1922/ 1994].* Routledge.
49 Greenwood, S. (2009). The wild hunt: A mythological language of magic. In *Handbook of Contemporary Paganism* (pp. 195–222). Brill, p. 8.
50 Crawford, K., & Joler, V. (2018). Anatomy of an AI system. Retrieved February 14, 2023.
51 https://adriancheok.info/category-media/kissenger/, accessed on October 5, 2021.
52 Norman, D. A. (1988). *The Psychology of Everyday Things.* Basic Books.

8

MARKETING AND ITS GRIP ON DESIGN

The Great Hack

The ancients saw earth as the center, Galileo replaced it with the sun and Darwin challenged the primacy of this species and assigned it to a humble lineage descendent from other animals. But then the *marketing revolution* came along and put us back in the center of the universe. It is all about us again. Everything revolves around humans again. No matter if the approach is qualitative, quantitative, operative or experimental; *marketing research* has been turned onto humans. All imaginable tools, from surveys to focus groups, from FRMI resonance to eye-tracking, telescopes to microscopes, are human-*centered.* They cut deeper and more precisely than ever before on their way to our emotions, thoughts and feelings. The human psyche is mined, refined and monetized while the *naked ape* still stands, staring empty at a messy campsite. It was called *person* but now it is simply a *consumer* and *user.*

If you want to know about human strength in accomplishing what they need, then ask the anthropologist, but if you want to know about human weakness to succumb to want, then ask the marketer! Marketing, as understood today, can talk more about the human being to anthropologists than vice versa; and that is probably the single reason why it took so long for the discipline of anthropology to be reckoned with in business schools. We can learn a lot about the human being from studying marketing, but as warning, it is not pretty! *Marketing research* figured out how to make humans give up their inner secrets and remaining vestibules of privacy in return for convenience, novelty and beauty. Through its rigor and empirical approach, it has thus amassed history's largest data set on humans. It is available, but not in psychology textbooks. Instead, it is on the hard drives of companies and embodied in gadgets, since much of modern design is but a helpful

DOI: 10.4324/9781003464754-11

accomplice, designated only to the embodiment of consumerism. In this sense marketing *is* applied anthropology and the *Anthropocene* is the manifestation of all material and ethereal manifestations of human behavior.

Marketing essentially "hacked" the human psyche. In the domain of information technology, "hacking" refers to an illegal entry into a network, and so I use the word cautiously. Pushing harmful goods such as cigarettes, alcohol or junk food has been outlawed by various governments at various times. Speaking of a marketing "hack" involves addressing the age, cultural background, addictive predisposition and neurodiversity of a *target group*, but it is usually legal. To be sure, life as we have come to expect it would change if advertisement were made entirely illegal. There would be no more free internet content, freelancers would have a much more difficult time making money and business locations would be the end-all of any competitive market. Worst of all, life would return to a jungle where only the most aggressive and largest company wins, likely as a monopoly. As we have seen in biology, signaling the quality of traits is a much more cost-efficient and milder strategy than just taking out rivals.

Of course it will always be a "chicken or egg" question, but let us start with people receiving the signals emitted by marketing and advertisement. When we feel bored, a part of our brain called *default mode network*, used for unfocused attention, fires up. But don't confuse binge-watching a series, surfing on the internet or doom scrolling with boredom. They are *answers* to boredom; they are attempts to escape it. It is as if we are just sitting around idly and our brain produces a feeling that screams, "here we are, now entertain us."[1] When we're bored, we actively seek out anything at all to provide a bit of purpose. Boredom motivates us to find new things to do, to explore novel experiences. It is a defense mechanism and all those activities – no matter how mindless – consist of focused attention. And they are, neurologically speaking, very pricey. It is not our boredom but constantly running away from it that is causing our mental fatigue. Smartphones and other tech gadgetry provide continual stimulation through constantly shifting streams of media, which capture our attention. Using such devices as a strategy to reduce boredom likely results in negative outcomes like depression and anxiety.[2]

According to neuroscientist Jaak Panksepp there are seven core instincts in the human brain (fear, anger, play, maternal care, panic-grief, pleasure/lust and seeking), and seeking is the most important. Through neurotransmitters like dopamine, humans are rewarded for seeking new information in their surroundings, anything that might help survival.[3] Marketers exploit such parameters to convert their products from something a person "wants" to something they "need." In corporate jargon this is called "customer education." The trick of modern marketing – their sleight of hand – is telling us that we *need* a new pair of pants because the ones we are wearing currently are so 2024! How do we take humans from *wanting* something to *needing* it? There is a neurological structure underneath the *logical cortex* in the *ventral striatum* called the *nucleus accumbens.* It helps us to want and pursue desired behaviors. This system receives information from the *amygdala* about the emotional intensity of a given situation and the *hippocampus* about memories on how good something was. Both streams of information are summarized by the *ventral striatum* and sent to the *hypothalamus,* which controls our archaic drives such as sex, food and sleep, our hormonal system and parts of the autonomic nervous system.

It is a little more complex still, and wanting alone is not going to drive consumerism. A *user* – whether of addictive drugs or shiny toys – needs to "like" the actual experience of the reward. In design it is measured as user experience, or UX. The wanting is fueled by dopamine, but the liking involves opiates with their analgesic (painkilling) effects. Both endogenous to the brain, dopamine is what makes you order the latest trinket, while opiates give you the intense pleasure of unboxing and experiencing it.[4] Rarely do these biological computations make it to consciousness, but they still drive us to go for something. If this system of "wanting" is pushed to the maximum, you get addictive behaviors. The *hedonic treadmill* is powered by reinforcing a constant state of un-satisfactoriness, which in turn is based on a constant chase of uppers and downers in our heads. Obviously, the best customer is the one who is never satisfied and always comes back for more, newer things.

Let us also quickly turn to marketing as a field of enquiry. Originally, *marketing* referred to the process of buying and selling. It was the activity taking place in the marketplace following the simple rules of supply and demand. Now, the term refers to the discipline or program of moving products, services and experiences from those who conceive them to those who consume them. Thus, the emphasis has shifted from the sale to advertising and creating the desire for those products, services and experiences. The evolutionary perspective, adopted here, sees marketing as an almost omnipotent force that uses an a priori human condition to exploit it, making the marketplace a mere mirage of supply and demand. Marketing does not coerce the end-user to consume; rather, it hacks the human psyche into consent. I don't think marketing is addressed much in such terms in business and design schools. Considering that in the early 1900s marketing courses were first offered at universities in the US, we are now over a century into marketing education, which has left an indelible stamp on culture.

A Short, but Design-Relevant, History of Marketing

During the second half of the 19th century and up to the years between the two world wars marketing was focused on production, which is to say that supply was believed to create its own demand. Just the mere fact that during the Industrial Revolution it became much easier for people to acquire commodities made elsewhere than making them themselves speaks for itself. The Industrial Revolution spawned modern marketing as the promotion of mass-produced consumer products. The famous quote from Henry Ford, "If you have a really good thing, it will advertise itself," really sums up this "first" period of marketing, as does the Model T – the company's most famous car. It truly was the perfect car for a newly developing market of horseless carriages, and it soon became the standard by which the citizenry could be judged. Incredibly, by 1918 half of all the cars driving around America were Model Ts! The company's marketing approach was purely descriptive and very heavy on text. Corporations such as Ford clearly placed their emphasis on creating economies of scale, to manufacture as many goods as possible, and marketing communication was limited to raising awareness of the product's existence.[5]

It was the dawn of the "age of me," these narcissistic times that we are living in. Sigmund Freud in 1914 introduced the concept of *narcissism* as a clinical pathology, and like so many of Freud's ideas it got its name from Greek mythology. Narcissus fends off all amorous pursuits and falls instead in love with his own reflection in a pool of water. The reflection is key to the myth because the protagonist does not fall in love with himself but rather with how *others* see him. After all, no one without the help of a reflective surface or photographic device can see what they see. It is the signal projected that the narcissist is in love with. Narcissus also had contempt for people who fall in love with non-superficial inner values.[6]

It seems worthwhile to ponder for a few minutes the relationship of the inside and the outside world. The inside version we have, which as we have seen depends also on an objective, societal version, is constantly in contact with a changing world. Inside, we think we are standing still and not moving, but that is obviously an illusion. It is known by all psychological traditions – Western and Eastern – that consuming sense objects from the outside world does not necessarily correlate positively with a happy inside world. Surely, we can experience pleasure from a great meal or an intoxicating substance, but that pleasure is fleeting and creates a state of never being fully satisfied. Narcissus of Greek mythology had no interest for such introspection, which although accessible requires contemplation and solitude. As a result, the narcissist retreats into social isolation, focusing instead on outside perception and attempts to make an "objective" social perspective synonymous with his own perspective. Narcissus did not fall in love; he fell into the pond and drowned, so beautiful was the image.

Interestingly, it was Freud's nephew Edward Bernays (1891–1995) who stands at the beginning of the discipline we now call *marketing*. Bernays was related to Sigmund Freud both biologically and by law: Bernays' mother was Freud's sister and his father was the brother of Freud's wife. Bernays had close contact with his uncle and often joined Freud for summer holidays. Anecdotally and ironically his career really started – I kid you not – with a cigar. After reading his uncle's "General Introductory Lectures," sent by Freud as thanks for a box of Havana cigars, he began his career as the original spin doctor. Bernays corresponded regularly with his uncle "Sigi" and began to understand the power of emotions, instinct and feeling tones. Using insights from psychoanalysis, he really put propaganda, public relations and advertisement on the map. Whatever it was that he was selling, he exploited what Freud labeled the *unconscious* and became the chief commander of persuasion.[7]

Although born in Austria, Bernays' family moved to New York right after his birth. He studied agriculture at Cornell but started a career in journalism before becoming famous as a consultant to the Woodrow Wilson administration, helping to promote the idea that the United States' World War I efforts were made only to bring democracy to Europe. After World War I, Bernays continued with his efforts during peacetime. The first genius move was morphing the term *propaganda* into *public relations* – now simply known as *PR* – dodging the bad reputation the former term had acquired. Insights from his uncle helped him develop an approach he dubbed "the engineering of consent." In a tone far more overt than modern business jargon, he had the following message for industrial leaders: "If we understand the mechanism and motives of the group mind, it is now possible to control and regiment the masses according to our will without them knowing it."[8]

To do that, Bernays used what is called "third-party technique" where apart from the brand and the end-user, a third party – usually a celebrity, hierarchically superior – is used as the mouthpiece for the client's interests. As revolutionary as this might have been, it has become the status quo. Think of George Clooney and you think of Nespresso! Think of product placement and social media influencers! Bernays pioneered the strategy of symbolic figures manipulated to play upon archaic human aspirations and fears. Bernays is also in part responsible for the absurdity of throw-away culture by scaring people into thinking that only disposable cups were sanitary and that drinking out of glass caused diseases. But this was no ordinary ad campaign; for it he founded the *Committee for the Study and Promotion of the Sanitary Dispensing of Food and Drink*. According to him the masses could easily be manipulated. He wrote:

> The conscious and intelligent manipulation of the organised habits and opinions of the masses is an important element in democratic society. Those who manipulate this unseen mechanism of society constitute an invisible government which is the true ruling power of our country. We are governed, our minds are moulded, our tastes formed, and our ideas suggested, largely by men we have never heard of. ... It is they who pull the wires that control the public mind.[9]

He was using his uncle's terminology, but his ambitions were clearly manipulative. Bernays led companies to the goldmine of the human psyche by showing them that they could simultaneously produce things that people desire as well as convince people that they desire something. This was a very useful insight when a post–World War I recession began in 1920. During the war, average citizens had reduced their overheads dramatically and purchased only what they really needed, much to the exasperation of industry moguls. The logic is striking in its straightforwardness: *need* and *want* had to be made synonymous. In 1927, a Wall Street banker and business partner of Bernays called Paul Mazur wrote in the *Harvard Business Review*:

> We must shift America from a needs to a desires culture ... People must be trained to desire, to want new things even before the old have been entirely consumed. We must shape a new mentality. Man's desires must overshadow his needs."[10]

With hindsight we know that this goal went beyond Mazur's wildest dreams. Marketing, as a strategy and embodied marketing in design, is increasingly in the business of satisfying desires and, hence, generating new ones. We are now obsessed with possession, with primal, violent desires seeking to have rather than be. To get there we ignore any ping of resentment, remorse or doubt. What Bernays did, sinister as it may be, was scientifically accurate. The quote below explains very clearly the terror we all feel from being ostracized and mobbed, which in ancestral times was equivalent to the death penalty:

> Physical loneliness is a real terror to the gregarious animal, and that association with the herd causes a feeling of security. In man this fear of loneliness creates a desire for identification with the herd in matters of opinion.[11]

Bernays' knowledge and strategy made him an influential man. Not only did he consult the advertisement campaigns of huge companies such as General Electric, Dodge and Procter & Gamble, but he also helped Chiquita – now known as the United Fruit Company – overthrow the Guatemalan government in 1954. He was a genius at finding *corporate identity* (CI), whether in the public sector, the private sector or the political arena. Thus, when President Coolidge's stiff image needed an overhaul, he organized "pancake breakfasts," including live music in the White House. Coolidge won the 1924 election, in large part due to Bernays. Cute, compared to the algorithmically aided manipulations of the democratic process we see now.

Some of Bernays' publicity campaigns would now be called *guerilla marketing*, clandestine and radical as they were. Let us consider a famous example from the tobacco sector. It was not socially accepted in the 1920s and 1930s for women to smoke, and so he marched into action to overcome *sales resistance* to cigarettes among women. Bernays was starting to become a well-known consultant and one of his clients was George Washington Hill, president of the American Tobacco Company. Hill wanted to broaden the market for his Lucky Strike brand by selling to women. Bernays consulted with Freud disciple and New York's leading psychoanalyst Dr. A. A. Brill. Stereotypical of Freudian psychoanalysis, Brill told Bernays that cigarettes symbolized male power. As a result, Bernays staged a demonstration during a parade in 1929 where fashionable young women smoked publicly. They were not just smoking the cigarettes of a patriarchal society; they were flaunting their "torches of freedom." The parade was sold as a political statement of the liberation of women, but the underlying motivation was otherwise. More than just showing women smoking, it demonstrated that the forest green hue of the Lucky Strike cigarette pack was far more fashionable than other colors of the day. The campaign proved very successful and soon that color was seen on the mannequins in the shops and the models of the fashion shows. Using his powerful techniques of persuasion, Bernays convinced the public that cigarettes acted soothingly on the throat and slimmed the waistline, and that the color of the cigarette pack looked really good.

The "Torches of Freedom Parade" was a sensation, covered by local, national and even international papers. While Freud studied the psyche, Bernays mined it. Whereas Freud had a backbone, Bernays did not. When Bernays suggested his uncle promote himself in America by writing popular articles for *Cosmopolitan* magazine, Freud was apparently shocked by the idea and refused. Just like his uncle, Bernays believed that thoughts and actions are just placeholders for unconscious desires that humans have found crucial to suppress. According to him, people cannot see things for their intrinsic worth but only as representations of something else, and that most people cannot face up to their real motives. Basically, he believed that the general public – himself excluded – were dumb and thus the public's opinion must be created using symbols and clichés. Smoke and mirrors.

Later, in 1940, one of history's most famous industrial designers Raymond Loewy helped complete the packaging and with it the corporate identity of this particular brand of cigarettes. Loewy was challenged by company president George Washington Hill to make even more recognizable the green and red package, with a $50,000 bet at stake. Loewy changed the order and weight of the colors, making the background white with the black logo inside red and surrounded by concentric circles of white and green. Lowie won the bet, as the cigarettes were adopted primarily by women and printing costs went down since less green dye was needed. The target logo was placed on both sides of the package, making it more visible. Of course, we have come a long way and anyone with a social conscience would take on just about any other gig before contributing to the tobacco industry. But back in the 1930s and 1940s graphic and industrial designers apparently did not think twice about designing cigarette packages. Bernays and Lowie, by tweaking the appearance of the packaging, made more people fall into the throes of nicotine addiction. The irony of the Lucky Strike being like a bull's eye for cancer was apparently lost! Privately, Bernays was against women smoking and tried to persuade his wife to kick the habit. It is said that he would destroy the cigarettes he found around the house by breaking them in half and throwing them down the toilet. He must have been aware of some of the emerging studies linking smoking to cancer. This all seems so benign compared to the designers of highly addictive software in Silicon Valley who will not allow their own children anywhere near social media accounts.

Bernays lived to be 103, eight decades of which he worked. It is hard to overstate the significance of this man in marketing, advertisement and design; his insights dictated some of the strongest consumerist currents of the 20th and 21st centuries. Now, in the early 21st century we live in a *post-truth* time, where reality itself is subject to debate and authentic events might as well be fake. Explicitly or not, his work is in the curricula of hundreds of design schools across the globe, his messages pumped into the heads of thousands of students, conceiving millions of products, services and other distractions. Historian Stuart Ewen writes in the introduction to Bernays' classic text *Crystallizing Public Opinion*: "If anything, the 21st century has witnessed the encroachment of Bernays' ideas into every crevice of our lives."[12]

There is an even darker area that Bernays influenced. Joseph Goebbels, minister of Nazi propaganda, greatly admired his books, using their insights in the 20th century's most horrific of all propagandas: the final solution that became known as the Holocaust. Looking back, we now know what is possible with propaganda and thus have no excuse for looking away but "Design History" courses offered in design schools often conveniently jump such historical chapters. Students are told of the marvels of the *Bauhaus* movement and other periods of creativity, and then there is a sudden break in the late '30s only to pick up again in post–World War II Europe. Running a very high danger of being misquoted and misunderstood, I do believe it is important to teach design students about the psychopathic genius of Goebbels, Himmler, Speer and Bernays. I cannot improve or agree more with the words of Richard Gunderman of Indiana University:

> In a world from which respect for objective truth has been expunged, we are left with nothing but biases and the propagandists who mold them. To withstand Bernays' cynical vision, democracies need fewer manipulable consumers and more citizens worthy of self-government. They must care about separating truth from falsehood, be able to recognise spin when they see it, and jealously guard their liberties and responsibilities. Among other things, the development of such citizens would require childrearing and education practices that esteem ends over means, prioritising knowing and serving the good over merely getting what one wants. One way of fostering an appreciation for the importance of such knowledge is to introduce students to Bernays' work, inviting them to behold life in the dystopia he describes.[13]

During the Great Depression and later, marketing orientation shifted towards selling products that were not known or desired enough, with most of the emphasis on the market transaction itself. It also became increasingly important to develop a recognizable brand when more and more competitors crowded the field. In this second phase of marketing, we see a push towards creating demand first and then supplying the commodities. Perhaps the most famous example is the Coca-Cola company, which tried to move their beverage away from a summer-only refreshment to be enjoyed all year round. The company's success in doing so hinged on associating their brand with Santa Claus. For such an ambitious and profane strategy to be successful, the Christian saint himself needed to be modified into the jovial, round character instantly recognized today. He was first illustrated by artist Haddon Sundblom and incidentally based on the artist's friend, a salesman. This is especially ironic since in the 1930s we see the birth of the classic "salesman" who convinces people of the benefit of something hitherto unknown or undesired. The modern marketing concept itself emerged in the 1950s and tried to understand customers' needs, wants and behaviors in order to form new strategies or course-correct old ones.[14]

By the 1960s a global move away from production of goods towards marketing was well under way and can be considered a paradigm shift as large as any scientific revolution has caused. As predicted by Robert Keith's 1960 article "The Marketing Revolution," consumption – not production – became the focus of corporations.[15] More and more companies raised marketers to the position of CEOs, and the mission of many firms was making customers like and demand future innovations. Interestingly, this revolution is not talked about much by the intelligentsia on either the left or right. While the former tends to acknowledge it as a kind of evil monster manipulating people to change their ways towards ever greater consumption, the latter-day saints of libertarianism – Hayek, Friedman and Becker – ignored it and continued insisting that prizes alone carry all the information about supply and demand that a market needs.

Also in the 1960s, IT departments sprang up all over the US, and programmers began to describe their craft as far more than nerdy mechanics, and their fundamental tool was the *algorithm*. The word – nothing but namedropping the Persian polymath Muhammad ibn Musa al-Khwarizmi, or Algoritmi – sounds philosophical and pristinely removed. But an algorithm is not beyond good and evil like a mathematical formula or axiom. After all, it is programmed by a human being full of biases and covert objectives. Outside the realm of IT and the coding of algorithms, we mere mortals use the vague and slippery term *technology*. We never use it for describing a hammer, a bicycle or an extension cord, but instead for all the transactions that leave us in awe because they allow us to do more with less effort. Basically, we use *technology* like we use the word *magic*. And if the price for asking Amazon Echo to play our favorite track and order Uber Eats without lifting our domesticated behinds is some algorithmic authoritarianism, so be it.

Algorithms became entangled with marketing, since they can quickly find patterns in vast data sets without relying on hypotheses or even scientists. Silicon Valley tech entrepreneurs avoided capitalizing on them directly and decided early on that profit would be made via marketing and advertisement. As we now know, the promise of a free search engine, maps and email services (Google), connectivity (Meta and X), unlimited shopping possibilities and digital, personal assistances (Amazon, Apple and Google) allow for our personal behavior change to be easily harvested and sold.

Starting in the 1990s, relationships between customers and a companies moved to the forefront. The consumer is still the center of attention, but not only for short transactions; rather for as long as possible. The consumer demonstrates loyalty as well as a lasting interaction with a brand, becoming what has been called a *prosumer*. A great example of the dichotomy between consumer and company becoming fuzzy beyond recognition comes from the outdoors company REI, where customers enter a co-op model, and after an initial membership fee receive many perks. Of course, marketing channels became much bigger and easier to use with widespread digitalization in the late '90s. Since it is far pricier to recruit a new customer than to keep an old one, such relationships must be based on trust and commitment. Instead of focusing on a single transaction of a good or service, here emphasis is shifted to the lifetime of relationships.

Planned Obsolescence

One question I now ask my first semester bachelor students is, "what are some of the tricks that you will learn on how to make people throw away products as soon as possible?" I admit it; it is a mean question to ask the bright-eyed creatives at the very beginning of their design career. But it gets their attention. Their look is a complex mixture of brief disappointment and confusion followed by apathy. I repeat the question, wording it slightly differently: "What are the techniques that designers use so that customers are forced to buy new things and throw the old ones away?" Both questions demand answers because if designers tell manufacturers how to make things that go bust prematurely, then the techniques to do so were taught at some point.

Planned obsolescence sounds conspiratorial. The term reeks of boardroom meetings, cold war, and stale cigarette smoke. That is actually not far off the mark, since the phrase first appeared in 1954 when Brooks Stevens, an American industrial designer, gave a talk with the name "Planned Obsolescence" at a Minneapolis advertising conference. He defined it as, "instilling in the buyer the desire to own something a little newer, a little better, a little sooner than is necessary."[16] Maybe he was the first to use the term, but, as we will see below, the history of this sinister industrial practice goes back quite a bit further. If you, the reader, doubt the reality of commodities deliberately made to be obsolete, take a second and look at the cellars, drawers and attics of your lives and ask yourself how much of the stuff you find you still use. If the answer is all of it, then you can skip to the next chapter. But if you are like most others living in this Western world of abundance, then you find staring back at you hundreds or thousands of items floating in this "limbo of things." (We are revisiting my Catholic analogies here because I think it illustrates nicely the complex, but fleeting, relationship we have with our objects.) The day of spring cleaning is "purgatory" for your things, and then you ship them to their last station, the incinerator, "hell." Sometimes, you decide to use them again or give them to someone else to use – "heaven" for things.

The definitive guide to *planned obsolescence*, or *built-in obsolescence*, is *Made to Break: Technology and Obsolescence* by Giles Slade, published in 2009.[17] According to Slade, deliberate obsolescence in all its forms – technological, psychological or planned – goes back to the early 20th century. A classic case of *path dependency*, the advance of this practice was coevolutionary: as company executives learned the tricks of obsolescence, manufactures applied them, and consumers increasingly fell for them, and demanded more. The first item that Slade traces historically was the electric starter in automobiles introduced in 1913, which did not just make the handheld crank but an entire car obsolete. Like Bernays using female emancipation as proxy to increase the market for smoking, women were also targeted here. After all, it was really not very ladylike to hand-crank a car!

Also in the year 1913, Henry Ford had famously revolutionized the manufacturing of cars through the principle of conveyer belt assembly, a far more effective version of Adam Smith's model of scaling, introduced in the *Wealth of Nations*. There, he argued – using a pin-making company as example – that the unskilled laborer could focus on one endlessly repeated task instead of acquiring all the knowledge required for making the whole pin. As a result, far more pins could be produced, and the company would not have to transfer much monetary capital into human capital. In order to produce the famous Ford Model T, the production process was broken down into just 45 steps taking 93 minutes! Henry Ford didn't invent the assembly line, but he used it so efficiently that he was able to produce – and sell – ten million Model Ts by 1924. At least in part, Henry Ford is responsible for mass consumerism and even the stupefaction of his workforce through relatively good money for brainless work, but he is *not* to blame for *planned obsolescence*. After all, it is claimed that he said, "Any customer can have a car painted any color that he wants, so long as it is black."

General Motors, the other big car house in America and Ford's nemesis, was really starting to sweat, and what followed was the most famous design arms race in history. It was also, I think, where design lost its innocence. Managers and executives who had changed from the sectors of textile and dyes to GM, brought with them the oldest trick of creating novelty: *styling*. This term is rightfully frowned upon in the world of design because rather than actual innovation, shapes, forms and colors are rearranged to give the superficial appearance of the new. George Nelson, considered the founder of American modernist design, wrote: "Design ... is an attempt to make a contribution through change. When no contribution is made or can be made, the only process available for giving the illusion of change is 'styling'!"[18]

Styling as a technique for selling works well on humans; don't forget we are novelty-seeking creatures with strong impulses to display. In any case, GM turned to slick styling, changing the appearance of their cars on almost a yearly basis, going from long tail fins to short ones, from aluminum to chrome mirrors. Alfred P. Sloan, the CEO of General Motors, apparently did not like the word *planned* and so called his company's approach *dynamic obsolescence*. This version is also sometimes called *psychological obsolescence*, a mechanism to manipulate consumers to feel that their products are so "last year," and that they should buy new ones. To this day this is the main driver behind fashion, a term used here to include all sectors. By the end of the 1920s, GM had overtaken Ford and *planned obsolescence* started to conquer the world.

A third kind of obsolescence strategy is that of making a product break prematurely to bring the customer back into the store. This one is called *technical* or *functional obsolescence* and we can start by talking about a small blue disposable razor that most men after puberty will have seen. Its inventor, an eccentric man called King Camp Gillette, called himself both a utopian socialist and captain of industry (this oxymoronic pairing of terms discussed above) with disastrous consequences. He wrote books on an ideal world of no competition and no wars, with corporations providing employment and welfare for all. Unfortunately, he is remembered for none of that and only for all those little razors sticking out of our bathrooms' garbage cans. Gillette's idealism becomes even more pathetic when considering that GDP (gross domestic product) never even measures utopian ideals such as health, happiness, welfare, human progress or environmental sustainability. Instead, it is based on the sale of un-wholesome things like weapons and end-user goods such as disposable items. Put simply, producing and selling thousands of throwaway items makes a country rank higher than one with industries based on products that last.

It is well known that war – especially in foreign lands – is great for a national economy since all the destructive machinery needs to be manufactured in companies across many sectors. Also, reconstructive efforts, such as the Marshall Plan after World War II, helped the USA economically. Indeed, *planned obsolescence* could be used as a very dark euphemism for war, since when it is over it serves as the best strategy for jumpstarting an economy. In times of peace, people are forced to turn to their private property and prematurely discard what might otherwise still work. After all, "consumption is the sole end and purpose of all production," as Adam Smith, the father of modern economics, wrote. In the 1950s, for the *Council of Economic Advisers to the President* under Dwight Eisenhower, consumption became the engine of the economy. In the words of retailing analyst Victor Lebow:

> Our enormously productive economy demands that we make consumption our way of life, that we convert the buying and use of goods into rituals, that we seek our spiritual satisfaction and our ego satisfaction in consumption. We need things consumed, burned up, worn out, replaced and discarded at an ever-increasing rate.[19]

And thus, we have been transformed once again, this time from users of things to "customers," "shoppers" or "consumers." Rather than being credited with our societal roles, we are encouraged to support economic growth by burning up materials. We are sold increased status when we buy things; instead of *being* we define ourselves as *having*, as Erich Fromm pointed out.[20] It is a self-propelling feedback cycle. Planned obsolescence practiced by corporations turns people into obsessive and stupid consumers, who in turn keep the corporations running. But worst of all: we are continuously forced to waste our products and their packaging. The mountains of waste and pollution usually end up in underdeveloped countries. Slowly, things are changing as countries are seeing the absurdity of such practices. France, for example, has outlawed it. As anyone can imagine, this is a judicial nightmare that will easily lead to drawn out, he-said-she-said battles between company and end-user, but working together with the French government is the success story of *Back Market*, a company that was a mere start-up eight years ago and, as of writing, has expanded to 25 countries. By addressing what CEO Thibaud Hug de Larauze calls the *trust gap*, they sell refurbished consumer electronics for a fraction of their original prices and with guarantees.

Not Like 1984: How Orwell Was Wrong

Today's most powerful private companies – the Big 5 tech giants – are stronger in revenue than many nation states, including Switzerland, Spain or Russia. But far more frightening than economic might is their rule over the largest human database ever compiled, and its implications for systematic behavioral change and the undermining of a democratic and open society. Big Tech, concentrated in Silicon Valley, is built on a truly strange ideological mixture of *libertarianism*, Ayn Randian dogmatic egoism, Skinnerian *behavioral utopianism* and *woke* political activism that spawned from Marxist and post-modernist critiques of power differentials. To understand and possibly escape from the powerful information hold companies have on private lives and democratic practices, we must untangle the various components and reconsider regulation.

In 1984, Apple spent one million dollars on a sixty-second advertisement during the famous *Super Bowl* halftime show. Back then the company was a nobody in the world of IT, but the ad changed computing forever. Directed by Ridley Scott, it was a powerful dystopian short, an Orwellian scene in which brainwashed clones, dressed in uniform gray and blue, mindlessly stare at a screen with "Big Brother" uttering monotonous mantras of conformity and obedience. Suddenly, an athlete comes charging down the aisle with a sledgehammer in her hands. As agents of the thought-police chase her, she stops, swings her hammer and throws it onto the screen. Immediately after the words "we shall prevail," the image explodes into a mess of smoke and dust. The scene is an epic struggle for the control of information technology between personal computing and an authoritarian monopoly, probably representing IBM. The Macintosh – original, empowering and free – is victorious as the commercial ends with the scrolling text, "you'll see why 1984 won't be like 1984." Indeed! As we now know what came to pass is not Orwellian but rather Skinnerian because the world is not coerced into submission by an authoritarian government but consents happily to the massive behavioral conditioning of private companies.

Besides Orwell's *1984*,[21] there are two other important books that came during the aftermath of totalitarian atrocity: *Walden Two*[22] by B. F. Skinner and *The Road to Serfdom*[23] by F. A. Hayek. The former is a novel published in 1948, a year before Orwell's classic, and the latter a philosophical treatise published in 1944. *The Road to Serfdom* stands as a staunch and logical warning of the horrors of totalitarian regimes. It "[warns] of the danger of tyranny that inevitably results from government control of economic decision-making through central planning."[24]

Hayek saw coercive state planning as an inferior method of social regulation and recommended instead competition in a free market system, "because it is the only method by which our activities can be adjusted to each other without coercive or arbitrary intervention of authority."[25] Skinner dismissed such notions as empty dreams and found free market economics dangerous, as it pitted individuals against one another in corrosive contention. Neither did he believe religion or even democracy to hold the key for peace on earth. Rather, he thought it was behavioral techniques that would nudge people into an equitable and harmonious society. His dream was behavioral engineering of a perfect society working like a *superorganism*. In *Walden Two*, the fictional protagonist and avatar of Skinner himself, Frazier, dreams of such a community "running as smoothly and efficiently as champion football teams."[26] Perhaps Skinner came closest, but none of the three authors envisioned the operators behind the machine, as it turns out they are neither an inflated state nor a Walden-like commune. Shoshana Zuboff has labeled this age the *Age of Surveillance Capitalism*[27] and identifies a dangerous collision of extreme individualism and neoliberalism as key for understanding the birth of the media giants.

Let us return to Silicon Valley to see what happened. Hippy tech-nerds genuinely wanted to improve the world, but they were also drawn to dogmatic individualism and the concept of *laissez faire* capitalism. It is well known that Steve Jobs, Peter Thiel and other celebrated entrepreneurs saw Ayn Rand's *Atlas Shrugged*[28] and *The Fountainhead*[29] as their moral north stars. Technocracy – governance in the spirit of science, rationality and order – is an old fantasy of a world free of corrupt power structures. The sort coming out of Silicon Valley, however, acts more like *millenarianism* by presenting the digital revolution as the answer to all our economic, social and spiritual problems. In 2011 amid the *Arab Spring* and the global *occupy* movement, techno-optimism was at a highpoint and social media was seen as purely supportive of all things democratic. After all, a wired, interconnected citizenry could only be every dictator's nightmare as no wall could ever contain the internet.

Or so we thought. With hindsight we now know that social media is threatening democracy by spreading false news, creating distrust and atomizing our stories. British consulting firm *Cambridge Analytica*, for example, taught us that digital democratization was just a dream as they meddled in both the referendum that led up to Brexit and the fateful 2016 US election. The consultancy collected personal data of millions of Facebook users without their consent, predominantly to be used for political campaigning. Then CEO Alexander Nix famously bragged – but he wasn't lying – that with only a few dozen "likes" the company knew more about us than we do ourselves. By knitting together the most trivial postings – the emoticons and hearts we carelessly leave as we browse sites – and more sensitive personal information such as sexual orientation, gender, the color of our skin, intelligence and even childhood trauma, the company steered voting behavior with targeted advertisements. This most famous data heist is documented in *The Great Hack*, an unfortunate title because the company did not *hack* but merely used Facebook.[30]

On the internet, content caters to our cognitive pitfalls at an unprecedented scale. It is harmful for modern individuals and society, but incredibly profitable. Monetization works through advertising, and the amount of money generated correlates with user engagement. It follows that most social media platforms use algorithms to amplify content that captivates users as much as possible. Facebook specifically employs machine learning in its algorithms. Regardless of the issue at hand, the code adapts to feed users' increasingly extreme viewpoints and thus measurably polarizes them. With algorithms programmed to spread false news at least five times as fast as truth, science becomes a matter of opinion and the cults of *QAnon* or *flat earth* just alternative discourses. Disinformation and conspiracy theories are particularly engaging because they trigger our *flight or fight* instinct, forcing us to pay attention; the algorithms amplify them more than other content and the cycle starts over again.[31]

To see the many affinities between traditional governance and that which can be called *algorithmic governance*, one must overcome an antiquated and silly *libertarian* dogma, which states that only governments can ever pose a real threat to liberty. Silicon Valley already represents quasi-governmental power untouched by either the democratic process or the actual government in charge. A correlation – or effect – is the disappearance of many forms of in-person social interactions used to create, curate and evolve the fabric of social life. Democracies simply cannot work in countries of atomized individuals and must feature extensive networks that share a high level of trust in shared institutions and stories. Whereas in the waning years of the 20th century, the ruling of the people was still a strong ethos that kept Western culture and much of the polity together, 21st century tech companies have flooded the world with products corrosive to democracy, or even a shared epistemology. While homeland security is beefed up, cyber security is weaker than ever, and any adversary of democracy will embrace machines sowing discontent, mistrust and polarization. We have seen it in the US elections of 2016, 2020 and 2024. But it is not just foreign entities, as any politician would be stupid not to use social media platforms, as they are the most effective tools ever designed to clearly mark the lines of *in* and *out groups*.

Serious anti-democratic tendencies started to appear in 2009 when Facebook allowed the public to show approval of content by tapping a "like" button. In the same year Twitter rolled out their "retweet" button for endorsing and sharing a post with one's followers. Facebook then copied that with their own "share" function, making it available to smartphone users by 2012. Such buttons – now standard features of most media platforms – allow for maximum product engagement and the viral dissemination of controversy, misinformation and extremism. While it is true that technology has always outpaced regulation, this is breaking democracy!

Sometime in the early '90s, the internet was turned from a maverick idea like the *Whole Earth Catalog* into a gigantic shopping mall. After ditching other strategies for generating revenue, advertising became the default business model, simply because it was easy for businesses to start up as well as promote themselves to investors. Basically, the reins for generating revenue streams were given to marketing and digital designers. Above all else what mattered was (and is) *audience growth*, which is business jargon for gluing human attention to screens. The ad-based model of extracting revenue can be seen as a sort of fall from grace, a time when all dignity and shame was lost, and internet consumption was turned into a vast data set used to power the machine learning devices and to mine human behavior for possible avenues of seduction. We ended up with surveillance as the new status quo internet business model. A notable antidote to the current situation is Jaron Lanier's excellent book, simply called *Ten Arguments for Deleting Your Social Media Accounts Right Now.*[32]

The problem is not the screens, and it is not even the amount of time on them. Today, the average American spends 11 hours/day, or 65 percent of their only life, consuming digital media, but it is not deep-diving into one subject. Instead, the screen time is spent on tiny and multiple streams of content, making us lose the ability to focus attention. The elements fueling economic growth are no longer rare earth metals but human attention, and just like the former becomes depleted so thus the latter. When the ability to focus attention on any one thing decreases, then marketers need to chop it up more and more. The data mining turns to data fracking! The most successful players in the Attention Economy are Meta and Google. The former is a half-trillion-dollar business where 98 percent of its revenue is generated through advertisements and its very name implies the diversion of attention away from physical life to its applications. The latter got its name from a misspelling of "googol," a number represented by a 1 followed by one hundred zeros, and while that number originally referred to the amount of search queries, Google morphed into a digital Times Square – or *Blade Runner* scene – hiding behind a search engine. As of this writing, about 60 percent of its revenue comes from ads.

Online advertising doesn't follow your interest; that would be great. Instead, it competes for your attention by becoming a barrier to overcome. Just think of the constant clicking to minimize, make something go away and consent to get to finish reading an article. And more often than not you simply don't finish that article, as you fall prey to *clickbait*. Any outrage over the manipulation of personal data is short-lived and hasn't shrunk the use of ad-based services. End-users have simply accepted that some manipulation is to be expected and tolerated in return for a "free" online experience. Basically, tempted by "free" services and software, we have opted for convenience over free will and surveillance over privacy. As Gillian Tett points out in her *Anthro-Vision*, this makes little sense until we scrutinize the word "free" and understand the exchange of private data for convenience not as monetary but bartering. Through an incredibly consequential sleight of hand, capitalism cannot be blamed for the current situation because the transfer of services for data is not capitalist![33] After all, as the great Marcel Mauss remarked, "there is no such thing as a free gift." As this manuscript goes to press, Meta and other tech giants are introducing options of user payments as trade-offs for advertisements. We will have to see how the public will choose.

What Orwell absolutely got right was his observation of the connection between power and language and a resulting dystopia. When it becomes too confusing and too risky for our reputation to talk about certain issues, society tends to avoid them. And what Marshal McLuhan got right – although he made his predictions before this age of algorithmically powered exchange of opinions – is that the *medium really is the message.*

In all fairness, back in the '90s Silicon Valley probably had good intentions by offering people free webpage hosting and a way to make money. Paywalls would have blocked most potential customers since most people did not have credit cards – much of the world still doesn't. *PayPal* and the whole slew of online payment systems did not appear until the turn of the millennium. Ad support also allows us to "try before we buy," which through a powerful network effect allows platform services to scale to hundreds of millions of users. It also provides incredible content on blogs, podcasts and video sites to nourish our minds. There is no doubt about that.

Of course, the tech giants are all competing in a race towards artificial general intelligence (AGI) as well. After the success of *OpenAI's ChatGPT*,

Google's umbrella company Alphabet announced its own AI chatbot called *Bard*, and Meta is set to release its version in 2025. But this arms race of capturing and monetizing any remaining human attention will likely have dire consequences. In the aggregate, corporations spend billions of dollars and people spend millions of years filling human minds with disjointed flickers of information. And the welfare states cannot keep up as they try to repair their burnt-out husks of citizens. The actual money is made by designing attention deficit on the one hand, and gadgets that directly cause climate change on the other. My concern remains the same: should we hand over this incredible power to some tech bros with hoodies and moustaches? Sure, since they know a lot more about these matters than me, but only after training them in ethics, sustainability and anthropology!

Surveillance Capitalism

In *surveillance capitalism* there exist two types of knowledge, one expressed in text and images available to anyone online, and another, consisting of all the behavioral *data surplus*, accessible only by companies themselves. Internet *cookies* – chunks of code essential for convenient browsing – allow websites to remember the user, any log-ins and shopping cart contents. But they are also a treasure trove of private information for criminals and corporations to spy on. Typical of Silicon Valley euphemism, the data points on a meta level above our search queries – such as the time we spend on a site, our emotional response and shopping patterns – are simply called *data exhaust*. On so-called *behavioral future markets*, the final mile on the freeway to serfdom, *surveillance capitalists* then trade *prediction products* that are made from the public's *behavioral surplus* data. In the words of Geoffrey Miller: "Adam Smith's invisible hand has spawned the invisible eye."[34]

The largest of them all, Google's "database of intentions," understandably has antitrust authorities alarmed, as it can squeeze out competitors from search results once it becomes part of a business venture or stands for a given ideology. Obviously, Google knows what we all search for, but it also knows which businesses are communicating, and what businesses are searching, buying, emailing and planning. While their services are branded as progressive forces, they are instruments of despotism.

Unfolding in front of our eyes is the biggest natural social experiment ever. We are seeing what happens when smart machines insistently prey on human *evolutionary biases* such as for *confirmation* (search, focus on and remembering information that confirms one's preconceptions), *salience* (focus on items more prominent or emotionally striking) and *in-group* (favoring those who share our views) with a sample of probands numbering over three billion people. Everyone has been given a media feed that shows only what they like seeing and what keeps their attention as well as a megaphone to yell about their opinions, identity and achievements. One outcome of this experiment is the terrifying case of Myanmar. Viral fake news and hate speech about the *Rohingya* Muslim minority spread faster than all other content and escalated the country's religious conflict into full-blown genocide.[35]

Big Tech companies often know our choices before we do, and it is only a matter of time before they start understanding human feelings and emotions. In this writing the very real phenomenon of Big Tech also entering financial services has not even been discussed. Financial technology (*Fintech*) already offers payment systems, insurance, credit, wealth management and alternative currencies. Even the most vehement small-state libertarians would probably not object to counter-surveillance on the operations of Big Tech companies. Such scrutiny – representing one regulative approach – is noxiously difficult, though, because many of the services provided are "free" of charge and thus avoid legal bindings between companies and users. Sure, there are the famously complex *shrink wrap* texts that we all scroll down rapidly to "agree" and "consent." Similarly, we are asked whether we "accept" software cookies, but usually, not doing so renders the webpage useless. In other words, we can try to provide new adjustments to data protection rules, but companies will quickly find loopholes by annoying end-users into compliance. Paywalls, where users compensate Google or Facebook for the services they provide, would solve many of the before-mentioned problems. Another approach is imposing entity-based obligations and restrictions. It is to treat Big Tech like utility companies who often enjoy near monopolies by providing an essential service from which it is expensive or impossible to switch.[36] Especially during the COVID-19 pandemic – by providing connection tools – it can easily be argued that Big Tech services are essential and that we can no longer do without them. (After all, there are no longer public phone booths in case of emergency and working without a massive search engine renders business impossible.) Obviously, internet services are less vital, but the regulation of the water sector might be an instructive analogy because of the concept of a RAB (*regulated asset base*). It would not make any sense to dig for another water source – artificially creating competition – and thus water monopolies are sometimes accepted but checked for authoritarian tendencies. The monopolist's profits may not exceed the level that a (fictitious) competitive market would allow. The cost to an imaginary new entrant must be those of the incumbent's assets and then profits of the newcomer can be calculated. Current monopolies are then capped at that amount. In short, just like a water, plumbing or electricity company is watched very closely, so should internet companies. Such a utility approach would also require companies to "unbundle" their products, thus giving back users' control over their personal data and allowing them and not the corporation to sell it.

In terms of revenue, influence and power, the world's five most valuable brands are Apple, Microsoft, Google, Meta and Amazon. Collectively, they account for roughly one trillion dollars and they, more than any other company, organize human behavior in respect of what we surround ourselves with in material and digital products. Ironically – or cynically – they also all promise to empower people. Microsoft's mission statement is "to empower every person and every organization on the planet to achieve more," and Apple suggests that "technology is most powerful when it empowers everyone." Google "organizes the world's information and makes it universally accessible and useful," while Facebook wants to help people by giving them "the power to build community and bring the world closer together." Amazon has its infamous mission "to be Earth's most customer-centric company." Jeff Bezos, when asked about the secret of Amazon's success, has said that he is "obsessively concerned with his users."

It seems that the model *homo economicus*, a self-serving, always rational creature that always wants more, has been digitalized in the playing field of the internet. Adam Smith's "invisible hand" was the guiding metaphor for much of classical economic theory since the impossibility of total knowledge on where the market is going justifies market capitalism's insistence on minimal regulative interventions. That idea was completely wrong, as was another idea of Adam Smith, namely that human exchange moved from "primitive" barter to money and finally credit. Precisely the opposite seems to be happening. Big Tech exists because of the fertile soil provided by unregulated capitalism, but we must be wary of committing the naturalist fallacy, which is to say they exist and therefore they should exist. Simply letting things be – the *laissez faire* approach – will likely lead to abhorrent totalitarian outcomes. As we have seen, this industry carries a long tail of externalities, many of which are toxic for an open society and democratic practices.

Marketing, advertisement and design are employed as *behavioral architecture*, encroaching on the last vestibules of human action and always as a means to an end of capital accumulation. We have created a world full of distractions where everyone wants a piece of your attention and marketing agencies want to monetize it. It is everywhere, on the internet and out in the world, but like the air all around us we don't see marketing. Or maybe "mirror" is a more appropriate metaphor; when it is held up to our species, we see not what we are, but what we *want* to be. Marketing is extremely seductive because it offers empowerment through the display of our traits through the flaunting of different products. It represents the Darwinian paradox of the loudest sender of information. A conspicuous consumer who receives the most societal fringe benefits – just like a peacock displaying the most ornamental of feathers – is also the most hindered in a situation of adversity or predation. Likewise, we allow just about anything to be known about ourselves through the promise of getting what we want.

In the words of Gad Saad, author of *The Parasitic Mind*, "it is not hyperbole to say that [Big Tech] have more collective power, in terms of the information they control, than all the rulers, priests and politicians of history."[37] As stated above, through near complete market penetration, diversification and the transformation of products into services, Apple, Microsoft, Amazon,

Google and Meta have all reached market capitalization of one trillion dollars, which is a thousand billion dollars or a one with 12 zeros. Based on 4.72 billion internet users, 4.3 billion users worldwide use Google, which makes an incredibly frightening market share of 92.2 percent.[38] With roughly three billion monthly active users, Facebook is currently the most used online social network platform.[39] The vast data sets on human behavior, action and interactions generated by our use of internet search engines and social media platforms as well as mobile apps, virtual assistants, wearable gadgets and smart devices are called *behavioral big data* (BBD). As individuals move around, offline and online, the searchlight is inverted and their billions of tracks "educate" *artificial intelligence* on patterns of human behavior and eventually create prediction products, to be sold to *data brokers* and marketers, or capitalized internally.

Social media, history's biggest social experiment, is far from over. At the time of writing, it is a usability and UX research experiment with *n* being over 4.59 billion people, a number projected to increase to six billion by 2027.[40] About half of the global human population has been seduced into constantly boasting about and comparing themselves. Not surprisingly, during the lockdown measures of the COVID-19 pandemic, social media use spiked.[41] The problem is that the research results are not in the name of knowledge and science but sold to marketing and advertisement firms to cater further to shame, envy and desire. But what are we the subjects given? What is the carrot? It is the ability to address the biggest human population that anyone has ever been able to address in the history of humanity. Anyone can yell about their opinions, identity and achievements. Most everything written here has already been said in the brilliant documentary *The Social Dilemma*.[42]

Where compliance breaks down the stick is used for coercion through the threat of punishment. Not a stick but an especially big and bright carrot is needed, argues Yuval Harari, to make the proverbial donkey go into uncharted and dangerous territories. Big Tech giants are promising a utopia of convenience and equity that most likely will come at the expense of democracy and free will. Dystopia and utopia are not mutually exclusive and are rather more like two sides of one coin.[43] Through complacency, not coercion, we the people upgraded to wearable gadgets, smart home devices and powerful algorithms to help companies track, predict and shape our every move. The possibility of central planning was made real, but Hayekian zealots can rest assured that it was not a top-down governmental coup. More like a boomerang, it started bottom-up and then came top-down from massive firms. In defense of an open society and democracy, Big Tech's unfolding digital encroachment must be watched very closely.

Innovation

There is a string of words that have been totally overused in our society: "awesome," "amazing," "like" and "literally" are near the top of my list. But there is one – "innovation" – that has reached hyperinflation. It seems that every few weeks there is an innovation around the corner, disrupting all other things and pretending to make life impossible without it. Some things are truly innovative, others are just masqueraded versions of prior things. That in and of itself is not problematic since technically nothing is really invented and always a conglomeration of prior somethings. I call innovations *fake* when they paradoxically deserve their title but only by cannibalizing other true innovations. Everything is innovation these days. Products get marketed as being disruptive, game-changing and innovative, no matter if it is a genuine new invention or just a new breakfast cereal. Or the way the cereal morsel is photographed! Post Foods has demonstrated the power of fake innovation through marketing with their classic Shreddies breakfast cereals. Originally, Shreddies was sold as square-shaped pieces, but when sales started to stagnate and then decline, the pieces were rebranded by literally rotating the pieces on their heads and selling them as "diamonds." Although mind-numbing in its cheekiness, this example stands as transparent and even humorous in its approach.[44]

Consider the espresso machine as a second example. The fist patent of pushing water steam through a bed of ground coffee was given to Angelo Moriondo of Turin, but the "Moriondo" machine does not really exist; there are none left in existence, not even photographs of his work. Because he failed to brand his invention, Moriondo was basically lost to history. Business partners Luigi Bezzera and Desiderio Pavoni are sometimes called the Steve Wozniak and Steve Jobs of espresso because they did not make the same mistake. Bezzera deserved a new patent by introducing a filter and multiple brew-heads, and many other innovations still associated with espresso machines today. Pavoni ended up buying the patent and finalized – more or less – one of the biggest joys of modern life: the single-shot espresso machine sporting a pressure release valve was born and introduced at the 1906 Milan Fair. And it works well! Then in 1976 capsule coffee was born. After much street research, Nespresso employee Éric Favre concluded that the best espresso is a frothy espresso, a mixture of coffee oil, air and water; coming with trapped air from the get-go, the water is forced through after insertion. The result is a frothy espresso with no mess … in the place of making the coffee. Nestlé thus disrupted societal trends and made an extremely user-friendly product and created a very successful business model and service, which in turn is changing society's consumption of coffee. Drinkers of filter coffee mutated (with the help of George Clooney) to aficionados of espresso drinks.

It is estimated that every minute about 39,000 capsules are made worldwide and 29,000 are dumped in landfill sites. Most are made of aluminum or plastics. In its wake are an estimated 6,000 tons/year of aluminum waste from households worldwide.[45] Meanwhile, in Brazil vast stretches of indigenous territories are threatened by the proposed construction of the Belo Monte dam, designed specifically to aid the aluminum industry.[46] In all fairness – and when assessing the whole life cycle of a shot of espresso – capsule coffee does better than the baristas' machines. But that is precisely why I use

Nespresso as an example of fake innovation: why not try to reduce the upstream environmental impact of a clean downstream design? If the design brief was to make something that is used for about two seconds fully aware that people tend to be too lazy to return anything to a company, not to mention composting it, then I would say 6g of coffee in 3g of packaging is a design fail. Fake innovation!

Buddha's Nightmare

The Dalai Lama often leaves the refuge of his palace in the Himalayan foot-hills of Dharamshala, India to go on lecture tours in the secular world. One day he was passing a shop of electronic gadgetry on such an outing and said that he was desiring things that he did not know existed. With that statement he summarizes the human predicament of living with very primal software in a world dominated by the advertised signal. It is a very simple observation that any child could make but it has added gravitas when considered in the Buddhist context. The Dalai Lama also said, "We need to learn how to want what we have, NOT to have what we want," a slogan that would definitely not win him a job in a marketing agency.[47]

Over 2,600 years ago, Siddhartha Gautama is said to have reached a state of full realization of the nature of reality. The "awakened one" – the literal translation of the word *Buddha* – then told of this extraordinary spiritual experience in what is called the *Sermon of the Deer Park* in Sarnath, India. Most significant about this first sermon is not the account of the Buddha's experience – a total cessation of a separation of time and space and melting into an eternal here and now – but his instructions for any mortal to reach the same. The Buddha taught the so-called *four noble truths*, the foundation of what has been called Buddhism ever since: the existence of suffering, the cause of suffering, that the cause of suffering can end and the path to the end of suffering. *Suffering* is an unfortunate English translation of *dukkha*, from Pali, the language spoken in the days of the Buddha. A better, more revealing translation of this word is the "state of not being satisfied." While *dukkha* draws its affective texture and coloring from its connection with pain and suffering, and includes these, it refers to *un-satisfactoriness* of everything conditioned. This un-satisfactoriness is a result of the impermanence of lit-erally everything in the universe. It refers to the eternal itch of always wanting more and never being fully satisfied with the present moment. According to the Buddha, life leads to un-satisfactoriness whether we cling to the things that we like or run away with aversion from the things we dislike. In the first case we are bound to eventually lose all things cherished, leading to unhap-piness and in the second case the aversion itself is painful.

Brief mental states of satisfaction in the here and now, a state sometimes labeled as *flow*, is experienced as pleasant, even blissful.[48] But not desiring anything to improve the utility of the moment is a mental state diametrically opposed to the current economic order. It is poison for a society based on endless consumption. It is the nemesis to teachings of marketing and especially advertisement. Eloquently stated by evolutionary psychologist Geofrey Miller:

> On the downside, marketing is the Buddha's worst nightmare. It is the grand illusion, the veil of Maya, turned pseudoscientific and backed by billion-dollar advertising campaigns. It perpetuates the delusion that desire leads to fulfilment. It is the enemy of mindful human consciousness, because consciousness is content with its own company, and needs little from the world.[49]

Millenia before the label of the *hedonic treadmill*, the Buddha understood these mechanisms. One does not have to be spiritually inclined to see in this first noble truth an objective truth. Welcome to the *dukkha machine*!

Notes

1 Nirvana. (1991). *Nevermind*. DGC Records.
2 Elhai, J. D., Dvorak, R. D., Levine, J. C. & Hall, B. J. (2017). Problematic smartphone use: A conceptual overview and systematic review of relations with anxiety and depression psychopathology. *Journal of Affective Disorders*, 207, 251–259.
3 Panksepp, J. (2005). Affective consciousness: Core emotional feelings in animals and humans. *Consciousness and Cognition*, 14(1), 30–80.
4 Haber, S. N., & Knutson, B. (2010). The reward circuit; linking primate anatomy and human imaging. *Neuropsychopharmacology*, 35, 4–26.
5 Levitt, T. (1986). *Marketing Imagination: New*. Simon and Schuster.
6 Freud, S. (2014). *On Narcissism: An introduction*. Read Books.
7 Hrelja, D. (2017). *Marketing Is Persuasion and Persuasion is Marketing* (Doctoral dissertation, University of Rijeka. Faculty of Humanities and Social Sciences. Department of English Language and Literature).
8 St. John III, B., & Opdycke Lamme, M. (2011). The evolution of an idea: Charting the early public relations ideology of Edward L. Bernays. *Journal of Communication Management*, 15(3), 223–235.
9 Bernays, E. L. (2008). *Propaganda*. Melusina.
10 Häring, N., & Douglas, N. (2012). *Economists and the Powerful: Convenient theories, distorted facts, ample rewards*. Anthem Press.
11 Bernays, E. L. (2008). *Propaganda*. Melusina.
12 Bernays, E. L. (2015). *Crystallizing Public Opinion*. Open Road Media.
13 https://lawliberty.org/edward-bernays-prophet-of-spin/, accessed on September 20, 2021.
14 Elmore, B. J. (2013). Citizen Coke: An environmental and political history of the Coca-Cola Company. *Enterprise & Society*, 14(4), 717–731.
15 Keith, R. J. (1960). The marketing revolution. *Journal of Marketing*, 24(3), 35–38.
16 Adamson, G. (2003). *Industrial Strength Design: How Brooks Stevens shaped your world*. MIT Press, p. 145.
17 Slade, G. (2009). *Made to Break*. Harvard University Press.
18 Nelson, G. (1956, December). Obsolescence. *Industrial Design*, 3(6), 81–82, 86–89; Packard, V., & McKibben, B. (1963). *The Waste Makers*. Penguin.
19 https://www.newscientist.com/article/dn17569-consumerism-is-eating-the-future/, accessed on October 13, 2021.
20 Fromm, E. (2013). *To Have or to Be?* A&C Black.

21 Orwell, G. (1990). *1984* (1949). *The Complete Novels.* Penguin, p. 7.
22 Skinner, B. F. (1969). *Walden Two.* Hackett.
23 Hayek, F. A. (1994). *The Road to Serfdom.* University of Chicago Press.
24 Ebeling, R. M. (1999, May). Friedrich A. Hayek: A centenary appreciation. *The Freeman*, 49(5). Archived from the original on April 15, 2013.
25 Ibid, p. 41.
26 Skinner, B. F. (1969). *Walden Two.* Hackett, pp. 275–276.
27 Zuboff, S. (2023). The age of surveillance capitalism. In *Social Theory Re-Wired* (pp. 203–213). Routledge.
28 Rand, A. (2005). *Atlas Shrugged.* Penguin.
29 Rand, A. (2014). *The Fountainhead.* Penguin.
30 Amer, K., & Noujaim, J. (2019). *The Great Hack.* Netflix.
31 https://www.theguardian.com/technology/2017/sep/19/facebooks-war-on-free-will, accessed on April 20, 2022.
32 Lanier, J. (2018). *Ten Arguments for Deleting Your Social Media Accounts Right Now.* Random House.
33 Tett, G. (2021). *Anthro-Vision: A new way to see in business and life.* Simon and Schuster.
34 https://www.youtube.com/watch?v=spiB9wBRUps, accessed on May 4, 2021.
35 https://www.theguardian.com/technology/2021/dec/06/rohingya-sue-facebook-myanmar-genocide-us-uk-legal-action-social-media-violence, accessed on May 9, 2022.
36 https://www.economist.com/business/2017/09/23/what-if-large-tech-firms-were-regulated-like-sewage-companies, accessed on May 24, 2022.
37 Saad, G. (2020). *The Parasitic Mind: How infectious ideas are killing common sense.* Simon and Schuster, p. 42.
38 https://www.semrush.com/blog/google-search-statistics/, accessed on May 13, 2022.
39 https://www.statista.com/statistics/264810/number-of-monthly-active-facebook-users-worldwide/, accessed on November 22, 2023.
40 https://www.statista.com/statistics/278414/number-of-worldwide-social-network-users/, accessed on November 22, 2023.
41 Haigney, S. (2020). TikTok is the perfect medium for the splintered attention spans of lockdown. *The Guardian*, p. 16.
42 Orlowski, J. (2020). *The Social Dilemma.* Netflix.
43 Harari, Y. N. (2020). The world after coronavirus. *Financial Times*, March 20.
44 https://fameable.com/diamond-shreddies-rebranding-case-study/144/, accessed on May 10, 2022.
45 Kontio, C. (2012). Schweizer start-up greift Nestlé an. *Handelsblatt.* https://www.handelsblatt.com/unternehmen/handel-konsumgueter/nespresso-konkurrenz-schweizer-start-up-greift-nestle-an/7289618.html, accessed on January 30, 2024.
46 Calvi, M. F., Moran, E. F., da Silva, R. F. B. & Batistella, M. (2020). The construction of the Belo Monte dam in the Brazilian Amazon and its consequences on regional rural labor. *Land Use Policy*, 90, 104327.
47 Lama, D. (2009). *The Art of Happiness: A handbook for living.* Penguin.
48 Csikszentmihalyi, M., Abuhamdeh, S. & Nakamura, J. (2005). Flow. In *Handbook of Competence and Motivation* (pp. 598–608). Guilford Publications.
49 Miller, G. (2009). *Spent: Sex, evolution, and consumer behavior.* Penguin, p. 43.

9

MODERN OBSESSIONS

The Holy Trinity of Design

Far too heterogenous a group, *Design* – with a capital "D" – would never literally qualify as a religious body. It has no leaders, although some charismatic figures are imitated *ad nauseam*. Generally, and perhaps unfortunately, it lacks commandments or even moral codes. And putting aside college graduation, there are no *rites of passage*. However, I do see some common denominators when it comes to metaphysical ideals or guiding principles that influence designers to steer their creative process to go into one or another way. They are a complex mixture of cultural expectations and biological biases, consumer demand and creative supply. Metaphorically, I see *novelty, convenience* and *beauty* like a trinity of God-like principles worshiped at the altars of design. On top of this trinity sits another behemoth called marketing, whose singular goal is to monetize the matching of the trinity on the world's marketplaces. Perhaps the tone of the last few chapters is so bitter simply because I find very few other books that dare to criticize marketing. It is sacrosanct. As we have seen, it has reached near omnipotence in our economic order, and it is understandable that designers act in the safety zone of trends rather than in the risk-prone zone of true innovation to solve existing problems. After all, they too must pay bills.

Novelty

Without novelty there is boredom, and it is truly horrible. As we have seen in the previous chapter, a lot of modern marketing is based on the creation of un-satisfactoriness, which in turn is based on a constant pursuit of dopamine and opiates manufactured by the brain. Without any reference to or awareness of neurological processes, philosopher Martin Heidegger called boredom "an insidious creature." When there is nothing to do, we are left with only our

DOI: 10.4324/9781003464754-12

racing mind, and its uncontrolled chatter is unbearable to most of us. We prefer anything, even nasty things, to that. For instance, in one shocking (pun intended) study, Timothy D. Wilson et al. found that people preferred receiving mild electric shocks to being left alone with nothing to do.[1] It may sound utterly counterintuitive, but when we are bored, we are in a state of motivation. It is dopamine-opioid driven cycles of behavior that make us get new stuff. We are wired for *neophilia*, but it is cultivated and monetized.

Once again, we find ourselves in a situation of *evolutionary mismatch*. Behaviors and emotions once adaptive become maladaptive in modern environments.[2] Meaning in an ancestral setting was reduced to survival and reproduction and attention was dedicated to find food sources, not become prey, and have offspring. In modern society challenges have shifted and with them meaning has shifted.[3] Boredom as a negative emotion increases *novelty seeking*. It does so by motivating the pursuit of new experiences which differ from those that resulted in the boredom.[4] In an ancestral environment it likely made sense to escape boredom and take risks on new things. There is a lot of money in the realization that we have not changed that much.

The human trait of *novelty seeking* stands for the demand side in the marketplace of the new. As for the supply side – *novelty pushing* – much of the creative sector's efforts cater to this human vice. I think to escape the reality of a saturated marketplace we keep adding, no *duct-taping*, new designs to older ones. Don't get me wrong, *duct tape* is one of the greatest inventions of human civilization, on par with the wheel, fire and beer. Unlike just about every other tool needed in a given moment, it should never be missing from a toolkit. This American institution – part cloth, part glue – has an amazing ability to connect, seal and patch disjointed parts. But that is it: *duct tape* does not have its own, inherent function. I use it here as a metaphor for much of the design that I have seen produced and sold in recent years. Just like the tape is used to continue without fixing any root problems, a lot of design is dedicated to the concept of fixes to artificial problems. I borrow the term from anthropologist David Graeber's work on *Bullshit Jobs*. In the informative and entertaining book, Graeber presents a taxonomy of such utterly meaningless and soul-destroying work that a large part of our society performs on a daily basis, and one of his job descriptions is the *duct taper*. He writes: "Duct Tapers are employees whose jobs exist only because of a glitch or fault in the organization, who are there to solve a problem that ought not to exist."[5] Since there are always flaws in systems, a necessary amount of duct taping will always be required to keep an organization running smoothly. It is similar with many designed objects. Instead of being stand-alone systems conceived to solve problems of the real world, they all too often are like duct tape for created problems. What was the last object you bought or received that intrinsically, by itself, solved a human problem? Your hands-free device? While it lets you talk on your cell phone and drive at the same time, both the cell phone and the necessity to talk to someone not in the car are invented problems and the hands-free gizmo is the *duct tape*.

I am frequently part of the recruitment process for students at design universities. My role is to ask about their design attitude, or why they want to be designers in the first place. "To you, what is the biggest societal problem and how might design solve it?" I frequently ask. One candidate answered that during the Austrian winter it was hard to use the smartphone, because the fingers get so cold. "Put on some gloves," I snapped. "But then the touchscreen function no longer works," she answered. "I think we should make some kind of a see-through cell phone pouch that warms the hand and lets us use our phones!" I am proud to say that that design brief was aborted immediately after conception (and the student was not admitted to the department of design). Unfortunately, numerous such devices have been conceived, produced and marketed since then. *Duct tape.*

In 2016, in a totally transparent move, Apple removed the headphone jack on their iPhone 7, forcing loyal users to make a decision. They could either buy a ridiculously overpriced *dongle adapter* that fits into the lightning port and acts as a bridge – *or duct tape* – to wired headphones, or they could go like sheep to the shop to buy wireless headphones. Back then a petition to keep the 3.5 mm socket attracted over 290,000 signatures but obviously had no effect whatsoever.[6] Either way users decided, the design decision meant a lot of revenue for Apple and an immeasurable amount of e-waste. Apple has a history of changing component design in order to make older technology obsolete. Just consider the DVD/CD drives or data and charging ports in their laptops. Are these perfect examples of *disruptive innovations* coming out of Silicon Valley or incredibly irresponsible *duct taping*? Probably both, and definitely they illustrate the awesome power of design to change culture.

It is true: in my resistance to the *first cell phones*, I have often said that I would wait until there is one gadget that can do it all. I wanted the *Walkman*, the *Leica camera*, the *moleskin* notebook, the map, the compass, the encyclopedia and the phone all in one convenient super gadget. I would never, ever get lost and neither would any beautiful images or interesting thoughts. And I would have a soundtrack to my life. Now, I have one hand on the *super gadget* in my pocket and the other no longer needs to hail a taxi. All the old stuff was banished to the *limbo of things* or burned. In the Prologue of *Enchanted Objects: Design, Human Desire, and the Internet of Things*, David Rose writes of his "recurring nightmare." It is exceptionally well written and describes the new status quo. It is worth reading in full.

> All the wonderful everyday objects we once treasured have disappeared, gobbled up by an unstoppable interface: a slim slab of black glass. Books, calculators, clocks, compasses, maps, musical instruments, pencils, and paintbrushes, all are gone. The artefacts, tools, toys, and appliances we love and rely on today have converged into this slice of shiny glass, its face filled with tiny, inscrutable icons that now define and control our lives … Desks are decluttered and paperless. Pens are nowhere to be

found. We no longer carry wallets or keys or wear watches. Heirloom objects have been digitised and then atomised. Framed photos, sports trophies, lovely cameras with leather straps, creased maps, spinning globes and compasses, even binoculars and books – the signifiers of our past and triggers of our memory – have been consumed by the cold glass interface and blinking search field. Future life looks like a *Dwell* magazine photo shoot. Rectilinear spaces, devoid of people. No furniture. No objects. Just hard, intersecting planes – Corbusier's Utopia. The lack of objects has had an icy effect on us. Human relationships, too, have become more transactional, sharply punctuated, thin and curt. Less nostalgic … In my nightmare, the cold, black slab has re-architected everything – our living and working spaces, our schools, airports, even bars and restaurants. We interact with screens 90 percent of our waking hours. The result is a colder, more isolated, less humane world. Perhaps it is more efficient, but we are less happy.[7]

I will add another observation here: it has become so quiet in restaurants as the few children stare without emotions into screens. Fiction author Dave Eggers picked up on this theme of replacing our many everyday objects with just a few slick and convenient ones in his book *The Every*,[8] a delicious sequel to his dystopian novel *The Circle*.[9] One of the first scenes deals with an entire corporate department dedicated to first digitalizing and then incinerating objects of sentiment. In a kind of holocaust of the past all memories are annihilated to create a vast database used to direct consumer choice. *The Every* belongs to a particularly feasible type of futuristic fiction called *hard science fiction*.

Stanford University's computer scientist and long-time head of *the Institute for the Future*, Roy Amara, gave his name to a "law" of innovation. It states that we tend to overestimate the impact of a new technology in the short run, but we underestimate it in the long run.[10] The internet serves as a good example. When William Gibson imagined a world where all computers of the world were linked in his 1984 novel *Neuromancer*,[11] he predicted the profoundest of effects on society. Fifteen years later, when the *dot-com bubble* burst, this was clearly overrated. But now, another twenty-five years later, it has become impossible to think away the internet. Autonomous cars are in the early stages of such an Amara cycle. We are told that truck drivers, taxi drivers or any driver really will soon be redundant. But designing a society with self-driving cars is technically and ethically extremely difficult and likely will lead to huge disappointments and reports about how the forecast has been wrong. But then another ten years or so out, the pessimists will again look foolish as autonomous vehicles become a reality.

Of course, not all novelty is terrible and there are some very promising examples in what is called humanitarian design. I was lucky to mentor a truly inspiring master's thesis concerned with a novel solution for fresh water supply in Africa. The design student spent three weeks living with the Maasai of rural Kenya to gain insights into their problems concerning water transportation. She employed *cultural probes* using cheap, throwaway cameras to capture the day-to-day experiences of her subjects. This went well beyond *participant observation*, practiced almost a hundred years ago by the founding fathers of cultural anthropology Bronislaw Malinowski and Franz Boas; it was *human-centered design research*. Local design thinking combined with European capabilities proved to be extremely fertile ground for a sustainable solution in water transportation. Another student completed her master's thesis on schools for special education and again saw that the children themselves were able to spark her imagination just as she was able to empower them with modular furniture for the classroom. Or take two master's theses for improving the life of asylum seekers in Austria. There is hope.

Named after the 20th century philosopher, G. K. Chesterton, *Chesterton's fence* is a parable of caution. He argued that before demolishing a fence built across a road, sufficient information is needed. He wrote: "Don't ever take a fence down before you know why it was built!"[12] Designers are all too hasty in being novel and disruptive and often don't consider why certain things might make sense the way they are. Designs, especially re-designs, should ideally start with a workshop full of stakeholders. Simply reading a design brief, and then trying to make improvements on a given project, will likely crash a design project into an iceberg of unknown needs, expectations and constraints. However, I still witness a lot of designers putting the design brief in the beginning of the process with minimal or no considerations of other stakeholders. The classic espresso machines made perfect sense because Italians wanted coffee and did not have lots of aluminum to make capsules. As society, we are constantly violating Chesterton's fence, and that goes a long way towards explaining the situation we have referred to as *evolutionary mismatch*. Evolutionarily speaking, novelty seeking makes perfect sense – it helped us find new territories and liberated us from the caves – but when it is employed primarily as a way to drive consumption I cannot stand on the side and applaud.

Beauty

Thankfully, designers care deeply about beauty. Design is about composition, form, space and color; and rhythm, texture and flow. It is an incredible craft that takes talent, experience and vision, but the praise given to completed design often involves beauty only. The very word "design," as understood on the street, implies foremost aesthetics. The Goddess of Beauty (I will use the stereotypical female exuberance of aestheticism) wants the production of beautiful objects that are talked about for decades and illustrated in coffee table books. She also wants gorgeous spaces and buildings that make people feel healthy and grateful to be alive. To this day, international design focuses heavily on visual surfaces, and by simply looking at the curricula of design schools around the world, one can see that even non-industrial aspects of design, such as service, experience or social innovation are still subordinate to a worship of aesthetics.[13] Often, such worship is covert – few designers would admit to it – and they often display latent hostility towards art which they call a purely functionless endeavor. The very definition of design is often in juxtaposition to art.

In design – so the *Bauhaus* mantra – *form follows function*; in reality, however, form often follows fantasy. But there is no need for insecurity here, since beauty never was a separate component of some grand recipe to make paintings, products, food or ideas. It is not purposefully "put into" the object by the designer. Instead, it is an emergent property in the consciousness of the beholder. Considering that design is based to a large extent on the *phenotype*, so much should be clear. But instead of looking at *whether* beauty is used, we need to beware of *how* this powerful force is used. More often than not beauty is simply used to sell something. Beauty is a double-edged sword. It is the magnet that draws people to objects, just like it draws them to other people through *mate choice*. But it also gives design a bad reputation. By focusing on it, the discipline is seen as superficial, shallow and frivolous. This is unfortunate because it distracts from what design is capable of.

Arguably the greatest designer who ever lived, Leonardo da Vinci, defined aesthetic perfection as the state where nothing else can be taken away. This principle is called *irreducible complexity* and it has been addressed by many other great designers such as Dieter Rams. In economics, E. F. Schumacher long ago wrote that "small is beautiful"[14] and *minimalism* has become an important countertrend to *run-away consumerism* and materialism. In spiritual practices most traditions agree that personal growth is a subtraction, rather than addition, of mental and worldly content because personal enlightenment might be found in asceticism, not hedonism. Lao Tsu stated that in order to gain knowledge we must add things, but in order to gain wisdom we must subtract.

Many design objects are overly – instead of irreducibly – complex. It may be over-engineered, crowded with levers, buttons and functions. How many of the buttons on your remote control have you pushed? Indeed, products are afflicted with a terrible "disease" that Don Norman has labeled "*featuritis*, whose major symptom is creeping *featurism*."[15] The subtle art of taking away from an existing invention or prototype is so much harder in design (or any other creative endeavor, such as writing this book) than adding ever more features. Part of the explanation lies in the fact that design sits right in the middle of a highly competitive and saturated marketplace where each new device aims to stand out.

Or might *featuritis* be yet another *heuristic*, a universal cognitive shortcut with evolutionary roots? Fascinating research by Leidy Klotz and his colleagues at the University of Virginia seems to suggest just that. In an elegant experiment, subjects were asked to make a *Lego* model symmetrical, without any further instructions. They were not obliged to add pieces and could have perfectly well taken some away. Yet, the vast majority opted for addition rather than subtraction. In another experiment subjects received additional cognitive load and were asked to also complete an unrelated second task simultaneously. In that situation, they opted for even more addition. A classic example to demonstrate the power of subtraction in the context of design is the *strider bike*, which has proved far more efficient in teaching toddlers how to ride a bicycle than traditional training wheels and other clunky gadgetry attached to the bike. The design breakthrough came when something was taken away from the bicycles: the pedals. It is beautiful.[16]

New York–based creative duo Stefan Sagmeister and Jessica Walsh dedicated a whole exhibition and book in defense of beauty at the *Museum of Applied Art* in Vienna.[17] It was an immersion into all things beautiful and was supported by theories of psychological aesthetics. There is some irony here. After all, Vienna is where the before-mentioned Adolf Loos rebelled against the use of ornaments. Over a hundred years ago he argued that architecture belongs to the domain of culture, whereas art transcends it. It was his criterion for all forms of "applied art" to remain practical. Anything else is a prostitution of art and a failure to appreciate the functional.

Okay, slowly, let us look at this age-old conundrum from an evolutionary point of view. Indeed, decoration and ornamentation pose a riddle to anyone moving inside a Darwinian framework. Strictly speaking, art lacks functionality and trying to find an individualist survival advantage can be challenging. In his book *The Art Instinct*, American philosopher and art critic Denis Dutton posits that art appreciation is not culturally learned but instead an evolutionary adaption made during the Pleistocene. Dutton speaks of the *art instinct* and argues that the production and acquisition of aesthetic objects has brought our ancestors a survival advantage.[18] The blueprint for the things we humans design – hand axes, houses or smartphones – is never genetically anchored, but the potential to shape existing matter into new forms and in new ways likely is. As we have seen above, *evolutionary psychology* claims that modern aesthetic sensibility is a product of natural selection of those ancestors who responded positively to the environment of their time. It is also likely that humans value uniqueness in their appraisal of aesthetics. A bright blue flower in a bed of red ones is seen as beautiful, as is the small blemish on Marilyn Monroe's otherwise flawless face. We have individual tastes and value uniqueness, all the while wanting to fit in. This is why in the world of business we have come up with such oxymorons as *mass customization*.[19]

Philosophical aversion to assigning aesthetics anything functional dates back centuries. Already in his *Critique of Judgement*, Immanuel Kant (1790) wrote that a sense of beauty was *disinterested*, and therefore functionless. When utility comes into play, Kant spoke of *mediated pleasure*, while beauty causes *immediate pleasure* to the subject. Nevertheless, it seems perfectly reasonable to assume that the pleasure caused by viewing something beautiful is immediate – even when functionless from the observer's point of view – and at the same time serves a function for the well-being and survival of the same observer. Evolutionary reasoning challenges the Kantian notion because *proximate* and *ultimate* causation are not mutually exclusive, but rather mutually reinforcing.[20] Thus, I stand with Darwin and disagree with Loos: design has every right – no, obligation – to beautify our lives. I love it for that. Once again, I just don't think it should be yoked to beauty just for the sake of sales.

Convenience > Free Will

Above all others, in a brand-new throne, both beautiful and comfortable, sits the supreme ruler, the king of kings in the pantheon of design deities: Lord of *Convenience*. Here, akin to the paradox of the Christian trinity, novelty, beauty and convenience are collapsed into on, and thus some arguments I have made before are revisited. The new is always sold to us as more convenient and beauty often just serves as temptation. Convenience is cloaked seductively in layers of technological features. It caters to a whole suite of human vices, including laziness, boredom and apathy. Settings and situations are comfortable; the path to them is convenient. From our comfortable lounge chairs we can ask *Alexa* to order from *Uber Eats*. Convenience coordinates the affairs of families, clans and companies via *WhatsApp*, while making *Meta's* dubious business plan justifiable. *Wearables* conveniently quantify our heartbeat, while we stop feeling it beat out loud and put pins in all the places we have been to but not seen. But don't worry, dear reader who has made it this far: this is the last section of "darkness." There is an arc to this story and Part III of this book is dedicated entirely to "the light," to constructive input.

What really is at hand is what authors Gray and Suri call the *paradox of automation's last mile*.[21] Human progress is usually measured along lines of the tools and machines that we build to solve problems. But as one problem is solved, novel ones arise and thus we make more machines to solve those. But in automation, people are plugged in to do the work the machines cannot do. This is nothing new – after all, majestic steam-powered ships like the *Titanic* depended on more than 150 people shoveling coal into boilers day and night – but it is also the logic behind *machine learning*. End users are not spared as we shovel more and more data into machines that make themselves better. In a race to *singularity*, engineers, using on-demand *ghost work*, try hard to advance the frontier of automation. What make automation so difficult are not its technical barriers but rather that every time something like *voice recognition* or *self-driving cars* is close to being solved another social need or desire pops up. We could send self-driving cars to the curb of stressed-out office workers, but what to do with them once they are being driven around? They must be entertained, no? Or consider facial recognition capabilities. What seemed just a few years ago as horrible technology stemming from surveillance and war efforts was readily adopted for conveniently unlocking your phone. How did it get so good, so fast? Companies get rich from both sides of the *point of sale*. People *pay* (a lot of money) to *work* (by continuously showing their faces). The word *prosumer* lost its sparkle; it isn't the same. We keep making progress only to find new problems to tackle.

Michael Easter, author of *The Comfort Crisis*,[22] tells the story of two Harvard psychologists, David Levari and Daniel Gilbert, who a few years ago had a revelation while waiting in an airport security line. A security agent was just doing his job when he makes a child give up her prized mini pocketknife or, in the words of Easter, "a wheelchair-bound 90-year-old who can't walk or see gets the full-body pat down after forgetting she had a half-filled bottle of hairspray in her purse."[23] Levari and Gilbert thought about what would happen if everyone always stuck to the rules and never brought anything on the lists. Would security agents just take it easy, sit back and do nothing? They decided to conduct a study that explains why we are so bad at appreciating how cushy we have it. The study showed that the human response to a decrease in prevalent stimuli is simply expanding the concept of the stimuli. In other words, we just find new problems. The scientists showed a bunch of blue dots and then slowly phased them out. Instead of seeing fewer blue dots, participants stated seeing purple dots as blue. In another experiment, when instead of blue dots threatening faces became rarer, participants saw neutral faces as more threatening. Finally, in a third experiment, when unethical requests became rare, participants began to see completely innocent ones as unethical. Even when participants were told about what would happen, they reacted with what David Levari and Daniel Gilbert called *prevalence-induced concept change*. Michael Easter simply calls it *comfort creep*. Social problems may thus seem bigger than they are just because there are less of them in part because reductions in their prevalence lead people to see more of them.[24] What is comfortable today is totally unacceptable tomorrow. The goalpost is constantly moved, end-users never reach happiness and lots of money is made in the process. Make it all pretty and you have the *perpetual mobile* that dominates modern design. In the words of designer Jonathan Chapman, "True joy never comes from banishing all negative emotions and, to persist in blindly promoting positive emotional experience at all costs is to push toward an artificial future with no place left for sentient beings."[25] Decades of research by architects and designers, as well as geographers and sociologists, warn of a dystopian future where humans lose all agency through a mindless pursuit of convenience and efficiency.

As of late, products and services configure users to always opt for the path of *least resistance*. Everything is accessible: easy to reach and consume. Not just food, or media; everything has in fact become *bingeable*. Less friction equals more consumption. Let us take a modern use case, one that transpires a million times across the world. Consider it like a story, but instead of "character" we will use the word "actant" to stand for a person, creature or even object playing an active role in a narrative. In this story one actant (user Joe) interacts with another actant (a non-human device called *Amazon Echo Dot*). Joe is hungry and wants to eat immediately, but feels very lazy about cooking, heavy on his couch. In other words, his "program of action" – the "intention" to take up food quickly – is blocked by laziness. This is not a problem, however, since Joe can enter a relationship with *Amazon Echo Dot*, which mediates the *program of action* of Joe, based on its own *program of action* – ordering food. Now the plot thickens. As Joe and his gadget interact a third *actant* is born (actant 1 + actant 2 = actant 3), with a new, translated program: *ordering food for the hungry person who is too lazy to cook*. *Program of action* is a symmetrical concept since it refers equally to the intentions of Joe and his gadget, without having to distinguish between human and non-human on the level in which the terms are applied. Both Joe and *Amazon Echo Dot* change in the mediated situation. Joe is different with his gadget and the gadget is different with Joe. Both still exist but their essence has been transformed in their relation to one another. Obviously, artifacts are not authors of such *scripts* but rather their messengers. Designers together with engineers have written a script with a *program of action* they desire ("let people conveniently order food as we collect their data") into the cute, little machine we can buy for US $34.99 on Amazon.com.

At a school of industrial design, students were asked to brand a drinking bottle for two different companies of their choice. One student came to my office to ask my advice as an anthropologist. She clicked through her *mood-board* of pictures to give me a better sense. There were the stock pictures of tired office workers falling asleep on their desks, traffic jams and the soft cold glow of computer screens to show the urgency of her design intervention. She recited a design mantra, this time about work–life imbalance. We sit too long, spend too much of our time in artificial environments and become so sad, we don't get enough sunlight and don't drink enough fluids. As for the framing of the problem, she was spot on. The modern work environment really is a great example of an *evolutionary mismatch*.

It was the solution space that I found disturbing. Beautiful renderings showed a sleek steel bottle with a USB cable connecting it to a personal computer. The cable allowed for charging electronics inside the bottle and recording metrics of its own usage, she explained. Apparently, she imagined some intelligence, a little genie in her bottle. It would give friendly feedback as to how much water a user has drunk and advice on how much more they should drink. She also designed an application to serve as a beautiful inter-face between the bottle and its user. It was then that I lost my cool. As an office worker I am part of her target group but fail to see any kind of added value in a *smart bottle*. As the drinker of water, I am aware of drinking. And as a human being, I know when to drink again. "I personally also use an app. It is called thirst!" I blurted out. "My application went through rigorous UX testing of life and death over the last seven million years. Those ancestors who used the application, who downloaded it free of charge and open-source before birth, knew when to drink water. The ones who neglected to heed the warning of the application did not pass their genes on." By taking user responsibility away, was this design not exacerbating the *evolutionary mismatch* of office work further?

Design students gravitate towards a default of convenience. It is fetishized and leveraged by magic no matter what the design brief is. Tell them to come up with a future scenario of something mundane like buying a loaf of bread and they will invariably produce a scenario involving holograms, NFTs (non-fungible tokens) and wearables. Apparently, the future will not be analogue but digital, connected and convenient. The students are probably right and that is the bitter takeaway here. Not through random evolution but a disturbing kind of *technophile teleological bias* will designers make it happen. I guess Buckminster Fuller's statement of the best way of proving a prophecy is by designing a future is true.

Do I really need a little wrist band that tells me how many steps I walked? No, because I walked them! Or how about the sleep tracker that tells me I slept poorly? No, as I fumble to make another strong coffee! The *Apple Watch* telling me to breathe? Nope, nope, nope. Much of our novel gadgets seem to have one function only, and that is solving problems created by other gadgets. Unless of course the function is to gather data on users to send them more tailored advertisement to sell them more bullshit they did not know existed. But that would be considered dark, conspiratorial and anti-capitalist thinking.

Let us revisit Joe from above, living quite conveniently in the *Anthropocene*. He has ordered and eaten his *Uber Eats*, and now as he blissfully enters *food coma*, he tells *Amazon Echo Dot* to play some early noughties *Cafe del Mar*. An instant later soft beats and sampled sitar licks are playing on his *Sonar* system. So easy! So convenient! Actually, the effort exerted in this transaction is immeasurably greater than walking over to the stereo and selecting a song. That statement seems absurd to Joe, but only from his myopic and egocentric point of view. After all, speaking across a room to a little device resulted in Punjab *tabla* floating back to him.

The magic of this *artificial intelligence* keeps Joe blissfully ignorant of an immense network driving its interactive capacities. Only when we embody the experience can we understand that *no man is an island* and that *nothing is free*. That split second of modern luxury is literally based on scraping Earth's deep history since it requires batteries, microphones and network routers, made of elements that took billions of years to produce. It also took an immense amount of other, less tangible resources such as labor and data. It seems incredible that an *Amazon Echo* device sells in Media Market for under twenty dollars, or even that any money can be made on digital products at all. It might help to think of modern power relations in the shape of a gigantic pyramid: from indentured labor in mines for the extraction of minerals to the work of manufacture and assembly of hardware to workers cleaning up toxic waste dumps in underdeveloped countries, wealth and power is accumulated and concentrated in a tiny sliver of a social layer. Somewhere between the wide bottom and the pointy tip of Amazon – where a pharaoh named Jeff Bezos resides – are all the *Alexa* users. Seen in such a manner, the scale of the effort required dwarfs the energy and labor of Joe getting off his butt to select a song.

But Joe sprawled out on his couch is many things. By engaging in interactions with AI, he is a *user*, but also *used* as supplier of resources, as his voice commands are collected, analyzed and saved for the compilation of an ever-larger data set of human behavior. There, from his couch, he provides labor through his service of contributing feedback mechanisms on the overall quality of the AI system. Joe is a trainer of the *neural networks* at the heart of *Big Tech*.

The other side of human–machine interaction is that any details of the birth, life and death of networked devices are hidden. Thus, the *Alexa Echo* is a dark Skinnerian box. Also known as an *operant conditioning chamber*, the original Skinner box allowed researchers to study rats' and pigeons' behavior and their response to conditioning. Once an animal is taught to perform an action in response to specific stimuli, the correct action is reinforced through the provision of food or other rewards. The digital footprint of Joe's every interaction with his teched-out *smart building* is tracked, quantified, analyzed, and sold on the marketplace. *Alexa* is an artificial intelligence and fed into it are all the command lines that run a household, from manipulating light switches and thermostats to selecting entertainment and ordering food or maintenance. The Japanese phenomenon of *Hikikomori*, which means "pulling inward, being confined", might be a dark omen of things to come in other parts if the world, especially in the aftermath of COVID-19. *Hikikomori* refers to a total withdrawal from society and voluntary solitary confinement and includes up to a million Japanese people. Joe is different. He orders an Uber to leave. But before stepping out he pushes a button to close his window and quickly asks his wearable about the weather out there. It would have been more convenient to stick his arm out the window, but it meant a great catch of data for Amazon.

Home assistants are like black holes of data since the stuff we say does not *only* precede an action; it is also monetizes in the form of *surplus data* long after the action. While users are feeding and training the neural networks with behavioral data, companies like *Amazon* obviously use that same data to work with third parties such as pizza restaurants or media providers, as well as smart home device manufacturers, from dishwashers and lighting systems to stereo systems. By 2018, Amazon aggressively entered the service sector by selling *Alexa* as *Amazon Lex*, which allows companies to use its brain to be built into their products. *Amazon* is quite open about its aim to build a pervasive neural network where all forms of biodata – biometric, sociometric, forensic and psychometric – are being captured by their devices and logged into databases for AI training.

The range of things we can ask *Alexa* is always expanding since millions of households serve as unpaid labor by shoveling data into a machine that learns. *Alexa* is just a physical end-product, representing the interactions between humans and AI. It is the interface of an immensely complex set of information processing based on an inference-driven feedback cycle between human and machine. Every single response that *Alexa* gives is measured against what happens right after. Is the question repeated? Then the user did not feel heard. What if subsequent questions are reworded? Then the user did not feel understood. Did something happen after the question was asked, like a light turned on, a song played or a new product was purchased? *Alexa* is training to hear, understand and respond better to the user's commands and to build a more complete data set of their preferences, habits and desires. The machine learns more and more about humans and becomes a great tool for modern marketing efforts. The key difference between *artificial intelligence* systems and other forms of consumer technology is that they need to be fed massive amounts of human generated texts, images and videos in order to analyze and optimize their performance.

Couch potato Joe is also a buyer of gadgets, which gives him a set of comfortable *affordances*, but he is kept in absolute darkness about any supply chains required to power his devices. Even the corporations themselves often don't know much about what is happening, as is demonstrated by semi-conductor chip manufacturer Intel. With more than 19,000 suppliers in over 100 countries, they supply companies like Apple with processors. Apparently, it took Intel more than four years to understand its own supply chains, before it could start any efforts to clean them up.[26] Indeed, merely speaking about this subject we are forced to address a fractal structure of supply chains within supply chains, each with tens of thousands of suppliers. And the elements of components that make parts of products travel millions of land and sea miles and involve hundreds of thousands of workers before any product is even assembled.

And what about the *cloud*? All Joe's vital bio statistics, his taste in media, food and ideology, his purchasing history and ripples of life, will be safely stored in the cloud, that little fluffy icon. Where is that cloud? Certainly not above and insofar we can assign a location it might be an artificially cooled server farm of some corporation in the Utah desert. Vincent Mosco shows how the metaphor of "cloud" might be the most hypocritical of Silicon Valley New Speak: it stands in total contradiction to the physical realities of extraction of minerals, dispossession of human populations and the working conditions of the mines and factory floors along corporate supply chains.[27] Modern extraction to power the *cloud* requires thinking about labor, resources and data just as much as trying to understand European imperialism or the Industrial Revolution, but such processes are hard to grasp for the individual sitting on the couch. How much energy is consumed when using cloud services? According to a recent *Greenpeace* report:

One of the single biggest obstacles to sector transparency is *Amazon Web Services* (AWS). The world's biggest cloud computer company remains almost completely non-transparent about the energy footprint of its massive operations. Among the global cloud providers, only AWS still refuses to make public basic details on the energy performance and environmental impact associated with its operations.[28]

As to the storage of data, it is safe … mostly from Joe, provider of the data! The commodification of Joe happens in a series of steps. First, he quickly bartered his data for convenience. Secondly, the data is monetized as his behavior change is sold to third parties, like advertisement agencies or ideological institutions, who in turn encourage him to change his behavior of consumption and ideology. *Product placement* is no longer an ugly trick, as *influencers* have become a lucrative business model, never mind that many of its actors are minors. Any incentives to live outside of the domain of mega companies like *Meta* or *Amazon* are dwindling, as any parent who buckles under the pressure of buying their children smart devices knows.

Dave Eggers' *The Circle* is based in Silicon Valley of the near future and paints a dark picture of a mega corporation formed from merged companies like *Meta, Google, X* and other social media sites. It is based in a circular headquarters, enjoys greater influence over the public than the government and has as its corporate identity this mantra: "Secrets are lies, sharing is caring, privacy is theft." Incidentally, a few years after *The Circle* was published, in 2017 the Apple headquarters *Apple Park* opened its doors in Cupertino. It is shaped in a perfect circle. In the book's sequel, the *Circle* buys up a mega company ominously called *The Jungle*, obviously standing for Amazon. The Circle turns into *The Every*, a company with aspirations for world domination based on the simple formula of "convenience > free will." I was so moved by Dave Eggers' books that I started a correspondence with him using old-fashioned mail. In a handwritten letter to me, Eggers writes: "Always I have been less interested in what terrible ideas these companies come up with and more interested in how readily the vast majority of humanity embraces them." In *The Every*, humans are turned into domesticated pets – mild, neutered and docile but always ready to consume. Through conformism, sanitization, shame and surveillance they become spiritually bankrupt and utterly incapable of creativity. The characters of the book are a nightmarish but still strangely funny version of Nietzsche's "last man." *The Every* is the fictitious counterpart to *The Age of Surveillance Capitalism* by Shoshana Zuboff.

Techno-utopian promises carry inside of them dark dystopias just like the black yin in the heart of white yang. Big Tech giants are promising a utopia of convenience and equity that comes at the expense of democracy and free will. Through complacency, not coercion, Joe and the rest of us upgraded to wearable gadgets, smart home devices and powerful algorithms to help companies track, predict and shape our every move.

Although it primarily addresses the intangible business plans and algorithms employed by the likes of *Google* and *Meta, The Age of Surveillance Capitalism* is immensely important, scary and required reading for everyone; those conceiving and developing the trinkets, gadgets and devices we strap around ourselves, and all the webpages and services that track our behavior as well as those using all these things. *Surveillance capitalism* is defined as "an economic system centered around the commodification of personal data with the core purpose of profit-making."[29] We are becoming zombies, which have outsourced their very life to applications, devices and wearables all in order to not think, work and hurt. In defense of an open society and democracy, we need to keep a close eye on Big Tech's unfolding digital encroachment. I cannot say it better than Peter Schwartz, founder and executive chairman of Kognitiv, in his blog:

> Complicated times call for those willing to run headlong into the complexity rather than scurrying for the sanctity of simple. Hard problems require people willing to do the hard work, not those who'd prefer to lean back into the air-conditioned luxury of convenience.[30]

The emphasis on convenience has shifted *user-centered design* easy-to-use to easy-to-want. As design theorist Jonathan Chapman points out, so-called *user experience* is entirely biased on joyous, seamless and smooth interactions. Any inconveniences such as sadness, confusion or anger are designed out. He writes: "Designers have developed an unhealthy preoccupation with positive emotions and wholly constructive product experience."[31] For the user the experience becomes sleek, but not realistic. Design is focused on getting things done fast, but while time in each task might be reduced, so is the experience we call life. While obviously a huge benefit in many situations, such constraints shelter us users from some of life's most joyous opportunities and real moments.

Diversity?

The world is diverse, but cultural differences, idiosyncrasies and contradictions are shrinking. Back in the mid-1990s, Marc Augé wrote in his fabulous *Nonplaces* that there exist places without identity, almost like pockets of cultural vacuum. They are places were "people are always, and never, at home."[32] This interchangeability and symbolic blankness, once reserved for hotels and airports, has now leaked into the rest of our cities. Bars, coffee shops and co-working spaces all seem to be part of a global chain, cut like corporate cookies. Don't they share an aesthetic of modern comfort and retro-novelty: exposed piping, reclaimed wood, industrial lighting, minimalist furniture, chalkboard menu and fast internet? Even when they are not actual franchises, digital platforms like *Foursquare* and *Instagram* direct you to the same sort of place all over the world. A wonderful blog by Alex Murrell called "The age of average" describes how exterior and interior spaces, cars, products and even brands all look the same. Thus, a certain "Brooklyn Look" has become instantly recognizable as "International Airbnb Style" with its lofty sense of urban authenticity and *sans serif* slogans on the walls. If someone dropped Joe – or me – by parachute over a random city of the world, we might not instantly know where we landed, but we would get to a *poke bowl* and *flat white* in a flash. A kind of *urban monoculture* is spreading through our cities, leaving me yearning for the local. Many *mom-and-pop shops* selling products crafted with care have not updated and thus folded. *The Verge* calls this technologically created geography "AirSpace," homogeneous spaces that make traveling frictionless, a value much prized in Silicon Valley. And as we move around this world, posting trillions of pictures on channels, like *Instagram* and *Pinterest*, of course establishments about to open also want to look like the images of popular places that go viral; we have entered a feedback loop that will likely end in loud distortion.

Trend-scouts and *cool-hunters* are paid good money to study successful restaurants and hotels so that their data can then be copied and pasted into another cultural context. But as we saw in our excursion to the *cargo-cults*, copying successful business stories won't necessarily result in innovation, and as consumers we are all duped into being cultists of globalization. Human culture is not universal and generally humans don't behave exactly the same as others and thus any lasting addition to the fabric of culture must be sensitive to context. Stuff that works in one place will not necessarily work in another.

Are we designing a WEIRDer world? The cultures we label as WEIRD are not only where many engineers, architects and designers are raised and schooled; they also form a major marketplace for the products and services such makers conceive. Just like in the social sciences, drawing on a very unrepresentative, WEIRD-based sample, design research massively skews our understanding and prediction of human usership and consumerism. We are dealing with a massive sampling bias here, because as loud as the data might be screaming about this or that trend, it is often distilled from a WEIRD target group. Consequently, services, products or websites have limited value when applied to markets of other cultures. European and American design is to a large degree conceived by WEIRD people after conducting research on WEIRD people. And so, I ask again: through the forces of globalized media, labor and trade, is all this making the world WEIRDer?

Like modernism a century ago, modern *design thinking* offers "good" design, and whether purposefully or not, it excludes other approaches, schools and ethnicities. The result often is a homogenous design landscape increasingly full of WEIRD biases. None of this would be a problem were it not for the fact that designers see themselves as a separate "creative" class, one that knows best. This process of cultural homogeneity is really a process of gentrification by design. Local culture must be shared and cannot be possessed by an elitist minority because it needs to be learned and passed on to survive. For a thing, idea or behavior to qualify as cultural, it has to be understood by others. By all those criteria, we are seeing a massive diffusion of a rather homogenous culture all over the world. It is no coincidence that, regardless of my students' backgrounds, their English is always colored by two localities: their specific upbringing and Californian technophile slang. It seems that the world is getting a makeover based on a feedback loop between producers and consumers of designed objects, algorithmically amplified.

Notes

1 Wilson, T. D., Reinhard, D. A., Westgate, E. C., Gilbert, D. T., Ellerbeck, N., Hahn, C., Brown, C. L. & Shaked, A. (2014). Just think: The challenges of the disengaged mind. *Science*, 345(6192), 75–77.
2 Al-Shawaf, L., & Lewis, D. M. (2020). Evolutionary psychology and the emotions. In *Encyclopedia of Personality and Individual Differences* (pp. 1452–1461). Springer.
3 Lin, Y., & Westgate, E. (2021). The origins of boredom. osf.io/preprints/psyarxiv/bz6n8, accessed on January 30, 2024.
4 Bench, S. W., & Lench, H. C. (2019). Boredom as a seeking state: Boredom prompts the pursuit of novel (even negative) experiences. *Emotion*, 19(2), 242.
5 Graeber, D. (2018). *Bullshit Jobs: A theory*. Simon and Schuster, p. 40.
6 https://www.reddit.com/r/iphone/comments/405em0/a_petition_against_apple_removing_the_35mm/, accessed on November 23, 2023.
7 Rose, D. (2014). *Enchanted Objects: Design, human desire, and the internet of things*. Scribner Book Company.
8 Eggers, D. (2021). *The Every*. Vintage.
9 Eggers, D. (2004). *The Circle*. Penguin.
10 D'Este, P., Amara, N. & Olmos-Peñuela, J. (2016). Fostering novelty while reducing failure: Balancing the twin challenges of product innovation. *Technological Forecasting and Social Change*, 113, 280–292.
11 Gibson, W. (2019). Neuromancer (1984). In *Crime and Media* (pp. 86–94). Routledge.
12 Munger, M. C. (2023). Wild problems: A guide to the decisions that define us. *The Independent Review*, 27(4), 630–634.
13 Keitsch, M. M., & Bjørstad, N. (2010). Ethics in product design curriculum: An example from the Oslo School of Architecture and Design. In *DS 62: Proceedings of E&PDE 2010, the 12th International Conference on Engineering and Product Design Education-When Design Education and Design Research meet…, Trondheim, Norway, September 2–3, 2010* (pp. 120–125).
14 Schumacher, E. F. (2011). *Small Is Beautiful: A study of economics as if people mattered*. Random House.
15 Norman, D. (2013). *The Design of Everyday Things* (revised and expanded edition). Basic Books, p. 258.
16 Klotz, L. (2021). *Subtract: The untapped science of less*. Flatiron Books.
17 Sagmeister, S., & Walsh, J. (2018). *Beauty*. Phaidon Press.
18 Dutton, D. (2009). *The Art Instinct: Beauty, pleasure, and human evolution*. Oxford University Press.
19 Walcher, D., Leube, M. & Blazek, P. (2016). Gender differences in online mass customization: An empirical consumer study which considers gift-giving. *International Journal of Industrial Engineering and Management*, 7(4), 153.
20 Kant, I. (1949). *The Philosophy of Immanuel Kant*. Modern Library.

21 Gray, M. L., & Suri, S. (2019). *Ghost Work: How to stop Silicon Valley from building a new global underclass*. Eamon Dolan Books.
22 Easter, M. (2021). *The Comfort Crisis: Embrace discomfort to reclaim your wild, happy, healthy self*. Rodale Books.
23 https://forge.medium.com/the-science-of-your-stupid-first-world-problems-19a47dd78efd, accessed on October 12, 2023.
24 Levari, D. E., Gilbert, D. T., Wilson, T. D., Sievers, B., Amodio, D. M. & Wheatley, T. (2018). Prevalence-induced concept change in human judgment. *Science*, 360(6396), 1465–1467.
25 Chapman, J. (2021). *Meaningful Stuff: Design that lasts*. MIT Press, p. 95.
26 https://www.intel.com/content/www/us/en/corporate-responsibility/conflict-minerals-white-paper.html, accessed on December 12, 2023.
27 Mosco, V. (2015). *To the Cloud: Big data in a turbulent world*. Routledge.
28 Cook, G., Lee, J., Tsai, T., Kong, A., Deans, J., Johnson, B. & Jardim, E. (2017). *Clicking Clean: Who is winning the race to build a green internet?* Greenpeace, p. 30.
29 https://en.wikipedia.org/wiki/Surveillance_capitalism.
30 https://www.linkedin.com/pulse/simplicity-convenience-our-problem-solution-peter-schwartz/.
31 Chapman, J. (2021). *Meaningful Stuff: Design that lasts*. MIT Press, p. 92.
32 Augé, M. (1996). About non-places. *Architectural Design*, 66, 82–83.

10

HOW DESIGN STUDENTS CAN RECOVER MEANING

Anxiety

These are the best of times and the worst of times depending on where you live. While most of the world's population struggles to get by, the West is obsessed with novelty, beauty and convenience. It is a luxury obsession that only works by ignoring world consequences and treating them as mere externalities or collateral damage. The weather reporting app lets us plan our picnic but leaves us ignorant about climate change, and asking Alexa to sort out food obliterates the inconvenience of hunger. Momentary transactions can be so divorced of error and nuisance that worldly problems become ethereal. Still, or because of this magically convenient life of instant gratification, I find it hard to keep peace of mind these days. As a father, I am very anxious about the state of the world my two daughters will inhabit. As a citizen coming back from a garbage run with the dirty sludge of our civilization on my hands, I feel guilty. I am increasingly embarrassed to be human, and that is problematic when you are an anthropologist. As a college professor of mid-twenty-year-olds, I feel deceptive when I pretend optimism.

Students are gifted, they are creative and they are anxious to start their careers. They are also quite anxious in the other sense of the word. It is not surprising that they experience feelings of *anomie* and *cognitive dissonance* when they are trained to seduce us into buying new things in the face of societal challenges! When you combine these conditions and throw in some mood-stabilizing drugs, then you get *apathy*. I know from university psychologists, other professors as well as from proud exclamations of entitled students that Prozac, Zoloft, Adderall and Ritalin – all tailor-made to ensure that modern work demands don't render us dysfunctional – are becoming the norm on our campuses. Especially Adderall and Ritalin are stimulants that

DOI: 10.4324/9781003464754-13

help control levels of chemicals in our brains, which affect how well we concentrate. It is all so darkly ironic; many design students have a very hard time concentrating as we train them in distracting end-users!

Let us zoom in on our students. So here are young designers on the verge of becoming professionals from a generation that we have labeled "Z"! Why care about the future of anything when you are the last in line? Let us not get started on the ridiculous concept of generations (a child is born every second), but how stupid to start with the letter X? I know the term comes from Douglas Coupland's novel *Generation X*, but how dumb of the marketers to gobble it up for their peddling purposes. Why not start somewhere in the middle of the alphabet like the letter "H"? Or better yet, "A"? Anyways, enough of this rant.

At the time of writing, my students are all natives to a digital world that is always on and where everything is at reach all the time. Many of them belong to a cohort born between 1996 and 2010 of parents who stopped hovering around them (*helicopter parents*) and instead made sure that any hardship or discomfort is removed from their paths (*snowplow parents*). Many have been told that outside is very, very dangerous and thus they have spent a considerable part of their childhood and adolescence staring at screens and being otherwise coddled. They were told that they are fragile and need protection from anything that might make them uncomfortable. Now they demand protection because of a new iteration of an old saying: "what does not kill you makes you weaker." On our high school and college campuses we have installed safe spaces, and *offices for diversity, equity and inclusion* (DEIs) have made sure that only un-controversial professors stay. *Trigger warnings* have preemptively shielded students from emotional discomfort, the very symptom and only hope for someone to ever overcome a traumatic experience. Such developments do remind me of the so-called *hygiene hypothesis*, which suggests that our obsession with cleanliness and sanitation has dramatically increased cases of food allergies worldwide.[1] Similarly, we banish all emotional discomfort form our lives. Content warnings in our universities and works of art are what allergy information is to food. Just like allergens, triggers are on the rise, and just like there are more autoimmune overreactions to foods, there is more anxiety in the face of emotional discomfort. Such trends move in lockstep with our obsession with convenience and comfort in our products and services; all of it has only increased fragility and anxiety.

Truly heavy words like "trauma," "anxiety" and "safety" are now used far outside of their original, clinical settings. Such *concept creep* has led to everyday feelings of discomfort to sound like physical harm. Of course, there is a whole slew of banned or rephrased words on our campuses. For example, "walk in" or "white paper" are considered hurtful because they prioritize people without disabilities or white skin, respectively. On the notion of language as a political tool of manipulation, George Orwell was spot on.[2] But not feeling good all the time or being emotionally challenged is not the same thing as being in danger of physical violence or sexual predation. If my students don't like something I said, that's a problem for me the professor, maybe even the administration or the reputation of the university. Today, on this important learning journey that is university, we are preparing the road for the student instead of the student for the road.[3]

Many students are obsessed with group identity. They often start sentences with "as a woman," "as a member of the queer community" or "as a depressed person with suicidal tendencies," even when the conversation is about something that has nothing whatsoever to do with sex, gender or *neurodiversity*. At the center of political and cultural life now stands a strange ideology where everything is seen through a prism of one's identity. It becomes hard to have a conversation when influences are seen as cultural appropriation and influencers as culture! In such a climate, members of different groups can never, ever truly understand each other. Human universals and humanist values no longer serve as guiding lights for true equality, but instead offend. When I speak of the biological fact that we have more genetic variance within groups than between groups, students are confused. Wait, he is saying we should not racialize. Wait, as a pink person with polka dots, am I triggered? When everything is seen in terms of identity politics, then the whole project of anthropology, no of diversity, goes out the window.[4]

Design students are not trained in ethics and so all they have in the way of a moral compass is what they bring with them from before college. Designers hold a massive and global responsibility but are trained with a curriculum providing few, if any, moral regulatives. Of course, they are not told about externalities and consequences of their designs when the bottom line is scalability and net income. Why the hell do we teach *ethics* exclusively to philosophy majors, notoriously ineffective in changing the world? Why do we even have a field labeled *ethics* if not to use it in the practical sense? Was it not conceived as a way for a wholesome, examined and effective life?

Design students cannot wait to get out of school and work. They measure success on heavy workload, tight deadlines and as much output as possible; not *outcome*, which might be solving some urgent societal issues, but output! I am talking about mid-twenty-year-olds that multitask and obsess with building a portfolio that is more competitive than others'. Depressing as it may sound, once they are out, most will end up making impossible-to-recycle, meaningless objects to be used for as short a while as possible. I know for a fact that only a tiny minority of my students will go into the world with agency to stop wasting food, saving species from extinction, helping developing nations or easing the pain of suffering and dying that all of us face. The primary explanation for this is that year after year whole armies of bright young minds are stuffed to the brim with the aggressive art of marketing and advertisement for an unchallenged paradigm of limitless growth in GDP. What a squandering of design's awesome power in a pointless pursuit of increasing consumerism!

They are very aware of the competitive edge they must bring to the game. In an essay alarmingly called "Creative Burnout: Suffocating the Future of Design," Kayla Roles and Byungsoo Kim of Kansas State University found that while designers still enjoy the hands-on creative nature of their field, they dislike the competitiveness, high expectation and perfectionism.[5] The problem is that they are not immune to stress and the creative sector seems to be among the highest in terms of burnout.[6] In an ongoing query by the statistics company *Comparably*, based on the responses of more than 5,000 design workers across the tech industry, more than half say they feel burnt out at work. In the middle distance, in their early thirties, many find themselves empty, devoid of creative ideas and self-destructive.[7] There are other quantitative and qualitative studies reporting similar findings.[8] I have personally talked to several early-career designers who have hit the wall by burning out, but they all talked about it with some pride.

None of this should be terribly surprising. Whatever the symptoms and the number of patients, we must look at the incentives that drive creativity. When we consider creations as part of the self and see modern design as the dizzying whirl of trends that come and go, then design is implicitly self-destructive. If all you care about is to stay relevant, you will sooner or later undermine your self-worth – by default. As a result, a designer's shimmering euphoria and ingenuity often lacks depth because it lacks purpose. Or better yet, it is full of despair. To describe what I see among design students, three psychological terms come to mind: *anomie, cognitive dissonance* and *apathy*.

When the sky is the limit and "anything goes," one inevitably experiences unsettling frustration, for the simple fact that many things will fail. The general lack of purpose or ideals, standards and norms is called *anomie*, sometimes spelled *anomy*. In 1893, Émile Durkheim first used the term to describe the mismatch of collective guild labor to changing societal needs. Later, in his famous study of suicide, Durkheim associated *anomie* with the influence of normlessness: "One does not advance when one walks toward no goal, or … when his goal is infinity."[9]

I believe it is an apt term for students of design since their schooling misses most of the parameters provided by ethics and urgency of the real world, but while there exists sociological theory on the link between greater society and anomie,[10] none on the discipline of design and anomie. These are obvious generalizations, but I see current design curricula simply encouraging students to make stuff for a market completely saturated. In a discipline perceived as a major driver of growth in GDP per capita by accelerating consumption, students are often told to use as many resources as necessary to come up with ideas that can be build out of anything, manufactured anywhere and disposed of in unknown ways. They are working away on their semester projects and theses under an extremely myopic framing of the field; they have been given defective job descriptions. Outcomes, such as business success by way of industrialized empathy, thus often fall short. Whether it is an individual or group project, the jury of professors judge not along lines of usefulness for society but more short-sighted goals like return of investment and UX. There exist infinite ways to solve a problem, and design consists of a set of choices among them. The quality of design depends on how skillfully those choices were made. The more value those choices create or provide access to, the better the design is not just for end-users but also for business and society. When incentives are turned towards the creation of value rather than wealth, cooperation instead of competition things might change because, after all – as argued throughout this book – changing context changes behavior.

Beyond normlessness, I have many students who experience profound mental struggles, and I think I know why. For a professional designer, failure on moral grounds often coincides with success on commercial ones. The more agency you have for doing good or bad in this world, the worse the pain must be when you make things worse. There must be an inner war between inter-nalized awareness of a connection between throwaway consumer society and various socio-ecological crises and the striving to become successful designers. There must be! Rather than particularly traumatic backgrounds, design stu-dents often come from places of privilege. As a matter of fact, they either have a WEIRD background or aspire to be WEIRD, but none of that diminishes their suffering.

In short, by holding two inconsistent cognitions and actions, I think my students suffer from *cognitive dissonance*. In the mid-1950s, Leon Festinger developed this concept when observing members of a doomsday cult. When the leader's prophecy failed, Festinger noted strong proselytization by the members.[11] Design schools are obviously not cults, but their students are often tasked with simultaneously working in diametrically opposed directions, as they are asked to be part of the problem and at the same time help to solve it. When the preferred *consonance* is not achieved, they experience unease and anxiety. While *cognitive dissonance* has been studied among many societal sectors such as religion[12] or economics,[13] design has been a blind spot.

Much of what I say in class, much of its brutal realism and urgent idealism, resonates with students of design. But those are the good days. On the bad ones, I look at a sea of *Apple* laptop backs, and cheaper products that try to look like *Apple*, the crown of heads lowered as if about to dive into screens. Next to them or on their knees lie the latest iPhones or cheaper, black rec-tangles that imitate them. When the wall of apathy comes crashing down it is quiet in the classroom except for the sound of technology in use. Tapping, clicking, binging; an un-choreographed drone. Some are simultaneously *doom-scrolling* social media on their knees. From my point of view that is the random white noise I hear, and that is the harsh fluorescent glow of screens on foreheads I see. From their point of view, I am the white noise of someone rambling on. Only when I stop talking and when I shut down my PowerPoint presentation do they look up and see me. Sometimes the silliest anecdotes or angriest of rants don't work and it is a simple turn to their inner world that engages them in discussion. When the screen goes blank, when I stop pacing, then I ask a simple question: "How are you feeling?"

Reflections concerning feelings and elements of healing have become part of my pedagogy … out of necessity. There are days when classes simply cannot proceed any other way. I empathize with my students as I have occasionally also fallen into apathy. I believe we share a kind of *Weltschmerz*, a pain coming from seeing all that is happening to our living environment. Such pain can block any helpful stimuli or even good news from even reaching you. Worse still, it can lead to very unhealthy behaviors of seeking peace and finding oblivion. I know, because at moments I have stopped caring and then hope turns to cynicism. When it gets personal in class, the story of Parsifal comes to mind.

The 13th century chivalric romance made famous by Richard Wagner tells the story of a young knight who wanders into a kingdom, totally devastated and parched. He wants to understand the reasons for all the despair and goes to the capital to find out. There, the citizens are going about their *business as usual* and behaving as if everything were perfectly normal. But when Parsifal looks closer, nothing at all is growing, the whole place is a wasteland, and the people lack all joy or zeal. Instead, they are dull and apathetic, lifeless, as if under a spell. Parsifal goes to the castle and finds a pale king lying in his bed and dying. Since Parsifal was taught that asking personal questions is improper for a knight of his rank, he keeps quiet. Instead, he continues his journey and has an encounter with a witch called Kundry, who becomes completely enraged when she finds out that Parsifal did not even address the king's well-being. "How could you be so cowardly?" she asks. "You could have saved the king and the kingdom by only extending yourself." Parsifal is shaken up and returns to the dying king, gets on his bent knees and gently asks, "Oh, My King, what aileth thee?" As soon as he uttered this question, color returns to the King's cheeks as he begins to heal. And with that, everything else comes back to life; even all the people who were walking like zombies wake up from their slumber with agency.

Apathy is protective. *Apathy* is a coping mechanism to deal with both *anomie* and *cognitive dissonance*. It helps you cover up any inner turmoil with a protective attitude to distance you from situations out of your control. An attitude of "I can't be bothered because none of this matters" provides a sense of control. To illustrate, when it comes to choosing a topic for their theses, design students lose sleep over what to design. I have witnessed doors slammed in anger and tears flowing in existential fear. It is tragic that in these overwhelming times, students cannot find an issue to dedicate their time and incredible design skills on. Design must be infused with meaning again, and that can only happen when it is based on optimism.

As Karl Popper has stated many times, if we wish to have a brighter future, such optimism becomes our duty. In a lecture entitled "The History of Our Time: An Optimist's View," Popper said:

What the future will bring us, we do not know. But the achievements of the past and of our own time show us what is humanly possible. And they can teach us that although ideas are dangerous, we may learn from our mistakes how to handle them; how to approach them critically, how to tame them, and how to use them in our struggles, including our struggle to get a little nearer to the hidden truth.[14]

Nowhere is such an outlook more important than in a discipline that literally designs the future. Although, as I hopefully showed, some very careless design decisions have led to less than optimal outcomes in the present, there is no reason to commit the same mistakes now. While I strongly believe that global change must come from a shift in our mindset from parts to systems, we should never forget the parts. It is more important to change a small part of a larger story than do nothing at all. Let us emphasize this change with the people whose very job is to change things: designers, architects and engineers. Human life is regulated economically, politically and socially and all three domains seek to discourage selfishness and *free riding*, but for regulation to be successful we need to ask which human needs to consider, and how to address individual differences in the pursuit of public policy. In this book, it is my ambition to elevate the importance of current design practices. Rather than creators of unsatisfiable desires, I want my design students to become ambassadors of social and ecological sustainability.

Notes

1 Stiemsma, L., Reynolds, L., Turvey, S. & Finlay, B. (2015, July). The hygiene hypothesis: Current perspectives and future therapies. *ImmunoTargets and Therapy*, 4, 143–157.
2 Orwell, G. (2021). *Politics and the English language* (Vol. 2). Renard Press.
3 Haidt, J., & Lukianoff, G. (2018). *The Coddling of the American Mind: How good intentions and bad ideas are setting up a generation for failure.* Penguin.
4 Mounk, Y. (2023). *The Identity Trap: A story of ideas and power in our time.* Penguin.
5 Roles, K., & Kim, B. (2022). *Creative Burnout: Suffocating the future of design.* https://www.idsa.org/wp-content/uploads/Creative%20Burnout%20-%20Suffocating%20The%20Future%20Of%20Design.pdf, accessed on January 31, 2024.
6 https://www.limeade.com/resources/blog/employee-burnout-statistics-for-2023/, accessed on November 12, 2023.
7 https://www.comparably.com/blog/most-burnt-out/#, accessed on November 25, 2023.
8 Hill, C., Hegde, A. L., Matthews, C. & Reed, S. J. (2014). Seasons of our discontent: Do age, gender, partnership, and parental status affect burnout among interior designers? *Journal of Family & Consumer Sciences*, 106(1), 15–23; Pueschel, A., Tucker, M. L., Rosado-Fager, A., Taylor-Bianco, A. & Sullivan, G. (2018). Priming students for success through energy management: The balancing act. *Journal of Instructional Pedagogies*, 20.
9 Durkheim, É. (1979). *Suicide: A study in sociology* [1897]. Translated by J. A. Spaulding and G. Simpson. The Free Press, p. 248.

10 Marks, S. (1974). Durkheim's theory of anomie. *American Journal of Sociology*, 329–363.
11 Festinger, L., & Riecken, H. W. & Schachter, S. (1956). *When Prophecy Fails.* University of Minnesota Press, pp. 252–259.
12 Burris, C. T., Harmon-Jones, E. & Tarpley, W. R. (1997). By faith alone: Religious agitation and cognitive dissonance. *Basic and Applied Social Psychology*, 19, 17–31.
13 Akerlof, G. A., & Dickens, W. T. (1982). *The Economic Consequences of Cognitive Dissonance.* The American Economic Review.
14 Popper, K. R. (1986). The history of our time: An optimist's view. *World Affs.*, 149 (3), 119.

PART III

The Department of the Future Designer

11

A NEW CURRICULUM FOR DESIGN SCHOOLS

Evolution is, to use Richard Dawkins' metaphor, a *blind watchmaker*. Every type of evolution always leads to an outcome, albeit not necessarily a desirable one. For example, cancer cells are adaptive relative to others but certainly not desirable for their host. But all treatments of cancer agree on the basic evolutionary principle of selecting for cooperative units and fighting dysfunctional cancer cells. Similarly, albeit on a much larger scale, Thomas Hobbes' *Leviathan* shows that cooperation works well in times of peace and war but only when there is cohesion among individuals. Individuals are always connected to one another, be it cooperation, competition or aggressive conflict, depending on the situational context. It is the social norms and the structure of institutions that help reduce individual level variation and competition, thereby shifting selection principles to the level of the group. For groups to prosper in the evolutionary process, the same regulative principles for individuals are required to thrive. At the most macroscopic position, global challenges urgently call for international institutions enabling multilateral cooperation. Such a multilateral and supra-national approach will be weaker than the national ones, but hopefully sufficient for addressing global problems such as climate change.

Humans have guided evolution for millennia by conducting its different streams to their liking. For example, we have agreed on rules of grammar and syntax for our language, in trade we have come up with rules of economic conduct and we have changed our plants and animals in what is known as domestication. Humans have always tried just a little bit harder and reached for solutions in what is called *culture change*. But rather than *utopia*, which literally means "no place," let us use Kevin Kelly's *protopia* for that place, just a little bit better than before.[1] No matter the term, if we want to steer our human evolution into a better rather than worse future, we must do just that:

DOI: 10.4324/9781003464754-15

steer. Regrettably, *culture change* is often likened with the horrors of *social Darwinism* where one group of people is selected to live and proliferate, and another is not. But if we take the other extreme stance, that of agnostics and apathy, culture will take its course anyway. In our current system of unregulated pursuit of self-interest, we will most probably not like the outcome because ecological devastation, just like unregulated proliferation of cancer cells, often leads to death.

Systems analyst Donella Meadows has identified different "leverage points" within complex social systems where relatively small changes can produce seismic shifts. She considers "parameters" such as governmental taxes, norms and subsidies to be of a lower level because they rarely cause substantial changes. Meadows believes that far more effective are changes in punishments, incentives and constraints, the "rules" of the system and in "self-organization," basically the ability to re-design the structure of the system itself. Finally, on top of Meadows' list of effective culture change are "goals" (the system's purpose) and "paradigms" (the mindset and shared agreements about the nature of the system).[2] We now have an immense database on when humans act in a kind and respectful way with each other and their environment and when no such behavior is displayed. If we want a certain human behavior to thrive without falling into the throes of populist politics on both the left and right, "we must play the role of selective agent for self-organizing processes in modern life," in the words of David Sloan Wilson.[3]

In case you have not noticed, this book is quite opinionated. Certain human behavioral traits are presented as "better" than others, but this is because I am an evolutionist and appreciate what has brought human happiness in the past, what hasn't and the circumstances responsible. I have done my best to support their adaptiveness for humans and the rest of the planet through scientific sources. Let us revisit *pro-sociality* as an example. It is no coincidence that small tribes have been the ideal size for humans throughout evolutionary history, but this can only happen when individual goals align with other individuals of the group and when resource allocation is managed in a fair and equitable manner. Only then can productive and pro-social *communities be formed. Pro-sociality* must be fostered, and groups must be granted the right to manage their own use of resources, language, currency, food and other raw materials without stepping on the toes of other groups of individuals. Such groupings can comprise a functioning society, which in turn can live in harmony with other societies. Thus, *pro-sociality*, more than an idea, forms a prerequisite for sustainable life on earth.

Another important behavioral trait I favor is sustainability. Currently, in the *linear economy*, we are designing to sustain the garbage bin, used here in the wider sense to include landfills and incinerators. If that sounds like a strange sentence, think about the fact that in no natural systems are garbage bins found. We are the only species that conceived them! Every system produces *waste*, but we produce *garbage*, mountains of it. We produce it because we are lazy apes and when given the path of least resistance, we will take our Starbucks coffee "to go" instead of lugging a mug around. And we produce it because the brief possession and annihilation of resources strangely remains a signal of affluence when done conspicuously. But then the garbage lies all around, looks gross and smells yucky and we try to get rid of it by throwing it up, down, left and right. Throwing it *away* is impossible in a hermetically sealed system, which this planet is. The human species really is full of irony, because tidy streets are a country's pride and joy; they act like a developmental patch of honor to show that everything is *thrown away*. If, on the other hand, incentives for repairability, reuse, sharing and recycling of commodities were fostered through the very design of those commodities, things would change.

Okay, let us address the gigantic *elephant in this book*. It is everywhere and all over this book. Can you spot it? Indeed, we are faced with a *platonic dilemma*, since I want to elevate designers to the level of politics, to be gatekeepers of the reasonable and wholesome. But who selects and educates them in our universities? Should it be private companies, with decisions based on portfolios? From the bridges that we drive over, the smartphones we use and the check-in procedure of an airline, design affects us all. It seems crazy to base decisions concerning the hiring of designers entirely on for-profit motivations since a lot of their creations are in the public sphere. Instead, should the state select the best designers top-down? And once they have been admitted to university, who chooses the content of their curriculum? This is not an argument for a kind of super-national system of *platonic philosopher kings*. Instead, I see designers as representatives of the general public, experts who help the establishment and maintenance of smaller, local units of self-governance. I take notions of *co-creation, participatory design* and *inclusive design* very seriously and see the role of designers changing in line with technological advances and societal development towards a participation society.

Before we go any further, let us revisit David Sloan Wilson's metaphor of the *ivory archipelago*, introduced in the first part of this book. Members of academic disciplines tend to deal only with each other and thus develop idiosyncrasies, dialects and disciplinary jargon, all too often indiscernible to anyone outside. Unfortunately, the same holds true for design. Does the *service designer* talk with the *product designer* and *transportation designer* to conceive cleaner cities? Sometimes, but do they then go over and talk with ecologists, behavioral scientists and psychologists? Rarely! It seems so obvious that especially those designing cities, or software, or hardware – all of which mandate our collective future – should study lots and lots of ecology, behavioral science and psychology. And then they should head over and speak to ethicists and anthropologists, or really anyone else who might provide some insights. As all stakeholders, from designers and product managers to end-users, are marooned on their own islands, their thoughts and opinions are unnecessarily partitioned. The water between the islands acts as barriers to any kind of unification of design wisdom. As we have seen, when left alone on its island, design tends to migrate towards human folly and vice through a focus on novelty, beauty and convenience. Only when the design process is truly democratized can ignorance and the fear of looming technocracy be lessened.

To build necessary bridges between the islands of the archipelago, I thus propose to move the design department. Literally! I don't think it should be in the arts department building, nor should it be in the engineering one. Neither should it be in the business department. Instead, let us move it to the department of public policy! Why? For the simple reason that design creates the future more predictably and more powerfully than art, engineering and business combined. Better yet, let us make our own "department of the future designer"! It could be like a hive of creativity populated with designers and engineers alongside anthropologists, sociologists and ecologists, to name but a few. This department might also be called the "department of the humanities of the future," since always looking in the past for ancient codes of ethics and ways of building things, although important, is much less important than turning to the people creating the future. Should we not be concerned with the machines and forms of intelligence we are building now? Whatever the name, in the new department we must teach a value system based on human sciences combined with the skill set surrounding *design thinking*. But to tackle the really big problems, we need an army of economists, biologists, anthropologists and designers to leave their respective islands to meet on common ground and work together. The overarching theme of the department is the design of alternative cultural *symbotypes.*

Teachers in the *department of the future designer* would be a rotating assembly of experts who are prevented from grabbing power through either the type of task they have or the time they are active in each task, and the curriculum would be based on systemic, human, ethical and qualitative thinking. Upon graduation, students should roll up their sleeves and contribute to the most important challenge of our times, which can only happen with a fluid connection between science, design and public policy. We must stop cloaking agendas in jargon of complexity and design with informed intention, because while complexity makes a small selection of people feel smart, simple stories get lots of people to act together. In the final pages of this book, I will create a kind of prototype for a curriculum of a *department of future designers*. Obviously design skills like modeling, rendering, business planning and marketing would be taught alongside, or better yet intertwined with, the content I am suggesting here.

Paleo Design Camp

In the words of health and fitness journalist Michael Easter, "we are living progressively sheltered, sterile, temperature-controlled, overfed, underchallenged, safety-netted lives."[4] On the one hand this is great, because we no longer face the calamities of the past, but on the other we have become increasingly vulnerable to what failures of the edifices we built around us might bring. I also believe that as a species, more than ever, we must keep our dignity and integrity; we must also show gratitude since every single one of us is the descendant of surviving groups, testimonials of incredible trials and tribulations. Science basically confirms that our ancestors were on one enormous camping trip, one that spanned thousands of generations and hundreds of thousands of miles. Daily, early hunters and gatherers ran and walked about 30 km a day, and while we call such a feat "marathon," they were "getting dinner." As they walked, they were carrying tools, food, water canisters and babies.[5] We have degenerated to probably being the least fit ever; now that we have constant access to shelter and food, we have turned soft and unimaginative in the face of challenges. We prefer to be entertained than have our own adventures. In many industrialized nations, few physical challenges remain. Throughout this book I have suggested that the original designers were our hominid ancestors and that design thinking as a creative process is archaic. I have also argued that so many of the things designed to make our lives easier are actually causes of physical and mental problems.

While all such ideas might be understood rationally, they must also be felt viscerally. There is no better place to learn all of that, and much more, than out in nature. I suggest that students in the very first semester go on a camping trip. Welcome to *Paleo Design Camp*! And I am not talking about luxurious *glamping*, but rather a no-frills adventure into the outback. Students will leave all tools of distraction (phones, tablets, books) at home and only take the essentials for survival (food, material for building shelters, clothing and sleeping bags). *Evolutionary mismatch* theory would become blatantly obvious when the comfort of home is removed. The trip would occur before any of the formal academic courses so that students could experience important principles before intellectualizing them. After pitching the *Paleo Design Camp* here, I will introduce the parts of the design curriculum below. Students also need get to know each other and bond as a group by working together. And most of all, they need to understand deeply what it is to be human. The group would have to take care of getting to the campsite, building shelters, organizing and rationing food, dividing labor and getting along, which is to say become product, strategic and circular designers.

A popular exercise for teaching design thinking and encouraging group work is the *spaghetti challenge*. The task is simple: teams must build a free-standing structure out of some sticks of uncooked spaghetti, some masking tape, some string and one marshmallow. The challenge is usually done with a time constraint and as a competition, where the team with the largest tower and the marshmallow at the very top wins. Forget spaghetti and forget marshmallows! Let us not be divisive and as one team let us walk out of the classroom and into the wild. In *Paleo Design Camp* we would build one shelter in one group and the time constraint would be darkness falling. There could be endless variations on what students are allowed to bring in terms of material, from tarps, sticks and nails to absolutely nothing.

Students would naturally become acquainted with *jugaad*, or *frugal innovation* – defined as improvisational problem solving with limited resources – because that is basically the essence of camping. They would adopt principles of the *circular economy* simply because there is no extra supply coming in from the outside. As we saw, there is much reason to put our bets on the creative sector for coming up with and implementing sustainable solutions, but they need to learn it for themselves. Like the *experimental archaeologist* we briefly met in the first section, students would test any hypotheses by replicating or approximating the circumstances of ancient cultures as they deal with the various discomforts of camping.

The *eight design principles for successful commoning* by Elinor Ostrom perfectly align with the basic evolutionary dynamics of cooperation generally, and the history of the human species specifically. Just like I am only mentioning them superficially here and will go into depth in Chapter 13, our cohort of students would *experience* the validity of the *design principles* on the ground, in the field, before learning about them in the classroom.

Clearly defined groups. Here the group is a cohort of young design students in the very first weeks of their education. *Paleo Design Camp* would show students what Nicholas Christakis means by the *social suite of humanity* because strangers helping strangers occurs mostly during communal challenges.[6]

Proportional equivalence between benefits and costs. There should be a fair relationship between costs put into the camp facilities (construction and maintenance duties of camp) and the benefits received from them (enjoyable camp experience). Students will learn very quickly that "divided they fall and together they stand" and experience first-hand why the *free rider* is problematic in any communal effort.

Collective-choice arrangements. Rules should be dictated by campers and local ecological needs. Practitioners should use the resources (time, space, technology and the quantity of a resource) available in a given and appropriate context. Consensual drafting of policy prevents bullying of single group members and mobbing of many against one. So-called townhall meetings are extremely important in any democratic process and campsites were likely the perfect "townhalls" for most of human evolution.

Monitoring. For the maintenance of *Paleo Design Camp*, the allocation of resources and the safety of the practitioners, there must be a supervisor or a board of trustees. Some kind of monitoring system must be in place for the simple fact that an individual sneaking into the supply tent at night to binge on all the energy bars jeopardizes the success of the group.

Graduated sanctions. A free rider or otherwise offender of the rules and regulations of a group can face expulsion from the group. Since expulsion from hominid campsites surely meant death, it still causes much anxiety for modern humans when facing the aspect of leaving a group. In *Paleo Design Camp* there must exist a system of warnings and feedback sessions followed by formal and informal sanctions for those who break the rules (of not gorging on everyone's energy bars).

Conflict resolution mechanisms. All members of *Paleo Design Camp* should be granted the right for mediation where nobody is shut out. Conflict resolution is especially important in a camping situation since the very success of the undertaking hinges on group harmony. Since group conflict tends to arise in challenging situations (storm coming), it must be fast and efficient. But since *Paleo Design Camp* is also about bonding, a feedback session can be fun.

Minimal recognition of rights to organize. For most of our evolutionary history, everyone lived in small groups responsible for their own organization and only in a recent development have groups lived within larger structures like nation states. The failure to comply with subordinate laws is one of the reasons communes, sects and cults of the past have imploded. *Paleo Design Camp* rules count for nothing if a higher local authority (e.g., the university campus) doesn't recognize them as legitimate. However, camp should remain independent of its own affairs.

For a world of groups within a larger social system, there must be coordination and communication among all. Though issues can usually be managed locally, some might need wider regional attention. Just as an irrigation network might depend on a river that others also draw on upstream, *Paleo Design Camp* might relate to other campers locally, the closest city or the state regionally.

Paleo Design Camp will be tough and existential at times. But it will also be fun and surely it will be pedagogically valuable. After many failures – or might we call them iterations – students *will* succeed as they set up – and maintain – a working campsite. Their approach will be *open-source* and it will be *strategic.* As they come up with creative solutions they will come up with a mini version of *pro-social* and *circular* life. I predict all of this simply because the students are human and everything mentioned in this section has been proven to work for humans cooperating on common challenges. How do I know this? Because we are all here as living proof!

Notes

1 Kelly, K. (2011). *What Technology Wants.* Penguin.
2 Meadows D. (2010). Leverage points: Places to intervene in a system. *Solutions*, 1, 41–49.
3 Wilson, D. S. (2015). *Does Altruism Exist? Culture, genes, and the welfare of others.* Yale University Press, p. 147.
4 Easter, M. (2021). *The Comfort Crisis: Embrace discomfort to reclaim your wild, happy, healthy self.* Rodale Books, p. 6.
5 Pontzer, H., Wood, B. M. & Raichlen, D. A. (2018). Hunter-gatherers as models in public health. *Obesity Reviews*, 19, 24–35.
6 Christakis, N. A. (2019). *Blueprint: The evolutionary origins of a good society.* Hachette.

12

MODULE ONE: DESIGN FOR SUSTAINABLE SYSTEMS

Once our students are back from *Paleo Design Camp*, they are ready to begin their formal education in design, and one of the first lessons will be on the reality of limited scalability. Growth and development are both good. Of course they are, because without them we would all still sit in some Paleolithic cave (or remain blissfully but stagnantly in our design camp). It is the doctrine of "infinite and at-all-costs" growth that cannot work and must change. Economic systems with never-ending growth are impossible, but they can thrive within limits. Nothing short of a re-design for global industrialism based on value rather than only growth in GDP, Kate Raworth's *Doughnut Economics* is required reading for the *future designer*. The entire book is based on an incredibly simple illustration of a doughnut or a circle within a larger circle. The goal for 21st century economists, Raworth argues, is to reach the figuratively sweet (just, safe and dignified) spot between the social foundation of human striving and the outside circle, which represents the ecological ceiling imposed by planetary limits. The doughnut illustration is held against the illustration of our current economic order of a line going towards higher GDP over time at all costs. On a planet of finite resources, the worst ecological and social disasters can be avoided while maintaining economic progress only through truly *planet-centered design*.

Just like economics, design must be seen as affecting everyone, user and non-user alike. Even when designers are making choices about a small part, they are also making choices about the whole system. A failure to think systemically will likely lead to an extraordinary user experience but the exploitation of people and planet. The most pressing issues faced by humans today – the so-called *wicked problems* – simply cannot be solved by designing for individual needs. World hunger, the environmental crises or global pandemics cannot be tackled by *human-centered design* and instead require a systemic, *planet-centered* approach.

DOI: 10.4324/9781003464754-16

Humans more than any other species have changed every aspect of earth's systems and thus interfered with the functionality of natural behavior. Anthropogenic global change causes a myriad of *evolutionary mismatches,* since finely tuned features adapted for an earlier environment have become bugs in a new environment. Unfortunately, the *Anthropocene* story is empirically real, as our ability to change the world climate shows, but it is not the only story that could have unfolded. And neither does it predict the only possible future. Designers are left with three moral stances: 1) don't care about natural problems and conceive more artifacts; 2) outsource responsibility to governmental or non-governmental organizations dedicated to conservation and sustainability; or 3) roll up their sleeves and conceive interventions to remedy the situation.

Thus, the criterion for good design needs to shift to a level higher than humans to earth's biosphere, which includes all aspects of sustainability: ecological, social and economic.

Although working in lockstep, design culture and business culture are different. While business dies in the absence of positive numbers, design thrives on human experience. In short, value is measured quantitatively in the former and qualitatively in the latter. Business can get value expressed in money *because* users get value expressed in meaning. Design is all about value proposition to all stakeholders, but most companies have not figured out how to design communally for the simple reason that such an undertaking is very hard to monetize. For this reason, it is still to a very large degree focused on selling individual units of products and services for private ownership, with a total disregard for externalities caused in the production, use and disposal of them. What energy is used to produce them and run their functions? What will happen at the end of their life cycle? Where will used material go? We must stop the myopia of seeing isolated manifestations of materials and consider production, use and waste management. When you are making design decisions about complex systems, it's easy to get lost in the details. It's also comforting to focus on getting the details right while ignoring the larger implications. If the model only draws attention to itself, it tends to be no good. After all, the map should never be as intricate as the territory. To quote an economist, the Nobel Prize–winning Peter Diamond, "taking a model literally is not taking a model seriously."[1]

Most current business practice is based on identifying an underutilized resource to extract value from it, in the process depleting the given resource, whether we are speaking about petroleum reserves, forests or human attention. Privatizing profits and outsourcing losses are usually better for the single bottom-line profit, but rarely better for people and planet. Such reluctance is completely understandable, since designing a *human-centered* product is hard enough and thus the responsibility to address communal needs are ultimately outsourced to governmental regulation and public policy. The *future designer* must make intentional and informed choices from the beginning of the process. In a very real sense, they must visualize the complete narrative, thus influencing it. Designers have to step up to the plate. In the words of co-founder of Mule Design Erika Hall, "[they] either need to participate in defining the business model or they will simply be its tool."[2]

The market is not a self-contained system but rather a collection of several intertwined systems. Unlimited growth in one system cannot work on a planet with finite and equal amounts of resources. It is not only outdated but simply wrong to think otherwise. It is the space between the lines – the doughnut – we must design for. I will follow Raworth's logic and suggest that we should "think like 21st century designers." Albeit different, the *department of the future designer* also follows seven points, each one a title of a course.

Course One: Design for Needs

Designers need to be taught the mechanics behind an economic system based on infinite growth in GDP per capita, before there might ever be hope to change anything. Mainstream economic theory promises that the solution to most social ills is growth. The idea behind the *Wealth of Nations*[3] or Reagan's *trickle-down economics* is that through economic growth and development all people benefit even if welfare discrepancy rises at first. According to the infamous *Kuznets curve*, as countries get richer inequality first rises as rural labor migrates to urban areas, and then eventually falls. Developing countries tend to concentrate income among the wealthiest, because it is hoped that they then invest much of it to kick-start growth in GDP. It is supposed, more poetically, "a rising tide lifts all boats." Unfortunately, the metaphor does not translate to reality. In 1955, Simon Kuznets explicitly warned that his work was 5 percent empirical, 95 percent speculation and "some of it possibly tainted by wishful thinking," but his findings were soon taught to every economics student for the next sixty years.[4] There is another trend running counter to *Kuznets curve*, the so-called *Matthew effect*, coined by sociologist Robert K. Merton. In reference to the biblical adage "the rich get richer and the poor get poorer," it describes the tendency of individuals to enjoy more social and economic benefits if they already had a bigger net worth at birth due to their rich upbringing.[5] The reality is that most OECD countries are now facing their highest levels of income inequality in thirty years and their ecological footprints are so large that it would require about six planet earths if every country followed the same historic trajectory.

Oligarchic accumulation of wealth might actually be the principal reason for the collapse of history's great civilizations, as is argued by scholars like Jared Diamond[6] and Peter Turchin.[7] In short, history proves that egalitarianism does not come from development automatically but must be designed. We must move from "growth will even it all out" to "distributive by design." For starters, national economic rankings need to move from those centered around GDP per capita to wider conceptions of human welfare such as the *OECD Better Life Index, Index of Sustainable Economic Welfare* or the

Human Development Index because such indices try to address not only environmental but also social sustainability, manifested by social cohesion. When future designers take such welfare measures seriously, they might bring human social needs to the forefront, which in turn forces us to address common resources. To tackle such problems, an army of economists, biologists, anthropologists and designers need to descend from their ivory towers and work together in our *department of the future designer.*

Most of the built environment loses value with time, especially in an economic system obsessed with faster and faster material throughput by way of planned obsolescence and marketing-driven fashion cycles. Money, on the other hand, is often hoarded. But since shopping is trading – money for commodities – shoppers are caught in an emotional war between the ecstasy of acquisition and the pain of paying for it. They are victims of another cognitive bias called *loss aversion*, which describes why the pain of losing is psychologically twice as powerful as the pleasure of gaining. That inner battle can only be won by the heart, or what Daniel Kahneman called *system 2*, which is conscious and slow. It is also precisely why advertisement and marketing appeals to *it* and not *system 1*, which is unconscious and fast. Designers have learned to leverage system 1 very successfully and that is precisely the reason they add so much value to business. And, they have done so for quite some time now. Without a doubt, much of that leverage has helped us escape a life that is "solitary, poor, nasty, brutish, and short," but in recent history it has been used for one purpose and one purpose only: to consume. Taglines such as "designing desire" are ironic since they require a strong emphasis on research. Design frequently adopts the deductive research of marketing as its legitimization to show the world what humans desire by pushing commodities onto people instead of asking them what they need. Research is seen as a means to an end, which is *consumption* not *use*. Spurred on by marketing techniques and a system geared exclusively towards economic growth as measured by GDP, understanding human beings with all their nuances is not a helpful means to an end. Rather than learning what a human might need or want, items are given to users, and it is then seen as something that works or not, as successful or a failure.

Course Two: Design Research

A qualitative field-based approach is indispensable because user behavior is always contextual and individual interactions with products and services need to be mapped vis-à-vis larger, communal issues. The marketing toolbox includes many very clever tools such as *user journeys, personas* and *empathy maps* to contextualize a given service or product, but rather than assessing the immediate environment an end-user finds him-/herself in, *context mapping* needs to be extended to assess a broader *use case*. *How* we can change the behavior of individuals is studied like nothing else on this planet – it is well understood – and the knowledge is widely implemented. But how do we change the behavior of individuals in service of the collective? No matter the field, *change facilitation* starts with a target and ends with measurable change of that target. It is evolutionary. Governmental and non-governmental organizations often use the theory of change framework to plan and implement collective change.

Many indigenous cultures have disappeared, and most craftsmanship has been industrialized. Yet, perhaps more than ever before, this globalized and disruptive post-modern world has urban, visual, economic, corporate and cyber-anthropologists poring over new mysteries. The more designers want to create magical experiences, the more empathic they must become. And to make such experiences accessible to people across cultural divides, they must be open to the field of ethnology, or cultural anthropology. This is nothing new, and ethnography – literally the description of an ethnic group – has long been established as an integral part of design research. The problem is an age-old tension between design and business based on the type of data used to make decisions. A designer of a system that persuades millions of individuals to share videos or buy teapots has a hard time persuading a boardroom full of businesspeople to trust qualitative research. It is just so hard to fit a story into a spreadsheet. If we do not conduct user research, then we can only design things that by chance – and not metrics – are needed. Sometimes designers employ a sleight of hand conversion of notions to numbers by quantifying content, and sometimes it even results in profit. Even when the numbers are meaningless – the amount of time spoken about the frustration with an old teapot – managers love the math because of an irrational addiction to measurements.

The reason for designers' resistance and skepticism to scientific fieldwork may be the current emphasis on deductive exploration.[8] The marketing sciences tend to use such a top-down approach of going from the general to the specific; when a product is accepted, a given strategy is repeated, and when not, it is dropped. Why, designers ask, should they do such research when marketers already do it better? Well, because marketing-driven research is skewed on behalf of the seller rather than the user, and on behalf of profit rather than progress. Ideally, the design process is exploratory and neither inductive nor deductive, but rather abductive. John Chris Jones, one of the first design science thinkers, defines the discipline of design as holistic, centered primarily on problem solving, and thus the basic steps of research in the anthropological sciences and design are similar.[9] Any empirical insights concerning human action and motivation could be foundational for the design process, and conversely design thinking could be studied by all kinds of anthropologists because only then does design return to being *human-centered*.

In the past the relationship between the disciplines ethnology and design was rather one-sided, where ethnology offered designers ethnography as its most valuable tool for observing, understanding and predicting human action. In short, the designer has to become an ethnographer in order to become a better designer. It is also true that qualitative, descriptive "ethnography" as a term has become inflationary; it leads Tim Ingold to exclaim "that's enough about ethnography." Thankfully, ethnology is changing from a purely transcriptive and categorizing art to part of culture generation itself.[10] Instead of only observing and evaluating the objects coming out of a workshop, the ethnologist is now inside the workshop. Thinking of design as a participatory, emphatic discipline calls for optimism and reminds us that in many ways *design thinking* is social science thinking.

In recent years the relationship has become deeper, leading to the ethnologist learning much from the designer. The study of things has also deepened a lot and modern product design is scrutinized similarly to how a bow and arrow of an indigenous person was in the past. Much more than any theoretical considerations and metaphysical mental acrobatics, the relationship between ethnology and design is thickening due to a shift from theory to practice. If it is difficult to imagine a classical ethnographer building artifacts with the people that he/she is studying, that is exactly what is starting to happen in design schools around the world. The participation might range from mentorship in the design process to helping in building *mock-ups* and mental prototypes. A systematic methodology known as *grounded theory*, to construct hypotheses and readjust them while conducting fieldwork, is actually similar to the design process itself through its iterative nature.[11] Due to their similarly, the *grounded theory* approach thus works very well with that of *design thinking*.

A promising contribution to fieldwork is the *cultural probe* devised by design professor Bill Gaver, where a potential end-user is asked to actively participate in the research phase of a project.[12] This tool can consist of a simple notebook, a cheap camera or even a WhatsApp profile and acts like a drone going where the researcher has limited access

One master's thesis project stands as an example of how qualitative research techniques may be combined with *design thinking*. Initially the question was how cooperation between traditional handicraft and design can be improved. Or rather: how could it be re-established since the two disciplines used to be one and the same? In a truly open and iterative approach, a viable design process was created and thus two innovative products: a spindle to make stools and a stool itself. Here the designer became ethnographer to become a better designer. After a phase of desktop research, qualitative ethnographic research was undertaken. The chosen craft – basket weaving – was observed from the outside using quantitative and qualitative research methods. However, it soon became apparent that the research would be thoroughly intertwined with the research phase of the project. Two workshops were organized to teach design students the art of traditional basket weaving. In the first one held in Salzburg Austria, Roma and Sinti from Rumania led the students from simple basket shapes to complex design objects. The team was multidisciplinary, consisting of a designer (student), a design professor (mentor) and an anthropologist (me), and we worked well together. In this first phase the emphasis was obviously on the theory and methodology of the humanities. The design student in the team observed and recorded the workshop, but also participated in it and in a way reversed the Malinowskian *participant observation* to *observational participation*. In a second workshop the same was repeated in Istanbul. This time the weaving was employed to make boat-like structures. In both workshops the master's student focused on documenting the events by qualitatively interviewing the participating students and photographing the resulting objects. The next step was to learn the art of weaving from two experts, one time in Bavaria and one time in Istanbul. The designer became a disciple or student of a designer, here a craftsman of the basketry tradition. As a result, two stools were created. After the completion of the stool, the packaging was designed as well.

Design students must leave the classrooms to really use any qualitative research tools such as *individual interviews, focus groups, cultural probes* and others by speaking to real people on the streets. Only once data has been collected should they come back to the classrooms to break all of it down into insights – to debrief. From my experience working with research-driven design projects, two tools have proved to be especially helpful: the *empathy map* and formal *content analyses. Empathy maps* should not be confused with *personas*, as the former are used at an earlier stage of the research process, and when used properly they can be a way into users' hearts and heads. *Empathy maps* help in understanding use cases in their context, which is paramount for any consideration of what adjustments to future researches might be needed. In essence they are quick-and-dirty content analyses. For longer data sets (resulting from an expert interview or focus group) I find the *content analysis* of Philipp Mayring the best fit for design research.[13] Canvases, especially *Value Proposition Design* provided by Alexander Osterwalder, are also useful tools for understanding context of human behavior and appropriate design interventions.[14] It really is all about context!

Course Three: Design for Demographics

In the so-called WEIRD societies, there still exist largely areas of plenitude, peace and cleanliness, because for centuries the labor- and resource-intensive parts of the global value chain have been conveniently outsourced through systems such as colonialism and unregulated global capitalism. But these are not truths we like to look at and for many of us globalization means little more than yoga on Monday and sushi on Friday. Logos of corporations loom larger than logos, the biblical word; churches stand empty as shopping centers burst at their seams. Many of the Western countries are societies and not communities, as individuals stand atomized and without common direction. We WEIRD ones experience fear surrounding overpopulation and being the center of a series of asylum crises. Indeed, it is getting tighter on these pockets of privilege, and when the fear of the Other grows, we rally around our flags, we bawl our hymns and split into political tribes. We then try to exorcise anything foreign, and when that does not work we project our fears onto scapegoats, ostracized as tax burdens into the far corners of our empires. We need emigrants more than ever because local people don't like working with their hands anymore. We need them to help with our ageing and morbid populations. We need them now because we are wrought with chronic diseases while conservative family planning, even abstinence from having kids, has become a kind of moral high ground.

Part of this paranoia of the encroaching hordes can be traced back to 1968. In the year of the moon landing, assassinations, riots and Hardin's "The Tragedy of the Commons," Paul Ehrlich's *The Population Bomb* described the planet as simply too crowded. The book with the sensational-ist subtitle "Population Control or Race to Oblivion" sold millions of copies and really shaped the opinion on world demographics for several genera-tions after its publication. It stands in a long tradition of doomsday fore-casts starting with Thomas Malthus' prediction that since the population grew exponentially while food output grew linearly, we are bound to hit *carrying capacity*. Simply shown on a graph, an exponential and a linear line inevitably cross.[15] The inability to feed the world's population would thus lead to mass starvation and crisis mortality. What Malthus and the so-called *Neo-Malthusians* got wrong, however, is that a rise in development strongly correlates with a *drop* in global fertility. There actually has been a steady decrease since the mid-1950s. At the time of this writing the global fertility rate is around 2.4. That number refers to the global average of the *total fertility rate*, which in turn is an average number of children born to a female during her reproductive period. More precisely, that means if a woman lives to the end of her menopause and experiences the exact current age-specific fertility rates throughout her lifetime, on average she would have 2.4 children, who in turn live to have babies.

In most European countries the total fertility rate is below the replacement rate of 2.1, which means that were it not for immigration and local longevity, our populations would die out. Oblivious to any of this, a lot of current design still caters to the *wants* of affluent individuals or small nuclear families at best while it seems abundantly clear that far more important would be to focus on the needs of the disenfranchised. But more than just a moral appeal, this is hard *Realpolitik*. The *demographic transition* shows the historical shift from high birth rates and high death rates in societies with minimal infra-structural development and education (especially for women) to low birth rates and low death rates in societies with advanced infrastructural develop-ment and education. While in absolute numbers most of the world's popula-tion still finds itself at an earlier stage of this *transition* with a disproportionately large percentage of minors depending on a small working-age cohort, the most developed countries are getting older, which is to say that in the near future the majority of their population will depend on a minority. Such trends clearly show that the best way to future-proof design studies is to focus on these rapidly increasing cohorts of young in the developing world and elderly in the developed world. Expressed in cold, economic logic: together they will be the biggest user group the world has ever seen.

Improving material and social infrastructure inversely correlate with lower birth rates. Studies even show a slower reproductive strategy in benign environments with a stable supply of resources and a faster reproductive strategy with more resource competition in relatively hostile and unstable environments.[16] For example, one striking study conducted in different parts of Chicago shows the median age of first-time maternity to be 22.6 years in neighborhoods with lower life expectancy, and 27.3 years in neighborhoods with higher life expectancy.[17]

Scholarly research shows that rather than biological, cultural or geographical considerations, citizens of less-developed countries (LDCs) are victims of historical circumstances, which lead to infrastructural shortcomings. Improving material and social infrastructure correlates with lower birth rates.[18] Regarding this global trend of sinking birth rates, there are also reasons for optimism, and it just might be design that has the most agency in implementing positive change. Is this not the best possible way to *decolonize* design and repair wrongs of the past? The book *A New Reality: Human Evolution for a Sustainable Future*, co-authored by Jonas and Jonathan Salk – the latter being the inventor of the polio vaccine – addresses falling global fertility rates and the potential of a highly educated age cohort of young adults. The rate of population growth has begun to slow and is trending toward equilibrium, a change that may coincide with an equally significant shift in values based on limits, interdependence, cooperation and long-term thinking.[19] Let us link these arguments to Amartya Sen and Martha Nussbaum's *capability approach*, a normative perspective to human welfare, which concentrates on individuals' actual capability for self-realization rather than only having rights and freedom. While income inequality is an important issue, other non-income outcomes of well-being (such as nutrition or education) must be addressed with infrastructural changes.[20] We can only imagine what would happen when we help emancipate local communities by showing them skill sets to design their own destiny. Interdisciplinary research points to the role of institutions (for example, ineffective delivery of services) as another key driver of inequalities of material well-being,[21] and this should be part of any discussion on *service design*. Calling all designers, the biggest population of youth the world has ever experience needs help for self-help! Of course, there are plenty of brave design projects helping the most underprivileged and it will be those that are taught in the *department of the future designer*. We will move from "design for" to "design with" the underprivileged majority.

Course Four: Design for Sustainability

Right now, we are all screaming apocalypse and the end of humanity, but as a species we are but toddlers with a mere three hundred thousand years under our belts. If the human species survives for many millennia into the future, and considering world demographics of the past, there will be more people alive in the future than all who have lived in the past and are living currently – combined. Such considerations are generally considered *population ethics* and were brought to the attention of the academic community by moral philosopher Derek Parfit.[22] From that tradition came *longtermism*, the moral responsibility of those living now to make sure that those living in the future survive and flourish. Philosopher William MacAskill writes of this type of moral philosophy in his book *What We Owe the Future* as "the view that positively influencing the long-term future is a key moral priority of our time."[23] The term *longtermism* is recent – Oxford philosophers William MacAskill and Toby Ord coined it a few years ago – but the concept has been subject to philosophical scrutiny for centuries. For example, the *Iroquois Confederacy* encourages all decision-making to be made to be of benefit for people living about 525 years in the future, a number reached by multiplying a life expectancy of 75 years by 7. This is often called *seventh generation* sustainability and is very similar to *Our Common Future*, or *Brundtland Report*, published in October 1987 by the United Nations. There *sustainability* is defined as: "meeting the needs of the present without compromising the ability of future generations to meet their own needs."[24]

Technically (no pun intended) most designed objects are really a form of technology conceived to help humans, but we have become very spoiled indeed. The late science fiction author Ursula Le Guin – incidentally daughter of the great anthropologist Alfred Kroeber – wrote about this tendency in a rant-turned-blog:

> "Technology" and "hi tech" are not synonymous, and a technology that isn't "hi," isn't necessarily "low" in any meaningful sense. We have been so desensitised by a hundred and fifty years of ceaselessly expanding technical prowess that we think nothing less complex and showy than a computer or a jet bomber deserves to be called "technology" at all.[25]

Cell phones with more computing power than what *Nasa* had when they put a man on the moon are used for only a year before ending up in the drawers and attics of our lives; incredible devices, from washing machines to microwave ovens to cars, are piling up in our junkyards. It is said that technology and design have been democratized as it was made available to the masses. But at the same time it has become far more difficult to maintain – and prolong – the life of commodities than to simply buy a new unit. But given that the word *sustainability* literally means "the ability to sustain something," designers can also sustain desired situations. Rather than only focusing on innovation disruption, products and their use need to be sustained for as long as possible. While we are really good at designing enchanting objects, is there not also some hope for designing a deeper, more sustainable connection between things and users of things? As our gadgets have become more and more awesome, we have become less and less full of awe! Somehow, when users are in daily contact with the unexplainable "magic" of things, they have turned careless and wasteful with the things producing such magic.

Have we become so detached from the creation of the objects around us that we have dropped all parent-like affection? Yes, because industrialization and in a sense industrial design have removed the production of things by one degree, it has created a system where things are mothered by things. Repair of consumer goods is equally removed and made exceedingly difficult. In the words of Jonathan Chapman:

> This is because we have been designed out of our material worlds and banned from participation. As users we are relegated to the role of passive button pusher, an obedient spectator. All we can do is pay for the show, sit back and gawp in awe at the brilliance of others, meanwhile reflecting on our own failings and inadequacies as individuals.[26]

As Chapman points out, maintenance has both *preventative* and *corrective* implications. But, while the state is constantly taking care of things such as the infrastructure of our built environment, users of privately owned products have been discouraged to offer any love for the machines in their lives. You don't really own your machine if there's no chance of opening, hacking or fixing it! The Californian company *ifixit* has realized this modern shortcoming as a market niche and now specializes in selling kits for entering the obnoxiously closed membranes of *Apple* products. But, even if you do get to the motherboard of your device, you will likely not be able to hack or manipulate it. Constant software updates make the hardware from companies such as Apple go obsolete. Their continuous changes in cables, adapters and ports render older versions useless and the myriad models and short fashion cycles makes the user constantly feel inadequate and so "last year." Indeed, a lot of design has become prey to the doctrine of *planned obsolescence*. If you still don't believe me, open your drawers—but really this time—and explain to me the tangly cable-and-gadget spaghetti you find there.

Just like design can give objects magical qualities, it can also provide meaning, though such meaning is rarely allowed to foster and mature in fast-paced times. There are relationships to be built between a designed object and its user. Chapman's *Emotionally Durable Design: Objects, Experiences and Empathy,*[27] as well as the later *Meaningful Stuff,*[28] serve as priceless countercurrents to speedy consumption and planned obsolescence. Just like a person-to-person relationship lasts only through maintenance and tender care, the relationship between object and user cannot ever be taken for granted. Immediately after reading his work, I wrote an email to Chapman inviting him to host one of his *object-handling sessions* at our design school I was working at. I was excited and the excitement only increased when he responded and we arranged for his trip. Together with Jonathan, I have hosted several such workshops since.

There are a few objects in our lives that we cherish, and they are far outnumbered by those that we throw away quickly. Saying that we only keep the valuable ones would be jumping the gun. After all, we have no problem discarding perfectly working smartphones or cars. Let us take a quick detour into moral philosophy, where *instrumental* and *intrinsic* value are distinguished. The former is a *means to an end* because it helps us achieve a particular goal, and the latter is as an *end in itself* because it is desirable in and of itself. Such terms were coined by Max Weber, one of the founders of modern sociology. Although he studied the meanings people assigned to their actions and beliefs, *intrinsic* and *instrumental value* can readily be transferred to things. Thus, a washing machine and a screwdriver are objects with *instrumental value* because they help you clean your clothes or drill a screw into a board. A teddy bear, on the other hand, is charged with *intrinsic value*.[29] Although only a piece of textile, it holds all the emotional comfort a child needs at night when the lights go off and the boogieman lurks. Asking my teenage kids why they continue to sleep with theirs makes little sense: Lou and Ka (their names) are desirable for their own sake irrespective of their possible instrumental value. The shiniest, fluffiest and newest replacement from *Toys R Us* would be flatly rejected by my daughters. According to Max Weber, objects hold value for us because of their intrinsic function of giving comfort.

Emotions are also key in understanding – and influencing – human behavior regarding sustainability. Right now, design often resorts to truly desperate measures to transform people into cogs of the throwaway society. Both superficial styling and behavioral science are used as a means to exactly that end, the former often unintentional and the latter mostly intentional. Chapman's emotional durability serves as a solid theoretical foundation. Research has shown that emotional bonds with consumer goods reduce the likelihood of such goods to be discarded. *Emotional durability* seeks to create stronger emotionality and enduring interaction with things, which in turn can lead to a more sustainable use of resources. Our everyday things might also be made to be longer lasting by adding animacy.[30]

As I have hopefully demonstrated – because I have definitely tried – evolutionary preferences should never be reduced to aesthetics alone; they also apply to other aspects of human society, such as morality, cognition or human inventiveness. Indeed, civilization looks very different once you entertain the notion that the human mind and its manifestations are all subjects of evolutionary forces. One beacon of hope for behavior change away from the throwaway society might just come from *animism*, and so let us revisit it here.

It can be regarded as something that could be shared by all peoples regardless of their technological advances, something that can lead to more emotional attachment to things, and in turn more sustainability. For modern product design, there might thus lurk an opportunity rather than a problem since animistic tendencies could potentially lead to more product attachment and consumer satisfaction. Thus, Graham Harvey has used such a renewed appraisal of animism as a way to describe more sound ecological harmony with all things, since for humans it is likely easier to exploit and abuse a soulless entity. Treating things better, using them as long as possible and repairing them whenever possible is a core aspect of the circular economy, which we will turn to in the next section.[31]

The idea of "designed animism" actually dates back to the 1970s when design theorists treated the impact of pervasive computing on the human experience and design as a discipline. Recent approaches in design research have been steered towards purposely increasing *emotional durability* of products through design. One type of design, *interactive design*, requires a level of animistic thinking for the user experience to be a positive one. As shown in a recent conference paper, animism can be used as an appropriate design metaphor for interactive design. Not all types of design share such intrinsic relationships with animism, but all would arguably benefit from the ongoing discussion of a *new animism*. In the end we can ask if animism is a vice or a virtue. Is it something to be encouraged or renounced for society to develop? Humans have a deeply ingrained fascination with stuff, which has become a serious concern when considering the resources required in making all such stuff. I believe that animism, understood as a deeply rooted understanding of a world unfolding, alive with things, could very well lead to a more sustainable future.[32]

Course Five: Design for Circularity

In 1946, the same year that Hayek organized the very consequential Mont-Pelerín society, a young sociology and economics student with the peculiar name Bill Housego Phillips did something truly strange. He was a student at the London School of Economics – where both Hayek and Karl Popper held positions – when he built a large machine meant to not only show how the UK economy worked but also how to make predictions by tweaking variables like consumption spending, tax rates, interest rates, etc. The machine became known as MONIAC – an acronym for *Monetary National Income Analogue Computer* – or the *Phillips Hydraulic Computer* or, less flattering, the *Financephalograph*. Phillips faced a genuine design challenge: macro-economics was all theoretical at that point and he wanted to create a physical model of an economy to demonstrate its mathematical complexities and mechanical logic to people who don't have much of a sense for numbers. Thus, he drew on his background as an undergraduate engineering student to design a three-dimensional analogue computer.

The result was spectacular. Standing two meters tall, Phillips' machine showed how money flowed in an economy – literally, because the direction of money was shown by water running through the machine, and with pipes, valves and pumps, it could be manipulated to represent policy effects, such as interest and taxation as well as social effects, such as consumption or saving. It was meant to be a teaching aid to illustrate how the UK economy worked, but with its small error rate the MONIAC offered an effective way of modeling a very complex system and became a simulator. By adding or subtracting certain amounts of water in certain places, the computer showed the aggregate behavior of the economy. Phillips also proved to be a product manager and after the first simple prototype, he made 14 more MONIACs and even sold them to places like the New Zealand Reserve Bank, Harvard Business School, Istanbul University and the Ford Motor Company. Bill Housego Phillips became a hero of sorts by showing how an economy worked in a beautiful mechanical fashion as predicted by the godfathers of economics Adam Smith, Thomas Malthus and David Ricardo and later the *neo-classicists*. There was only one major shortcoming to this marvelous model and demonstration of economics; one feature that instantly rendered it useless. Can you guess?

It seems subtle, but the truly embarrassing moment came when Phillips needed to go to the back of the machine and flick on a little electrical switch. The reason this detail is significant is because an economy can never be modeled and no economy can ever work without an external power source. Incidentally, the same happens with just about all design presentations from students and professionals: they always show splendid renderings or models of objects, houses and cities as if in a vacuum, disconnected from any power source. The whole point of a model is to be a gross simplification of reality and thus a geographical map is a rudimentary depiction of topography. Similarly, a simple mock-up is a demonstration of a product or service. But the mock-up cannot be understood, not to mention developed, without an understanding of the system the product or service is embedded in.

Our department would train students into designers of a 21st century regenerative economy instead of last century's degenerative economy. Easier said than done, but designers need to shift from sustaining the linear economy, where the garbage bin is just that semi-convenient spot where externalities land, to sustaining the bio-system. That is not to say we must stop producing all products; it is the garbage bin that needs to become obsolete, not our products. By once again looking at nature as an entity to exploit for infinite inspiration and knowledge rather than finite resources, humans can redesign a society based on circular production and consumption; a society where the waste of one commodity becomes food for the next. Nature is the mother of prototyping and every second of every day under the sun new forms of life are created through the process of selection. We don't have a garbage problem; we have a design problem!

Regenerative design, as would be taught in our department, would ensure that instead of exhausting the earth's resources, we use them over and over. We would teach to work with, not against, the cyclical processes of life on earth, such as those displayed by water or carbon. A green movement should never be based on austerity, and to the contrary can be one of abundance if the "technical nutrients" are kept in a healthy cycle.[33] Evolution as an innovative process is very wasteful, and experimentation tends to trump conservatism. Similarly, humans could enjoy a life of abundance as long as the design of our everyday things considers several lives instead of just one. Instead of doing "less bad," designers should be encouraged to do "more good," to *upcycle* rather than recycle.[34]

Nature is the supreme master of recycling materials. But it has a very hard time and takes an exceedingly long time to break down artificial things built to *not* come apart. If we stop for a moment and ask a small child to give a definition of glue, it would probably say something to the extent of "a sticky substance that puts different thing together forever." Idealistic and naive, the child does not know any chemistry, but it's definition points to the biggest problem we face in our efforts to recycle matter! Designers must provide incentives for *repairability* as well as be incentivized to do so. Provision of incentives can include some simple rules of the craft such as avoiding glue, which makes compounded products next to impossible to disassemble and therefore recycle. Instead, consumer goods must be fashioned using screws or, even better, return to joint systems, developed through craftsmanship around the world for millennia. Japan has an especially rich tradition of mono-materialistic connectors of products' parts. Smartphone company *Fairphone* has boldly gone where no other smartphone providers have gone; they attempt to build a highly complex smartphone fairly. Like fair-trade coffee or chocolate, they avoid all supply chains that don't comply with their standards. What is most impressive here, however, is that the phone is made in a modular fashion and can easily be disassembled with standard screwdrivers. The end-user is encouraged to configure and maintain their devices for as long as possible. Such design is radically different to, for example, *Samsung*, who make sure that we end-users cannot take them apart, not to mention repair. In short, *Fairphone* design their devices to be *used* and *Samsung* design them to be *consumed*.

We put things together in ways that are very hard to reverse-engineer or take apart, and then ask consumers to please, please place them into one of four or five colored bins after their use. If designed objects were made of one biodegradable material, we would not have a problem and I would not have to write this section. But they are not; most are incredibly complex compounds of hundreds of non-biodegradable materials, and that is why I must continue writing. The mixing of different materials into compounds is why recycling is so very hard, but since our artifacts are mixtures, we have to design in ways to easily separate materials. To put it as simply as this: we train creatives to design and manufacture complex goods that cannot be separated into their parts, sell them to someone with a promise of improving their looks and rank, and then, when a newer, hotter version reaches the marketplace, we ask end-users to please recycle the old stuff properly.

Indeed, the most compelling transformation of the current linear "take-make-waste" economy towards a system driven by "intelligent" production and consumption is the *circular economy*, but as an anthropologist, I will go further. If we continue to champion an open society and allow people to keep their standard of life and not force them into frugality, it is the only chance this species has! The *circular economy* is based on the ideas of closing resource loops for large volumes of finite resources (used by organizations) to be captured and reused while opening flows of innovation and information.[35] As an exemplary introduction, I use Adidas with its *Futurecraft-loop* running shoe. Manufactured from only one material – laces included – the running shoe can be discarded and reused. Naturally, the manufacture of the following shoe also requires resource and energy input, but far less than traditional running shoes. When objects are made of non-natural materials such as various polymers, then those need to be returned, a challenge far greater.[36] When successful, the extraction of virgin materials is kept to a minimum since the materials would be owned and reused by companies. As for the business plan, sale of individual products stops being a top priority in what has been called a *performance economy*.[37] In a *circular economy*, the disposal stage (of commodities) is replaced by a circulation stage. While biodegradable material returns to the biosphere – for example by composting – technical material is recycled either on the level of raw material (e.g., used glass is melted and new glass is produced) or on the level of *components* (e.g., electronic components of laptops are remanufactured and reused in TV sets), *redistributed* (e.g., a used cell phone is sold via eBay to another user) or *reused* by the original user (e.g., the life of a broken cell phone is extended by repair).

Currently, supply chains, working conditions and externalities related to production of designed objects are outsourced to unknown third parties, a process largely kept hidden from our creative class. But we need to point at all of that; point it out to students. In the words of economic geographer Mark Graham:

> contemporary capitalism conceals the histories and geographies of most commodities from consumers. They can only see commodities in the here and now of time and space, and rarely have any opportunities to gaze backwards through the chains of production in order to gain knowledge about the sites of production, transformation, and distribution.[38]

In a future-oriented design department we need to point to how, where and by whom something was produced because true circular design goes well beyond products and entails production processes and business models.

Designers must become "system thinkers," making informed decisions about which circular strategies to use according to the business model, and consider transition processes and socio-cultural aspects in which the circular model will be implemented. They also need to design attractive services for users to return the material to their sources, the manufacturer. In addition to obvious positive ecological effects, superior economic advantages, such as the creation of new jobs and savings in the purchase of raw materials, are stressed in the circular economy.[39] Design is key for accelerating a transformation towards circularity as it stands between users below and the government above. Right before this manuscript went to press, on February 2, 2024, the European Commission passed a new law giving end-users the right to have their devices repaired after the expiration of their warranties. Both bottom-up demands and top-down legislation for the circular economy requires *more* not *less* creativity.[40]

Course Six: Design for *Usership* …

… not ownership is taught in a future-worthy design school. Skills on how to sell something for profit, how to scale production, how to distribute and how to make revenue are also taught because they are all essential for design to be successful. But we must stop spreading the falsehood that profitability and scalability is intrinsically linked to, and only possible through, the sale of individual units for private ownership. Indeed, it is *product–service–systems* that own the future! Designers have significant responsibility in shaping the current status quo of more and more people sharing, swishing, leasing and renting. They are moving away from private ownership due to the novelty, beauty and convenience of our products and services. Designed as *product–service–systems* this type of culture change is admirable.

The corresponding business model is the access and performance approach.[41] Nestled within the *circular economy* lies what is commonly labeled the *sharing economy* with business models based on *use* rather than *property*. Individuals, for instance, do not own a car but have access to a fleet of mobility offerings with the help of car sharing systems and smartphone apps such as Car2Go and Uber. In short, access trumps ownership! What is "owning" something as opposed to claiming it as private property? The basic difference is that in the former one *uses* material, while in the latter the materials – along with all the responsibilities implicated – become private assets. When users rent and lease things, revenue can be created by selling utility rather than material. Here collaborative consumption allows two or (many) more parties to create mutual value.[42] Take as an isolated example *Bundles*, a small company that came to the brilliant but simple realization that households *need* to have clean clothes and sheets rather than bulky washing machines. Thus, in cooperation with other stakeholders such as *Miele* they came up with a *pay-per-wash* business model. Instead of the washing machine being owned by individuals, its use is granted. Anyone who has moved a household would appreciate the service of a company that comes over to pick up *their* back-breaking machine. Other examples among many are *Airbnb* (apartment sharing) and *Kickstarter* (crowdfunding). The common denominators of such diverse business models are that they are very disruptive, accumulate revenue from services (and experiences) rather than sale of units, most are very lean platform-based enterprises and they are typically highly successful.

Design is the interface between object and user. By interface I mean the "place at which independent and often unrelated systems meet and act on or communicate with each other," not just screens and buttons.[43] To clarify, ask yourself the following questions: would you rent scooters, cars or movies? You probably answer yes, yes and yes and have done so many times. Would you *rent* for a few hours an old mattress that hundreds of people have slept on and otherwise used? If that thought made you viscerally recoil in disgust you are certainly human, but wrong. That transaction is called a hotel! The bed sheets are literally the interface between the user and the object, in this case a rancid old mattress. If we extend that interface to include a great minibar, a little dinner mint on the pillow and the seamless check-in procedure, then humans can enjoy the magic of comfort away from home. When its magic works, design can make everyday life easy and joyous; when it does not it can burn you in the hotel shower or it can make you actually throw an overcomplicated remote control against the wall.

Once again, the traditional view of tangible products sold as units for private ownership must be replaced by a more holistic view of *product–service–systems* and that can only happen through the magic of design – clearly, because not everyone can own everything; not eight billion people and not on a hermetically sealed planet. However, sustainability is much more than just ecological, and some societal aspects leave much to be desired. They are summed up by Arvind Malhotra and Marshall Van Alstyne: 1) services can quickly become exclusive, and people are often ostracized; 2) many platforms use loopholes to avoid taxes and regulations; 3) the *sharing economy* often goes together with the *gig economy* where the smallest of tasks are outsourced to workers with no insurance or other work benefits; 4) subletting can be taken to extremes when a user "sells" a service to a secondary or tertiary user; 5) shared apartments can raise real-estate prices beyond the capability of residents; 6) often the platforms outsource responsibility by claiming to only match supply and demand, such as *Uber* claiming to not be responsible for a person run over by a contracted driver; and 7) since cars, bikes, apartments and anything else are not privately owned, the service invites vandalism and theft. Thus, abandoned e-scooters lie broken and abandoned in cities the world over. Still, the question is not whether to prohibit sharing models because they are here to stay and they are multiplying. Rather, a lot more sociological, political, economic and legal research is needed in order to foster the immense benefits of the *sharing economy* while reducing some very negative social externalities.[44]

Course Seven: Open Design

Creators and decision-makers, such as designers, engineers and managers, play a crucial role in successful change. Besides closing the value creation chain (e.g., repair, refurbishment and recycling), the *opening* of different life cycle stages, for example by *open innovation* in the development phase, is deemed crucial.[45] The idea is not new. Surely *co-creation* is archaic in its nature; it is a *return* to truly *human-centered design* because human culture in its entirety is based on cooperative learning. In the past innovation was an open process depending equally on the knowledge of manufacturers and users. Products and services may have been developed by a kind of guild we now label "manufacturer," but always with an eye on use rather than sale. Currently "user" often stands for someone whose needs have been satisfied by a "manufacturer." Protective agents such as patents and copyrights are meant to prevent imitations. Can or should property rights be applied to the realm of ideas? Or should the government stay totally out of such matters? It is a Western system, but should we extend it worldwide? Are patent rights to blame for millions dying of HIV in Africa? These and many more questions are screaming for answers and obviously of huge importance to the world of design.

However, these imitations have and will always be the second-most essential ingredient in an innovative process.[46] New tools, or rather new ways of conceiving the market, have raised awareness in the process of *co-creation*.[47] By returning to it, "users that innovate can develop exactly what they want, rather than relying on manufacturers to act as their (often very imperfect) agents."[48] More than just a process, such an approach is seen as a necessary program and it seems plausible that on any economic level, it adds value to commodities for both consumer and supplier. Perhaps the best way to illustrate the intersection of design, *co-creation* and the *do-it-yourself* (*DIY*) movement should go back fifty years to Enzo Mari. In 1974 the Italian designer created the *Autoprogettazione* manual for non-designers to create chairs and tables just using wood, hammer and nails. Literally *Autoprogettazione* means "self-design," a translation perhaps a bit misleading since Mari saw the project as a critique of the estrangement resulting from industrial production. This was long before DIY became cool and the original title *Autoprogettazione* did include a "?" at the end. Has Mari's question been answered by *mass customization* and other marketing schemes à la IKEA?[49] CUCULA (also called the Refugees Company for Crafts and Design), a humanitarian organization based in Berlin, received the rights to use the manual during the European refugee crisis of the mid-2010s. In an inspirational display of co-creation and clever business plans, refugees built, personalized and sold pieces of furniture, all the while gaining legality. In 2014, the CUCULA team launched a crowdfunding campaign on *Startnext*. Prominent ambassadors along with numerous volunteers raised more than 120,000 euros and showed that such creative models work; the campaign garnered international support for reforms in refugee policy.[50]

Perhaps the best way to illustrate the necessity of synergetic and cooperative work is given by what is called the *internet of things*, the extension of internet connectivity to everyday objects such as our word-processing or smartphone devices. Currently, companies are encouraging users to inhabit a world of objects made by them to ensure usability and comfort and discouraging the mixing of operating systems by guaranteeing a world of pain. Since companies are seldom able to produce all things desired by individual consumers, a ceiling will always be hit. Increased data sharing would allow organizations to overcome challenges and profit more effectively beyond such ceilings. In a world where the idea of manufactured obsolescence has become the default business plan, and externalities are hidden by economic policies in order to allow low pricing, such information stinginess makes sense, but a transparent and truly free market economy would render such introversion self-defeating.

Companies could make a lot of money if they sold branded replacement parts to the public. Teaming up with the businesses already processing their products would allow a symbiotic creation of value since resources would be kept in a closed loop.[51] Based on the powerful developments within information technology, more and more internal corporate processes would be opened for external stakeholders, such as customers, and it could be argued that the consumer would mutate into a value-creating *prosumer*.[52] *Lead-users* – individuals who recognize a personal need earlier than the majority – can profit from a conceived remedy first and can generate solutions themselves; they have received much attention in innovation management.[53] For example, many of the most disruptive innovations in the sports industry were not developed by companies but by *lead-users*, who were eagerly striving for something new and an additional "kick."[54] In short, moving towards *open innovation* could enable value creation far beyond what is seen today. Michele Boldrin and David K. Levine actually compare the invention of the steam engine after the expiration of the Watt patents to modern *open-source* software development.[55] Admittedly, I have a moral quandary over the idea of artificial intelligence opensourced in 2022 by the likes of *OpenAI*. Making a gigantesque database through users is not what I see as a wholesome use of group intelligence, as it gives agency to all actors, benevolent and malicious. Whatever our intent, it is *us* who are feeding the machine, but one thing is for sure, opening artificial intelligence to the public will surely outcompete any closed approaches.[56]

Distributive economic design ensures that any value created is spread equitably among those who helped generate it. For example, community-owned renewable energy grids can generate electricity along with income for a community, and all the while they would avoid the so-called *intermittency problem*: renewable energy sources such as the sun, wind, rivers or even the earth's internal heat are all affected by astronomical, seasonal and daily cycles, which can limit their efficiency. Privately, some households can generate more electricity than others simply because of the direction their houses face, or the amount of shade they receive from the neighbors' trees. A final example of the advantages of an open-source approach is the *WikiHouse*. Here, the design and construction of resource-light dwellings is democratized and simplified.[57] Due to the rise of digital networks, designers have more opportunities than ever before to turn last century's divisive economy into one that is distributive.

Designers need to be more like gardeners in their approach. You reap what you sow. If you don't like the way a community deals with its resources, then the designer must sow methods and tools that are different. Small-scale policy experiments are set up to test out a plethora of interventions; the ones that work are scaled up while the ones that don't are halted. Such an adapting portfolio of experiments is the very essence of *biomimicry*, where we imitate nature. After all, nature's process of natural selection is summed up as *variation–selection–replication*. Adopting an evolutionary perspective for designing the built environment is urgent because, as Elinor Ostrom puts it, "we have never had to deal with problems of the scale facing today's globally inter-connected society. No one knows for sure what will work, so it is important to build a system that can evolve and adapt rapidly."[58] Contrary to a closed innovation process, in an open system the boundaries – or "membranes" to again borrow from biology – are permeable, making the exchange of infor-mation with other organizations possible. Businesses, government and inno-vators must realize that it is more profitable to collaborate in a vast ecosystem than innovate as individual entities. *Co-creation*, as the purposeful diffusion of terms like *user* and *producer* through open innovation, is a central factor of the circular economy, but it needs to be taught – just like any other design methodology – with a keen eye on ethics.

Notes

1 Diamond, P. (2011). Unemployment, vacancies, wages. *American Economic Review*, 101(4), 1045–1072.
2 https://medium.com/mule-design/a-three-part-plan-to-save-the-world-98653a20a 12f, accessed on October 12, 2023.
3 Smith, A. (2002). *The Wealth of Nations*. Bibliomania.com [Web]. Retrieved from the Library of Congress, https://lccn.loc.gov/2002564559, accessed on February 16, 2024.
4 Kuznetsk, S. (1955) Economic growth and income inequality. *American Economic Review*, 45(1), 1–28.
5 Merton, R. K. (1995). The Thomas theorem and the Matthews effect. *Social Forces*, 74, 379.
6 Diamond, J. (2011). *Collapse: How societies choose to fail or succeed* (revised edition). Penguin.
7 Turchin, P. (2023). *End Times: Elites, counter-elites, and the path of political disin-tegration*. Penguin.
8 Müller, F. (2021). *Design Ethnography: Epistemology and methodology*. Springer Nature, p. 93.
9 Jones, J. C. (1970). Method 5.6: Functional innovation. In *Design Methods: Seeds of Human Futures* (pp. 331–340). John Wiley & Sons.
10 Niinimäki, K., & Koskinen, I. (2011). I love this dress, it makes me feel beautiful! Empathic knowledge in sustainable design. *The Design Journal*, 14(2), 165–186.
11 Glaser, B., & Strauss, A. (2017). *Discovery of Grounded Theory: Strategies for qualitative research*. Routledge.

12 Gaver, B., Dunne, T. & Pacenti, E. (1999). Design: Cultural probes. *Interactions*, 6 (1), 21–29.
13 Mayring, P. (2014). *Qualitative Content Analysis: Theoretical foundation, basic procedures and software solution*. Klagenfurt.
14 Osterwalder, A., Pigneur, Y., Bernarda, G. & Smith, A. (2015). *Value Proposition Design: How to create products and services customers want* (Vol. 2). John Wiley & Sons.
15 Ehrlich, P. R., & Ehrlich, A. H. (2009). The population bomb revisited. *The Electronic Journal of Sustainable Development*, 1(3), 63–71.
16 Ellis, B. J., Figueredo, A. J., Brumbach, B. H. & Schlomer, G. L. (2009). Fundamental dimensions of environmental risk: The impact of harsh versus unpredictable environments on the evolution and development of life history strategies. *Humam Nature*, 20(2), 204–268.
17 Wilson, M., & Daly, M. (1997). Life expectancy, economic inequality, homicide, and reproductive timing in Chicago neighbourhoods. *British Medical Journal*, 314 (7989), 1271–1274.
18 Weinstein, J., & Pillai, V. K. (2015). *Demography: The science of population*. Rowman & Littlefield.
19 Salk, J., & Salk, J. (2018). *A New Reality: Human evolution for a sustainable future*. Simon and Schuster.
20 Sen, A. (2014). Development as freedom (1999). In *The Globalization and Development Reader: Perspectives on development and global change* (p. 525). John Wiley & Sons.
21 CECODES, VFF-CRT & UNDP (2013). *The Viet Nam Governance and Public Administration Performance Index (PAPI) 2012*. Centre for Research and Training of the Viet Nam Fatherland Front (VFF-CRT) and United Nations Development Programme (UNDP).
22 Parfit, D. (1984). *Reasons and Persons*. Oxford University Press.
23 MacAskill, W. (2022). *What We Owe the Future*. Basic Books.
24 Brundtland, G. H. (1987). Our common future – call for action. *Environmental Conservation*, 14(4), 291–294.
25 http://www.ursulakleguinarchive.com/Note-Technology.html, accessed on May 8, 2022.
26 Chapman, J. (2014). Meaningful stuff: Toward longer lasting products. In *Materials Experience* (p. 45). Butterworth-Heinemann.
27 Chapman, J. (2012). *Emotionally Durable Design: Objects, experiences and empathy*. Routledge.
28 Chapman, J. (2021). *Meaningful Stuff: Design that lasts*. MIT Press.
29 Schiermer, B. (2019). Weber's alternative theory of action: Relationalism and object-oriented action in Max Weber's work. *European Journal of Sociology/Archives Européennes de Sociologie*, 60(2), 239–281.
30 Norman, D. A. (1995). The psychopathology of everyday things. In *Readings in Human–Computer Interaction* (pp. 5–21). Morgan Kaufmann.
31 Harvey, G. (2005). *Animism: Respecting the living world*. Columbia University Press.
32 Leube, M. (2017). A meditation on the relationship between things and their makers. In *Routledge Handbook of Sustainable Product Design* (p. 41). Routledge.
33 McDonough, W., & Braungart, M. (2010). *Cradle to Cradle: Remaking the way we make things*. North Point Press.
34 McDonough, W., & Braungart, M. (2013). *The Upcycle: Beyond sustainability – designing for abundance*. Macmillan.
35 Leube, M., & Walcher, D. (2017). Designing for the next (circular) economy. An appeal to renew the curricula of design schools. *The Design Journal*, 20(sup1), S492–S501.
36 Bartle, P. N. (2021). *The Adidas Futurecraft Loop: A product innovation challenging the attitude-behavior gap in sustainable footwear consumption* (Doctoral dissertation).
37 Stahel, W. (2010). *The Performance Economy*. Springer.

38 Graham, M., & Haarstad, H. (2011). Transparency and development: Ethical consumption through Web 2.0 and the internet of things. *Information Technologies & International Development*, 7(1), 1.

39 Walcher, D., & Leube, M. (2017). Circular economy by co-creation. In *Preparing Designers and Decision Makers for Upcoming Transformations Salzburg University of Applied Sciences/Design and Product Management Submitted 20th April 2017 to the 15th International Open and User Innovation Conference, Innsbruck.* http://ouisociety.org.

40 https://www.euractiv.com/section/energy-environment/news/eu-agrees-new-law-granting-consumers-a-right-to-repair-products/

41 Oghazi, P., & Mostaghel, R. (2018). Circular business model challenges and lessons learned – an industrial perspective. *Sustainability*, 10(3), 739.

42 Prahalad, C. K., & Ramaswamy, V. (2004). Co-creation experiences: The next practice in value creation. *Journal of Interactive Marketing*, 18(3), 5–14.

43 https://www.merriam-webster.com/dictionary/interface, accessed on August 20, 23.

44 Malhotra, A., & Van Alstyne, M. (2014). The dark side of the sharing economy ... and how to lighten it. *Communications of the ACM*, 57(11), 24–27.

45 Burmeister, C., Lüttgens, D. & Piller, F. T. (2016). Business model innovation for industrie 4.0: Why the "industrial internet" mandates a new perspective on innovation. *Die Unternehmung*, 2.

46 Schumpeter, J. A. (2000). Entrepreneurship as innovation. *University of Illinois at Urbana-Champaign's Academy for Entrepreneurial Leadership Historical Research Reference in Entrepreneurship.*

47 Prahalad, C. K., & Ramaswamy, V. (2004). Co-creation experiences: The next practice in value creation. *Journal of Interactive Marketing*, 18(3), 5–14.

48 Von Hippel, E. (2005). Democratizing innovation: The evolving phenomenon of user innovation. *Journal für Betriebswirtschaft*, 55, 63–78.

49 Rajagopal, A., & Sacchetti, V. (2019). The Unmaking of *Autoprogettazione*. In *The Culture of Nature in the History of Design* (pp. 237–247). Routledge.

50 https://www.cucula.org/geschichte/, accessed on May 4, 2022.

51 Kurilova-Palisaitiene, J., Lindkvist, L. & Sundin, E. (2015). Towards facilitating circular product life-cycle information flow via remanufacturing. *Procedia CIRP*, 29, 780–785.

52 Ritzer, G. (2015). Prosumer capitalism. *The Sociological Quarterly*, 56(3), 413–445.

53 Von Hippel, E. (2005). Democratizing innovation: The evolving phenomenon of user innovation. *Journal für Betriebswirtschaft*, 55, 63–78.

54 Franke, N., Von Hippel, E. & Schreier, M. (2006). Finding commercially attractive user innovations: A test of lead-user theory. *Journal of Product Innovation Management*, 23(4), 301–315.

55 Boldrin, M., & Levine, D. K. (2008). *Against Intellectual Monopoly* (Vol. 62). Cambridge University Press.

56 https://www.wired.com/story/generative-ai-systems-arent-just-open-or-closed-source/.

57 LaBarre, S. (2011, August 25). WikiHouse, an online building kit, shows how to make a house in 24 hours. Co.Design. Fast Company, Inc.

58 https://www.project-syndicate.org/commentary/green-from-the-grassroots-2012-06, accessed on October 29, 2023.

13

MODULE TWO: DESIGN FOR HUMANS NOT MODELS

Matching Evolution

Certain environmental and societal affordances likely secured a better chance for survival and reproduction, but humans evolve infinitely more slowly biologically speaking – and I do include human consciousness here – than they do culturally. Said differently, what has changed over the millennia is the interface between physical world and cognition, not cognition. The result is the *uncanny*, as we move in a state of *evolutionary mismatch*, our minds trying to adjust to the world we built around ourselves. However, since cultural evolution has been much faster than biological evolution, our mental algorithms are often inapt for the transactions of modern life. Science writer Michael Shermer puts it this way:

> What may seem like irrational behaviour today may have actually been rational 100,000 years ago. Without an evolutionary perspective, the assumptions of Homo economicus – that "Economic Man" is rational, self-maximizing and efficient in making choices – make no sense.[1]

Humans are more than *users, customers* or *consumers* exploited for increasing GDP. As I have hopefully demonstrated, *Homo economicus* is but a caricature, and we know that humans are incredibly social, obsessed with reputation and predictably irrational. Simply put, humans are not *Econs* – a term sometimes used to stand for *Economic man* (and woman) – because they are not models. Neither are they perfectly rational agents. And they do not behave like cogs in a machine. We make decisions based on a complex network of premises and not just cost–benefit analyses. Should we replace this with *Homo faber*, the designing human, *Homo ludens*, the playing human, or *Homo altruistic*? All are absurd because all are models and humans are not.

DOI: 10.4324/9781003464754-17

Instead, we are irrational, often wildly unpredictable, and we were selected during the Pleistocene, a time radically different to today. The traits that made perfect sense back then – were features then – are bugs now. We call them *cognitive biases* and they serve as reminders of the need for a more naturalist appraisal of the human animal, especially with a focus on modern consumerism. Two very close friends, both grandsons of rabbis, psychologists Amos Tversky and Daniel Kahneman, expanded such insights and presented experimental research on cognitive biases in the 1970s. So creative and yet rigorous was their teamwork that they have been labeled the "John Lennon and Paul McCartney of psychology." For example, through simple social experiments they came up with the famous concept of *loss aversion*, the human tendency to prefer avoiding a loss to acquiring an equivalent gain. In other words, losing 10 euros will cause me more suffering than the joy of winning the same amount could ever compensate. As simple as this might sound, it poses a serious risk to standard economic theory since two commodities equal in value should be readily interchangeable.[2]

Tversky and Kahneman found many other such mental shortcuts to lead to totally illogical and irrational decisions. Their proposition was revolutionary because it shows that everyone is steered in their judgments by such biases. Obviously, such outcomes are not based on rational choices, but they make good sense when we look at *resource allocation* in the light of an ancestral environment. Another example is *framing*: an airline company could tell me that I will board an airplane and safely land in the destination airport with a 99 percent probability, or it could present the same data and tell me that there is a 1 percent chance of the airplane falling out of the sky, leading to the violent deaths of all passengers. Obviously, the former framing of information is the better sales pitch! Another bias is that of the *in-group* where we tend to rate our "tribe" as superior to others.[3] However, in these strange times our "tribes" overlap constantly, and individuals will always prefer ideological "echo chambers" for their safety and comfort, but never have they been as ripe for manipulation and misinformation as today. Similarly, being shunned by a group still feels terrible today, because it is a psychological remnant of a former age when ostracism meant certain death.[4] The *negativity bias* makes sense of the fact that we devote much more cognitive power to unusual, dangerous and negative events than usual, safe and positive ones. (Driving a long distance, we will remember one crash and not a single of the thousands of cars courteously and safely passing each other.) Those more attuned to danger were more likely to survive, but in a far safer present tense, such a negativity bias has us descendants unnecessarily fixated on the bad. Or take the *confirmation bias*, the tendency to rate information more favorably if it comes from within our own social spheres. Whatever the *ultimate*, the *proximate* motivation for human action is a need to fit in.

In his bestseller *Thinking, Fast and Slow*, Daniel Kahneman consolidates his research into a scientific treaty, arguing that the human mind works along two different pathways of processing information and computing decisions he called *system 1* and *system 2*. *System 1* is unconscious, fast, automatic and effortless and works without self-awareness or control. According to Kahneman, it does up to 98 percent of all our "thinking," a word I put inside quotation marks because it is often considered to be done by the gut and not the brain. *System 2* is slow, deliberate and conscious. It takes a lot of effort, control and rationale. It is what logic and skepticism are based on, and it is what makes our final decisions, but it only accounts for 2 percent of all our thinking.[5]

Let me be as clear as possible. I am not defending a human model along the lines of Jean Jacques Rousseau's *noble savage*, living in perfect ecological equilibrium until industrialization came along. Evolutionary traits can only be considered vices or virtues by judging their resultant behavior in the real world. Actually, many of the wicked environmental and social problems are caused and exasperated by human adaptive tendencies with long evolutionary roots such as 1) an extremely ego-centric wish to survive, 2) a strong motivation for high status, 3) a tendency to consciously and unconsciously copy others, 4) to be very short-sighted in our decision-making and 5) a proneness to disregard concerns that are abstract rather than real. I have shown all such anthropological constants at length and tried to paint as objective a picture of human nature as possible. But I am not a genetic determinist and I have also tried to show how important context is in strengthening or weakening any or all such tendencies. They are constantly exploited and monetized in the service of marketing, advertisement and even design. But just as likely, they could be harnessed for sustainability and pro-sociality.

There isn't much hope to get back to the same situation that nature designed us for, but since we have a kind of archaic memory of what was good for us and what we liked, we can recreate surroundings better fit for us today. This memory is manifested in universal cross-cultural preferences, and it seems obvious that *artifice* and *artifact* should be conceived to align with as many of them as possible. However, to realign the economic and social domains, *design thinking* will need to shift from selfish materialism to a more holistic approach of interconnectedness.

Course One: Design for *Paleorithms*

A great introduction to how evolutionary logic is useful for design students might be Jay Appleton's *prospect–refuge theory* of human aesthetics, this "acquired preference for particular methods of satisfying inborn desires."[6] Philosopher Dietrich von Hildebrand expanded Appleton's definition of prospect–refuge and included *mystery, complexity, enticement* and *illumination*, four elements especially important for design and architectural considerations since they suggest that environments that provide opportunities for collecting more information allow for better, safer living conditions.[7] Architects and designers have since developed a model which suggests that spaces must have views and outlooks, partially framed or enclosed, and that visual complexity enhances feelings of safety, while a sense of mystery is preferred.[8] Over ten years ago, I was able to apply such evolutionary criteria to a landscape architecture project in Vienna. Together with *GP designpartners*, we turned an unattractive piece of land into a *naturally* more appealing park, and while we have not tested whether the surrounding offices reported a higher output from their human resource departments, aesthetically the project might convince you on a very primal level.[9]

Evolutionary logic serves as a kind of template for designers to make appropriate decisions for solving real-life problems. Especially inspirational is David Sloan Wilson's *The Neighborhood Project*, a fascinating book about using evolutionary theory to improve social situations. In a lower-income, largely rundown district of upstate New York, Wilson and his team used the aforementioned *multilevel selection theory* to help different neighborhoods to design and implement their perfect community garden. He "[used] evolution to change [his] city one block at a time." Together with his colleagues he surveyed different aspects relating to corrosive social behavior and rundown infrastructure to fix them in collective efforts. The outcomes were vibrant, communal projects that could only come into existence because people started acting as cooperating wholes, as organisms.[10]

Indeed, there is much reason for optimism. For example, in Barcelona the design school *Elisava* has its own *Design for City Making Research Lab*, an institute that investigates the role of design in the material and social construction of our habitats through projects run by professors, students and researchers. The projects are always in collaboration with the private sector, public administration and NGOs. Design is seen as a "plug-in" which aims to enrich the complex system that is a city.[11] Another encouraging example comes from Boston's ongoing *Tactical Public Realm Guidelines*, which aim to use design interventions to make its city a more enjoyable and pro-social place.[12]

Interior designers can also glean much from studies pointing to the positive effects the presence and cues of nature in our habitats has on us, the inhabitants. Even concentration and productivity seem to go up with students and workers in offices with plants.[13] Architect Roger Ulrich has also conducted numerous investigations into the positive effects of plants. One example is an elegant priming experiment where subjects were shown scary videoclips of work-related accidents featuring loads of blood and fear. Afterwards the group was divided into two groups and the first was shown a film with scenes of nature and the second was shown a film of cityscapes. As predicted, stress indicators such as heart rate and skin conductance fell more rapidly in the group submerged in images of nature.[14] Ulrich is also known for his studies of records of patients recovering from cholecystectomies in Pennsylvanian hospital between 1972 and 1981. Twenty-three surgical patients who stayed in rooms with views of natural scenery had shorter hospital recovery stays, received fewer negative evaluative comments by nurses and had to take less pain medication than 23 other patients in rooms very similar with the exception that the windows faced brick building walls.[15] There is even scientific evidence that the flowers we bring to our loved ones in the hospital have a measurable physiological effect on recovery. Of course, because the giver, the receiver and the flowers are all kindred – designed by nature.[16]

Designers can also create interior concepts to foster learning. By adding flexible and ergonomic furniture and using graphics, students can engage in co-creation activities known to foster pro-social behavior. Anyone who has ever been to school understands that lighting and acoustics are crucial for an optimal environment of learning. As we have seen above, *biophilia* is the natural need to connect with nature. Arguably more than for adults – children are still closer to nature and have had less time to adjust to the artificial environment – it is essential for children's cognitive functioning and well-being.[17] *Biophilia* is not just a desire but a human need, especially for children in urban environments; and designers' ability to include nature in classrooms is an obvious solution to address this issue.[18]

Neuroscientists have teamed up with designers in Europe to show how an affinity for round shapes is human not just cultural. Led by psychologist Oshin Vartanian of the University of Toronto at Scarborough, the team compiled 200 images of interior architecture contrasting in curvature. This was not just a survey-based experiment, but involved brain imaging. Participants were slid into a functional magnetic resonance imaging (fMRI) machine and where then shown the pictures and asked to label them as either "beautiful" or "not beautiful." Rooms were considered far more beautiful when full of curves instead of straight lines and right angles. The study also showed much more brain activity, especially in the *anterior cingulate cortex* when looking at curvy spaces. There is nothing sexual going on here as the group was evenly divided between the sexes.[19]

It is immensely exciting to see studies on landscape preferences used to support design decisions for architectural exteriors and interiors. *Biophilic display*, such as vertical gardens, window-farming and interior plants, have become hugely popular and *Instagrammable* in hipster cafés the world over, but upon closer inspection such efforts rarely go far enough because they are still largely based on bringing nature *into* our built environment and technology is still seen as contrary to nature. But what if we stop thinking in such binary terms and think of nature *as* technology. After all, nature is the "mother of invention" and master of prototyping. It was able to produce and scale every living thing on this planet in a carbon-neutral way and without producing garbage. In the words of award-winning green architect Eric Corey Freed, "nature knows how to build structures that grow, heal, breathe and regenerate."[20] The research of science, coupled with the creativity of designers and architects, allows humans to be part of a natural technology with radical resource efficiency, closed material loops and regenerative energy. Concepts of *cradle to cradle* and *biomimicry* can and should be part of the roadmap.

Let us get back to a question asked at the beginning: are we inherently sustainable or unsustainable? Yes, we are all trashing the planet, and, true, we are not exactly subtle, as we leave behind our garbage and stench. But we do so only because we are constantly nudged to do so. No doubt that human behavior is biased towards maximizing personal gain and rank but the specific strategy for achieving either is always contextual. *If,* in a given society, rank and affluence are allocated to those displaying the shiniest, newest objects, *then* citizens will aspire to do so. Are we not told from an early age to express ourselves, not by what we are but rather by what we have? It is not surprising to see people impatiently burning through products, clothing and food when they are strongly encouraged to do exactly that.

Behavioral sciences (prevention science, cognitive psychology, neurology and experimental economics) could be used for good, and interventions can prevent many of the dysfunctions of modern society. The basic argument behind *nudge theory* is that non-forced compliance can be achieved at least as effectively by positive reinforcement as by negative sanctions. Let us imagine that we are hungry and walk into a self-service cafeteria. If the slices of pizza are found immediately after the entrance and the salad bar at the very end before the cashier, we will likely not eat many greens. But, for a designer wanting to fight a rising trend of diabetes, the environment of the cafeteria could be restructured in a way to encourage eating more greens and less lard. Especially designers of *services* and *social innovation* – but also those of commodities – can thus become *choice architects* by shaping the situations in which people make choices.[21] Of course, marketers, advertisers and shop designers have been excellent *choice architects* for decades, but their motivation has been on behalf of the seller. Designers could just as easily study human behavior and use choice architecture on behalf of the chooser. The fact is that the choices we make about the built and natural environment today will affect all generations of the future.

Course Two: Paleolithic Jiu Jitsu

The *British Behavioral Design Lab*, a collaboration between Warwick Business School and the Design Council, uses human sciences to design better products, services and places.[22] But we don't need universities to show that culture change is steered by design. It is the very definition of both. Again, this is not only a moral argument, and we don't need to get our heads chopped off by *Hume's guillotine.* Just as well we can use cold economic logic because maladaptive designs are pricey for society. Conversely, designs that reduce morbidity rates will reduce our tax burdens. Graduates of the *department of the future designer* would practice a kind of *soft paternalism.* Such an approach has already been tried when Cass Sunstein was in the Obama administration advising on how to manage the health of a population.

From neuroscience, anthropology and sociology we have a pretty good idea of how nature has designed humans to behave when. We also know how to exploit ancient behavioral algorithms in the service of consumption; that comes from marketing. But how can we use all this data to steer away from situations generally referred to as *tragedies of the commons*? In the vein of martial art Jiu jitsu, a priori tendencies that will likely lead to negative outcomes can gently be redirected towards the good. Let us consider climate change, the biggest tragedy of them all. We know that current fossil fuel–based consumption patterns drive climate change and will have dire effects on all human civilization; so why do so few people care about it? To explain we must introduce yet another evolutionary concept, *future-discounting*. Humans take the future far less seriously than the present, and even less seriously the more distant that future is. All this makes sense because the further away a reward is, the higher are the chances that it does not materialize, and so we likely evolved psychological biases to devalue future gratification. In short, we have a clear bias for today over tomorrow, for reaching the end of the month over setting up a pension plan. By *discounting the future*, we tilt the gravitas of decisions toward the present, making it less likely that society will undertake any real actions to mitigate climate change as well as other global environmental threats.[23]

Let us look at a famous experiment, this time involving marshmallows. Kids love them, they are soft and cute and most importantly, sweet. They love them so much that they literally cannot wait to eat them, even when promised a second one. In the famous *Stanford Marshmallow Experiment* by Professor Walter Mischel, children sat in a room with a marshmallow placed in front of them. They were told that if they just waited a little while they would get another, provided they had not eaten the original. Very few of these poor little kids could wait. What about adults? When someone is offered 100 euros today or 110 euros in a few weeks, most people will opt for the immediate reward, even if it is perfectly clear that waiting literally pays off. The reason is that the value 110 seems lower than the 100 because we assign the waiting period a cost, a process called *temporal discounting*. Basically, the larger the "psychological distance" – temporal or geographical – between a person and an event, the more unreal the event seems. We give immediate rewards no discount penalties and thus we can procrastinate doing important chores and do fun ones immediately.[24]

If we now take climate change and break it down into billions of individual contributory actions involving carbon emissions, we see that it is inherently caused by this psychological distance between rewards (a beautiful, green future) and costs (giving up our luxurious, fun ways of living). The very concept of burning up fossil fuels serves as an example here: it provides an immediate output of energy to make us move around, use gadgets and warm our homes. No wonder we are still struggling to delay energy gratification,

234 The Department of the Future Designer

which is the basic role of a battery! It just never seemed important enough. Why wait? But opting for the immediate benefit *will* have future ecological and economic costs, which are delayed by time and thus the future cost is discounted heavily. Putting all this together, the most effective method of internalizing the long-distance costs of burning fossil fuels is likely a negative sanction in the present through heavy carbon taxes. If we go back to the *Stanford Marshmallow Experiment*, such a tax would be like cutting off part of the first marshmallow, making the immediate reward smaller compared to the future one. Policymakers and economic experts need to decide how much of the first marshmallow to remove, for everyone to resist temptation and wait.

Evolutionary studies suggest that humans – just like other organisms – respond adaptively to environmental cues associated with threats and opportunities, but since we don't immediately smell, hear, feel or see global climate change, it fails to activate an immediate self-protection response. Designers might contribute here by giving climate change on the spot visionary, olfactory and acoustic cues. Energy research, for example, shows that visualizing thermal energy does increase the willingness of individual households to save energy.[25] However, I believe that for social and economic policies to be effective, it requires drawing on aspects of the human behavioral suite, which emphasize cooperation, sustainability and a shared sense of responsibility. Public shaming – as brutal as it sounds – is a powerful negative sanction that can be both official (written into law) or unofficial (expressed by friends and relatives), and likely works so well as a corrective measure because for our ancestors public shaming and the related ostracizing meant certain death. Thus, psychological research revealed that people contributed 50 percent more to goals set up by groups when they were told that the names of the most selfish individuals of the group would be publicized. In a similar vein, the least and most polluting companies can be publicized in national rankings. Such behavioral nudges could easily be combined with one catering to our evolved tendency to follow role models and influencers.[26] And let us not forget our *in-group bias*: seeing close friends and family members care about climate change can even reduce the enormous gap in beliefs on climate change between people on both sides of the political spectrum.[27] Strong identification with people concerned with sustainability matters brings out the same in us.

Interesting *priming* studies confirm this. First some participants were told to read a story in which they were the protagonists and were offered a work promotion. After reading the story, which triggered archaic longings for status, they were given a choice of products, including a car, a washing machine and a backpack, each of which had an ecological and non-ecological version. More people chose the eco-friendly option, especially if it was more expensive than the standard model when expectations of status were triggered. Interestingly, the eco-friendly choices were made more often when observed in a store rather than at home and online. It seems that products should be of high quality, not too cheap and consumers should be given the opportunity to show they both care for the planet and are able to spend – or have – money.[28]

Indeed, I have seen the rise of *conspicuous conservation*, a kind of reverse Veblen effect amongst my students as they virtue-signal slick drinking bottles and vintage clothes. Basically, the more people are willing to sacrifice to save the environment, the higher they are valued as partners in relationships. Such data is revealed by dating sites and there are also specific sites filtering for ecologists such as Greensingles.com and Meetmindful.com to match eco-conscious romantic partners. Following such logic, ecological designs can also become viral and consumer culture could follow a virtuous cycle.[29] Of course, the danger of "greenwashing" exists since companies thus have incentives to *pretend* to be better than they are. Volkswagen faking their emissions or McDonald's literally painting their franchises green come to mind.

As we have seen, people have a strong *aversion to loss* and will not give up any of their ways if the incentives are stacked the way they are. The drab, hemp shopping bag–toting, patchouli-smelling ecology of the '60s, '70s and '80s is most definitely not appealing. And it's not working. What if, instead, we use the desire to *conspicuously consume* and redirect it towards sustainability? What if we shift our efforts from a strategy of sacrifice and austerity to desire? Since our genes tell us to seek novelty and impress others, sustainability must be sexualized by making it into Darwin's status-enhancing peacock tail. Perhaps the true genius of Elon Musk is his insight that people want to virtue-signal their environmentalism, but in a slick, luxurious and sexy Tesla S. Musk has succeeded in making electric cars some of the most desirable vehicles available, and someone would have to spend nearly two million dollars to get a combustion engine car that accelerates and goes as fast as the Tesla Model S.[30]

Course Three: Design for Commoning

For humans, territorial markings are undoubtedly important to establish and protect, but a holistic and evolutionary view of life shows that nature can never be fully compartmentalized. For example, bees pollinate flowers and other plants far away from their stocks and trees draw CO_2 from the atmosphere, providing everyone with fresh oxygen; should the beekeeper and tree owner not be compensated for such positive externalities? Individuals and all they consider theirs will always include externalities far beyond any fences. Outside the yard, the so-called *common resources* cannot be parceled into neat packages either, since water and air flow and all creatures move.

Natural cycles are complex, and they are adaptive, continuously changing. More than that, cycles tend to be self-enforcing feedbacks, sometimes corrected by other cycles running counter to them. "It is out of these interactions of stocks, flows, feedbacks and delays," writes Kate Raworth, "that complex adaptive systems arise: complex due to their unpredictable emergent behaviour, and adaptive because they keep evolving over time."[31]

In the global *tragedy of the commons*, users of global commons (air, water, light, etc.) receive the full marginal benefit from their use but bear only part of the marginal cost. There have been efforts to resolve such issues through a rigorous campaign for property rights. While free trade and competition resolve issues concerning the value of resources to various parties, the issue of who owns the property right to a scarce resource remains unresolved. Can property rights really be established for things interconnected with other things beyond fences and frontiers? And if they are, what would the transaction costs of bargaining, conflict resolution or transfer be? The *Accordino Treaty* of 1949 between Austria and Italy as well as many others chartered by the UN are hopeful examples of transnational, regional initiatives to enhance cooperation. But can such agreements really settle all disputes over resources and their externalities? (After all, enjoying the warmth of the fire produced in the oven of one cabin results in pollution of common air.) Of course, property does not need to apply only to individuals and often community property rights arise to resolve issues of externalities. Whether they are privatized or owned by the state, land use affects us all since humans have always been and will continue being entirely dependent on each other, on society.

Nationally, *tragedy of the commons* situations have typically been tackled using either centralized top-down governance or *laissez faire* free-market economics, but both approaches have failed in terms of protecting global biospheres. For over half a century, human biology together with economic theory have told a mutually enforcing narrative of the individual as a legitimate unit of study, which we have seen is not only wrong but dangerous. What was meant to be a description of human behavior has turned into a program promoting selfishness with very maladaptive outcomes, the global climate crisis being the premier example. In fact, it is argued here that catering to individuals stands diametrically in the way of solving such issues since individualism makes us fall back on egocentric and narrow concerns instead of looking up to see the wider picture. (I believe that was the main takeaway of the excellent movie *Don't Look Up.*[32]) As we have seen in the theory, the collective efforts that we can broadly call *civilization* very often require individual sacrifice. The way forward must be an updated scientific account, liberated from outdated political categories of left and right and cleared of reductionist axioms. A managed process of cultural evolution using a more accurate understanding of human nature and evolutionary forces might be the only viable way for global sustainability. I sympathize with Austrian Leopold Kohr, who on New Year's Eve in 1983 said the following in his acceptance speech for the *Right Livelihood Award*:

> So let us solve the great problem of our time, the disease of excessive size and uncontrollable proportions, by going back to the alternative to both

right and left – that is, to a small-scale social environment with all its potential for global pluralistic cooperation and largely unaffiliated self-sufficiency, by extending not centralized control but by decontrolling locally centered and nourished communities, each with its own institutional nucleus and a limited but strong and independent gravitational field.[33]

The main impact of Nobel Prize winner Elinor Ostrom's work was to show that when certain conditions are met, groups of people are capable of sustainably managing their common resources. She defined common pool resources as "a natural or man-made resource system that is sufficiently large as to make it costly (but not impossible) to exclude potential beneficiaries from obtaining benefits from its use."[34] In "Governing the Commons," Ostrom sees that the problems arising from a *common pool resource* are like those arising from the *free rider* problem. She showed that the tragedy of the commons can be avoided within groups without privatization or top-down regulation. Evolutionary biologist David Sloan Wilson, ecologist Michael Cox and Ostrom have recently written a synthesis of her eight core design principles and the anthropological sciences.[35]

As we have seen, the linear system of production and consumption of our designed objects has led to systems we call *tragedies of the commons.* Remember, for example: the heat given off by millions of air-conditioning units warms the planet's atmosphere, which increases the need for more air-conditioning. Just like it is possible to optimize the traffic flow of a city not by focusing on individual driving behaviors but rather by looking at the whole system as the target of selection aligned with the driving behavior of the individuals, the same holds true for larger goals such as sustainable and coordinated economies. Ostrom's *core design principles* are a promising starting point for conceiving the multilevel governance that promotes human cooperation and sustainability at local, regional, national and global levels. They need to be firmly anchored in design curricula around the world! Although our cohort of students likely experienced the benefit of the *core design principles* first-hand on their *Paleo Design Camp*, let us revisit them here in more detail. I will use what authors David Sloan Wilson, Paul Atkins and Steven Hayes have called the *core design principles version 2.0* in their book *Prosocial.*[36]

Shared Identity and Purpose (formerly known as *clearly defined groups*): All examples of major evolutionary transitions involve groups of organisms with clear boundaries, such as the cell wall for cells or nests for social insects. But just marking a territory as an in-group is not enough; well-functioning groups also need to share a vison. Ancestral human life typically took place in small groups where membership, emotional attachment and tasks were obvious to everyone and present-day hunter-gatherer societies – although more fluid – also show strong group identity and sense of shared purpose. This important principle applies for any other group, no matter if they are living in an industrialized society or not. It is the logic behind why *corporate identity* (CI) and *brand identity* are so important in the world of business.

Equitable Distribution of Contributions and Benefits (formerly known as *proportional equivalence between benefits and costs*): In general, people feel strongly about equity and when costs and benefits are not fairly distributed, within-group selection and competition are bound to be the result. Everyone who has ever worked on a team project knows the feeling of some people carrying most of the workload, while others – the *free riders* – just do the bare minimum but enjoy any praise given on the day of the final presentation. When costs and benefits are evened out proportionally and selection differentials within the group are eliminated, however, the group will prevail.

Fair and Inclusive Decision-Making (formerly known as *collective-choice arrangements*): As Alexis de Tocqueville pointed out in his *Democracy in America*, the ideal setting for decision-making was the townhall meeting of a small group. It was not a random sidenote of a detached sociologist but a key observation of an important ingredient for people working on the success of a cohesive group, in this case democracy of the United States.[37]

But no matter what the size of the group might be, to ensure commitment and well-being, people must be given agency in decision-making. As I have mentioned numerous times, the existence of discussion groups around campsites of relatively small tribes are not just archaeological and ethnographic curiosities but evolutionary common denominators.

Monitoring Agreed Behaviors (formerly known as *monitoring*): The reason problems of common resource use arise in the first place is a failure to monitor free riders. A watchful eye on agreed-upon behavior is an essential ingredient for the success of any group because the successful management of *commons* doesn't run on good will but on accountability. It is easy to mistake this principle with the top-down surveillance of managers or states, but accountability is usually warranted best between peers.

Graduated Responding to Helpful and Unhelpful Behavior (formerly known as *graduated sanctions*): As Ostrom observed, successful *commons* worked best when participants were given a way to learn from their mistakes and primary offenders were not immediately ostracized. No one is perfect and often transgression from agreed upon behavior are simply mistakes resulting from misunderstandings, not bad intentions. Reminders and nudges for individuals to obey the rules of the group can be extremely effective, but more stringent sanctions must also be available. In group feedback sessions, such positive and negative reinforcements can lead to individual behavior change.

Fast and Fair Conflict Resolution (formerly known as *conflict resolution mechanisms*): Everyone has different interests and access to different information and thus, like the second design principle, conflict resolution must be democratic and proportional. Such mechanisms act as a safeguard against non-corporation inside groups. When issues of misconduct come up, resolving them should be informal, cheap and easily accessible. Rules of conduct might be detailed in a waiver to be signed by each member and problems are solved rather than ignored since nobody wants to be the source of trouble.

Authority to Self-Govern According to Principles 1–6 (formerly known as *minimal recognition of rights to organize***):** This one is outward-looking because every group is embedded in larger groups and society as a whole. A group must comply with laws as mandated by trade unions, syndicates or government. There are many methods to secure the self-governance of a group, such as *sociocracy* or *holacracy*. In a volatile world, flexibility and spontaneity in a team are key.

Collaborative Relations with Other Groups Using Principles 1–7 (formerly known as *for a world of groups within a larger social system, there must be coordination and communication among all***):** Though issues can usually be managed locally, some might need wider regional attention, and thus, authors Wilson, Atkins and Hayes call this principle, "a meta-principle that allows all the other principles to be scaled to groups of groups."[38] Cooperation between groups will only be successful if each respects and practices principles one through seven within their own group.

Course Four: Mindful Design Not Design for Full Minds

Mental morbidity is consistently and painfully made clear by presentations from my students of a demography class. The assignment was to report on morbidity and mortality rates of real countries of their choice and every single one of the reports presented self-harm and suicide in the top 10 list of global morbidity trends. Today, there is a lot of mental pain, and I don't think it is controversial to say that internationally people are self-medicating on many numbing substances. There is the raging opioid epidemic of the United States of America, but also milder drugs – prescribed or not – are very widely used. The psycho-pharmaceutical industry is having its heyday with sales going through the roof and it has recently been reported that mood stabilizing drugs such as Prozac are so common that they have been detected after passing through the internal organs of their users in the drinking water re-sanitized in Britain.[39]

By focusing on an objective societal image of ourselves and confusing that image with a very incomplete inner version of self, we can never be satisfied. Since in modern society end-users are constantly reminded of our old-fashionability, unsuitableness, unsuccessfulness and body-dysphoria, we consume the products, services and experiences laid out in front of us to compensate. Every future moment and every future purchase promises satisfaction. It is the anticipation of purchasing something that makes us go from moment to moment, and as soon as we have gone through the transaction at the point of sale and have a material good in our hands, our happiness starts to diminish as we are anticipating the next purchase. If marketing is the engine behind growth in GDP, the culture of inadequacy is the fuel. More precisely, what really is ignited to drive this engine is our faltering attention and eye on the next purchase. Designers: don't add to the confusion and stop filling our heads!

For the *future designers* themselves to work, to conceive, it will also be helpful to stay mindful, instead of stuffing their minds. A healthy inner world is crucial for the creation of a better outer world, as is suggested by the *Inner Development Goals* (IDGs), a non-profit organization based on science-based skills for living more purposeful and sustainable lives, which in turn could go some way towards meeting the UN *Sustainable Development Goals.*[40] Design students often fall into a mode of thinking where they assume that blindly copying functions, features and styles of existing successful products is the only *modus operandi*. When I ask my students to "research" a topic, they open *Pinterest* and *Instagram*! And even if they religiously follow every part of a research-driven design process – from exploration to ideation to proto-typing to delivery – good design cannot be guaranteed. That can only be measured by looking at its performance in the real world. Blind imitation and adoption of business practices without a shift in mindset and culture is as useless as the straw airplanes of cargo-cults.

When approaching a new design challenge, added biases can interfere with the creative process. Instead, an approach of open-mindedness, or mindfulness, can tap the roots of creativity by embracing the infinity that is the creative mind. The Buddhist principle of *beginner's mind* could mean here to start fresh without assumptions, norms and trends, because as counterintuitively as it may sound, the lack of expertise on a topic can be an opportunity for creativity. Trying to stay on top of every trend and every celebrity, my students are addicted to various *black mirrors* by displaying illusions of light and shadow to escape as much of the present moments as possible. (Yes, I stole that metaphor from the Netflix series.) Like junkies, they find focused sobriety so unbearable that they consume more and more of this illusionary flickering.

Designers also need to sit with uncomfortable truths and ethical dilemmas, to try and approach a problem from every angle – its *Gestalt* – before racing to solve it. For example, designers must look hard at the inconvenient truth that stoking desires requires ever greater material throughput, which in turn is ripping through our natural resources and encroaching on the rest of earth's biodiversity. Species are dying at alarming rates, and as their pain is not released into a vacuum unseen and unheard, it touches us all on subtle levels, adding to our distress and distraction.

Only by accepting such a situation can the *future designer* commit to do better. Speculation, *out-of-the-box* thinking, brainstorming – all are great tools of ideation, but the best is still inspiration grounded in reality, and driven by clear moral intentions.

Different schools of mindfulness – especially non-dual approaches – speak of *ego death*, the sudden realization that the "I" and "me" themselves are mere illusions. Our ego, that voice in our heads that demands to be "right" about lifestyle choices, is not the only one since most people walk around with similar voices in their heads. Our desire to be glamorous, gorgeous and awesome is reflected by what we watch, read, feel, think and speak. We are flustered and unsatisfied, always thirsty and hungry for more, wanting things faster, steeper, brighter, louder. But when the mind settles down, even for just a few moments, we can appreciate the fact that sight, sound, smell, taste and touch just *are*, prior to subjective judgment.[41] Designs don't even have to please their creator, because that is not who they are meant for.

Only when such a state of mind is experienced can anyone ever hope to practice true empathy and be open to the feedback from the people they are designing for. Designers, please stop pitching everything and just design! The end-user will like it or not, use it or not – but let *them* decide. If we continuously focus on what we might respond to, it is easy to miss everything the world around us is trying to tell us.

The human predicament as diagnosed by both spirituality and modern science is that we are not equipped with a default mechanism of happiness; instead, we are wired by nature to constantly try to improve our current state of being by leaning into the next moment. Still, every individual has the potential to be *psychologically flexible*, allowing them to increase behaviors that are rewarding and discontinue behaviors that are punishing. Like epigenetic processes, which regulate gene expression, there now exist many behavioral psychology methods that help to regulate the expression of adaptive or maladaptive behavior in individuals. The common denominator of such approaches is: rather than trying to solve problems by eliminating difficult thoughts and feelings, they select from their vast variety through what B. F. Skinner called "evolution by consequence."[42] For instance, acceptance and commitment therapy (ACT) is highly successful in treating maladaptive individual behavior because of its evolutionary foundation.[43] The ways you want individual players to behave needs to be designed and only then can you start deliberately practicing and reinforcing those behavior patterns. Stepping it up one level, managing the change of a team's culture also requires managed evolution.

Notes

1 Shermer, M. (2009). *The Mind of the Market: How biology and psychology shape our economic lives*. Macmillan, p. 35–36.

2 Shefrin, H., & Statman, M. (2003). The contributions of Daniel Kahneman and Amos Tversky. *The Journal of Behavioral Finance*, 4(2), 54–58.

3 De Dreu, C. K., & Triki, Z. (2022). Intergroup conflict: Origins, dynamics and consequences across taxa. *Philosophical Transactions of the Royal Society B*, 377 (1851), 20210134.

4 Boehm, C. (1999). Hierarchy in the forest. In *Hierarchy in the Forest*. Harvard University Press.

5 Kahneman, D. (2011). *Thinking, Fast and Slow*. Macmillan.

6 Crawford, D. W. (1976). The experience of landscape. *Journal of Aesthetics and Art Criticism*, 34(3), 367–369.

7 Spencer, M. K. (2019). Dietrich von Hildebrand's aesthetics and the value of modern art. *Quaestiones Disputatae*, 10(1), 52–71.

8 Dosen, A. S., & Ostwald, M. J. (2013). Methodological characteristics of research testing prospect–refuge theory: A comparative analysis. *Architectural Science Review*, 56(3), 232–241.

9 http://gp.co.at/index.php/projekte_detail_en.html?proj_id=97, accessed on February 20, 2015.

10 Wilson, D. S. (2011). *The Neighborhood Project: Using evolution to improve my city, one block at a time*. Hachette.

11 Manzini, E., Fuster, A. & Paez, R. (2022). *Plug-Ins: Design for city making in Barcelona*. Actar.

12 https://www.boston.gov/transportation/tactical-public-realm, accessed on February 1, 2024.

13 Mann, M., Oberzaucher, E. & Grammer, K. (2008, July). Phytophilia: Effects of plants on human cognition and room perception. In *XIX Biennial Conference of the International Society for Human Ethology*, p. 114.

14 Ulrich, R. S., Simons, R. F., Losito, B. D., Fiorito, E., Miles, M. A. & Zelson, M. (1991). Stress recovery during exposure to natural and urban environments. *Journal of Environmental Psychology*, 11(3), 201–230.

15 Ulrich, R. S. (1984). View through a window may influence recovery from surgery. *Science*, 224(4647), 420–421.

16 Park, S. H., & Mattson, R. H. (2009). Therapeutic influences of plants in hospital rooms on surgical recovery. *HortScience*, 44(1), 102–105.

17 Wells, N. M., & Evans, G. W. (2003). Nearby nature: A buffer of life stress among rural children. *Environment and Behavior*, 35, 311–330.

18 Flouri, E., Midouhas, E. & Joshi, H. (2014). The role of urban neighbourhood green space in children's emotional and behavioural resilience. *Journal of Environmental Psychology*, 40, 179–186.

19 Vartanian, O., Navarrete, G., Chatterjee, A., Fich, L. B., Leder, H., Modroño, C., ... & Skov, M. (2013). Impact of contour on aesthetic judgments and approach-avoidance decisions in architecture. *Proceedings of the National Academy of Sciences*, 110(Supplement 2), 10446–10453.

20 http://prostruction.life/inspiration/, accessed on May 8, 2022.

21 Thaler, R. H., & Sunstein, C. R. (2021). *Nudge: The final edition*. Yale University Press.

22 http://www.behaviouraldesignlab.org, accessed on February 9, 2015.

23 Caney, S. (2009). Climate change and the future: Discounting for time, wealth, and risk. *Journal of Social Philosophy*, 40(2), 163–186.

24 Mischel, W. (2014). *The Marshmallow Test: Understanding self-control and how to master it*. Random House.

25 Steg, L. (2016). Behaviour: Seeing heat saves energy. *Nature Energy*, 1, 15013.

26 Braun Kohlová, M., & Urban, J. (2020). Buy green, gain prestige and social status. *Journal of Environmental Psychology*, 69, 101416.

27 Goldberg, M. H., van der Linden, S., Leiserowitz, A. & Maibach, E. (2020). Perceived social consensus can reduce ideological biases on climate change. *Environment and Behavior*, 52, 495–517.

28 Bouman, T., Steg, L. & Zawadzki, S. J. (2020). The value of what others value: When perceived biospheric group values influence individuals' pro-environmental engagement. *Journal of Environmental Psychology*, 71, 101470.

29 Palomo-Vélez, G., Tybur, J. & van Vugt, M. (2021). Is green the new sexy? Romantic of conspicuous conservation. *Journal of Environmental Psychology*, 73, 101530.

30 Greene, D. L. (2011). Uncertainty, loss aversion, and markets for energy efficiency. *Energy Economics*, 33(4), 608–616.

31 Raworth, K. (2017). *Doughnut Economics: Seven ways to think like a 21st-century economist*. Chelsea Green Publishing, p. 121.

32 McKay, A. (2021). *Don't Look Up*. Hyperobject Industries.
33 Acccptance speech, Right Livelihood Award, Stockholm, December 31, 1983.
34 Ostrom, E. (1990). *Governing the Commons: The evolution of institutions for collective action*. Cambridge University Press, p. 7.
35 Wilson, D. S., Ostrom, E. & Cox, M. E. (2013). Generalizing the core design principles for the efficacy of groups. *Journal of Economic Behavior & Organization*, 90, S21–S32.
36 Atkins, P. W., Wilson, D. S. & Hayes, S. C. (2019). *Prosocial: Using evolutionary science to build productive, equitable, and collaborative groups*. New Harbinger Publications.
37 Tocqueville, A. de (1838). *Democracy in America*. G. Dearborn & Co.
38 Atkins, P. W., Wilson, D. S. & Hayes, S. C. (2019). *Prosocial: Using evolutionary science to build productive, equitable, and collaborative groups*. New Harbinger Publications, p. 43.
39 https://www.theguardian.com/society/2004/aug/08/health.mentalhealth, accessed on December 20, 2021.
40 https://www.innerdevelopmentgoals.org, accessed on November 30, 2023.
41 Rahula, W. (2007). *What the Buddha Taught*. Grove/Atlantic.
42 Skinner, B. F. (2022). The evolution of behaviour 1. In *Behaviour Analysis and Contemporary Psychology* (pp. 33–40). Routledge.
43 Harris, R. (2006). Embracing your demons: An overview of acceptance and commitment therapy. *Psychotherapy in Australia*, 12(4), 70–76.

14

MODULE THREE: DESIGN AS APPLIED ETHICS

Course One: Finding a Moral Compass

Alas, we have come to the final – but difficult – section of this book. Sometimes design is fabulous for the user, lucrative for business and good for society, but very rarely are all three satisfied. It won't be unless our definition of good design undergoes a big expansion, and we intend to satisfy all three before even drawing a sketch. How we define, measure and optimize design has consequences in the real world and must therefore be a proto-thought. In philosophical *consequentialism*, an action that results in more benefit than harm is good, while another, causing more harm than benefit, is not. Every action has a future consequence, but every design decision carries in it a multitude of consequences, for the simple fact of scalability. Designed consequences thus matter a whole lot, but designers are still not asked to reckon with what their creativity entails. Market incentives like *return on investment, profit, break-even point* and *shareholder value* confuse our understanding of the products we conceive by providing incomplete metrics. But designers *can* make things better through their creations. In the *department of the future designer*, success would be measured and reported by the outcomes of design in terms of social impact – the double bottom line. Instead of just tossing the word "good" around like some universal axiom, we need to ask questions like "good for whom?", "good for how many?" and "why them?"

Already in the 17th century, enlightenment philosopher Baruch Spinoza pointed out that "good" is that which is useful to us and "evil" is that which hinders us from having anything that is "good." As far as the experience of a user is concerned, it is only as good as the action it enables, but designing a system that makes doing bad things easy is bad. By Spinoza's light, systems that automate distraction, overeating or discrimination would thus be evil.

DOI: 10.4324/9781003464754-18

Perhaps the most famous list of criteria for good design comes from industrial designer Dieter Rams, known for his beautiful *Braun* products. In 1995 he published his "10 theses for good product design," a moral treaty of design that clearly states that design is much more than just an aesthetic and technically feasible venture.[1] There also exist some attempts to create a kind of *Hippocratic Oath* for design, as can be seen, for example, on the webpage of the University of Berlin (www.oekologischer-eid.de). Designer and educator Emily Pilloton-Lam wrote *Design Revolution: 100 Products that Empower People*, where she includes a "designer's handshake," which can be torn out, signed and sent back to her, adding a certain weight of commitment.[2] Recently Mike Monteiro published *Ruined by Design*, a book far angrier than this one or any that I mentioned within it, which suggests that many of society's most pressing problems result from a lack of ethics in design. Monteiro also advocates for a code of ethics similar to the *Hippocratic Oath* guiding medical doctors.[3] I could not agree more with these designers, but their attempts of finding moral codes all miss the fact that individual morality is kept in check through group interaction. Although often used interchangeably, morality is defined as something that's personal and normative, and ethics as communal or social standards of "good and bad." At the level of the village, human society has always employed ethics to hold free riders and cheaters responsible. On a global level, such archaic mechanisms of accountability fall apart, but if success for the business means harm for society and planet, then every individual contributing to that success is doing harm. How often do designers actually create a new problem while they are solving a business problem or delighting an individual customer?

There is no profession more ethically thorny than design for the simple reason that it is more consequential on the lives of people both geographically and temporarily removed than others. Let us consider one of the most famous moral thought experiments. You are standing by a train track onto which three people are tied. With horror you notice that a train is approaching and look around for a lever to divert it to another track. However, before you pull it, you notice with even more horror that a single person is tied to the diversion track. What is the right thing for you to do? Ethics, usually understood and taught as a subjective and individual code of conduct, is already overpowered by this *trolley problem*. True, this as well as many other thought experiments conveniently exclude all real-world variables, but if anything that makes them easier, not harder. Let us now take the trolley problem out of our heads and quite literally onto the streets. Should autonomous cars, vehicles driven by robotics, save their passengers by running over the grandmother or the small child standing on either side of the tree? Human life will be lost, but who is responsible? The owner of the car? The car companies? Or the designer of the car and its algorithms? Moral thought experiments like the *trolley problem* ignore choice architecture and any other responsibility that designers actually have.

The designer of autonomous vehicles – or is it the programmer of its codes – is responsible for far more ramifications than the philosopher of academia, and so I ask once again: why the hell are we not teaching ethics *especially* to the makers of things, the ones designing the interfaces between us and the world? To be honest, I had to write this book because of the sad truth that most students of the applied arts and sciences graduate without having taken a single course in ethics or sustainability.

Donald Norman states in his essay, "Why design education must change," that:

> today … designers work on organizational structure and social problems, on interaction, service, and experience design. Many problems involve complex social and political issues. As a result, designers have become applied behavioral scientists, but they are woefully undereducated for the task.[4]

Let us not forget that Norman's quote, coming from 2010, could only have anticipated the incredible crusade *persuasive technology* has made in our society. Such technologies take the agency of design very seriously by encoding the insights of behavioral science. Take B. J. Fogg, head of the *Stanford Behavioral Lab*. As a behavioral scientist, he pioneered an entire field of research showing that simple behaviorist techniques combined with computer tech easily manipulate human behavior. His *Fogg behavior model* (FBM) describes three conditions – (1) motivation, (2) ability and (3) a prompt or trigger – that are needed for a behavioral manipulation to occur. It is easy to see why he is venerated like a guru in tech circles and nicknamed "millionaire maker." His knowledge on how to create and prey on individuals' desires by triggering them into action proved to be extremely lucrative indeed when appended to the webpages and applications we visit and the smart devices we surround ourselves with.[5] Tristan Harris, former "design ethicist" at Google and founder of the *Center for Humane Technology* was also a student of B. J. Fogg at Stanford. More than most people, he is thus closely acquainted with behaviorist techniques of nudging, herding, influencing and reinforcement, all of which are used by Google and Facebook. They are techniques of social control employed by cults, and they make social media as effective and dangerous as they are. In this writing, we are not even addressing the alarming rise in teenage body dysphoria, self-harm and suicide, as Harris and many other whistle-blowers attest in the documentary *The Social Dilemma*.[6]

Viewed at a finer scale, the process of exploiting human vices can be broken into four simple steps, known as the *hook model* and described in Nir Eyal's book *Hooked*. These steps – *trigger, action, variable reward* and *investment* – are the basic steps of behavioral science used to hook people to products and services. They are designed features making (metaphorically, not literally) consumption robots out of all of us. Eyal and so many other libertarian defenders of free will have spoken out against measures to regulate habit-forming technologies, arguing that it is an individual user's responsibility to control their will to use or ignore such products. But is that not like asking a novice chess player to try really hard to beat Gary Kasparov? Is it not exactly like handing out additive narcotics to minors and people with mental disabilities? I mean the book is called *Hooked*, for the love of God![7]

Designers don't make unique pieces for individual users; that would be craftsmanship. To the contrary, design is all about scalability. Just that, combined with the fact that design success is usually measured in the aggregate, makes it a strong candidate for ethical considerations. Now more than ever, all forms of design are saturating a global market be it digital or analogue. As an example of how behavioral science has morphed into a kind of marketing of complacency, consider Alex Pentland. The behavioral scientist and director of MIT's *Human Dynamics Lab* is often referred to as the "godfather of wearables." The methodological foundation and business plan of such devices designed to track individuals' location and biometrics is behavioral science and the model of *Homo economicus* applied to IT and sold to data brokers. Pentland neatly summarizes his take on human sciences in his book *Social Physics*: "Social phenomena are really just aggregations of billions of small transactions between individuals."[8] Such a (flawed) appraisal of human society comes from and is even more radical than Margaret Thatcher's notorious claim, which at least made room for "families" in addition to "individual men and women." In a purely materialist and behaviorist worldview, human brains are just complex computers that not only need outsourced memory (cloud computing) but also programming through behavioral architecture. Of course, wearables are an integral part of *surveillance capitalism*, which is a different beast altogether.

Unlike other forms of capitalism, *surveillance capitalism* demands freedom (for corporations to do as they please) and total knowledge of present and future market behavior. Its sight is set on collectivism and monopolistic control of information, and it simply cannot be argued that it needs to escape regulation to work best. In the words of Zuboff, "surveillance capitalists know too much to qualify for freedom."[9] Another major difference to classical capitalism is that *surveillance capitalism* doesn't rely on end-users but instead on private businesses as customers. The old moniker "if something is free, you are the product" is wrong. It is data on our *behavior change*, our attention deficit, that is peddled on the marketplace. How can this possibly have happened? Looking at the etymology of the word "data" sheds some light: it originates from Latin datum "(thing) given." The transfer of data is not free of charge in a monetary sense, but rather belongs to a whole other system, namely barter. The incredible accumulation of wealth we have witnessed in high tech and its subsidiaries fintech and the app economy of smartphones starts to make sense when we understand that service providers make a lot more money on end-users using something free than they would paying for it. As Gilian Tett points out, it all seems like magic until the "social silence" of an intermediary barter between users and data brokers is addressed.[10]

Course Two: Ethical Things

But not all types of design are *persuasive technology*! Are you sure? After all, if a designed object or service does not manipulate its user into action, then it is a failure. Actively or inactively, the designer influences society by changing industry, consumer behavior and people's attitudes. Designers of the past have caused me to sit a certain way, to drink exactly a certain amount of beer in a bottle and to move my fingers along this QWERTY keyboard in a way to write this sentence. They manipulated me and reduced my already fleeting sense of free will and thus it seems to me that far beyond the goals for which artifacts are designed or the quality of their functioning, designers need to think about user action in accordance with artifacts. While the field of ethics concerns the question on how to act, designed objects often give material answers to this question. Artifacts functionally influence human actions extrinsically through the linguistic message they carry – such as a road sign – but also intrinsically as materials. They often function *for* us, passively.

We can even go beyond such considerations, as did the before-mentioned Akrich (1992) and Latour (1992), and address other roles artifacts play in their use contexts.[11] According to such authors, artifacts carry in themselves a kind of "script," which dictates the actions of the user. Thus, a takeaway coffee cup has inscribed a script that says, "throw me away right after use," whereas the ceramic cup "wants" to be cleaned, handled with care and used again. It goes without saying that those examples have a lot to do with sustainability. But, to drive the point home, let us take another horrible scenario, that of homicide. Which entity kills a human – a gunman or a gun? Although sounding absurd, this question is definitely not an easy one. Neither the gun nor the gunman is the sole actor in a shooting since there would be no shooting without a weapon, and also without a user of the gun. Bruno Latour calls such a situation "technical mediation." Rather than seeing the gun as an intermediary, neutral object between the gunman and the object, it is a mediator actively contributing to the way in which the homicide is realized.[12]

Once we treat designed objects as moral entities, then designers are automatically *doing* ethics and the real question becomes *how* to do it? They could explicitly and purposefully build specific scenarios of mediation, which they consider desirable. Morality would then become materialized and an explicit part of a product's functionality. Such a direction was taken by Dutch philosopher Hans Achterhuis who pleads for an explicit "moralisation of technology."[13] Thus, instead of moralizing only people and asking them to not waste so much water, we could also moralize our material environment and conceive a water-saving showerhead. The burden of moral responsibility is eased as humans delegate some of it to their artifacts but freely willed morality would probably decline. Such notions are heavily criticized as the specter of an Orwellian technocracy looms large. But even without such ambitions, design cannot ever be neutral, as it eloquently moves from *is* to *ought* and by embodying ethics, it thus evades *Hume's guillotine*. As individuals, our liberties and choices are mediated tremendously and continuously through technical systems created and maintained by designers. This, by definition, is power that needs to be wielded wisely.

Design always has consequences, and therefore ethics ought to be an intentional part of the process. Before I get crucified for committing the *is–ought fallacy*, I will add to the sentence above , "… if designers want to avoid unintended harm, or do good." The disciplines of design, far beyond others' disciplines, affect not only millions of people anonymous and far removed; they also affect people of the future. It is for this reason that I suggest the most logical moral matrix for designers to be *consequentialism*, which holds that judgment on whether something is good or bad always depends on its outcomes. Why should designers not steer their design decisions by considering possible consequences the production, use and disposal of their products might have? Like never before, human distance is bridged through means of communication and transportation. Should we not also worry about those not yet born?

A designer's ego can be effectively kept in check through what is known as *co-creation*. When we allocate design decisions outwards to as many stakeholders as possible, the design automatically moves from *human-centered* to *humanity-centered*. It is up to everyone affected to make sure designed objects increase the well-being of users, community and planet.

Course Three: Design *as* Effective Altruism

As we have seen, "Everyone designs who devises courses of action aimed at changing existing situations into preferred ones."[14] Design is all about care, by definition. No one would call themselves a designer if their business was making things worse and most designers and product managers I have met will say they are in the business to create positive impact in the world. They always talk about solving "pain points." Sure, many times those are just hollow phrases, just lip service. If designers are sincere, however, then they are part of the *caring class* because at its heart their craft holds the very ethos of altruism.

I consider Peter Singer the most practical, living moral philosopher and his work of utmost relevance to design. He is the patriarch of the *effective altruism* (EA) movement, the definition of which (from EffectiveAltruism.org) is how to "use our resources to help others the most" that we possibly can.[15] It might be counter-intuitive at first, but designers and *effective altruists* have many common denominators. For example, both designers and *effective altruists* know it is best to regard a problem from as many possible angles to address root causes rather than symptoms. Design and *effective altruism* must understand why users might experience pain, and then seek to address the root of that pain. Such insights are always gleaned from data, which is a result of research. *Effective altruists* and designers focus on prevention rather than treatment of problems because the former is more cost-effective than the latter.

I do feel obliged to clarify expressing design as part of the *caring class*, because that is usually associated with the Marxist concept of grossly underpaid kindergarten teachers or nurses. I am trying equally hard to steer clear of right-leaning tendencies of *laissez fair* policies. Neither the extreme right nor left is useful in ethical considerations, and precisely for this reason evolutionary thinking plays such an important part of this book. Putting on an evolutionary lens allows us to zoom out and view both the left and right narratives without getting caught up in either one. Applied ethicist Peter Singers addresses this exact conundrum in his very much underrated *A Darwinian Left*.[16] Besides the concept of *effective altruism*, Singer is also responsible for the *animal liberation* movement. He considers himself politically left-winged but at the same time a strong Darwinian. After all, he often champions the *selfish gene theory* of his friend Richard Dawkins!

The logic of altruism, once a feature, is now a bug. The reason we are far more likely to donate money to a cause when we are shown the image of a single suffering child than thousands of anonymous people affected elsewhere is that our evolutionary feature of empathy is gamed. We care deeply about people whom we can empathize with, and for countless millennia they just happen to be the ones closest geographically. Throughout deep history those were typically also the people we were either related to and/or shared production and consumption of resources with. The tribe living in the next valley we treated with skepticism and xenophobia. Research has shown that *parochial altruism* – defined as individual sacrifice to benefit the in-group and harm an out-group – is a behavioral pattern that not only undermines intergroup cooperation but stokes fear and hatred. It is the dark side of patriotism, nationalism nepotism and religious zealousness. Empathy precedes sympathy and stands as the foundation of morality, but needs to be practiced, especially when it comes to strangers. And because morality follows, an evolutionary logic is hierarchical. Akin to seeing distant objects as smaller, no matter how large they actually are, the less of a relationship we have with living or non-living entities, the less we care about them. Singer's book *The Expanding Circle* explains that over the course of human evolution, humans have expanded the circle of beings whose interests they are willing to defend, from self, family and tribe to all other humans.[17] That circle can expand to include plants, animals and non-living entities. For morality to be effective, we thus must compensate for distance and anonymity, basically what David Hume meant in his moral philosophy. Design can be a very *effective* type of *altruism*, one that overcomes such an evolutionary glitch. I see designed objects and services as *humanitarian drones* of sorts. They boldly go where volunteers cannot, to bring joy to people removed by both distance and time.

Designers level great importance on creating products of novelty, beauty and convenience, and just maybe all three aspects can be used for giving effectively. Creating something new is only a success for designers if others hear about it, which is why they employ the incredible power of marketing combined with *network theory* to spread their conceptions. After all, as they say: "Your network is your net worth!" Currently, the outcomes of *effective altruism* projects are tailored to and reach only those already converted. As we have seen, the *confirmation bias* leads people to get involved with causes they already identify with. In short, *effective altruism* could easily be appended to our obsession with novelty.

First impressions matter. They set the feeling tone for the rest of all relationships, whether human or non-human. Thus, digital content as well as physical objects need to make good impressions; they need to look good. Unfortunately, to say the least, the content and "products" created in the *effective altruism* community often lack the luster provided by design. They usually are scientific texts and data analyses, which are difficult to digest and lack imagination for a new recipient. Attractive infographics (communication design) and web development (interaction design) could help *effective altruism* reach its highest goal of becoming a high-impact organization. It needs industry-standard design. It needs strong branding, graphic design and content curation. Unfortunately, *effective altruism* does not often reach people with a design skill set, and as a result its ecosystem severely lacks quality design services.

Doing good is anything but convenient for one very specific reason: it lacks the *user-centered approach* of design. Most altruistic organizations are (or work with) clumsy agencies who don't understand the first thing about *UX*, accounting, finance or marketing. Instead, they often rely on volunteers or unpaid interns to create their interactions with the world. So, it should be of little surprise that the results are often terrible. I can speak from experience as I have spent many summers on voluntary humanitarian missions, but ended up sitting around waiting, doing random and useless work, or learning how to do something. Designers and product managers could translate research insights into design concepts for novel products and features. As far as *interaction design* is concerned, wireframes, mock-ups and prototypes must be optimized for devices and interfaces, to be easily understood not only by engineers but end-users, too. In short, rapid prototyping and iteration techniques so useful for the creation of innovation must be applied to *effective altruism*. Let us go beyond *effective* and make altruism *convenient*!

Course Four: Guided Ethical Evolution

To reach a desirable target, the design process needs to be pre-emptive. Current design processes such as the *double diamond* have proved to be incredibly effective in squeezing out ideas in a short period of time, but they do follow a rather rigid process. Changes tend to be allowed only in what is called the *ideation* and *mock-up* phase, and the focus undeniably remains on process reproducibility. I always encourage designers to follow the iterative *grounded theory* approach in research as well, but such is not commonplace. In a planned evolutionary process, on the other hand, insights of product short-comings would flow upstream throughout the process by identifying critical material attributes and process parameters. Design flourishes best in environments that encourage learning, testing and iteration, all of which reduce the risk of pricey misses, but such approaches stand in contrast to the prevailing norms in many companies, which still emphasize discrete and irreversible design phases in product development.

An interesting approach to consider is *constructive technology assessment* (CTA) where social problems surrounding technology are addressed by different stakeholders, including external expertise, designers and end-users.[18] CTA is based on an evolutionary view insofar as the process of technology development is seen as a kind of generator of variations, which in turn are exposed to selection by entities such as the market and government regulations. Only the best-fitting variations survive. There exists an important difference to biological evolution, however. Designers anticipate and pre-empt the selection environment for the technologies they conceive, since exerting so much effort into research and development of new artifacts that will not be accepted by consumers or permitted by government regulations would be silly. In this, it is teleological, but it also allows stakeholders to set ethical and sustainable targets while it robs some of marketing's power. It is where my hope lies and what I wish to teach the *future designer*.

The CTA process is called "constructive" because technology assessment takes place *before* and not after something is released on the market. Designers, using ethnographic research, try to explain behavior in terms of a technological, man-made matrix. In other words, evolutionary algorithms collide with a world artificially designed, and resulting behavior can be measured. Akin to Skinnerian psychology, such a systematic approach requires a massive amount of data on the interaction of a product with its users. Such data exists in spades. Albeit primarily in fields of digital technology, such as the *internet of things, artificial intelligence* and *interaction design*, an enormous data set has been accumulated in just the last few decades. True, much of it is locked away on corporate hard drives, but some of it can be described as belonging to *open-source technology* (OST). It could be used for the analysis of trends on the basis of user behavior, and we could begin to deconstruct the logic of design choices behind them and discuss their implications on potential, alternative scenarios in the future. Thus, for the designer, OST is a subject worth grappling with and deemed an important aspect of ethical and sustainable *behavior change* generally, and the *circular economy* specifically.

After collecting human data, a group of relevant stakeholders (experts, designers and potential end-users) must now ask what they want to achieve with a design, how that goal might be achieved and which of the variations might be replicated. However, compartmentalization of this sort increases the risk of losing the voice of the consumer or of relying too heavily on one iteration of that voice. The best results come from constantly blending quantitative (such as conjoint analysis) and qualitative (such as ethnographic interviews) *user research*. This information can then be combined with reports from the market analytics group on the actions of competitors, patent scans to monitor emerging technologies, business concerns flagged by the finance team and the like. Without these tensions and interactions, research and development may end up in a vacuum, producing otherwise excellent work that never sees the light of day and delights customers.

Just like design, ethics is a quest to find solutions to the right problem. More and more designers rely on testing to validate their designs. Although a very admirable tendency, ushered in by a recent emphasis on *user-centered design, UX* and *UI* audits, applied metrics are still far too narrow, as they focus almost entirely on use cases. Wider consequences of product and services are still cloaked as externalities. *UX design* can thus produce an incredibly novel, beautiful and convenient interaction such as hailing an Uber ride but never considers any ecological impact or deplorable working conditions said interaction requires. This means that only a fraction of the design decision-making process is documented or measured. The remainder is externalized before and after the conception of the thing or service. If, for example, we judged McDonald's by applying only use-case metrics, it would do quite well. In *Corporate Identity* (CI), it is the top of the class, and the Golden Arches are likely the most recognizable brand now and the biggest mystery for the archaeologists of the future. (Will they associate them with a global cult, and will they be wrong about that?) *Usability*, the ability of a cultural system to allow its users to perform tasks effectively, efficiently and safely is also really good in McDonald's, especially since the introduction of the huge smartphone-shaped touchscreens for ordering. One must be severely limited physically and/or mentally to fail to select vast amounts of sugar, fat and salt in different shapes or forms to be administered to the body. *User experience?* Employed mostly in the context of digital products –unduly in my opinion – this is a measure of the overall, subjective experience of users of a system. It is a very apt term here because regular customers of McDonald's are more like *users* of substances (distillates of sugar, fat and salt) than eaters of food. Judging from the outside, the *UX* of McDonald's also ranks very high along metrics of satisfaction, engagement and loyalty. It is painfully obvious that I could list scores of cultural practices that thrive, while they physiologically and psychologically harm humans and other parts of the biosphere. The fruition of design consequences poses a massive burden on countries' welfare and thus taxpayers' pockets.

In our current industrial atmosphere of stress to market we tend to live with many gaps, such as those between what the producer thinks the customer needs and what the customer really needs, and between what the producer thinks the customer needs and what is designed. In other words, the final prototype tends to also be different to the initial design simply because many real-world variables in materials and processes along the way to completion were ignored. Consequently, when something goes terribly wrong, the unforeseen consequences can only be found through a kind of *reverse enquiring*, which really is a trial-and-error hunt for clues. Similarly, *UX* and *usability* testing often come at the very back-end of the industrial design process. It is an empirical approach relying on product testing and inspection to determine the quality of the product. If human society wants to limit dysfunctional, harmful cultural traits, more metric-based barriers to market are required and they must be applied throughout the process. Incentives would duly be steered towards the successful completion of such metrics. This *quality by design* is the norm in the pharmaceutical as well as large parts of the automobile industry. In standard design practice (industrial, service, interaction, etc.), mistakes are not immediately fatal like in pharmaceutical or automobile sectors, but in their production, use and disposal they do have dire externalities for society at large. We will regard quality by design in greater deal in the final section of this book, but let us conclude this section with a conservative list of metrics for ethical design that might serve as examples:

Accessibility: Can the product be found and used by anyone and everyone? Does it follow rules of *universal design*?

Reliability: Is the product trustworthy or does acquisition and use of it have undesirable consequences for users as well as the non-using community?

Usability: Can the product be used intuitively and easily by all?

Functionality: Do the contents and tools of a product work according to the needs of the user as well as the non-using community?

Sustainability: Can the product be produced, used and disposed of without harming society and the environment through its externalities?

Course Five: Quality by Design

In 2016, I visited my first car production plant. Situated in Győr, the gigantic Audi Hungary Motor Kft. develops and manufactures engines for most subsidiaries of the Volkswagen Group. A few years prior, the company's Audi 3 model became one of the first to be built entirely at Győr, an achievement our tour-guide was clearly very proud of. As someone normally interested in all things anthropological and psychological, and less interested in cars, this was new and strange territory. Or was it? Walking through the plant we were required to wear safety equipment for obvious reasons. Robot arms swung around, workers moved extremely fast and the roar of production was deafening. But then my mind managed to capture a wider aperture and the pounding onslaught of machinery turned into experimental industrial techno, of the *Einstürzende Neubauten* sort. It had to, because every soundbite was produced by precise and looping repetitions of workers and machines as car parts moved along the conveyer belts pioneered by Henry Ford. What at first seemed an ugly dystopia turned into a brimming hive. All of a sudden, the automobile manufacturing company resembled a social insect colony. Whereas the queen of a termite colony, fed and protected by an army of workers, manages to lay an egg every few seconds, the Győr plant squeezed out 155,157 cars in 2021 alone. This equates to over 600 vehicles produced in every one of Hungary's 254 working days.[19] Such impressive numbers are impossible to achieve democratically, and power structures are most certainly top-down, "command and control." But centralized planning only works well until a critical scale is reached. Then it runs into difficulties, because although errors in production can be pinpointed to a unit somewhere in the car plant, it will never be possible to amend the error mid-process. Incidentally, the same difficulty is faced by governments when a population becomes too large.

As for human effort, a manufacturing plant ebbs and flows, running smoothly until some worker carries less than his/her share. Also, an untimely delivery of parts can result in a halting process, similarly to one driver erratic braking on a freeway curve can result in a mile-long traffic jam. It is in bracing for this kind of issue that *Toyota*'s manufacturing has developed its famous "Toyota Way" for continuously improving operations. But rather than seeing failure as purely negative, the Japanese automaker regards it as an opportunity for improvement, just like nature does in its continuous process of selection. David Sloan Wilson writes: "Every figure provides an opportunity for a variation-and-selection process to go to work to improve the efficiency of the whole operation."[20]

In the past Toyota had cords called *andons* for operators to pull whenever an inefficiency was spotted along a particular process. For Toyota, employees didn't just have the right to pull the cord; they were obligated to pull it whenever a problem occurred. Of course, such cords are now replaced by high tech, but the idea remains the same: a part can cry out to help the whole system. This is akin to the "check engine" light in a car; it is also precisely the function of pain in the body. In the manufacturing plant, managers can go in real time to the exact location where the irregularity occurred and try and fix the issue at hand. Toyota had effectively invented a way to intervene in the production process before problems festered into something much worse downstream. Incidentally, the mega-retailer *Amazon* uses a similar innovation: when a product or supplier causes unwanted errors, a single employee can "pull the cord" and take an item entirely out of circulation until the problem is fixed.

The *Toyota production system* (TPS) is based on the *Jidoka* methodology, which empowered operators to not only recognize issues but also to stop work without management approval; this significantly contributed to what is now known as *lean management*. But the deeper meaning here is that Toyota's default assumption is systemic. Sure, a problem might have been caused by an individual, but only when all work is in harmony as part of a system will those errors become less frequent. Hiring and firing of workers and managers is cumbersome and simply takes too long. Again, the *andon* cord in *lean manufacturing* is designed to alert management in real time so that corrective steps can be taken immediately. Similarly, *quality by design* (QbD) is the process of researching and developing product quality while safeguarding for potential errors. Its principles are common in heavy industry, especially the pharmaceutical sector, for the discovery, development and manufacture of new drugs as well as the automotive sector. But surely, quality has always been the highest objective of any productive process, since mishaps in production, use and disposal were much riskier in past ages. As a matter of fact, rigorous control of quality can probably be traced to the mass manufacturing techniques of the Industrial Revolution. During both world wars the demand for huge amounts of interchangeable parts of military equipment created more rigorous requirements for safety, accuracy and precision. In times of peace, too, industry has learned to get it right the first time.

Indeed, and for centuries, most industrial processes could guarantee quality only by inspecting the end product. In the 1930s, Walter Shewhart, an American engineer and statistician, shifted the quality debate from the final product to the process creating the product. Shewhart argued for more engineering and statistics for quality assurance purposes. Basically scientific in its approach, the quality of something conceived was checked not so much by its design but by its process design. The stringent measurement of variation became the prime indicator of process stability. What did not work in the process was changed or disposed of, and what worked was replicated for ever greater results, making production of things a managed evolutionary process. Shewhart's methods were adopted and evangelized especially by his colleagues Dr. Joseph Juran and William Edwards Deming at Western Electric in Chicago.[21] While Shewhart brought the statistical parameters, Juran developed equally important perspectives of management commitment. Deming, belonging to the rare type of human who is a philosopher, engineer, idealist and realist, called his system of thought "System of Profound Knowledge," and it includes four corrective lenses through which to view the world: 1) systems thinking, 2) understanding and appreciation of variation, 3) human psychology and 4) epistemology, the theory of what we can know. According to Deming, profound knowledge was necessary for any production of anything useful.[22]

Whereas traditional processes have multiple handoffs from specialist to specialist, here a team works together in what can be labelled *concurrent engineering*. *QbD* was systemized into the "quality trilogy" by Dr. Joseph Juran and consists of three phases of a process:

Quality planning: In this design stage an organization takes a customer's needs, defines function, feature and form of the product or service, and actually designs the processes. Very similar to the double diamond's first stage, this is all about discovery and definition. The exact needs – not wants! – of the customers must be researched. There must be metrics to measure if the design is successful or not. To really understand what users need we need to see what the science has already researched and do rigorous and new scientific user research. We need to establish how users will relate to a product, how users' needs are met and how features will deliver. Addressing a larger framework, we need to see how well a product can be brought back into the system by closing resource loops as demanded by a *circular economy*. What is the product and what kind (s) of user(s) should it serve? What should the product achieve? In other words, what are the goals? Only then can inspiration hit brightly as new forms and functions are conceived. The creative spirit is let loose then and not earlier. The stringent, scientific framework holds creativity in check, on the one hand, but it can also give it wings through its very corset, on the other.

Quality control: Quality control involves surveillance, checks and inspections, to make sure the designed process is advancing as planned. Wherever problems are detected, root causes must be identified in order to correct and prevent further damage. In the double diamond design process, designers try to model a new product that meets all previously established metrics. Remember those metrics are put in place by a multidisciplinary, science-driven team. Once a product or service is designed, it's production needs to be designed as well. This is equally important and requires rigorous metrics to see how successful the process is. Process design is based on an understanding of variability, since things don't tend to go as planned. How do we know that the process is running ideally if we don't check it?

Quality improvement: Breakthrough quality improvement involves the identification of areas where processes can be optimized. Production goes ahead once all goals set out in advance are met. Once something is produced, the chances of meeting user needs are high. Delivery can only be effective when there is strong planning along all supply chains.

Quality by design is an approach both technical and human, and it is an approach that will be taught in the *department of the future designer*. Since product quality can only ever be designed in a multidisciplinary team, it could easily be practiced in various semester projects and implemented for the completion of final theses. Imagine a team presenting a final thesis and presenting all the difficulties, failures and victories that happened during the process. Students might be graded individually for their roles in a given project or for their managerial abilities as they summon and mediate their team of stakeholders.

Notes

1 Klemp, K. (2012). Dieter Rams: Ethics and modern philosophy. What legacy today? *Docomomo Journal*, 46, 68–75.
2 Pilloton, E., & Chochinov, A. (2009). *Design Revolution: 100 products that are changing people's lives*. Thames & Hudson.

3 Monteiro, M. (2019). *Ruined by Design: How designers destroyed the world, and what we can do to fix it.* Mule Design.
4 Norman, D. (2010). Why design education must change. *Core77*, November 26.
5 Fogg, B. J. (2019). Fogg behavior model. https://behaviormodel.org, accessed on December 14, 2020.
6 Orlowski, J. (2020). *The Social Dilemma*. Netflix.
7 Eyal, N. (2014). *Hooked: How to build habit-forming products.* Penguin.
8 Pentland, A. (2014). *Social Physics: How good ideas spread – the lessons from a new science.* Penguin, pp. 10–11.
9 Zuboff, S. (2019). *The Age of Surveillance Capitalism: The fight for a human future at the new frontier of power.* Profile Books, p. 467.
10 Tett, G. (2021). *Anthro-Vision: A new way to see in business and life.* Simon and Schuster.
11 Fallan, K. (2008). De-scribing design: Appropriating script analysis to design history. *Design Issues*, 24(4), 61–75.
12 Latour, B. (1994). On technical mediation. *Common Knowledge*, 3(2), 29–64.
13 Achterhuis, H. (Ed.) (2001). *American Philosophy of Technology: The empirical turn.* Indiana University Press.
14 Simon, H. A. (1988). The science of design: Creating the artificial. *Design Issues*, 67–82.
15 https://www.effectivealtruism.org, accessed on February 3, 2021.
16 Singer, P. (2000). *A Darwinian Left: Politics, evolution and cooperation.* Yale University Press.
17 Singer, P. (1981). *The Expanding Circle.* Clarendon Press.
18 Schot, J., & Rip, A. (1997). The past and future of constructive technology assessment. *Technological Forecasting and Social Change*, 54(2–3), 251–268.
19 https://www.audi.com/content/dam/gbp2/downloads/report/annual-reports/2020/en/audi-report-2020_desktop.pdf, accessed on May 3, 2021.
20 Wilson, D. S. (2020). *This View of Life: Completing the Darwinian revolution.* Vintage, p. 204.
21 Best, M., & Neuhauser, D. (2006). Walter A. Shewhart, 1924, and the Hawthorne factory. *Quality and Safety in Health Care*, 15(2), 142–143.
22 Korakianiti, E., & Rekkas, D. (2011). Statistical thinking and knowledge management for quality- driven design and manufacturing in pharmaceuticals. *Pharmaceutical Research*, 28(7), 1465–1479.

CONCLUSION

Design Optimism

My life has been incredibly enriched since stumbling into the world of design ten years ago, but I still can only supply the theoretical. This is the end of the book, but the end of the story cannot be told, as I need designers to take it into the future and give it shape and form. To let it unfold. We live in a confused and enraged world. As the so-called developed world is drowning in all our man-made stuff, the developing world is starving, but there are other stories to be told about the future. Instead of shades of brown and gray, we could paint the future with all the colors of nature. Instead of doom and suffering, we could have a future full of creativity and joy. Let us take the dark out of the future and paint in different, bright colors. To visualize this, I want to conclude with *solarpunk* as an antithesis to *cyberpunk* and *steampunk* aesthetics.

Instead of decay and toxic steam, the *solarpunk* future lacks existential threats like climate change or malignant AI. Here, a synergy is achieved between Homo sapiens and nature, and between biology and technology. *Solarpunk* backdrops are like a mixture of *art nouveau*-esque architecture and Milano's vertical forest tower from architect Stefano Boeri. Nature, as the greatest display of technology and creativity, is celebrated and harnessed but never exploited. In short, architecture is *biophilic*. By offering a solution to many of today's wicked problems, *solarpunk* aims for a brighter future ("solar") while rebelling against all current systems that might tamper with such a brighter future ("punk").

Speculative genres such as the science fiction of *solarpunk* provide a way out of the damning constraints and narrow futures provided by our non-renewable age. But this one goes beyond mere fantasy and is already in part responsible for a resurgence in principles of *biophilic design*.

DOI: 10.4324/9781003464754-19

More than simply an art genre, *solarpunk* has morphed into subculture of practical, regenerative ideas and innovations for the future. It is full of life-hackers taking energy exclusively from regenerative sources such as solar, wind and geo-thermal. Dirty emissions from burning fuels are "a thing of the past" – or is it our present? – since *solarpunk* is concerned with the future. Whether intentional or not, *solarpunk* is based on *circular economies*, where waste is always reused, and nothing becomes obsolete since commodities are always repurposed and refurbished. Following the principles of *biomicry*, rainwater is harvesting and farming follows the principles of *permaculture*.

Politically, the stories tend to go beyond rivaling left and right and offer instead a heterogeneous society fluid in race, gender and equality. There are differences, sure, but the focus lies on *recognition* and *acceptance*. The emphasis of *solarpunk* then lies in nourishing community, one that respects the potential of every individual. Not only is there a place for everyone, but the individual is an indispensable part of a greater whole. Instead of widespread dysphoria caused by some imaginary white *superstructure* of oppression, we see a *euphoric* display of gender and skin tones inhabiting the future. But the only thing explicitly political is the source of energy: the sun.

Whereas in *cyberpunk* fossil fuels have obscured the sun, here it shines bright and full of hope. In *cyberpunk*, dystopia is reaped from centuries of rape of the land. Hegemonic extraction of resources based on a story of dominance and control has led to a total estrangement with nature and a binary society of haves and have nots. At least since Copernicus, solar energy, on the other hand, is decentralized, inexhaustible and, most importantly, non-exclusive. At its root *solarpunk* is a culture based on creative energy and experiments. Instead of evil scientists with sinister plans, science is seen as the strongest skill set of this species to get out of all plights. Current technologies still fall short of expectations envisioned by us punks, where all designs are based on *repairability* and *reusability*, but much progress has been made. *Solar tech* is now more efficient and more easily scalable; prices have fallen to make solar the cheapest electricity in 2023. According to a report by the International Energy Agency (IEA),[1] solar is cheaper than all other sources of energy generated using gas, oil, and coal. This is true even when factoring in the cost of intermittency, the biggest downside of renewable energy sources.

Another interesting key principle of the *solarpunk* movement is decentralization. Whereas future scenarios of the *cyberpunk* variety are quite Marxist in tone- the world is usually dominated by evil and monopolistic corporations, controlled by *trans-humanoid* entities and powered by enslaved carbon-based humans- an alternative vision is one where society, people and the planet are prioritized over the individual and profit. In *solarpunk, Homo economicus* has died and human communities are based on cooperation and *polycentric governance*. Technologies are *open-source*, knowledge is shared synergistically. Instead of focusing on corporate greed or despotic governance, *solarpunk* counts on *commoning* for the management of resources. In this (possible) future, community gardening will be commonplace, and indigenous wisdom and practices celebrated. In short, the vision works well with Elinor Ostrom's work on the *management of common resources.*

Perhaps most importantly, the *solarpunk* story acts as a balm for a time rife with *climate anxiety* and apathy. Emotions of guilt, grief and anger amid heatwaves, droughts, wildfires and mass extinction tend to hinder real climate action due to feelings of personal insignificance. The *protopia* – not utopia-shown by *solarpunk* can be realized but it requires global action. *Circular economies* across all sectors must be adopted, our food systems need to be entirely overhauled and, most importantly, the growth of renewables and carbon capture technologies must be funded. Ultimately, humanity must undergo a massive and collective behavioral change. The seed for this change can be the future designer. Punk is not dead!

Communication for Good

I want to reach out a hand to advertisers and marketers. They were not spared any cynicism and anger in this text, and I still believe that their current role in the world of design and business needs to be throttled. I also stand by my position that it is marketing, advertising and design that feed our desire to consume, but I hope to have also been constructive in my criticism. Let me repeat a thought from the introduction of this book: If we stop for a second and think of ourselves as great apes, the tinder of our desires is always a return to natural systems. In order to feel protected, we are told to have houses, insurance plans and larger cars equipped with multiple airbags. We are told to change the stuff we wear and hold to be part of a welcoming tribe and to feel the embrace of a desired partner. We are told what to eat, think and say to get closer to some kind of ideal of human life. But the closer we get, the further it is removed. An industrial system based on the idea of the pursuit of pleasure as the highest goal – the definition of hedonism – has become a treadmill without exit.

But what if a counter-advertising campaign made *conspicuous consumption* a sinful activity? What if people felt ashamed to be seen as "future eaters"? This is clearly *utopian* and literally impossible in an economic order where consumption and the destruction of virgin materials drive the wealth of nations. What if, instead, marketing was seen as a multiplier? What if we had direct advertisement, campaigns and other tools aimed towards helping corporations spread wholesome products? For example, the success of *80,000 hours*, an offshoot of the *effective altruism* movement, relies on digital marketing that herds a massive audience to their sites and projects. That marketing strategy was offered by a marketing consultancy called userfriendly.org.uk! It is the same company that helped *Giving What We Can* and *High-Impact Athletes*. Or consider *Patagonia* with its "don't buy this jacket" campaign, first run in the *New York Times* for *Black Friday*! What seems risky and counterintuitive has helped establish *Patagonia* as an ambassador of sustainability and helped the company grow like never before. Marketers, advertisers – join the designers. Be punks!

Note

1   https://www.wtsenergy.com/solar-cheapest-energy-source-in-history-factor/#:~:text=
Solar%20energy%20has%20come%20a,International%20Energy%20Agency%20
(IEA), accessed on February 13, 2024.

INDEX